The Law and Harry Potter

The Law and Harry Potter

Edited by

Jeffrey E. Thomas

Franklin G. Snyder

CAROLINA ACADEMIC PRESS
Durham, North Carolina

Library of Congress Cataloging-in-Publication Data

The law and Harry Potter / [edited by] Jeffrey E. Thomas and Franklin G. Snyder.
    p. cm.
  Includes bibliographical references.
  ISBN 978-1-59460-645-8 (alk. paper)
  1. Rowling, J. K.--Criticism and interpretation. 2. Rowling, J. K.--Characters--Harry Potter. 3. Potter, Harry (Fictitious character) 4. Law in literature. 5. Magic in literature. 6. Wizards in literature. I. Thomas, Jeffrey E. II. Snyder, Franklin G. III. Title.

  PR6068.O93Z7565 2010
  823'.914--dc22

                                        2009041207

Carolina Academic Press
700 Kent Street
Durham, North Carolina 27701
Telephone (919) 489-7486
Fax (919) 493-5668
www.cap-press.com

Printed in the United States of America
2016 Printing

Contents

Part IV
The Wizard Economy

Part V
Harry Potter as an Archetype

Preface

The Law and Harry Potter? What does Harry Potter have to do with the law? Directly, nothing. Indirectly, however, a great deal. There is no denying that the Harry Potter franchise is an unprecedented cultural phenomenon: hundreds of millions of books in dozens of languages; six movies generating billions of dollars in revenue; a theme park.[1] This success shows that the narratives appeal to the public, children and adults alike. Within the narratives Rowling creates a "magical world" complete with laws and legal institutions. Although the stories are not directly about legal issues, law and legal institutions are important parts of the narratives. There are laws against certain curses and the underage use of magic, international treaties on a variety of topics, a wrongful conviction of Sirius Black, the ever powerful (or inept) Ministry of Magic, numerous crimes (by Lord Voldemort and others), a horrible prison (Azkaban), a tribunal that appears to be a combination of judge and jury (the Wizengamot), a banking system (Gringotts), etc.

Part of the appeal of the narratives is that the depictions resonate with readers and viewers. This may suggest that the depictions are consistent with readers' and viewers' values or opinions. Alternatively, if the depictions are not reflective, they may influence the development of values or opinions. This is not to say that the conditions of Azkaban will generate a movement for prison reform. Certainly any influence would be much more subtle that that. But perhaps readers and viewers will be more willing to consider the plight of those in prison, or to consider the possibility that a person was wrongfully convicted. Even if the depictions have little or no influence on their own, they can be used as examples or archetypes to advance the discourse on various issues, as

---

1. Originally, I tried to gather statistics to support this point, but it is a moving target. A recent news account puts the number of copies of the books at more than 400 million and the revenue from the first five films at $4.5 billion. *See* Michelle Nichols, *"Harry Potter" director says finale to be the best yet*, Reuters (July 13, 2009), available at http://www.reuters.com/article/entertainmentNews/idUSTRE5687D420090713 (last visited August 10, 2009). The theme park has its own website. *See* http://www.universalorlando.com/harrypotter/.

is demonstrated by several chapters included in this volume. There can be no doubt that the Harry Potter narratives have become a significant part of our popular culture, and our popular culture is the context within which our legal system operates and is reformed.[2]

The 22 chapters in this book have been grouped into five sections based on the content and approach of the chapters. The first section looks at legal traditions and institutions. It considers the role of law and legal institutions generally in the wizarding society, and includes a chapter on historical allusions. The second section considers crimes and punishments, and includes consideration of the wrongful conviction of Sirius Black and the application of human rights law. The third section includes chapters about identity in the narratives. It includes chapters about family relationships, moral development, and racial and other differences. The fourth section considers economic issues: the economy, money and banking. The fifth and final section contains chapters using the narratives as archetypes for law-related purposes: legal education, legal argument, and to illustrate legal principles.

This project is an outgrowth of a presentation made at the conference on *The Power of Stories: Intersections of Law, Culture and Literature,* co-sponsored by Texas Wesleyan University School of Law, the University of Gloucestershire, and the City of Gloucester, England. We therefore wish to express our appreciation to the conference organizers. Five of the original panelists stayed with the project and were joined by my co-editor, Frank Snyder, who was involved in organizing the conference, and a more than a dozen others.

I also wish to express my appreciation for assistance from an outstanding team of student assistants: Rachel Flaster, Erin Lawrence, and Scott Thein. They did a great job and without their assistance, I would have never finished. I also wish to thank our contributors for their patience. This project has taken longer than it should have, but the editorial delays (for which Frank and I are responsible) have a silver lining because it allowed us to account for *The Deathly Hallows* to make this volume complete.

Jeffrey E. Thomas
Kansas City, 2009

---

2. *See generally* Lawrence M. Friedman, *Law, Lawyers, and Popular Culture,* 98 YALE L.J. 1579 (1989).

Legal Traditions & Institutions

1

What Role Need Law Play in a Society with Magic?

John Gava & Jeannie Marie Paterson

Introduction

The magical world of Harry Potter is both heroic and intensely bureaucratic. It is also one where law seems relatively unimportant. Private law—the law providing for the rights and obligations owed by individuals to each other and in respect to property—is not as significant as it is in modern Muggle societies. While it is true that contract law is largely avoided even in Muggle societies, wizards and witches seem to need it even less than we do. Harry Potter and the rest of the wizarding community seem disinclined to use the law to deal with injury and harm caused by others. Perhaps this lesser use of law reflects the very nature of magic itself—hurts generally seem to be easily remedied by magical means. Perhaps it is a function of the nature of Harry Potter and his kind. The magical world is a heroic culture and this seems to be reflected in its inhabitants' attitude toward risk.

Public law, through the Ministry of Magic, has a much greater role than private law, but its role is still much less significant than in modern Muggle societies. The Ministry is the most important legal institution in Harry Potter's world. It is the major combined regulatory, legislative and judicial institution with an impressive reach. This is made clear when Harry is taken to his hearing by Arthur Weasley and gets, in effect, a tour of the Ministry's office and its many agencies—from international co-operation, to law enforcement and travel control. As we shall see, in constitutional terms the Ministry does not reflect, in either its structure or its operation, what we would understand as separation of powers. In fact, the Ministry is potentially a despotic organisation with very few legal limitations on its power.

The magic world of Harry Potter is also a world where there are no lawyers. Healers are the magical equivalents of doctors and we know that the magical

3

world has teachers and a form of police. However, there is no indication that lawyers are used either for civil work—the buying of property, drawing up of wills and the like—or as advocates in criminal trials. Law is unlikely to be important when there are no lawyers.

Private Law

Two prominent forms of private law are the law of torts and the law of contract. Contract law provides for the legal recognition and enforcement of agreements between individuals. Tort law provides compensation for those harmed by the wrongful action of another. There are plenty of incidents potentially arising under these areas of law in the Harry Potter books but only minor mention of contract law, which tends to depart from traditional principles of contract law, and no mention at all of the law of torts.

Contract Law

In *The Goblet of Fire*, George and Fred Weasley make a bet with Ludo Bagman about the outcome of the Quidditch World Cup. Bagman loses the bet and pays the twins. But his payment is in leprechaun gold which vanishes by the next morning. When the Weasley twins press their claim, Bagman refuses to pay on the ground that the Weasley twins are underage. A bet is a form of contract. However, this incident does not reveal a lack of law for enforcing contracts in the world of magic as compared with the non-magic world. Even in the Muggle world there has been a traditional hesitance to enforce gaming contracts and, as is apparently the case in the world of magic, there are limits on contracts with minors.

Another possible example of a contract in the magic world occurs in *The Order of the Phoenix*. The members of Dumbledore's Army sign a parchment which leads them to feel that they have signed "some kind of contract."[1] This contract is a little like the contract between members of a club in the Muggle world. It binds the members to comply with the rules of the club and, importantly in this case, to secrecy in respect to the existence of the club. The contract is never really tested as the members of the Army remain voluntarily loyal to its purposes. In *The Order of the Phoenix*, one member of Dumbledore's Army re-

---

1. *Order of the Phoenix* 347.

veals its existence and has the word "SNEAK" written in pustules across her face due to a charm placed on the "contract."[2] The beauty of magical contracts may be that the consequences for breach are self-executing so that lawyers need not be involved.

In *The Half-Blood Prince* Harry wonders while watching a scene through the Pensieve whether the "contract" between the house-elf Hokey and her mistress Hepzibah Smith (who Voldemort later murders and robs) obliges Hokey to lie and say her mistress looks lovely when she doesn't. Harry is clearly joking here, but his reference to a 'contract' is somewhat misleading. One of the most fundamental principles of contract law is that contracts should be voluntary, that is they should be made between consenting and informed individuals. Agreements which are entered into by individuals who cannot exercise relatively free choice or who have been subject to excessive or illegitimate pressure will be set aside. The issue over which Hermione becomes so concerned in *The Goblet of Fire* is that house-elves are not free and autonomous beings but are effectively slaves to the wizarding world. A house-elf has no real choice but to follow the orders of his or her master, a point illustrated by the protests of the house-elf Kreacher on being required to do the bidding of Harry Potter. Thus, a house-elf such as Hokey cannot in any real sense be said to have entered into a contract with the witch she serves.

Interestingly, the house-elves seem to be the most legalistic of the inhabitants we meet in the magical world. When Sirius Black shouts at Kreacher to "get out," Kreacher takes Sirius at his most literal interpretation. Kreacher leaves the house and goes to serve Narcissa Malfoy and the enemies of Sirius. When Harry tells Kreacher to follow Draco Malfoy he is careful to include detailed prohibitions on Kreacher in any way informing Malfoy of this mission. We are told that Kreacher struggles, unsuccessfully, to find a loophole in these instructions.

In *The Goblet of Fire* Dumbledore explains that when a student places his or her name in the Triwizard Tournament Goblet, it "constitutes a binding magical contract" which obliges that student, if selected, to see the Tournament through to the end.[3] A legally binding contract generally involves the exchange of promises by two contracting parties. Who is the other contracting party in the case of the magic contract nominations for the Triwizard Tournament? Perhaps it is the organizers of the event—the Departments of International Magical Cooperation and Magical Games and Sports—or perhaps the other

---

2. *Order of the Phoenix* 612.
3. *Goblet of Fire* 256.

contracting party is the panel of judges. It is also not clear what promises these other parties to the contract make in return for the undertaking by the Tournament contenders. Perhaps it is to apply the rules of the Tournament and to award the prize to the winner.

A contract is commonly understood as an agreement enforceable in law. The "contract" involved in the nominations for the Triwizard Tournament is binding but, as Dumbledore indicates, this is by magic rather than law. We might wonder how such a contract would be enforced. In the Muggle world, common law courts rarely order specific performance of a contract for personal services. It is considered undesirable to force a person to perform personal services as opposed to effectively buying his or her way out of the contract through a payment of damages to the other party. While magic could no doubt make a young witch or wizard participate in the Triwizard Tournament against his or her will, we might wonder how meaningful the participation would be in such a case? Some sort of magical order to perform would not necessarily compel in an otherwise recalcitrant witch or wizard the creative magical problem solving required by the tasks, which make up the Triwizard Tournament, though perhaps the high level of physical danger involved in the tasks would provide sufficient incentive for full and enthusiastic participation.

Perhaps the most chilling example of a binding agreement in the magic world concerns the "unbreakable vow" between Snape and Narcissa Malfoy whereby Snape undertakes to protect Narcissa's son Draco and to carry out the deed that Draco has been ordered to perform by Voldemort, namely the murder of Dumbledore. Is this something that could be described as a contract in the world of magic? The unbreakable vow is by definition a binding promise. However, as with the magical contract concerning the Triwizard Tournament, the agreement between Snape and Narcissa seems to be magically self-enforcing through the intermediary of Bellatrix Lestrange as bonder, rather than relying on a system of law. However, even in a Muggle world, a contract for the purpose envisioned by Snape and Narcissa would have to rely on some form of enforcement outside of the law. The law will not enforce a contract which is made for an illegal purpose or to perform an illegal act.

In the Muggle world contracts are usually of a fairly mundane character. Muggles make contracts to buy food and other necessities, to travel on public transport, to attend sporting or cultural events. In the world of magic many necessities seem to be conjured by magic. Mrs. Weasley produces meals for her very large family without shopping. On the other hand, there are numerous other dealings that we might expect to involve a contract between wizards and witches. The magic community deposits its money for safekeeping at the Gringotts Bank. The items needed for attendance at Hogwarts are purchased at the shops in Diagon Alley. Would these types of transactions need to rely on a law of contract, for example to provide basic consumer protection?

At the start of their third year at Hogwarts, Harry and his classmates purchase *The Monster Book of Monsters*. This is an unusually aggressive book that attacks all around it unless stroked along the spine. The book thus proves virtually unusable by the class. In the Muggle world, compensation for the purchase of defective goods might be available under the various conditions and warranties that are usually implied into contracts for the sale of goods. These terms commonly provide that goods are of merchantable quality and fit for their purpose. The maxim of buyer beware seems to apply to the purchase of *The Monster Book of Monsters* and, perhaps, this is appropriate. The implied terms protecting the rights of consumers in a Muggle world do not apply in cases where the purchaser had a chance to inspect the goods and identify the defects. In the case of *The Monster Book of Monsters,* which was stored in a cage at the bookshop, it would be readily apparent that the book had certain unusual features which might make normal use impossible. And given the nature of the magical world, it would not be all that surprising to the students to find that one of their schoolbooks was a little bit strange.

Issues of contract and consumer protection law also arise in relation to the products sold in "Weasleys' Wizard Wheezes," the joke shop run by Fred and George Weasley. Given the experiences of Hogwarts' students with the twins' inventions, it is possible that some of them might not work precisely as planned. Would there be any legal recourse for a disgruntled customer? Given that most of Fred and George's customers are themselves magical, there may be little need for a law of contract providing basic consumer protections. The customers themselves (or their parents) could presumably correct most defects in the goods sold to them. Or it may be that Fred and George would be obliged to accommodate and compensate disgruntled customers for reasons that go beyond the law. In the world of magic there must always be the threat of retaliation by a disgruntled customer in the form of a nasty curse. Moreover, and just as importantly, Fred and George might recognize that a reputation for fair dealing is important to the commercial success of their shop. One way such a reputation is built is by refunding, without dispute, the purchase price of defective goods and being prepared to throw in a little something extra as compensation for the inconvenience caused by defects in a product. In this sense, business in a magical world may be very similar to that in the Muggle world. In the Muggle world, contracting parties tend to use the law only as a last resort. Thus, in a now famous survey of contracting parties in the manufacturing industry, Macaulay concluded that "[d]isputes are frequently settled without reference to the contract or potential or actual legal sanctions. There is a hesitancy to speak of legal rights or to threaten to sue in these negotia-tions."[4] Contracting parties in a Muggle world tend instead to be influenced in mediating disputes by a range of factors outside the law, such as the value of reputation and the imperative of maintaining good business relationships.

Torts

Hogwarts students are injured fairly often in the Harry Potter books, but those injuries do not give rise to claims for compensation. For example, Neville falls off his broom in flying class and breaks his wrist; Harry falls 50 feet from a broomstick in a Quidditch match and Fleur Delacour and Viktor Krum are injured in the Triwizard Tournament. The Muggle parents of a child injured at school might well sue the school in tort for compensation for the injury to their child. Muggle schoolteachers and authorities owe their students a duty to take reasonable care to protect those students against any reasonably foresee-able risk of harm. No school in the United States or Australia would ever hold an event as dangerous as the Triwizard Tournament—and would never find in-surance if it did.

In the world of magic, the risk of harm in the course of a number of the school's activities is foreseeable, and few precautions against that harm seem to have been taken. Yet there is no mention of tort actions against the Hogwarts School on this basis. This lack of litigation is perhaps most telling in respect to the inci-dent in which Draco Malfoy is injured by the Hippogriff Buckbeak in Hagrid's class on the Care of Magical Beasts. Draco's father, Lucius Malfoy, dislikes Dumbledore and uses the incident as an excuse to vent these feelings to the school governors and the Ministry of Magic, with disastrous consequences for Buckbeak. From a Muggle perspective, suing Hogwarts and Dumbledore in tort for compensation for Malfoy's injury might have also been a very effective way of both attacking Dumbledore and effecting change in the organization of the school.

One reason for the lack of litigation may be that the magic world tolerates a higher level of risk than the Muggle world. Quidditch and the Triwizard Tournament are inherently risky activities and indeed seem to be embraced by the world of magic precisely for that reason. Another possible reason for a lack of tort law in the magical world is that magic renders redundant much of the

---

4. Stewart Macaulay, *Non-contractual Relations in Business: A Preliminary Study*, 28 Am. Sociological Rev. 55, 61 (1963). *See also* David Charny, *Nonlegal Sanctions in Commer-cial Relationships*, 104 Harv. L. Rev. 375 (1990).

need for compensation for injury. Damages in the law of tort are awarded primarily to compensate an individual for the harm caused by the wrong of another. In other words, the damages aim to restore the victim in a monetary sense to the position he or she would have been in had the tort not been committed. The accidental injuries occurring at Hogwarts are generally mended quite promptly by Madam Pomfrey, the Hogwarts Healer. There is then little need for a monetary award to compensate for the harm.

Tort law is sometimes applauded for its effect in providing incentives for individuals to take care and to reform careless or unsafe practices. The argument is that the one factor influencing us as members of society to take care in our dealings with each other is the threat of being liable for damages for the harm caused if we don't take care. Would a law of tort in a magic world also provide such an incentive? It seems unlikely that the impulsive Hagrid would have been dissuaded from introducing his class to the Hippogriffs by such an abstract possibility; much more effective was the resort by Lucius Malfoy to the regulatory authority. However, even in a Muggle world there are arguments that there are other factors that are at least as important as the law of torts in ensuring individuals take care in their dealings with each other. These factors include our respect for other members of the society, the importance of a good reputation in our interactions with other members of the community, and the role of regulatory authorities in policing undesirable or unsafe activities. We drive carefully not merely because we are concerned about being sued if we injure someone, but also, and perhaps primarily, because we do not want to injure other human beings or their property.

Public Law

Public law has a more prominent role in the Harry Potter books, which is very different from public law in the modern Muggle world and, in comparison, its role is relatively insignificant. Public law is law which involves relationships between individuals and the rulers in a society as well as those laws which are designed to guide and limit the exercise of power by that society's rulers. Criminal and constitutional law are two major forms of public law.

Criminal Law

The criminal law in Harry Potter's world is part of a complex, bureaucratic system that does not separate legislative, executive, and judicial powers. The system does not appear to distinguish between breaches of simple administrative regulations—for example, Arthur Weasley's magically tampering with a Muggle car; dragon breeding, outlawed by a Warlock's Convention of 1709; or operating as an unregistered Animagus—and behavior that might be understood as verging on criminal—for example, engaging in underage magic or use of a wand by a non-human—or what would be clearly considered as criminal—for example, the use of Unforgiveable Curses. In all these situations breaches are investigated, prosecuted and tried by the Ministry of Magic, except in more serious cases where the Wizard court, the Wizengamot, is used. However, even there the presence of the Ministry is all-pervasive.

Much of what we call policing is carried out by ordinary wizards and witches in the Ministry. Arthur Weasley, for example, as Head of the Misuse of Muggle Artifacts Office, is himself fined fifty Galleons for bewitching a Muggle car which was used by Harry and Ron to enter Hogwarts in *The Chamber of Secrets*. At another time, others are fined for Apparating without a licence. The discovery and apprehension of the wrongdoers seems to be the work of the officers of these departments.

More serious wrongdoing calls into aid a different office, that of the Improper Use of Magic. When Harry uses magic to ward off Dementors who attack him and his cousin Dudley, it is that Office that charges him with using magic in the presence of Muggles, breaching section 13 of the *International Confederation of Wizards' Statute of Secrecy*. When some Muggle baiters set off a backfiring jinx in the Elephant and Castle it is sorted out by the Magical Law Enforcement Squad (which is part of the Improper Use of Magic Office) and it is Bob Ogden as the head of that squad who attempts to arrest Morfin Gaunt, Voldemort's uncle.

Aurors are wizards whose sole function is the detection and apprehension of dark wizards; those wizards who threaten the lives of Muggles and magical folk alike. Aurors are similar to a SWAT team except that they have much more status in the magical world. To be accepted as an Auror demands one must have had high grades at school, such as normally needed to study law or medicine in the Muggle world.

The court process in the magical world is essentially bureaucratic. In several instances we are told that hearings have taken place and they seem to be entirely administrative and not curial (that is, they don't have the features that we would normally associate with a court). Arthur Weasley's hearing for bewitching a car does not seem to have been conducted by the Wizengamot, and the hearing to determine if Buckbeak is to be destroyed is conducted as an administrative matter, although it is apparent that some rules of natural justice apply—Harry, Ron and Hermione, with varying degrees of application, investigate evidence and advise Hagrid. The appeal from the decision to kill Buckbeak is cursory and ad hoc and would not pass any standard of natural justice. Fudge, after all, makes it quite clear that the appeal will fail. Having the executioner as a member of the appeal panel made it clear that the appeal was doomed.

We do have evidence of four more serious court processes. In *The Order of the Phoenix*, Harry is charged with a serious breach of the *Statute of Secrecy* and faces a complete trial. In fact, Arthur Weasley is astounded that Harry's alleged breach of wizarding law merited a full trial in the Wizengamot and Dumbledore voices a similar comment during the trial. The process is unusual to our eyes. Harry is still a minor, yet he is given neither a lawyer (perhaps not surprising given their absence in this world) nor the equivalent of a *guardian ad litem*.[5] Dumbledore presents himself as a witness for the defence although this is without Harry's knowledge (and, therefore, permission) but then acts, effectively, as Harry's defence counsel. The hearing is run by Fudge, who is the Minister for Magic, and Harry is questioned by a panel of three wizards who are the Interrogators for the trial and all of whom are members of the Ministry. Fudge acts as prosecutor in chief and he runs the trial, but the matter of guilt or innocence is decided by all the wizards in attendance, in this case about fifty or so, by a simple majority vote. Fudge and the other two Ministry wizards also vote. In common law jurisdictions, such as the United States and Australia, judges do not prosecute, and they do not participate in jury decision-making. Neither are they members of the administrative and executive parts of government. This example shows that the separation of powers is not apparent in the court processes of the magical world.

One intriguing aspect of criminal law in the magical world is raised by the issue of money. In all the books it is evident that some wizards and witches are richer, far richer, than others. Ron is forever bemoaning the fact that his parents are poor and cannot afford to buy him new robes, a fancy owl or a ritzier broomstick, and the Gaunts, the paternal ancestors of Voldemort, are clearly poverty stricken, while on the other hand, the Malfoys are clearly wealthy. Yet why can't all wizards be wealthy? As Harry notes when he discusses the death of Voldemort's mother with Dumbledore and how she had sold the family's sole treasure, Slytherin's locket, because she was broke, "But she could do magic ... She could have got food and everything for herself by magic, couldn't she?"[6] If this is the case, why is anyone poor? Several possible reasons come to mind.

---

5. A guardian appointed to represent the interests of a person in litigation is a *guardian ad litem*. In Latin this means "guardian for the proceeding."

6. *Half-Blood Prince* 245.

It is clear that magical skills vary greatly, from Dumbledore and Voldemort at one extreme to someone like Neville Longbottom who seems a poor wizard (apart from his speciality in Herbology), and, eventually, to squibs such as Filch the caretaker and Harry's neighbour in Little Whinging, Arabella Figg, who can do no magic at all. It may be that, relatively simple tasks apart, there is specialization in the magical world and money is used when a wizard or witch finds it difficult to conjure, transfigure or brew whatever it is that they want or need. It may be, for example, that while Mrs. Weasley can cook and clean by magic, she finds robe making far more difficult and is not confident in going beyond her evident pleasure in knitting. If this is the case, the use of money, to buy new robes for Ron for example, (*Goblet of Fire*) becomes necessary and explicable. Even in a magical world one will need money to buy that which one can't make.

This need for money raises the question: why don't the wizards and witches conjure or transfigure their way to a vault full of Galleons? We can assume that there is a law against counterfeiting, but the temptation to break it would be so great and the potential number of wizards and witches with sufficient skill and determination to counterfeit money would be large enough that law by itself would seem a poor guardian. In our world we rely mainly on technology as a barrier with some deterrent effect from the severity of the sanctions imposed by the law if one is caught. In the magical world we can imagine that the accumulated wisdom and power of generations of wizards have created spells so strong that counterfeiting is just impossible. Something similar, after all, prevents even Snape, a wizard of uncommon power and skill, from Disapparating from the grounds of Hogwarts when he escapes with Draco Malfoy after having killed Dumbledore. As a frustrated Hermione keeps reminding Harry and Ron, *Hogwarts: A History* explains that Hogwarts has been enchanted so no one can Apparate in or out of Hogwarts' castle or grounds.

Constitutional Law

A second significant area of public law is constitutional law, which has very little role in Harry Potter's world. Constitutional law deals with the legal restraints on the exercise of political power. In the United States and Australia, for example, we have constitutions which set out the legal structure of our political systems (the design and power of legislatures and their relationship to the citizens), the powers and limits given to and imposed on our executive leaders (the U.S. President and the Australian Prime Minister) and the nature and reach of our judicial systems. Ultimately, all constitutions are designed to allow for the exercise of political power, but they also, with varying degrees of success, are designed to protect the liberty of the citizens under the reach of this power.

To the extent that there is a constitutional law in the magical world, it is informal and largely unwritten. In this way it is similar to that of the United Kingdom which, until it joined the European Union, could be described as a potential parliamentary despotism partly controlled by the history of liberty embedded in the country's culture and institutions. The Ministry of Magic does not seem to have any constitutional constraints on its operation other than the vigilance of the population of wizards and witches and the widespread dislike of the Dark Arts. In the United States and Australia the limits on power are various. We both have a separation of powers with the legislative, executive, and judicial arms occupied by different people (in Australia the separation between the legislative and executive arms is not as clear-cut as in the U.S.). In addition we both have a federal system which splits these powers between the federal and the state governments. We both have an independent judiciary and, in addition, the U.S. has a Bill of Rights enforced by judges. All these devices are designed to limit governmental power to protect individual liberty.[7]

None of these devices exist in the magical world. Indeed, there does not even seem to be any provision for elections. It is not clear how the Ministry is staffed, and it appears to be the Minister of Magic, perhaps with senior colleagues, who decides who gets employed and who gets promoted. In *The Half-Blood Prince*, Fudge tells the Muggle Prime Minister that he has been sacked but does not explain by whom and neither does he explain how his successor, Rufus Scrimgeour, was chosen to succeed him. In *The Order of the Phoenix* Dumbledore is voted out of the Chairmanship of the International Confederation of Wizards by Ministry officials.

In essence, the magical world is run by an oligarchy of senior wizards with no clear, regular means of political participation by the population. However, public opinion seems to matter—Sirius Black tells Harry, Hermione and Ron that many witches and wizards wanted Barty Crouch Senior to become Minister of Magic, but that the discovery that his son had been a Death Eater had destroyed his support. Additionally, Fudge in his last meeting with the Prime Minister tells him that the wizarding community had been calling for his resignation for a fortnight. What is not clear is how this popular feeling trans-

---

7. A superb and accessible historical, legal, and political discussion of these issues is contained in *The Federalist*, a collection of essays written by Alexander Hamilton, John Jay and James Madison in support of ratification of the Constitution of the United States.

lates into an impact on government. In our world the people participate in governance by regular elections for our rulers.

There is no mention of an elected (or, indeed, an appointed) legislature in the world of magic. What information we are given is that bureaucrats such as Arthur Weasley "write" laws. In one example, Arthur Weasley seems to have drafted a law that would allow him to tinker with a Muggle car because of a loophole that he intentionally placed in it. Dolores Umbridge is responsible for drafting anti-werewolf legislation that makes it almost impossible for Remus Lupin to find a job, and at Harry's trial before the Wizengamot, in an exchange with Dumbledore about what laws were applicable in the present case, Fudge says, "Laws can be changed."[8] During Umbridge's reign of terror at Hogwarts the Ministry passes a number of laws giving her increased powers over Hogwarts, its teachers and its students. Law making appears to be the prerogative of the Ministry and the more powerful officials there.

As we have seen above, the Ministry and its most important officials have a strong, perhaps predominant, role in the trying of offenses tempered only in the Wizengamot by the jury system. Unlike our world there is no independent judiciary to interpret the laws and oversee criminal and civil trials. The potential for despotism and authoritarian rule in the magical world is obvious.

Indeed, as the books proceed and the danger from Voldemort increases, the Ministry does assume an authoritarian, sometimes even despotic, form. Certainly Fudge in his time as Minister of Magic has a flexible attitude toward his powers. For example, in *The Prisoner of Azkaban*, Fudge seemingly decides on his own not to prosecute Harry for his breach of the underage wizardry law and in the same book Fudge makes little attempt to hide the fact that the appeal against the sentence to destroy Buckbeak is a foregone conclusion by bringing along McNair, the executioner, as part of the appeal panel. The latitude assumed by Fudge gradually assumes more sinister forms. In *The Prisoner of Azkaban* the Ministry grants the Dementors permission to give the Dementors' Kiss if Sirius Black is captured, effectively imposing a death sentence without trial. In *The Goblet of Fire*, Fudge "interviews" Barty Crouch Junior after his capture and takes along a Dementor for "protection." The Dementor carries out the Kiss. In essence Fudge has issued and carried out a death sentence without any supervision and without Crouch being given the benefit of a trial. Fudge manipulates his power within the Ministry and the Wizengamot to deny Harry natural justice in his trial in *The Order of the Phoenix* by rescheduling his trial at the

---

8. *Order of the Phoenix* 137.

very last moment to keep Dumbledore away. Harry is only saved because Dumbledore anticipates this maneuver. Fudge is also behind Umbridge's ever-increasing authoritarian rule of Hogwarts. When Fudge is replaced by Scrimgeour, the Ministry gains in rigour but loses nothing in its authoritarian tendencies. The new Minister places great pressure on Harry to publicly nail his colors to the Ministry mast and shows his authoritarian streak by arresting Stan Shunpike, the Knight Bus conductor, even though it is generally conceded that Shunpike is not a Death Eater.

It is not only the Minister, however, who displays authoritarian tendencies. Barty Crouch Senior stuns his house elf to keep her quiet and uses his influence to persuade Amos Diggory not to question her about the Death Mark at the Quidditch World Cup despite it being within Diggory's duties to question the elf. Later on in the same book, Sirius Black tells Harry, Hermione, and Ron that Crouch Senior, when head of the Department of Magical Law Enforcement, had had Sirius sent to Azkaban without trial and had given the Aurors power to kill and use the Unforgiveable Curses against suspects. Umbridge's reign at Hogwarts is not only authoritarian, it is violent as well. When Umbridge wants to sack Hagrid, she and several other wizards attack him and in doing so stun Professor McGonagall to unconsciousness. Umbridge then prepares to use the Cruciatus Curse on Harry who is saved by some quick thinking from Hermione.

The power of the Minister or other senior Ministry wizards to act in this fashion is subject to few formal restraints. During Harry's trial before the Wizengamot, mention is made of a Wizengamot Charter of Rights but there is no indication that this is anything other than an administrative measure which can be changed by the Ministry. There is neither an entrenched Bill of Rights nor a written constitution setting out the rules by which government operates and neither is there an independent judiciary to interpret the laws and police the work of government free from that government's control.

The otherwise unbounded Ministry appears to be subject to only two forms of restraint. First, some in the wizarding world display an attachment to the rule of law. Even in as trivial an example as Arthur Weasley's drafting of a law to allow him to bewitch a Muggle car we see a desire to follow a legal path. Harry, Hermione and Ron act as junior advocates, searching for precedents to help Hagrid defend Buckbeak, and Hermione and Harry are clearly mindful of the illegality of their actions in going back in time to rescue Sirius and Buckbeak at the end of *The Prisoner of Azkaban*. Dumbledore's defense of Harry at his Wizengamot trial is pure legalism in action with Dumbledore constantly insisting that the court must consider the charge before it and *only that charge* without any reference to previous alleged wrongdoing by Harry. As we have seen, not all wizards, especially those in the Ministry, have the same appreciation of the rule of law, but the fact that many wizards do must act as a brake on the authoritarian potential of the wizarding form of government.

The second, and probably more important, restraint on authoritarianism is rebellion. This is the option taken by Dumbledore when Harry and Dumbledore's Army is threatened by Umbridge and the Ministry. He simply resists arrest by violently casting aside Umbridge and the wizards who try to arrest him. The Order and Dumbledore's Army are secret paramilitary forces and both effectively invade the Ministry when Voldemort attempts to obtain the Prophecy in the Department of Mysteries. Rebellion is not lightly entered into but neither is it a desperate, once in a lifetime option either. It is clearly considered a reasonable and not necessarily remarkable matter and much the same attitude is displayed by the members of Dumbledore's Army at Hogwarts who are, after all, still students. It is this feature of wizard society that is probably the strongest defence against the possibility of despotism that is inherent in its form of government.

Harry Potter's World as a Heroic Society

As we have seen, law is relatively unimportant in the magical world. Wizards and witches do not rely on it to transact business or to compensate for injuries caused by others. In part this reflects what happens in our world where use of contract law is unusual. In part this reflects the capacity of wizards and witches to heal injuries and damage to goods in ways that are denied to us, and, in part, it reflects a much more robust attitude toward risk than that to which we are accustomed; one that would be, perhaps, unattractive to many in our society.

In our world the law is central to the maintenance of liberty. Constitutions are designed to control governmental power through devices such as the separation of powers, the federal structure of government and the importance of an independent judiciary. None of these features is replicated in Harry Potter's world. It is not law that constrains Fudge and his kind, although some forms of law and legalistic thinking are important features of the magical world. Rather, it is the ready recourse to rebellion and, if necessary, violence which seems to be the most important constraint on governmental power.

This reliance on rebellion and, if necessary, violence, adds drama and mythic proportion to the Harry Potter books. The reader constantly wonders what will constrain the menace posed by Voldemort and his followers? In some ways the answer is similar to that given in our world when faced by the aggressive evil of Hitler. Ultimately, it is force that will defeat Voldemort, just as it was force that defeated Hitler. But whereas in that case, at least in the Western democracies, it was an organized, democratic form of force, in the magical world the use of force seems patterned on the attitudes and practices of Homeric or Viking Saga heroes or Arthurian legend. Dumbledore fights a long, somewhat solitary fight against Voldemort aided and abetted by a number of close friends and like-minded wizards, and Harry sees it as his destiny to battle to the death with Voldemort, perhaps in the company of his close friends Hermione and Ron.

There is much to admire in the figures of Dumbledore, the Order, and Harry, Hermione, Ron, and their friends, but they belong to a different world than us Muggles in more ways than one. They do not share the faith in law and constitutional government that we in the West treasure. In many ways, they are a throwback to earlier forms of battling evils, forms that were neither legalistic nor necessarily liberal, but certainly heroic.

Bots and *Gemots*: Anglo-Saxon Legal References in Harry Potter

Susan P. Liemer

Fans of the Harry Potter books know how carefully J.K. Rowling chooses names. She populates Harry's wizard world with characters whose names suggest their qualities and their roles in the plot. Rowling then fills that world with all manner of things for which she creates equally clever names. For older children and adults alike, one way the books engage readers is by allowing us to decipher meaning in the names of people and things. To fully appreciate what many of the names communicate, a reader needs some familiarity with Latin and French, or, at least, the linguistic roots they have leant to modern English. Fortunately, readers who do not know that "Voldemort" is French for "flight of death" likely will know someone else who can enlighten them. But fewer Harry Potter fans, including many American lawyers, catch one of the most prominent Anglo-Saxon legal references in the later books.

When I first read the word "Wizengamot," the reference brought me back to a childhood history lesson. I knew immediately that the "Wizengamot" was a wizard court, comprising the wisest of the wizard elders. I also knew that this court's name must refer back to the *witenagemot,* an important legal and political institution of Anglo-Saxon society.

I want to be clear from the outset what I mean by "Anglo-Saxon." Americans are probably most familiar with the term "Anglo-Saxon" as it is used, usually derogatorily, in the expression "W.A.S.P." or "white Anglo-Saxon Protestant," or the related adjective "waspy." Some Americans may also associate references to the Anglo-Saxon way of life with the beliefs of a few skin-headed radicals. I am not referring to either of those groups here. I am only referring to the peoples who inhabited much of what is now England, in the few hundred years before the Norman Conquest, i.e., before 1066. The Anglos and the Saxons were Germanic tribes who took over much of England from the Britons, Celts, and descendants of Romans who were previously living there. These Anglo-Saxons, quite naturally, built a society based on what they had known before arriving on the island, and then the society developed over time under the influences of local conditions, events, and leaders. Most Anglo-Saxons had a pagan religion until the arrival of St. Theodore of Tarsus, from the Continent, in the late seventh century.[1] Their tribes gradually merged into several small kingdoms, each led by its own king.

The Anglo-Saxon language shares its roots with other Germanic languages. It was the fusion of Anglo-Saxon and Norman French that created the English language with its huge vocabulary. The distance from the Anglo-Saxon language to modern English is great enough to make understanding the predecessor difficult for anyone not familiar with one of the Germanic languages. Thus, the first step in understanding the *witenagemot* is to simply translate it and borrow meaning from that term in order to better understand the Wizengamot. *Wit* in Anglo-Saxon referred to wisdom or knowledge. It is the root word of many similar English words, including "wits," "witty," and even "witness." Quite relevant to the world of Harry Potter, the Anglo-Saxon *wit* likely is also the origin of the English word "witch." There was a time in pagan Anglo-Saxon society when a witch was a respected female elder who had specialized knowledge of the natural world, such as how to heal with herbal remedies. *Wita* was a wise person. *Witen* simply referred to "wise people" or, more colloquially, "wise ones." And so by extrapolation "Wizen" becomes a play on words that means "wise wizards."

Like most words in early languages, *witen* had alternate spellings, including *witten* and *witan*. And like many words, it had a meaning beyond its literal translation. In Anglo-Saxon times, every king had his *witan*. Many of the surviving Anglo-Saxon documents that refer to some aspect of the laws or the legal system include references to actions taken by "the king with his *witan*" or gatherings of "the king and his *witan*."[2]

Exactly what the *witan* was and did has been explained differently by the great English legal historians of different time periods. Of course, some of those differences may be attributed to exactly which century a historian was examining because, like most human social institutions, the nature and function of the *witan* changed over time. Some of those differences can be explained by the century the historian lived in, as each was inevitably influenced by his

---

1. *See* G.O. SAYLES, THE MEDIEVAL FOUNDATIONS OF ENGLAND 52–53 (1950) (describing the tenuous state of the church in England at the time of Theodore's arrival).

2. Examples in English translation and in the original Anglo-Saxon can be found throughout most of the texts cited in this chapter.

own society's views of English history and the historiographical methods of their time.

I understood J.K. Rowling's tip of the hat to the *witenagemot* because I first learned about this legal institution in the sixth grade in the 1960s, in an American private school with an old-fashioned curriculum, modeled on the curriculum of similar British schools. After making some inquiries recently, I learned that adults in England who attended school in the 1950s likely would have learned about the *witenagemot* too, and were taught the same explanation I was. In contrast, I discovered, when I took a university course in English Constitutional History, that most of my American contemporaries never learned about the *witenagemot* in grade school. I later learned that most English schoolchildren no longer learn about it either. No wonder so many people miss this reference in the Harry Potter books.

Apparently, the version of *witan* history being taught to schoolchildren in the mid-twentieth century was the legacy of Victorian legal historians. The story went something like this: The *witan* was a group of village elders who heard and settled disputes. These elders were respected for their experience and wisdom; they were "wise ones." They formed the rudimentary legal system of each tribe, in each rural village. And (this is a very big *and*) they were a group of twelve men and the precursor of the jury as we know it today. Of course, here in the lesson, the grade school teacher would be obliged to emphasize the importance and enlightenment of the jury system.

More recent historians explain the *witan* as a council of important men that the Anglo-Saxon king gathered together for advice on important matters, including decisions on major legal infractions. In pagan times the *witan* was composed of the men who held the highest ranks in Anglo-Saxon society and the greatest wealth. Eventually, high-ranking ecclesiastics held sway in the *witan* too.[3]

The Anglo-Saxon writings are quite clear that the *witan* had to approve a new king before he took office. Anglo-Saxon kings did not reign with the sort of absolute monarchy known in the feudal societies developing contemporaneously on the continent. The seeds of that type of monarchy arrived in England with the Norman Conquest. The Anglo-Saxon kings apparently benefited from the political support gained by the formal approval process of the *witan*.[4] Although the consensus of the *witan* as to who was best suited to rule often followed the

---

3. *See* SAYLES, *supra* note 1, at 193 (explaining interplay of the *witan* and ecclesiastics in the eleventh century).

4. *See* SAYLES, *supra* note 1, at 179 (describing the *witan's* check on the king as political, not constitutional).

hereditary lines of leading families, it was not a requirement and not always the outcome.[5] Although some historians have said that the *witan* "elected" the king, it was not the type of election one would recognize in a modern democracy.

Parallels to this sort of *witan* are seen in the Harry Potter books. Although there is no king in these books, there are prominent families whose descendants historically tend to be in the important positions and inner circles that lead the wizard world. Perhaps the Order of the Phoenix is the wizard world's *witan*. Harry is obviously in line for an important position some day, even if we can only speculate as to exactly what roles he will play in his lifetime. Voldemort's reign can be seen as analogous to the brutal monarchy of William the Conqueror who turned parts of England, literally, into dead zones to obtain absolute control,[6] executing his own "flight of death." In contrast, we watch Harry learn to exercise leadership more in the manner of the Anglo-Saxon kings: with the support and counsel of his contemporaries. (Surely it is no coincidence that the last of the Anglo-Saxon kings was Harold, our protagonist's namesake. Of course, in the context of the book series, J.K. Rowling sees fit to turn the table on history and not let Voldemort, William I's reflection, prevail.)

So what of the *gemot* in *witenagemot* and Wizengamot? In the Anglo-Saxon language, *gemot* referred to a meeting or gathering. In a Germanic language, *ge* simply would denote a verb's past participle, and *mot* was an Anglo-Saxon form of the verb "meet." So *gemot* would have been a noun back-formed from a verb, originally meaning something like "having met" or "assembled" and eventually meaning "meeting," "assembly," or "gathering." Likely it is from *gemot* that we get the English words "meet" and "meeting."

The lesson I learned in grade school was that the *witenagemot* was a larger gathering of the wise men, particularly as the kingdoms started consolidating in later Anglo-Saxon times.[7] The *witenagemot* was supposed to have been the precursor to the Norman *curia regis*, council of the king, which later developed into the English Parliament. And so the mid-twentieth century school lesson neatly accounted for the origins of both the jury and Parliament with

---

5. *See* KURT VON S. KYNELL, SAXON AND MEDIEVAL ANTECEDENTS OF THE ENGLISH COMMON LAW 20 (2000) (explaining the selection of King Harold, successor to King Edward the Confessor, who was related by marriage not blood).

6. *See* SAYLES, *supra* note 1, at 221 ("He turned one thousand square miles and more of land into a wilderness and imposed upon it the peace of death....").

7. King Alfred the Great is usually described as the first king of all the tribes combined, "*Rex Anglorum et Saxonum*," from 871 to 899. R.H. HODGKIN, A HISTORY OF THE ANGLO-SAXONS, VOL. II, 582 (3d ed. 1959).

democratic representation in both the courts and the legislature, neatly separated.

Many types of *gemots* existed in the Anglo-Saxon world, such as the *folkgemots*, a lower level gathering of people to take care of local matters. There were also alternate spellings for *witenagemot*, including *witanagemot* and *wittenagemot*. Most likely the word *witenagemot* simply meant "a meeting or gathering of the *witan*" and did not refer to a different institution in Anglo-Saxon society. In Anglo-Saxon times there was no separation of powers into three branches of government and no true representational democracy. Stemming from the culture of rural Germanic tribes, the Anglo-Saxons did have a society that was a bit more egalitarian than England's post-Conquest, feudal society. They did not view their king as divinely-anointed, and the differences between the lowliest and loftiest members of society were not as extreme as they became post-Conquest. However, there was still a definite pecking order and a hierarchy of positions within society that were based on sheer physical power, wealth, and lineage. Furthermore, while the *witan* approved each new king, it was still just a council of leading men rallying behind their new leader.[8] While the tiny seeds of modern Anglo-American legal and political concepts may have been sown in Anglo-Saxon times, if transported back in time, we would likely not recognize them. The proto-parliamentary *witanagemot* I learned about in grade school probably was wishful thinking on the part of earlier legal historians.[9]

For Harry Potter fans, if the *witenagemot* was a meeting of the wise men to decide important judicial and political matters, then by analogy the Wizengamot is a meeting of the wise wizard leaders to decide important matters. Whether J.K. Rowling learned the typical post-Victorian school lesson in her youth, took a university course in English legal history, or studied the more nuanced interpretations of today's historians, I do not know. My guess would be she has not delved into the most recent scholarship, some of which I reviewed before writing this chapter, only because I do not picture her having the time to devote to it. Although today's scholars write in twenty-first century English, they are examining documents written in the Anglo-Saxon language. They

---

8. *See* SAYLES, *supra* note 1, at 175 ("The old views of the witan, which saw it as a kind of democratic parliament, deliberately devised to limit the king's power and to act as a constitutional check upon his authority, very largely make a botch of the evidence.").

9. *See* PATRICK WORMALD, THE MAKING OF ENGLISH LAW: KING ALFRED TO THE TWELFTH CENTURY, VOL. I, 1–27 (1999) (describing erroneous interpretations by leading English legal historians) and 277–85 (quoting and re-interpreting King Alfred's description of a legislative process).

tend to assume anyone reading their work has a working knowledge of Anglo-Saxon. Most texts about English legal history, whatever time period they were written in, are rife with quotes in medieval Latin and Old French, as well as a smattering of other Germanic and Norse languages. J.K. Rowling obviously knows some French and Latin, as she uses these languages frequently to name her characters and their spells. Whether she would choose to wade through explanations of legal concepts with names in Anglo-Saxon, medieval Latin, Norman French, early Danish, Viking, and other archaic languages, I can only speculate. Even those who have experience with the languages and concepts find the review arduous.[10]

Knowing that the Wizengamot derives its name from the *witenagemot* may help readers of the Harry Potter books to relax some concerns about certain procedural aspects of the trials held before that wizard body. For example, in Anglo-Saxon times, there were no appeals from legal decisions. Once the tribunal passed judgment on a matter, that was that.[11] The right to appeal developed after the Norman Conquest, likely with influence from the ecclesiastical courts. Likewise, in the wizard world, the Wizengamot appears to have no avenue of appeal.

Another important aspect of an Anglo-Saxon criminal trial was the swearing of oaths by *kin*, including relatives, the tribal chief, and sometimes close friends of the accused.[12] Gathering detailed evidence and sworn testimony by eyewitnesses in order to prove a matter beyond a reasonable doubt was not the goal. Instead, close relations would stand and vouch for the good character of the accused. Although some details about the events leading to the charges would likely surface, that was not the focus of the testimony. What the accused might have to say about the charge was not considered as important, if he spoke at all.[13] The oath swearing of *kin* was key; the more *kin* you got to show up and the more prominent they were in the social hierarchy, the more likely you were to successfully beat the rap. Conversely, if you were accused of break-

---

10. An eminent scholar of the Anglo-Saxons once confessed that the study "reduces me to a state of mental chaos." CHARLES PLUMMER, LIFE AND TIMES OF ALFRED THE GREAT 122 (1902).

11. *See* Henry Adams, *The Anglo Saxon Courts of Law, in* ESSAYS IN ANGLO-SAXON LAW 26 (1876) (suggesting the system's strictness encouraged arbitration both outside and during court proceedings).

12. *See generally* J. Laurence Laughlin, *The Anglo-Saxon Legal Procedure, in* ESSAYS IN ANGLO-SAXON LAW 186–87, 287–99 (1876) (describing types of oaths and oath supporters).

13. *See* SAYLES, *supra* note 1, at 122 ("[T]he assembly-courts would pay no attention to a mere individual and do nothing on his sole behalf. They required every litigant to be accompanied by his kindred to vouch for him.").

ing the law and had no one to stand up for you, you had little chance of success at trial.

In *The Order of the Phoenix*, Harry is put on trial before the Wizengamot. He had used magic in Little Whinging, the Muggle town where his aunt and uncle lived. He executed the Patronus spell to protect himself and his Muggle cousin, Dudley, from dementors that were blithely gliding down Privet Drive. Since dementors were supposed to be working for the Ministry of Magic, which forbid them from being in the Muggle realm, Harry understood their presence as evidence that they had started working for Voldemort. With the Patronus, Harry violated the prohibition on underage wizards using magic beyond the grounds of Hogwarts, as well as the general prohibition against using magic around Muggles.

When Harry's trial for these violations begins in *The Order of the Phoenix*, Dumbledore makes his presence known by introducing himself as "Witness for the defense, Albus Percival Wulfric Brian Dumbledore."[14] Note that Dumbledore's full name here summons to memory the major cultural roots of the English people, including, via "Wulfric," the Anglo-Saxons.[15] Interestingly, Dumbledore does not actually testify as a witness to the events that led to Harry's transgressions.

At times during the proceedings, Dumbledore seems to act as the defense attorney, calling an eye-witness and making arguments on Harry's behalf. At other times, he seems to join the three judges, the Inquisitors, as a co-equal, as if he were a member of the bench discussing how best to dispose of the case. The ease with which Dumbledore converses with the Inquisitors can be explained partially by the fact that until recently he held the position of Chief Warlock of the Wizengamot. Of course, Cornelius Fudge, the none-too-bright Minister of Magic, has now given himself the job. And so the wise Dumbledore sounds at times like a law professor patiently leading his student to discover the correct solution to a legal problem. The role of Inquisitor, a judge who asks fact-finding questions, resembles more the role of a civil law judge in Continental Europe than the role of an English common law judge. In Anglo-Saxon hearings too, the role of the judge would have resembled the modern civil law model more, descending as it did from the Germanic tribal customs. Above all other roles that Dumbledore plays at Harry's trial, it is his very presence, his arrival there on Harry's behalf, that counts most. At the outset of the proceedings, "[a] powerful emotion had risen in Harry's chest at the sight of Dumbledore, a fortified, hopeful feeling...."[16] Of course, Harry knew from past

---

14. *Order of the Phoenix* 139.

15. *Albus* is Latin, *Percival* is from Old French, *Brian* is of Celtic origin, and *Dumbledore* is Old English.

16. *Order of the Phoenix* 139.

experience that he could count on his mentor to help out brilliantly. Harry also knew the esteem with which Dumbledore was held by most good wizards. Dumbledore's magical powers were renowned, he was the longtime Headmaster of Hogwarts, and he had until quite recently presided over the Wizengamot as Chief Warlock. He needed only to clear his throat, and the entire Wizengamot fell silent.[17] Dumbledore was one of the most prominent people in wizarding society, exactly analogous to the ideal person an accused Anglo-Saxon would have wanted vouching for him at trial.

Towards the end of the trial, Harry realizes that "[h]e had not really said very much. He ought to have explained more fully...."[18] Readers are meant to share his anxiety about the imminent outcome of the proceedings, though we might worry a little less about the accused having little say before the Wizengamot, if we assume that the accused's word was not so very important before that tribunal, just as was so with its precursor, the *witenagemot*. When the likes of Dumbledore has stood up for the accused, who cares about the presumably self-serving protests of a fifteen-year-old boy? At the very end of Harry's court proceedings, the decision is put to the entire gathering, the *gemot* of wizards, just as it might have been put to the *gemot* of the *witan* in an important Anglo-Saxon legal proceeding.

Now compare this scene with the trials in *The Goblet of Fire*. After falling into Dumbledore's Pensieve, Harry watches three trials in that exact same courtroom, trials that actually took place a generation earlier. Because he is observing Dumbledore's stored memories, no one in the room can see him. These earlier trials take place at a grimmer time when the Ministry of Magic is tying up loose ends after fighting back Voldemort who, for awhile, had gained many followers and was extremely dangerous. Barty Crouch presides over these proceedings.

First, Igor Karkaroff is on trial. He shows remorse for having followed Voldemort and turns informant against some of the Death Eaters. When he fingers Severus Snape as a Death Eater, Crouch says that "Snape has been cleared by this council.... He has been vouched for by Albus Dumbledore."[19] This is an earlier instance of Dumbledore's vouching saving the accused. The weight of Dumbledore's word was enough to acquit an adult accused of a much more serious crime. Karkaroff is not at all convinced and repeats in strong terms that Snape really is a Death Eater. Even Mad-Eye Moody, who spent six months tracking down Karkaroff and very much would like Karkaroff's information to

---

17. *Order of the Phoenix* 142.
18. *Order of the Phoenix* 150.
19. *Goblet of Fire* 590.

be useless so that a sentence would stick, "was wearing a look of deep skepticism behind Dumbledore's back."[20] So at least two wizards disagree with Dumbledore's assessment of Snape. Nonetheless, Dumbledore vouched for Snape, and the court had no reason to doubt his word.

Of course, J.K. Rowling is setting up what seems like Snape's ultimate betrayal when he later kills Dumbledore in *The Half-Blood Prince*. But a reader who has gotten only as far as *The Goblet of Fire* also has no reason to doubt Dumbledore and tends to dismiss the naysayers instead. This frame of mind would be akin to that of an Anglo-Saxon, who had no reason to doubt an upstanding member of the community vouching for an accused person. Similarly, J.K. Rowling lures her audience into believing that the word of the wise and well-respected Dumbledore in these proceedings is equally as infallible. The easy trust of her readers is built up over the course of four books, and this confidence in Dumbledore's opinion may make the Anglo-Saxon legal procedures seem less naive to a modern audience.

The third of these earlier trials is also instructive because one of the defendants is, like Harry, just a boy. Unfortunately, the outcome of the other boy's trial differs dramatically from Harry's. This boy is Crouch's son. He and three adults are accused of subjecting Neville Longbottom's parents to the heinous Cruciatus Curse, to help restore Voldemort to power. No one comes forward to vouch or testify for these defendants. Crouch's son screams repeatedly that he was not involved, beseeching his father, as well as his mother, who sits in the courtroom absolutely shattered. Just as in Anglo-Saxon times, what the accused had to say did not matter much, and all four defendants are whisked away to Azkaban by their dementor guards.

Another aspect of Harry's trial that appears to lack procedural fairness is the full-court press (pun intended) imposed for a relatively minor offense by a juvenile. This practice likely was not typical of Anglo-Saxon habits. At least some surviving documents indicate that the law was allowed to apply differently to young people. For example, a law report from the year 924 indicates that King Aethelstan thought capital punishment was too cruel for a co-operative fifteen year old's first charge of theft,[21] even though capital punishment would not have been unusual for an uncooperative, recidivist adult thief.

The story of Harry's trial shows us that leniency for juvenile offenders is typical in the wizard world as well. First, right in the middle of the trial, we are carefully reminded how very young Harry still is. Madam Bones, one of the

---

20. *Goblet of Fire* 591.

21. Juvenile Offenders for a Thousand Years 3–4 (Wiley B. Sanders, ed., 1970) (quoting Ancient Laws and Institutes of England (Benjamin Thorpe, ed., 1840)).

Inquisitors, asks Harry a series of questions about the particular spell he performed outside of school: "You produced a fully fledged Patronus?..And you are fifteen years old? ... very impressive indeed."[22] Her line of questioning reminds readers just how unusual some of Harry's abilities are for a wizard his age, lest his past extraordinary exploits make us forget he is still just a kid.

We are then shown, quite pointedly, Mr. Weasley's surprise that the whole Wizengamot heard Harry's case. Mr. Weasley brought Harry to his trial but went no further than the courtroom door.[23] Presumably, Mr. Weasley was not of high enough status in wizard society to be a member of the Wizengamot. When the proceedings were over and the Wizengamot started filing out of the room, Mr. Weasley says to Harry, "Merlin's beard ... you were tried by the full court?"[24] His surprise indicates that the underage use of magic outside the school grounds usually is not an important enough offense for the full Wizengamot to consider. We are told that there were about fifty people[25] in the courtroom, wearing plum colored robes sporting a silver "W,"[26] which presumably stood for Wizengamot and identified each wearer as a member. Here, J.K. Rowling's choice evokes the Anglo-Saxon model only as a reminder that a full gathering usually was called only for more important matters. A large group of the Anglo-Saxon elite likely would not have gathered just to hear a charge stemming from a law that applied only to children.

Depicting the full gathering for Harry's trial does greater service to moving the plot line along, developing some characters further, and introducing some new faces. Within the plot, Cornelius Fudge wants a large crowd present to prove what he hopes is a lack of any basis for Harry's transgression and to dispel, as effectively as possible, reports that Voldemort is on the move again. Fudge characteristically tries to fudge the results by changing the time of the trial and sending word of the change to Harry and Dumbledore only at the last minute in the hope that neither will make it on time. The drama of a full and participatory courtroom does make good fiction. This scene already contains a full script for the film version. But the scene likely does not mimic the Anglo-Saxon standards for juveniles which, although quite rough by today's standards, did cut some slack for the young. It was Fudge's desire to make a point and J.K. Rowling's literary device that called for the full Wizengamot.

---

22. *Order of the Phoenix* 141.

23. *Order of the Phoenix* 136.

24. *Order of the Phoenix* 153.

25. *See* SAYLES, *supra* note 2, at 176 (reporting estimates at an average *witenagemot* of 30 to 40 people).

26. *Order of the Phoenix* 138.

In contrast, when Crouch's son is tried in the previous generation, he is cut no slack. He is accused of such an extremely serious crime that his frantic pleas are of no use, even with his own father. In addition, Crouch's son is tried with a group of adults, and the Wizengamot would have had to show up for the adults' trial anyway. Perhaps the most compelling reason for him to be tried in an adult manner, however, is that he was "in his late teens."[27] Although the ages at which children were held responsible for criminal behavior has varied throughout English history,[28] by the late teens they were no longer minors. Recall that King Aethelstan did not want to treat too cruelly a defendant who was fifteen years old (the same age Harry was at his trial). Add on a few years, and it is likely that the Anglo-Saxon king would have been less lenient too.

Curiously, during the trials in *The Goblet of Fire*, the court is never referred to as the Wizengamot. It is merely the court of the Ministry of Magic. When the court is first referred to in *The Order of the Phoenix*, Remus Lupin is explaining that Dumbledore has been demoted from Chief Warlock of the Wizengamot. He quickly adds "that's the Wizard High Court,"[29] to define the term "Wizengamot" for readers. Everything about the courts in the two books suggests they are the same court: same courtroom, same categories of participants, same procedures. The court that tries Harry cannot possibly be a higher level court than the one that hears the earlier trials because of the gravity of the charges against the defendants in the earlier trials. Perhaps J.K. Rowling did not recall the *witenagemot* name sooner or did not make the connection that allowed her to create an evocative name sooner. Perhaps in Dumbledore's Pensieve memories, through which Harry sees the earlier trials, the name Wizengamot just was not prominent. Or perhaps there is more reason to evoke cultural roots when it is Harry who is on trial, as he is quickly coming of age and defining his identity.

At the outset of the final book, *The Deathly Hallows*, references to the Wizengamot purposely refer back to earlier times in the wizard world. Harry rereads Dumbledore's newspaper obituary, in which Dumbledore's judgments as Chief Warlock of the Wizengamot are praised as likely to "benefit generations to come."[30] This obituary was written by Elphias Doge, who had been a Special Advisor to the Wizengamot.[31] The newspaper also mentions that when

---

27. *Goblet of Fire* 594.
28. *See generally* JUVENILE OFFENDERS, *supra* note 21.
29. *Order of the Phoenix* 95.
30. *Deathly Hallows* 20.
31. *Deathly Hallows* 24.

Dumbledore's brother, Aberforth, was convicted fifteen years earlier by the Wizengamot for the misuse of magic, it was "a minor scandal."[32] These quick references showing the influence of the Wizengamot remind readers of its role as a core, stabilizing, social institution. These reminders suggest obliquely just how far from normal the wizard world is at the outset of *The Deathly Hallows*, as Voldemort is rising in power and the old social order is falling apart. Indeed, Harry points out that this time no hearing at all has been called for his underage use of magic.[33]

In great contrast to the Wizengamot, a different type of tribunal operates in *The Deathly Hallows*. The Ministry of Magic now houses the Muggle-Born Registration Commission. All wizards and witches who are not from "pure blood" wizard families must register and be questioned, and each interview starts with the presumption that the summoned muggle-born somehow stole magic powers, i.e., committed theft to achieve a place in the wizard world. When their pedigree does not hold up under inspection, they are sent off to a tortured existence in Azkaban Prison. The echoes from dark periods of human history are hard to miss.

To find the room where the questioning takes place, at first Harry heads through "the doorway he remembered..., which opened onto the flight of stairs down to the court chambers."[34] It may be on the same floor, but the room in which this Commission holds its tribunal is not the same room in which the Wizengamot met. "This one was much smaller, though the ceiling was quite as high; it gave the claustrophobic sense of being stuck at the bottom of a deep well."[35] The bottom of a deep well seems a metaphor for being inexorably stuck, not for attaining justice. More than once the room of the Commission's tribunal is referred to as a "dungeon."[36] Because a dungeon is usually a location for prisoners whose fate has already been decided, the location alone of this tribunal suggests its judgments are reached before it conducts its hearings.

Another major difference in this tribunal is the almost overwhelming presence of dementor guards. They line the hallway outside the room, terrifying the muggle-born wizards awaiting interviews. In the court room, most of the proceedings take place on a high platform. Only two high-level death eaters, serving as prosecutors, and a scribe sit there, protected by a patronus. The

---

32. *Deathly Hallows* 25.
33. *Deathly Hallows* 91.
34. *Deathly Hallows* 256.
35. *Deathly Hallows* 258.
36. *Deathly Hallows* 257, 258.

moment the accused sits down, chains magically appear and lock into place. Instead of the Wizengamot's lively and diverse crowd of important wizards and witches, when the accused look out into this room, they see only more dementor guards, standing sentinel in the corners. Before any proceeding is described, the absence of the communal advice and decisionmaking of the Wizengamot is already obvious to readers. This hearing is set up to be an in-quisition, in the nastiest sense of the word.

At first glance, one aspect of witenagemot procedure does seem so deeply ingrained in wizard culture as to withstand Voldemort's renewed influence. Elsewhere in the Ministry of Magic building, Yaxley Slughorn encounters a wizard he thinks is Reg Cattermole (actually Ron Weasley disguised by polyjuice potion). Yaxley expresses surprise that "pureblood" Reg is not downstairs with his wife, Mary, who is awaiting interrogation, and Ron later expresses concern over what will happen to Mary if Reg is not there for her.[37] As the questioning of Mary Cattermole begins, when asked if she is married to Reginald Catter-mole of the Magical Maintenance Department, she cries: "I don't know where he is, he was supposed to meet me here!"[38] This repeated concern suggests the characters still appreciate the importance of *kin* vouching for the accused in the wizard world, much as in the Anglo-Saxon world.

As Mary's questioning continues, however, Reg vouching for her, albeit from the janitorial rung of the wizard world, is quickly forgotten. J.K. Rowl-ing describes a new proceeding in which readers see that no vouching will change the pre-determined outcome. We learn that Dolores Umbridge, con-ducting interrogation procedures and casting judgments as Head of the Mug-gle-Born Registration Commission, "was so happy here, in her element, upholding the twisted law she had helped to write." Her leading questions as-sume that Mary Cattermole stole the very wand that chose her at age eleven. Umbridge takes on the role of legislator, fact-finder, judge, and jury, and there is no mention of the Wizengamot, no communal participation in the deci-sion-making process, just the absolute concentration of raw power.[39]

Depicting this alternate tribunal allows J.K. Rowling to highlight just how totally disrupted the social order of the wizard world has become, and the ter-rifying results. At this point in the plot, the wizard society's future seems par-ticularly bleak without its Wizengamot, its *witanagemot*-like approach to handling political and legal matters. Readers accustomed to participatory

---

37. *Deathly Hallows* 243–244.
38. *Deathly Hallows* 259.
39. *Deathly Hallows* 259–260.

democracy and an independent judiciary now come to appreciate these institutions even in their more rudimentary forms. Once again, the legal institution based on early Anglo-Saxon practices no longer seems to lack procedural fairness; it seems enlightened compared to Umbridge's presumptive interrogations, with their predetermined outcomes and sentences. J.K. Rowling makes readers long for the days of the well-functioning Wizengamot.

There is another aspect of Anglo-Saxon law that the Harry Potter books call to mind, and maybe it also is not a coincidence. Among the legal remedies imposed by Anglo-Saxon tribunals were *wergilds* and *bots*. *Wergilds* (also spelled *wergelds* and *wergylds*) were monetary compensation to relatives of homicide victims. The *wergild* correlated with the status of the victim, increasing along with the status of the deceased. *Bots* sometimes referred to compensation generally. But *bots*, more specifically, were money awards given by the defendant to a harmed person and calculated to compensate for the person's physical or intangible injuries.[40] As one scholar explains it, "the 'wergild' was the sum paid to the kin of a slain man and varied in its rate with the victim's social status; the 'bot' was the sum paid to the injured man himself and varied with the parts of his body outraged and the kind of property damaged."[41]

Now, *bots* surely brings to mind "Botts," as in Bertie Botts Every Flavor Beans. In the Harry Potter books, these jelly beans come in a wide variety of flavors, including some very odd ones, like spaghetti and pepper. And then there are the truly gross Bertie Botts jelly bean flavors, like earwax, booger, and vomit. Parts of the body outraged, indeed!

The language used in the Harry Potter series tells a story in itself, for those who wish to delve into it. The names of people, places, and spells add depth to descriptions and reference aspects of English cultural, legal, and linguistic history. For the adult reader, these connections add a rich dimension beyond the story's plot line. This multi-dimensional use of language and scholarly references in an easy-to-read story for young adults may help to explain why the books have garnered such mass interest in readers of all ages. It provides a ready excuse for those adults with a children's book series hidden beneath their copies of *Beowulf*, *Ulysses*, and *Middlemarch*.

---

40. *See* Laughlin, *supra* note 12, at 278–80 (explaining various types of Anglo-Saxon legal remedies).

41. Sayles, *supra* note 1, at 122.

Harry Potter and the Half-Crazed Bureaucracy

Benjamin H. Barton[1]

What would you think of a government that engaged in this list of tyrannical activities: tortured children for lying;[2] designed its prison specifically to suck all life and hope out of the inmates;[3] placed citizens in that prison without a hearing;[4] ordered the death penalty without a trial;[5] allowed the powerful, rich or famous to control policy;[6] selectively prosecuted crimes (the powerful

---

1. Adapted from Benjamin H. Barton, *Harry Potter and the Half-Crazed Bureaucracy*, 104 MICH. L. REV. 1523 (2006) (reviewing J.K. Rowling, *Harry Potter and the Half-Blood Prince* (2005)).

2. Ministry employee (and evil bureaucrat extraordinaire) Dolores Umbridge forces Harry to write "I must not tell lies" over and over again with an enchanted quill that slices those words into his hand and writes in blood. The worst part of the punishment is that Harry was actually telling the truth and was punished for publicly announcing Voldemort's return. *See Half-Blood Prince* 219, 347; *Order of the Phoenix* 263–68.

3. The wizard prison, Azkaban, is staffed by Dementors, magical beings that suck all hope and life out of the inmates. *See, e.g., Prisoner of Azkaban* 97 (describing Azkaban as "the worst place" and stating that "[m]ost of the prisoners go mad in there").

4. In *The Half-Blood Prince* the Ministry arrests and holds a minor character named Stan Shunpike without a trial on "suspicion of Death Eater activity," although no one seems to think that Shunpike is actually guilty. *Half-Blood Prince* 221, 331, 346–47. Similarly, in *The Chamber of Secrets* the Minister of Magic, Cornelius Fudge, sends one of Harry's favorite teachers, Hagrid, to Azkaban without a hearing or any opportunity to present a defense because the "Ministry's got to do something" in response to attacks at Hogwarts. Fudge further defends the action by saying "I'm under a lot of pressure. Got to be seen doing something." *See Chamber of Secrets* 261.

5. In *The Prisoner of Azkaban* the Dementors have permission from the Ministry to kill Sirius Black upon capture, and without any further trial, with the "Dementor's Kiss." *See Prisoner of Azkaban* 247. Similarly, Barty Crouch was given the dementor's kiss without a trial in *The Goblet of Fire*. *Goblet of Fire* 703.

6. There are innumerable examples of this. Throughout the first five books, Lucius Malfoy (the father of Harry's schoolboy enemy Draco Malfoy) is shown to have inordinate gov-

go unpunished and the unpopular face trumped-up charges);[7] conducted criminal trials without defense counsel;[8] used truth serum to force confessions;[9] maintained constant surveillance over all citizens;[10] offered no elections and no democratic lawmaking process;[11] and controlled the press?[12]

You might assume that the above list is the work of some despotic central African nation, but it is actually the product of the Ministry of Magic, the magician's government in J.K. Rowling's Harry Potter series. When *Harry Potter and the Half-Blood Prince* was released in the summer of 2005, I, along with many others, bought and read it on the day of its release.[13] I was immediately struck by Rowling's unsparingly negative portrait of the Ministry of Magic and its bureaucrats. I decided to sit down and reread each of the Harry Potter books with an eye towards discerning what exactly J.K. Rowling's most recent novel tells us about the nature, societal role, and legitimacy of government.

I did this for several reasons. First, with all due respect to professors of law and political science, no book released in 2005 will have more influence on

---

ernmental access and influence. *See, e.g., Prisoner of Azkaban* 125, 218 (arranging to have Hagrid's Hippogriff executed by the Committee for the Disposal of Dangerous Creatures); *Goblet of Fire* 100–01 (appearing as the Minister of Magic's honored guest at the Quidditch World Cup).

7. The lengthy detention of Stan Shunpike on the mere suspicion of Death Eater activity is a good example. *See Half-Blood Prince* 221, 331, 346–47. Harry himself is another example. In Book Three, the Ministry of Magic pooh-poohs a charge of the improper underage use of magic, *see Prisoner of Azkaban* 43–46, and in Book Five they attempt to prosecute Harry to the limit of the law (and beyond) for the same charge. *See Order of the Phoenix* 26–27, 137–51.

8. Harry's trial in Book Five is an obvious example. *See Order of the Phoenix* 137–51.

9. *See Order of the Phoenix* 629–31 (Dolores Umbridge interrogating Harry); *Goblet of Fire* 683–91 (Dumbledore interrogating Barty Crouch).

10. The Ministry of Magic keeps tabs on all uses of magic in order to detect any improper or underage uses of magic. *See Order of the Phoenix* 368.

11. This requires an inference from the first chapter of *The Half-Blood Prince*. *See* discussion *infra* Part III.A.

12. In *The Order of the Phoenix* the *Daily Prophet* regularly disparages Harry and Professor Dumbledore as deranged for claiming that Voldemort has returned. *See Order of the Phoenix* 94, 306–8 (stating that the *Daily Prophet* is discrediting Dumbledore under pressure from the Ministry of Magic) and 73–75 (same for Harry).

13. I did not, however, dress up as a wizard or go to one of the local bookstore's midnight Harry Potter parties. *Cf.* Triumph the Insult Comic, *Triumph Versus Star Wars Geeks, available at* http://www.milkandcookies.com/links/2536/details/ (Video of Triumph insulting Star Wars geeks in costumes, including this question: "How do you explain this to your imaginary girlfriend?").

what kids and adults around the world think about government than *The Half-Blood Prince*. It would be difficult to overstate the influence and market penetration of the Harry Potter series. Somewhere over the last few years the Harry Potter novels passed from a children's literature sensation to a bona fide international happening.

Second, Rowling's scathing portrait of government is surprisingly strident and effective. This is partially because her critique works on so many levels: what the government does (see above), how the government is structured, and what kind of bureaucrats run the show. All three elements work together to depict a Ministry of Magic run by self-interested bureaucrats bent on increasing and protecting their power, often to the detriment of the public at large. In other words, Rowling creates a public-interest scholar's dream (or nightmare) government.

Her critique is also particularly effective because despite how awful Rowling's Ministry of Magic looks and acts, it bears such a tremendous resemblance to current Anglo-American government. Rowling's negative picture of government is thus both subtle and extraordinarily piercing. Taken in the context of the Harry Potter novels and the personalities of the bureaucrats involved, each of the above acts of government misconduct seem perfectly natural and familiar to the reader. The critique works because the reader identifies her own government with Rowling's Ministry of Magic.

Lastly, *The Half-Blood Prince* is a tremendous work of fiction that deserves a more careful reading of its themes and plot. It continues a trend in the Harry Potter novels: the Harry Potter novels have gotten longer, more complex, and much, much darker. The first two Harry Potter books tell straightforward stories of good triumphing over evil (Harry defeating the evil Lord Voldemort) at the magical Hogwarts School. The first two books, *The Sorcerer's Stone* and *The Chamber of Secrets*, clock in at a tidy 309 and 341 pages, respectively, and feature quite similar narratives: the attempts of Lord Voldemort to return to power through unlikely pawns (a teacher in *The Sorcerer's Stone* and a student in *The Chamber of Secrets*) are foiled by Harry and his friends. In moral tone these books are very black and white, and in subject matter they are basically circumscribed to happenings in or around Hogwarts.

The next five books present a more complex vision of an entire wizard society, including a wizard government, and an international struggle against Voldemort and his followers. The books do not feature easy answers, instant triumphs, unblemished heroes, or even clear lines between good and evil. Each of the last five books is longer and more complex than the first two, and all but the seventh abandons the "Harry triumphs over Voldemort" structure of the first two. *The Prisoner of Azkaban*, the third book, deals at length with a series of miscarriages of justice, and the recognition that all is not what it seems in the battle between good and evil. Book Four, *The Goblet of Fire*, tells the story of Voldemort's return to power and features the first of multiple deaths in the series (Cedric Diggory). Book Five, *The Order of the Phoenix*, is darker yet. Harry hits puberty and is a moody mess throughout the book. For the first time Harry's impetuousness and desire to confront Voldemort backfires, as Sirius Black is murdered and Harry leads his friends into a trap. In Book Six, *The Half-Blood Prince*, Harry's personality returns to form, but the lines between good and evil are further blurred, and the death of Dumbledore (easily the steadiest and most uniformly "good" character in the series) is stunning. In Book Seven, *The Deathly Hallows*, we learn of many more atrocities by Voldemort and the deatheaters, and we see their power and influence grow to the point of nearly taking over the wizarding world.

Rowling's decision to eschew the tried and true formula of her first two books in favor of longer books featuring deaths, imperfect characters, and moral ambiguity is both exceptional and refreshing. She could have repeated her formula from the first two books to great acclaim and financial success. Instead, she created a much richer world where the more typical elements of magic and childhood collide with satire and social commentary in the mold of Mark Twain or Jonathan Swift.

Given the overwhelming popularity and influence of the Harry Potter books, it is worth examining what Rowling has to say about government and its role in society. Part I of this chapter describes how *The Half-Blood Prince* cements Rowling's negative portrayal of government. Part II argues that *The Half-Blood Prince* presents a government that fits perfectly into the public choice model of self-interested bureaucrats running roughshod over the broader public interest. Part III asserts that *The Half-Blood Prince*'s unflattering depiction of government is particularly damning because it so closely resembles British and American governments, while it lacks the features that potentially undermine the "public choice" critique. Rowling's vision of government consists almost solely of bureaucracy, without elections to offer the sheen of democracy, without a free press or independent judiciary to act as a check on bureaucratic excess, and few true public servants to counteract craven bureaucrats. Part IV takes a brief look at how Rowling's personal story may explain her disdain for government and bureaucracy, and Part V concludes that Rowling's writings may do more for libertarianism than any since John Stuart Mill's *On Liberty* was released in 1859.

Harry Potter and the Repulsive Ministry of Magic

Rowling's Harry Potter books slowly but surely build an impregnable invective against government, while still telling exceptional fantasy stories about witches and wizards at a school for magic. The first three books take a relatively light-hearted view of the wizard government. Rowling gives us goofy and highly bureaucratic sounding government offices like "The Misuse of Muggle Artifacts Office" or "The Department of Magical Catastrophes" and a portrait of the Minister of Magic, Cornelius Fudge, as a bumbling, but well-meaning, political hack.

In *The Goblet of Fire* we have the first real hints of Rowling's darker vision for the Ministry of Magic. The depiction of how the Ministry handled Voldemort's first rise to power features overzealous prosecutions and the suspension of civil rights.[14] Most notably, at the end of the book the Ministry refuses to believe that Voldemort has returned to power and actually works to discredit and repress Harry's story.[15]

The end of *The Goblet of Fire* presages the open hostility between the Ministry of Magic and Harry and Dumbledore in *The Order of the Phoenix*. The Ministry attempts to kick Harry out of school, they strip Dumbledore of his various government positions (including headmaster of Hogwarts), send the evil-bureaucrat *par excellence* Dolores Umbridge to Hogwarts, and generally bring the full weight of the Ministry's powers to bear upon Harry and Dumbledore.[16]

Nevertheless, *The Order of the Phoenix* ends on a hopeful note: Fudge finally recognizes that Voldemort has returned to power. We are left with the impression that Fudge will now use the full powers of the Ministry to battle Voldemort and his followers, the Death Eaters.[17] After all, even the most hardened libertarian generally recognizes that government is best suited to fight wars against aggressors and pursue police actions against those who threaten the well-being of others.[18]

---

14. *See Goblet of Fire* 456–61, 508–18.

15. *See Goblet of Fire* 703–08. These steps are ostensibly taken to avoid "a panic that will destabilize everything [the Ministry has] worked for these last thirteen years." *Goblet of Fire* 707. Dumbledore offers a likelier explanation: Fudge is "blinded ... by the love of the office [he holds.]" *Goblet of Fire* 708.

16. *See, e.g., Order of the Phoenix* 26–27, 71–75, 93–95, 137–51, 212–14, 239–40, 265–68, 296–98, 306–8, 351–52, 415–16, 551, 567, 610–20, 624, 747.

17. *See Order of the Phoenix* 845–48.

18. *See, e.g.,* Libertarian Party, Issues and Positions: National Platform of the Libertarian Party, http://www.lp.org/issues/printer_platform_all.shtml (last visited September 16, 2005).

The Half-Blood Prince, however, offers no such succor to government. The Ministry remains remarkably ineffective in its battle against Voldemort.[19] Though Cornelius Fudge is replaced as Minister of Magic by Rufus Scrimgeour, a savvy veteran of the battles against Lord Voldemort, the tone and actions of the Ministry remain unchanged. In fact, Scrimgeour's decision to try to calm the public by detaining individuals who are likely innocent, and his attempts to use Harry as a "mascot" or "poster boy" for the ministry are arguably worse than Fudge's actions.[20]

The Half-Blood Prince's most devastating criticism of the Ministry has little to do with Voldemort, however. It is what service in the Ministry of Magic has done to Percy Weasley that is the most damning. Harry's best friend is Ron Weasley, of the large and likable magical family that informally adopts Harry as their own. Percy Weasley is Ron's older brother, and throughout the first three books he is depicted as a bit of a rule-loving stuffed shirt, but the portrait is sympathetic, and it is clear that he is still a lovable member of the Weasley family.

In *The Goblet of Fire* Percy goes to work for the Ministry of Magic in a junior capacity and at once finds a home for his love of rules and talent for minutiae.[21] In *The Order of the Phoenix*, however, Percy takes the side of the Ministry against Harry and Dumbledore and ends up alienating his entire family as a result. This offers the first object lesson in government service: Percy essentially loses his soul and all that should matter to him by following his blind ambition.

The Half-Blood Prince, however, offers Percy a chance at redemption. Now that the Ministry recognizes that Voldemort has returned and that Harry is the best chance of defeating him, Percy can admit he was wrong about Dumbledore and Harry and rejoin the family. Yet, Percy refuses to bend and remains estranged. Of course, that does not free Percy from the clutches of the government. The first encounter between Harry and Scrimgeour occurs at the Weasley family Christmas dinner, which Scrimgeour crashes with Percy as his excuse. The violation of the Weasley family, and Scrimgeour's callous use of Percy

---

19. *See Half-Blood Prince* 7–18, 648–49.

20. *See Half-Blood Prince* 7–18, 221, 331, 346–47, 650. Harry himself notes that it is hard to tell whether Fudge or Scrimgeour is more distasteful: "You never get it right, you people, do you? Either we've got Fudge, pretending everything's lovely while people get murdered right under his nose, or we've got you [Scrimgeour], chucking the wrong people into jail and trying to pretend you've got 'the Chosen One' working for you!" *Half-Blood Prince* 347.

21. *See Goblet of Fire* 55–56.

to gain access to Harry, is hardly lost on readers. The depths that Scrimgeour and Percy will plumb to co-opt Harry are more offensive and distasteful than even the list of government wrongdoing that began this chapter because we experience them directly through the eyes of Harry and the Weasley family.

This is likewise true when Scrimgeour reiterates his request to Harry at Dumbledore's funeral. What government official could be more tone-deaf? Scrimgeour asks Harry to betray everything Dumbledore has stood for on the very day of his funeral. Thus, we fully sympathize with Harry's refusal to help the Ministry. The replacement of Fudge with Scrimgeour and the hardening of Harry's negative feelings towards the Ministry finalizes Rowling's portrait of the Ministry of Magic and its bureaucrats. Before *The Half-Blood Prince* it was possible to imagine that the Ministry of Magic was trying hard, but was simply misguided or ineffectual. After *The Half-Blood Prince* the reader reaches the inexorable conclusion that Harry (and Rowling for that matter) has little use for government.

Harry Potter and the Public Choice Government

The odd thing about Rowling's Ministry of Magic is how closely it accords with what is known in academia as the "public choice" critique of government. The central tenet of public choice theory is that the best way to understand the actions of governmental actors is to assume they are primarily (or solely) motivated by self-interest.[22] The theory has been applied to the actions and incentives of virtually every government actor and sector,[23] but it seems to be most popular as an explanation of bureaucratic behavior. One of the earliest public choice scholars, William Niskanen, theorized that self-interested bureaucrats would seek to expand their budgets and influence at the expense of the public.[24] This theory has since spawned a cottage industry of public choice analyses of bureaucracy.

---

22. *See, e.g.,* Edward L. Rubin, *Getting Beyond Cynicism: New Theories of Regulatory Public Choice, Phenomenology, and the Meaning of the Modern State: Keep the Bathwater but Throw Out that Baby*, 87 CORNELL L. REV. 309, 310 (2002) ("The essential and familiar components of [the public choice] model are that human beings are instrumentally rational and motivated by self-interest.").

23. *See, e.g.,* Dennis C. Mueller, PUBLIC CHOICE II 43–373 (1989) (applying public choice scholarship to any and all types of democracy and areas of government); R. Douglas Arnold, CONGRESS AND THE BUREAUCRACY (1979) (exploring Congress' ability to influence and control bureaucracy).

24. *See* William A. Niskanen, BUREAUCRACY AND REPRESENTATIVE GOVERNMENT (1971). For an update and analysis of Niskanen's ground-breaking work, *see* THE BUDGET MAXI-

The greatest strength of the public choice theory is, of course, its simplicity, and the ease with which it comports with our own experience of government. The word bureaucrat itself has come to have a negative connotation,[25] and many would instinctively agree that bureaucrats look out for their own interests ahead of the interests of the public.

The power of Rowling's portrait of bureaucratic activity is, similarly, its believability. Given the list of Ministry of Magic activities at the start of this Chapter, this is no mean feat. Rowling makes the Ministry's actions reasonable with well-drawn characters and difficult situations. Fudge, the original Minister of Magic, is portrayed as a classic bumbling politician: not quite up to the job, but for the most part genial and harmless. Fudge's replacement, Scrimgeour, is described as the battle-hardened leader offering "an immediate impression of toughness and shrewdness."[26] Percy Weasley is the classic young striver, willing to adopt any position of the Ministry in order to get ahead.

Of all the self-interested bureaucrats in the Ministry of Magic, however, Dolores Umbridge takes the cake. In *The Order of the Phoenix*, she is sent to Hogwarts as a new professor and the "High Inquisitor." By the end of the book she has removed Dumbledore as headmaster and taken the position for herself, created an "inquisitorial squad" of students to act as student informants and enforcers, and has generally turned Hogwarts into a mini-fascist state. We eventually learn that in her thirst for power she sent Dementors to attack Harry and his cousin Dudley in Little Whinging, attempted to use an "unforgivable curse" on Harry, and has brazenly broken any and all laws in an effort to discredit Harry and gain favor with Fudge. Couple these hideous actions with Umbridge's portrayal as the über-bureaucrat, an unctuous climber who begins every discussion with a phony "Hem Hem" and ends each with multiple references to Ministry protocols, and one gets a real flavor for what Rowling thinks of bureaucrats.

When you combine these characters, different in every way except for their overweening self-interest, with the extreme circumstances of the return of

---

MIZING BUREAUCRAT: APPRAISALS AND EVIDENCE (Andre Blais & Stephanie Dion eds., 1991).

25. In researching this chapter, I came across a fascinating little book that discusses the long history of administrative arms of governments, and the relatively shorter history of bureaucracy as a concept. *See* BUREAUCRACY: THE CAREER OF A CONCEPT (Eugene Kamenka & Martin Krygier eds., 1979). It also covers the popular dislike of bureaucracy.

26. *Half-Blood Prince* 16. The public choice bureaucrats, however, look like rank amateurs next to Scrimgeour, who detains suspects indefinitely so that the government appears to be addressing Voldemort's return and asks the sixteen year-old Harry to act as a Ministry mascot to fulfill his "duty to be used by the Ministry." *Half-Blood Prince* 221, 331, 346.

Voldemort, the reader believes that the Ministry is capable of almost anything. Furthermore, anyone who has lived in post-9/11 England or America will recognize the themes raised by *The Half-Blood Prince*: government by and for public relations effect, the indefinite detention of suspects for show, obtrusive governmental searches,[27] and government pamphlets offering silly advice of little help.[28] Meanwhile, there is little in the way of actual help.

The most powerful aspect of Rowling's portrait of the Ministry of Magic as a corrupt, self-perpetuating bureaucracy is how natural it all seems. Rowling creates a government that fits (and actually exceeds) each of the public choice assumptions about government, and closely resembles our own government in personnel and activities.

Harry Potter and the Bureaucracy that Ate Government Whole

Despite the intuitive power of public choice theory, defenders of government and bureaucracy remain unconvinced and offer a spirited critique of public choice theory. Interestingly, Rowling foresees many of these defenses of government, and her portrayal of the Ministry of Magic parries them with ease.

The Democratic Defense

The first line of attack against public choice theory is always that bureaucrats must answer to elected officials who must in turn answer to the voters. This defense has both descriptive and normative aspects. As a descriptive/empirical matter, defenders of bureaucracy question whether bureaucrats really have the ability or capacity to hoodwink elected executives or legislators who have to answer to their constituents. As a normative matter, defenders of bureaucracy argue that democracy justifies bureaucracy as a result of deliberation and public buy-in.

---

27. *The Half-Blood Prince* features several scenes where the students are searched *leaving* Hogwarts, creating this response from Ron Weasley: " 'What does it matter if we're smuggling Dark stuff OUT?' demanded Ron, eyeing the long thin Secrecy Sensor with apprehension. 'Surely you ought to be checking what we bring back IN?' His cheek earned him a few extra jabs with the Sensor....." *Half-Blood Prince* 243.

28. Consider the Ministry's pamphlet "Protecting Your Home and Family against Dark Forces." *Half-Blood Prince* 42–43, 61–62.

Rowling strips the Ministry of Magic of even this most basic justification, as Fudge is replaced by Scrimgeour as the Minister of Magic with no mention of an election.[29] To the contrary, Rowling uses the passive voice of the verb "to sack" repeatedly to describe Fudge's fate.[30] In fact, Rowling's decision to not specify the who or the how of Fudge's sacking adds to the sense of something underhanded or behind the scenes occurring. It is as if a powerful, hidden, and deeply undemocratic force is really in charge of the government.

The lack of an election is further highlighted by a meeting between the Muggle Prime Minister (presumably Tony Blair) and Fudge and Scrimgeour. The description of the Muggle Prime Minister features a discussion of elections and political opponents, two elements of governmental life that are notably absent from the Ministry of Magic.

One mystery that remains after *The Half-Blood Prince* is the legislative or rule-making power of the Ministry of Magic. It is clear that the Ministry enforces the laws, and there are discussions in the books about adopting new laws, but there is never any mention of a legislature or legislative process. The hints that Rowling drops, however, are not encouraging.[31]

These omissions are purposeful authorial decisions by Rowling. A government that has no elections and no democratic process for lawmaking obviously lacks the legitimacy of a democratic regime. Nevertheless, the overall similarity of the Ministry of Magic to our own government in actions, motivation, and personnel suggests that elections and democratic lawmaking actually have little, if any, effect on government as experienced by its subjects.

The Structural Defense

Defenders of bureaucracy frequently note that bureaucrats are overseen by other governmental and non-governmental entities. In the American system,

---

29. Prior to *The Half-Blood Prince* it was an open question whether the wizarding world had any elections. The fact that the Ministry stripped Dumbledore of his titles and positions in *The Order of the Phoenix* made it seem unlikely, but not impossible, that elections occurred.

30. We first learn the news from Fudge himself: "I was sacked three days ago!" *Half-Blood Prince* 15. Harry later uses similar verbiage. *Half-Blood Prince* 60. Scrimgeour is described as "appointed Minister of Magic," again with no description of who made the "appointment." *Half-Blood Prince* 40–41.

31. Harry's trial in Book Five suggests that the laws are quite pliable and possibly subject to change at the Minister of Magic's whim. During the trial Fudge and Dumbledore argue over a point of law, and the following exchange occurs: " 'Laws can be changed,' said Fudge savagely. 'Of course they can,' said Dumbledore, inclining his head. 'And you certainly seem to be making many changes, Cornelius.' " *Order of the Phoenix* 149.

for example, bureaucrats are subject to varying levels of oversight by the President, Congress, a politically appointed head of the agency, and a free press to root out any wrongdoing.

The first thing to note about Rowling's Ministry of Magic is that she has created a government structure that appears to be 100% bureaucracy. There is a Minister of Magic, but he is appointed, not elected. It is unclear who appoints the Minister of Magic, perhaps the elites. There are multiple offices and committees below the Minister, but each of these appear to be classic bureaucracies within bureaucracies, each staffed by a junior minister with his own area of responsibility.

There is a judicial body, the Wizengamot, which Rowling describes as the "the Wizard High Court."[32] We have good reason to believe it is substantially controlled by the Minister of Magic, and it certainly does not seem to be an independent check on Ministry authority.[33]

There are thus no governmental bodies outside the Ministry of Magic to act as a check upon government abuses. Again, this suggests that neither governmental structure nor checks and balances matter much: bureaucracy will run roughshod regardless.

The Free Press

Free speech and freedom of the press are commonly taken as constitutional guarantees in America, and are seen as fundamental to a just and responsive government. In the narrower sense, a free press is considered another check on bureaucratic or governmental misconduct.

Humorously, Rowling even denies the magical world a free press (or even a functional press).[34] Both *The Half-Blood Prince* and *The Order of the Phoenix*

---

32. *Order of the Phoenix* 95.

33. In *The Order of the Phoenix,* Dumbledore is fired as Chief Warlock of the Wizengamot because of his criticism of Ministry policy. When Harry later appears before the Wizengamot to answer the trumped up charges of underage use of magic, Fudge appears to be the main officiator and leader. *See Order of the Phoenix* 137–51. Although Harry successfully pleads his case before the Wizengamot, the sheer procedural irregularities and Ministry domination of the proceeding offer little hope of an independent judiciary to stem government abuses.

34. If you think the depiction of the press as a government puppet in *The Order of the Phoenix* and *The Half-Blood Prince* is unflattering, Rowling has actually lightened up since her portrayal of the evil reporter Rita Skeeter (the reporter equivalent of Dolores Umbridge) in *The Goblet of Fire*. Throughout *The Goblet of Fire,* Skeeter followed a well-known pattern of the press: she built Harry up as a hero at first, only to tear him down later, with unfair

are replete with instances of the Ministry leaning on the press to print what is essentially government propaganda.[35] Again, this strips the government of even the possibility of press oversight, or realistically public oversight, since wizards (not unlike us poor Muggles) typically rely upon the press for information outside of their daily experience.

Bureaucrats Are People Too

Another line of defense is the public-minded bureaucrat. Some theorists argue that the public choice critique ignores what government officials are really like. They are not greedy, self-interested budget-maximizers. Instead, they are decent and publicly oriented.

Rowling rolls over this possibility in three ways. There are five main characters that are Ministry employees: Fudge, Scrimgeour, Umbridge, Percy Weasley, and Arthur Weasley (Ron and Percy's father).[36] The first four of these five characters are basically villains, and are unquestionably motivated by self-interest and a naked lust for power rather than the public interest.

The fifth of those characters, Arthur Weasley, is actually the exception that proves the rule. He is a decent, hard-working bureaucrat who loves his work at the Ministry. Of course, in Rowling's Ministry no good deed goes unpunished. Arthur Weasley is described as a relative failure. At one point in *The Order of the Phoenix,* Harry is taken to his office, which is in the basement, down several long hallways, and is "slightly smaller than a broom cupboard."[37] Lastly, in *The Half-Blood Prince* two of the most revered characters, Dumbledore and Harry, clearly have little use for the Ministry or its bureaucrats.[38]

---

and scurrilous selective reporting on both ends. *See Goblet of Fire* 303–07, 390–91, 451–52, 554. Just as I speculate later about why Rowling might not have much use for government, *see* discussion *infra* Part IV, I think Rowling's depiction of the press is likely a reaction to her own life. Rowling's abrupt arrival as a magnet for Britain's rough and tumble tabloids following her success as an author must have been brutal.

35. *See Half-Blood Prince* 221 (repeating *The Daily Prophet*'s uncritical reporting on the Stan Shunpike arrest); *Half-Blood Prince* 314 (alleging that the Ministry squashed a story that Scrimgeour is a vampire in the alternative press). *Order of the Phoenix* 94 ("[T]he Ministry's leaning heavily on the *Daily Prophet* not to report any of what they're calling Dumbledore's rumor-mongering.").

36. You could include Barty Crouch from *The Goblet of Fire* on this list although it would not improve the overall batting average for public-interested Ministry employees.

37. Arthur does get a small promotion (and presumably a better office) in *The Half-Blood Prince*.

38. In *The Half-Blood Prince* Dumbledore notes that he has been offered the job of Minister of Magic, "[b]ut the Ministry never attracted me as a career." *Half-Blood Prince* 442–43.

Love It or Leave It

There is not a strong scholarly tradition of what I am calling the "love it or leave it" defense, but I think it exists, and has actually come to the fore in recent years. This defense of government basically requires citizens to accept the legitimacy of the government and its actions as a duty of citizenship, and then rebukes any criticisms as unpatriotic. The interesting thing about this defense is that it explicitly raises the question of governmental legitimacy: if one assumes governmental legitimacy, it may be appropriate to ask a citizen to "love it or leave it." If one leaves open the possibility that governments and laws may lack legitimacy, it becomes much harder to simply order blind allegiance.

Rowling makes quick work of this potential defense. In *The Half-Blood Prince* Harry makes it clear that he feels no independent duty to be used by the Ministry for the benefit of the public. Harry's decision should come as no surprise: throughout the novels Harry seems to pick and choose certain school rules and even Ministry laws to follow or disregard depending on the situation and his own sense of morality or duty. Rowling treats these decisions by Harry as if they are natural and easy, but taken together with Harry's rejection of the Ministry's overtures in *The Half-Blood Prince,* Rowling presents a remarkably contingent and situational approach to both government and law.

In sum, Rowling has created a world where all of our negative governmental stereotypes have come true. She combines familiar character types and government structures with a vision of government by the bureaucrats and for the bureaucrats to create a devastating critique of Anglo-American government.

J.K. Rowling and the Libertarian Mindset

Anyone familiar with Rowling's personal story will know that when she started the Harry Potter series she spent a period of time unemployed and on public assistance in Edinborough and was divorced with a young child. These biographic details are frequently juxtaposed with Rowling's current financial status.

Dumbledore similarly disparages the Ministry's attempts at public safety through leaflet. *Half-Blood Prince* 61–62. Likewise, Harry declares his loyalty to Dumbledore over the Ministry twice in *The Half-Blood Prince,* making clear that Harry pledges his allegiance to those he respects and trusts instead of feeling any overriding obligation to the government. *Half-Blood Prince* 343–48, 647–50. Even Voldemort eschews a career as a bureaucrat, establishing that most competent folks, good or evil, have little use for Ministry service.

Rowling's personal story provides two insights into her feelings toward government. First, in both England and the U.S., there is no quicker route to hating the government than dealing with the various bureaucracies that handle public assistance. As a general rule you can predict how user-friendly a bureaucracy will be by determining whether the served constituency regularly votes and/or gives campaign contributions.[39] Naturally, those persons unfortunate enough to have to rely upon the government for assistance are unlikely to have sufficient funds to donate to political causes. Similarly, poor people are less likely to vote than other socio-economic groups.[40] As such, you can expect that the bureaucracies set up to deal with the poor will be relatively poorly run and user unfriendly.

If the public assistance bureaucracy does not answer to its customers, *e.g.* the poor, then to whom do they respond? The obvious answer is legislators and members of the executive branch. In times of tight government funding, it seems clear that these parties will exert pressure on the bureaucracy to grant fewer applications and to root out any fraud or waste in the system. As a result, the best scenario for poor people may be a disinterested bureaucracy, since an interested bureaucracy may meet them with skepticism or outright hostility. Moreover, since each approved application costs the government money, there is pressure to make the system as unwieldy and complicated as possible to deter applications. The American Social Security Disability system is a typical example. The application process for disabled individuals (including mentally disabled individuals) requires pages of paperwork, medical testimony and records, and months and years of perseverance. Thus, I think that Rowling's experience on public assistance likely soured her on bureaucracy for a lifetime.

Second, Rowling's story smacks of success through self-reliance and sheer force of will. The Harry Potter novels likewise show a strong strain of self-re-

---

39. Consider, for example, the American Social Security disability system, which has been described as "one of the least user-friendly bureaucracies known to the administrative state." Barbara A. Sheehy, *An Analysis of the Honorable Richard Posner's Social Security Law*, 7 Conn. Ins. L.J. 103, 104 (2001); *cf.* Bruce Ackerman & Ian Ayres, Voting with Dollars: A New Paradigm for Campaign Finance 14 (2002) (arguing that a campaign finance reform that would grant each voter "patriot dollars" to donate to politicians would "reshape the political marketplace and enable it to become more responsive to the judgments of equal citizens than to the preferences of unequal property owners").

40. Ironically, this may be partially because the least educated citizens are the least equipped to handle the bureaucratic process of registering and appearing to vote. *See* Jonathan Nagler, *The Effect of Registration Laws and Education on U.S. Voter Turnout*, 85 Am. Pol. Sci. Rev. 1393, 1395–1403 (1991).

liance and stubborn independence, and Rowling came upon these themes the hard way. Anyone who has pulled herself out of poverty as Rowling has is likely to believe that self-reliance and hard-work are the keys to success, and to be conversely wary of government intervention.

Harry Potter and the Future Libertarian Majority

The Libertarian Party claims to be the fastest growing political party in the United States. After reading *The Half-Blood Prince*, I am much more convinced. The libertarian movement relies upon two interrelated concepts to recruit: a) "that government is best which governs least";[41] and b) self-reliance and respect of individual rights should be paramount.[42] *The Half-Blood Prince* makes both of these points exceptionally well. Rowling taps into the current, generalized distrust of government in the U.S. and the U.K. and creates a Ministry of Magic that simultaneously echoes and critiques our own governments. On the one hand, she creates a government that is repulsive in its structure, personnel, and actions. On the other, she crafts this government to appear closely related to our own government. This juxtaposition creates a powerful and subtle critique of government.

The truly surprising aspect of *The Half-Blood Prince* is how effortlessly Rowling covers the questions of the nature, role, and legitimacy of government in what is ostensibly a work of children's literature. I must admit that when I sat down to reread the Harry Potter books in light of *The Half-Blood Prince*, I did not expect to find the overwhelming skepticism of government that seeps through Rowling's work. Of course, the ability to entertain first and foremost while providing other levels of discourse is the hallmark of great and thoughtful literature, and *The Half-Blood Prince* is both.

---

41. Henry David Thoreau, *Civil Disobedience, in* COLLECTED ESSAYS AND POEMS 203 (Elizabeth Hall Witherell ed., 2001).

42. *See* MURRAY N. ROTHBARD, FOR A NEW LIBERTY: THE LIBERTARIAN MANIFESTO (Hans-Hermann Hoppe ed., 2002) (stating a theory of libertarian political philosophy); MURRAY N. ROTHBARD, THE ETHICS OF LIBERTY (1982) (same, in a more academic structure); ROBERT NOZICK, ANARCHY, STATE, AND UTOPIA 183–231 (1974) (offering a libertarian critique of the Rawlsian state).

Moral Choice, Wizardry, Law and Liberty: A Classical Liberal Reading of the Role of Law in the Harry Potter Series

Andrew P. Morriss

As an economist rather than a literary theorist, my training is in models rather than literary analysis. Inspired by economist Tyler Cowen's suggestion that economists can add value by considering novels as models,[1] this chapter examines the world created by J.K. Rowling in the Harry Potter novels, treating them as a model of a legal system.

But why look at the Harry Potter novels to learn about law? The books rarely mention law, have no characters that are lawyers, and, perhaps most damningly, are children's literature. There are plenty of pop culture works that talk incessantly about law, feature lawyer characters, and are written for adults. As Naomi Mezey and Mark Niles put it: "American popular culture is saturated with legal themes."[2] There are even many "serious" literary works that consider legal themes; as Richard Posner notes in his landmark *Law and Literature*, "[l]aw's techniques and imagery have permeated Western culture from its earliest days."[3]

Despite the dearth of legal topics and total absence of lawyers, engaging in this exercise with the Harry Potter series is valuable for two reasons. First, the books' astounding popularity shows by revealed preference that many people,

---

1. Tyler Cowen, *Is a Novel a Model?, in* THE STREET PORTER AND THE PHILOSOPHER: CONVERSATIONS ON ANALYTICAL EGALITARIANISM 319 (David Levy and Sandra Peart, eds. 2008).

2. Naomi Mezey & Mark C. Niles, *Screening the Law: Ideology and Law in American Popular Culture*, 28 COLUM. J.L. & ARTS 91, 93 (2005).

3. Richard A. Posner, LAW AND LITERATURE 3 (rev. ed. 1998).

including many adults, find the books compelling. Second, the books' primary theme, the contest between good and evil, is one which has profound implications for many current legal debates. This theme, which forces readers to examine difficult questions such as what measures are acceptable in combating evil, lies at the heart of many important legal questions. Moreover, it is a theme where moral intuition, rather than, say, econometric analysis, may prove to be the most important tool—precisely the situation in which novels may prove superior to formal economic models. As Cowen notes, novels "are most useful where introspection is most likely to provide some insight, relative to measurement and formal scientific experimentation. We might read a novel to better understand the emotion of self-righteousness, but we would be ill-advised to read a novel to discover how the labor market works."[4] Finally, literature offers us the opportunity to go beyond the typical tests of propositions offered by economic theory.

At the same time, however, the varying interpretations of the Harry Potter series testify to the danger of constructing analyses of the texts that are overly dependent upon details within the texts themselves. Critics have described the series as an attack on great English literary traditions (Harold Bloom's critique) while others view the books as moral fables consistent with Christianity (Alan Jacobs' defense). J.K. Rowling may have plotted every detail of every novel to support a specific set of views on a wide range of subjects, but she also may have added particular details and plot twists purely for aesthetic purposes or to satisfy a personal whim. Thus, there is danger in picking and choosing specific textual details to construct a hypothesis about authorial intent. Indeed, Rowling's personal story of transformation from single mother on welfare to a happily married woman richer than Queen Elizabeth II, as well as the legal travails her success has brought her, are tempting invitations to read the stories as conscious or unconscious reflections of her life. Nonetheless, the treatment of these novels as akin to the specifications of a model demands that I resist such temptations.

Harry Potter as a Calibration Model

There are a variety of ways in which novels may be understood as, at least, quasi-models. First, a novel may be literally a model—an attempt to spell out the specifications of the mechanisms by which a cause leads to an effect. For

---

4. Cowen, *supra* note 1, at 333.

example, the *Mars* trilogy[5] by Kim Stanley Robinson is an extraordinarily effective example of such an approach. Robinson takes human society, removes it to an isolated location to insulate it from the rest of the world, and shocks the system with technological changes that alter fundamental human relationships to the natural world. In doing so, Robinson takes pains to specify in great detail how institutions work. Rowling takes a different approach in the Harry Potter books, which fall into Cowen's category of novels as simulation models. We may use a simulation to test either a model, by putting new data into it and determining whether the outputs are reasonable, or our data, by seeing if the data reflect the understanding of reality embodied in the model.

In the Harry Potter novels, I contend that we have a good example of what Cowen terms a calibration. That is, Rowling is not "play[ing] out the implications of ... her underlying worldview ... [which reflects her] understanding of society, psychology, and human behavior" as in a "novelistic estimation"[6] as Robinson does in the *Mars* trilogy. Instead, Rowling asks the reader to judge the validity of her underlying model of human behavior when faced with the data provided by her characters' choices.

Three characteristics of the Harry Potter books support this interpretation. First, the books are children's literature. While the Harry Potter books are rarely didactic, as some children's literature often is, the genre tends to offer the children who read the books the opportunity to examine the truthfulness of a way of thinking about moral questions. Children, particularly the pre-teens and teenagers who are major consumers of the Harry Potter series, are at a stage in life in which they are seeking to establish their own moral frameworks. They are not at a stage at which their comparatively limited life experiences (compared to adults) give them sufficient data to engage in an estimation model about such large-scale questions. However, they can engage in the introspective analysis of whether a particular moral framework resonates with the moral framework they are constructing for themselves, and they may consider why the proffered model does or does not do so. Such examinations are at the heart of the rationale for using literary devices to supplement economic analysis.

Second, the structure of the world Rowling creates argues against treating it as an estimation model. Harry Potter lives in a world much like the real world—except that it also includes effective, non-religious magic. As Alan Jacobs perceptively observes, Rowling:

---

5. KIM STANLEY ROBINSON, RED MARS (1993); GREEN MARS (1994); BLUE MARS (1996).

6. Cowen, *supra* note 1, at 328.

begins by positing a counterfactual history, a history in which magic was not a false and incompetent discipline, but rather a means of controlling the physical world at least as potent as experimental science. In Harry Potter's world, scientists think of magic in precisely the same way they do in our world, but they are wrong. The counterfactual "secondary world" that Rowling creates is one in which magic simply works, and works as reliably, in the hands of a trained wizard, as the technology that makes airplanes fly and refrigerators chill the air—those products of applied science being, by the way, sufficiently inscrutable to the people who use them that they might as well be the products of wizardry. As Arthur C. Clarke once wrote, "Any smoothly functioning technology gives the appearance of magic."[7]

The interesting question about such a world is not "what would we do differently if magic worked," since magic does not work and will not work regardless of the choices we make. What is interesting is using the idea of functioning magic to address the moral choices relating to our equivalent "magic" technology. Since we must make choices about how to use the enormous power technology grants us over the world, we can evaluate the choices characters make using our introspective abilities—and, as argued above, so can Rowling's primary intended readership.

Finally, the text itself supports the characterization of the stories as calibration. In a key passage in the second novel, Harry questions Albus Dumbledore about whether Harry belongs in Slytherin House, as the Sorting Hat initially suggested, rather than in Gryffindor. Dumbledore responds,

> "Listen to me, Harry. You happen to have many qualities Salazar Slytherin prized in his hand-picked students. His own very rare gift, Parseltongue—resourcefulness—determination—a certain disregard for rules," he added, his moustache quivering again. "Yet the Sorting Hat placed you in Gryffindor. You know why that was. Think."
>
> "It only put me in Gryffindor," said Harry in a defeated voice, "'because I asked not to go in Slytherin....'"
>
> "*Exactly*," said Dumbledore, beaming once more. "Which makes you *very different* from [Voldemort]. It is our choices, Harry, that show what we truly are, far more than our abilities."[8]

7. Alan Jacobs, *Harry Potter's Magic*, First Things, Jan. 2000, at 35, 37.
8. *Chamber of Secrets* 333.

Individual choice is central to the moral dilemmas the characters must face at many junctures. The centrality of individual moral choices at critical points in the novels provides the reader with the opportunity to evaluate Rowling's claims about the nature of moral choice, exactly the function of a calibration model. An important reading of the series is a means for the reader to compare her sense of the appropriate moral choices with those the characters make.

The Text

What can we learn from treating the Harry Potter series as a calibration model? My contention is that Rowling is offering readers a chance to compare their own moral sensibilities with the choices of the characters. By doing so, readers are not asked to evaluate a particular theory of human behavior or philosophy; instead they are challenged to form their own answers to the most basic questions of morality. For lawyers, this moral calibration allows us to ask two questions: (1) What kind of a world allows individuals the ability to engage in moral calibration? and (2) What are the appropriate roles rules should play?

What Kind of World Allows Calibration?

Creating a calibration model requires Rowling to make some choices about the society in which Harry lives. Consider the Ministry of Magic, for example. Some legal commentary is critical of Rowling's portrayal of bureaucracy as unduly harsh. To some extent Rowling's portrayal may merely reflect general social attitudes toward law and government, while some of it is merely necessary to advance the plot. For example, the removal of Dumbledore and Hagrid from Hogwarts just before the climax of *The Chamber of Secrets* is necessary to set up the final confrontation between Harry and Tom Riddle in the Chamber. Leaving Harry to his own resources (and those of Ron and Hermione, of course) is critical to the plot. Books in which Harry only discovers Voldemort's latest disguise and reports it to Dumbledore would be dull. The Ministry's arbitrary treatment of Dumbledore and Hagrid is a means of advancing the plot rather than a part of a social commentary on the nature of the state.

Indeed it is a central feature of the climaxes of each of the Harry Potter books that Harry is left alone to face Voldemort and his allies. This, in itself, is not novel. Children's literature regularly features the abandonment of children to their own devices in the face of varying degrees of peril. Virtually every

Disney movie, for example, seems to feature one or more absent or dead parents, and the Lemony Snicket series satirizes this feature of children's literature by making the allegedly responsible adults resolutely blind to the perils into which their inattention places the Baudelaire children. In the Harry Potter books, however, Harry's need to fight alone is essential to the theme of moral choice. Throughout the series, Harry is often left to battle Voldemort, rather than be rescued by Dumbledore or other adults, not because the adults are inept (although some are) but because Dumbledore trusts Harry to make the right choices. For example, in *The Chamber of Secrets*, as Dumbledore departs from Hagrid's hut, he gives Harry (hidden under the invisibility cloak) crucial information. Dumbledore's comments emphasize the theme of individual responsibility: "You will find that I have truly left this school when none here are loyal to me. You will also find that help will always be given at Hogwarts to those who ask for it."[9] Similarly, in *Deathly Hallows* Dumbledore offers Harry the ultimate choice of whether to live or die. After Voldemort "kills" Harry, he meets Dumbledore in an otherworldly place, where Dumbledore tells Harry he can go "on" or return to life to continue battling against Voldemort.[10]

In the Harry Potter series, the story has gone well. Harry and many others have made the right choices. Dumbledore trusts many who others do not trust, including Hagrid, Professor Lupin, Sirius Black (after the truth about his role in the death of Harry's parents comes out), Ron, Hermione, the Durmstrang students in *The Goblet of Fire*, and, most notably, Severus Snape. We are told repeatedly of such trust, and Harry and others are often asked to trust the very people they have every reason to fear or dislike, such as Snape, based solely on Dumbledore's confidence that the trusted individuals will make the right choices.

With this in mind, let us examine a pivotal scene from *The Prisoner of Azkaban*. Sirius Black, Professor Remus Lupin, Harry, Ron, and Hermione have unraveled some of the book's central plot devices during their encounter in the Shrieking Shack in Hogsmeade. They have unmasked Peter Pettigrew, who has been masquerading as Ron's pet rat, Scabbers, since the beginning of the series. Black, who Harry has just learned is not a crazed killer responsible for the deaths of Harry's parents, confronts Pettigrew, who we also just learned *is* the person responsible for James and Lily Potter's deaths. Pettigrew tells Black:

---

9. *Chamber of Secrets* 263–64.
10. *Deathly Hallows* 722.

"Sirius, Sirius, what could I have done? The Dark Lord ... you have no idea ... he has weapons you can't imagine.... I was scared, Sirius, I was never brave like you and Remus and James. I never meant it to happen.... He-Who-Must-Not-Be-Named forced me—"

"DON'T LIE!" bellowed Black. "YOU'D BEEN PASSING INFOR-MATION TO HIM FOR A YEAR BEFORE LILY AND JAMES DIED! YOU WERE HIS SPY!"

"He—he was taking over everywhere!" gasped Pettigrew. "Wh—what was there to be gained by refusing him?"

"What was there to be gained by fighting the most evil wizard who has ever existed?" said Black, with a terrible fury in his face. "Only in-nocent lives, Peter!"

"You don't understand!" whined Pettigrew. "He would have killed me, Sirius!"

"THEN YOU SHOULD HAVE DIED!" roared Black. "DIED RATHER THAN BETRAY YOUR FRIENDS, AS WE WOULD HAVE DONE FOR YOU!"[11]

This scene nicely captures the moral calibration. What would the reader do in Pettigrew's situation? Black, and by implication Lupin and the Potters, would have chosen death at Voldemort's hands rather than betraying friends and cooperating with evil. Pettigrew chose differently. Thus far, however, the scene is not particularly noteworthy among children's or adult literature. Faced with a choice between "the most evil wizard who ever lived" and one's friends, most readers will, I hope, conclude that Pettigrew made the wrong choice. And Pettigrew's Animagus form as a rat seems particularly apt given his bad choices.

The key is what happens next. Black and Lupin are prepared to kill Petti-grew to revenge Harry's parents. " 'You should have realized,' said Lupin qui-etly, 'if Voldemort didn't kill you, we would.' "[12] Hermione, often a voice of a rules-based legalism and rarely at a loss for words, turns her face away but does nothing to attempt to stop the killing, seemingly accepting that Lupin and Black are right to kill Pettigrew. But Harry acts, and he stops the killing by placing himself between Pettigrew and Black and Lupin.

Why does Harry intervene? Not for Pettigrew, who he tells "I'm not doing this for you." Harry does it "because—I don't reckon my dad would've wanted

---

11. *Prisoner of Azkaban* 374–75.
12. *Prisoner of Azkaban* 375.

them [Black and Lupin] to become killers—just for you [Pettigrew]."[13] Harry's choice is extraordinary. Who could blame him if he wanted Pettigrew's death, as he had wanted Black's a few moments before when he believed Black had killed his parents? Not only had Pettigrew denied Harry his family, the thing he desires most, but Pettigrew condemned Harry to a miserable childhood with the Dursleys. At this pivotal moment, Harry chooses law over vengeance: "He can go to Azkaban ... but don't kill him."[14] Indeed, throughout the series Harry repeatedly chooses not to kill people who are trying to kill him. In *Deathly Hallows*, Harry refuses to do more than disarm Stan Shunpike (who is acting under the Imperius curse),[15] rescues Crabbe, Goyle and Malfoy from the fire they caused while trying to kill Harry, Ron, and Hermione,[16] and uses only the Expelliarmus spell against Voldemort, who dies from his own *Avada Kedavra*.[17] Protecting the innocent Stan Shunpike is a relatively easy choice; protecting the detestable Crabbe, Goyle and Malfoy harder; and refusing to kill Voldemort is hardest of all.

Harry doesn't choose law because he has internalized the value of due process. He doesn't suggest that Pettigrew deserves a lawyer or should be presumed innocent. He doesn't even choose a trial over vengeance. Pettigrew *will* go to Azkaban if he is taken back to Hogwarts and turned over to Dumbledore, a terrible fate for the guilty, and we have no reason to believe that Pettigrew's trial will have any more constitutional safeguards than did the trials Harry saw earlier in the Pensieve. Harry doesn't choose law out of mercy either, saying "if anyone deserves [Azkaban], he [Pettigrew] does...."[18] Harry chooses law over vengeance because he does not want his parents' friends to act immorally to avenge his parents. This is a mature choice, one that many adults would be hard pressed to make. It is also a critical choice, since "law grows out of revenge."[19] Black and Lupin question Harry about his choice, making a good case for private justice, but Harry remains firm. Rowling's readers are then invited to compare their own reaction to Harry's and test themselves against his choice.

To make this scene work as a calibration, several things are necessary. First, Harry must end up in the Shrieking Shack with, at a minimum, Pettigrew and Sirius, so that he can make the choice. Second, adult authorities cannot burst

---

13. *Prisoner of Azkaban* 376.
14. *Prisoner of Azkaban* 375.
15. *Deathly Hallows* 70–71.
16. *Deathly Hallows* 633.
17. *Deathly Hallows* 743.
18. *Prisoner of Azkaban* 376.
19. Posner, *supra* note 3, at 49.

upon the scene and take Pettigrew away. Third, it must be a real choice: Black
and Lupin must be able to actually kill Pettigrew. All of these elements, in turn,
require that the Ministry of Magic be unable to capture Black, despite months
of its massive manhunt; that Black be wrongfully convicted of the Potters' murder; that Black and Lupin be willing to violate the law and kill Pettigrew themselves; that Harry violate school rules and go to the Shrieking Shack; as well as
a number of other plot details. Allowing Harry the space to make his choice
at the climax thus dictates a number of elements of the novel, including crucial legal details.

Confirming the centrality of the Shrieking Shack scene to the novel, Harry
and Dumbledore discuss Harry's choice at the novel's end. Seeing that Harry
is unhappy, Dumbledore asks him why, noting "You should be very proud of
yourself after last night." Harry responds "bitterly" that "[i]t didn't make any
difference," because "Pettigrew got away." Dumbledore rejects this: "'Didn't
make any difference?' said Dumbledore quietly. 'It made all the difference in the
world, Harry. You helped uncover the truth. You saved an innocent man [Black]
from a terrible fate.'"[20]

The point I want to emphasize here is that the result of structuring the plot
to bring Harry to the climactic moral choice is the creation of a society in
which the state is largely absent. The Ministry of Magic regulates cauldron
bottoms, organizes wizard tournaments (including the Tri-Wizard tournament
which goes awry in *The Goblet of Fire*), and is run for most of the series by a
bumbling and officious Cornelius Fudge. (Fudge's replacement is, if anything,
even worse.) It does not catch, or even seem to slow down, Lord Voldemort's
many attempts to return to power or perform *any* functions critical to everyday life.

Moreover, the state is not even an essential ally in the battle against evil and
by *The Deathly Hallows* has become evil itself. At the end of *The Goblet of Fire*,
Dumbledore calls upon Fudge, who has been refusing to accept the idea that
Voldemort has returned, to act against the Dark Lord. Fudge is shocked by the
request that he authorize a mission to recruit the giants to the fight, which he
sees as a threat to his career. In a passage that could easily have been written
by a public choice theorist, Dumbledore rebukes Fudge.

> "You are blinded," said Dumbledore, his voice rising now, the aura
> of power around him palpable, his eyes blazing once more, "by the
> love of the office you hold, Cornelius! You place too much impor-

---

20. *Prisoner of Azkaban* 425.

tance, and you always have done, on the so-called purity of blood! You fail to recognize that it matters not what someone is born, but what they grow to be! Your dementor has just destroyed the last remaining member of a pure-blood family as old as any—and see what that man chose to make of his life! I tell you now—take the steps I have suggested, and you will be remembered, in office or out, as one of the bravest and greatest Ministers of Magic we have ever known. Fail to act— and history will remember you as the man who stepped aside and allowed Voldemort a second chance to destroy the world we have tried to rebuild!"[21]

Fudge is clearly not up to the task Dumbledore sets for him; indeed Fudge counters with a vague threat to assert authority over the school if Dumbledore "is going to work against me." Dumbledore replies, "The only one against whom I intend to work ... is Lord Voldemort. If you are against him, then we remain, Cornelius, on the same side."[22] Note that Dumbledore does not seek to have Fudge replaced or appear to believe Fudge's official assistance is critical to the fight—he merely asks Fudge to choose sides.

Finally, consider the concluding assessment of Harry's choice in *The Prisoner of Azkaban*. Harry feels he has made the wrong choice because Pettigrew escaped. But Dumbledore corrects him—Harry's choice "made all the difference in the world" because he saved one innocent man from the Dementor's Kiss, "a terrible fate." Thus even though Voldemort's ally is free, which has terrible consequences in *The Goblet of Fire*, Dumbledore weighs Harry's actions and concludes that they are praiseworthy for saving a single life. There is no utilitarian calculus here, simply unadorned moral choice in a story focused on the individual making the choice.

A world which allows moral calibration is a world in which individuals are free. They are not able to rely on the state or grownups to solve their moral dilemmas for them, nor can they put problems off on others. Thus, one crucial thing readers can learn from the Harry Potter books is that moral choices require liberty.

The Role of Rules

The flip side of liberty is responsibility. Responsibility implies rules. Indeed, an excellent case can be made (and has been, by Friedrich Hayek) that liberty

---

21. *Goblet of Fire* 708.
22. *Goblet of Fire* 709.

requires rule-following even when the rules themselves have no immediate utilitarian justification.[23] Yet Harry Potter is not a child who readily follows rules (sufficiently so that his rule breaking is often cited as a major flaw by conservative critics of the books). More generally, rules do not come off well in the Harry Potter books. Many of the examples of rules that mimic real life regulations realistically (e.g., regulation of imported cauldron bottoms' thickness) are presented in a ridiculous light. What conclusions can we draw from the characters' attitudes toward such rules? Is Rowling constructing an anarchistic world in which rules are to be flouted with impunity? No.

Much of the rule-breaking in the Harry Potter books is breaking of the type of rules which will be immediately familiar to children: seemingly pointless rules, imposed by an outside authority which prevent children from having fun. Rowling has fun with these rules and allows her characters to break them without serious consequences. Indeed, the rules at Hogwarts are so numerous and arbitrary that Professor Snape is able to constantly take points from Gryffindor for such things as knowing the answer to a question. Again, even an expert on public choice theory could not better characterize the perils of excessive regulations. A clearer example of what Hayek terms legislation, rather than law, is hard to picture. Hayek defines law as "purpose-independent rules which govern the conduct of individuals towards each other, are intended to apply to an unknown number of further instances, and by defining a protected domain of each, enable an order of actions to form itself whenever individuals can make feasible plans."[24] It is readily apparent that most of the rules, as applied by characters like Snape or Dolores Umbridge, fail this test. Like our world, Harry's is awash in legislation serving special interests and allowing the arbitrary exercise of power.

Sometimes there are more serious rules at stake. In these instances the characters generally consider and justify their actions in moral terms. For example, Firenze the centaur breaks centaur law ("we are sworn not to set ourselves against the heavens")[25] to rescue Harry from Quirrell-Voldemort in the Forbidden Forest. When another centaur, Bane, challenges his action, Firenze justifies his actions with an appeal to higher law: "'Do you not see that [dead] unicorn?' Firenze bellowed at Bane. 'Do you not understand why it was killed? Or have the planets not let you in on that secret? I set myself against what is

---

23. Friedrich A. Hayek, Law, Legislation & Liberty, vol. 1, Rules and Order 108 (1973). *See also* Andrew P. Morriss, *Hayek & Cowboys: Customary Law in the American West*, 1 N.Y.U. J. L. & Liberty 35 (2005).

24. Hayek, *supra* note 23, at 85–86.

25. *Sorcerer's Stone* 257.

lurking in this forest, Bane, yes, with humans alongside me if I must.'"[26] Morality thus serves as a measure even for important rules.

Although there are not many serious rules, there are some. In particular, we are told that there is one critically important wizarding law (aside from simple translations of ordinary principles of criminal law into the novels' context): the ban on using the *Avada Kedavra*, Imperius, and Cruciatus curses, whose violation is punishable by a life sentence in Azkaban. The *Avada Kedavra* curse kills its victim; the Imperius curse makes the victim do the bidding of the one who cursed him; and the Cruciatus curse tortures the victim.

Why are these three curses singled out? Other curses that humiliate or hurt the victim are not banned—Harry is drawn to a book on cursing one's enemies in *The Sorcerer's Stone* whose existence suggests a market for cursing enemies; the fake 'Mad Eye' Moody turns Draco Malfoy into a ferret and bounces him on the stone floor in *The Goblet of Fire* without more than a verbal reprimand from another teacher; and characters routinely afflict each other with lesser but potentially dangerous or painful curses (jelly legs, etc.) without fear of serious punishment. Nor is this ban a reflection of a pacifist response to evil—Aurors fought Voldemort's supporters during his initial rise and killed some—and so some violence is presented positively, making killing itself insufficient to justify the ban on *Avada Kedavra*. The key, I think, is that these three Unforgivable Curses are different because they are used to destroy the victim's ability to choose, again highlighting the importance of moral choice.

Rules in the books thus fall into two categories: silly and minor rules, and important rules linked to morality. Silly rules are broken by characters for plot purposes and humor. These incidents tell us little about the morality of the characters. Important rules are broken only when characters consider the morality of their actions. Firenze's choice is typical of the choices faced by the characters between following formal rules and obeying a higher law.

The right choice in the Harry Potter books is always to follow the higher law. For example, Harry, Ron, and Hermione face critical moral choices at the climax of *The Sorcerer's Stone*. Dumbledore is away and unavailable to help, and their initial plan to stake out the entrance to the room guarded by Fluffy and track Snape's whereabouts is foiled by Snape. Harry then announces to the others that he will have to get the Stone first, before Snape, who the children believe is working for Voldemort. Ron exclaims "You're mad!" and Hermione protests that Harry will be expelled if he is caught and Harry responds:

---

26. *Sorcerer's Stone* 257.

"Don't you understand? If Snape gets hold of the Stone, Voldemort's coming back! Haven't you heard what it was like when he was trying to take over? There won't be any Hogwarts to get expelled from! He'll flatten it, or turn it into a school for the Dark Arts! Losing points does-n't matter anymore, can't you see? D'you think he'll leave you and your families alone if Gryffindor wins the house cup? If I get caught before I can get to the Stone, well, I'll have to go back to the Dursleys and wait for Voldemort to find me there, it's only dying a bit later than I would have, because I'm never going over to the Dark Side! I'm going through that trapdoor tonight and nothing you two say is going to stop me! Voldemort killed my parents, remember?"[27]

Hermione and Ron relent, agree with Harry that they must act, and insist on accompanying him. Everyone has these choices; even Voldemort, the person-ification of evil, has a chance to make a choice at the end. In their final con-frontation, Harry tells Voldemort: "before you try to kill me, I'd advise you to think about what you've done.... Think, and try for some remorse, Riddle...." and "It's your one last chance, it's all you've got left.... I've seen what you'll be otherwise.... Be a man ... try ... Try for some remorse...."[28]

There are two crucial scenes dealing with rules outside the silly/important categories. The first takes place as the first years begin their initial flying les-son in *The Sorcerer's Stone*. Neville Longbottom breaks his wrist and Madam Hooch, the instructor, has to leave the others to take Neville to the infirmary. Before leaving she tells the others "None of you is to move while I take this boy to the hospital wing! You leave those brooms where they are or you'll be out of Hogwarts before you can say 'Quidditch.'"[29] Nonetheless, when Draco Malfoy steals the Remembrall Neville dropped and takes to the air to put it in a tree, Harry jumps on a broom for the first time and flies after him. As he does so,

> in a rush of fierce joy he realized he'd found something he could do without being taught—this was easy, this was *wonderful*. He pulled his broomstick up a little to take it even higher, and heard screams and gasps of girls back on the ground and an admiring whoop from Ron.[30]

We can see several important themes that recur throughout the novels in this scene. First, Harry acts without thinking and without regard for the rules.

---

27. *Sorcerer's Stone* 270.
28. *Deathly Hallows* 741.
29. *Sorcerer's Stone* 147.
30. *Sorcerer's Stone* 148.

Clearly the "legal" approach to Malfoy's behavior would be for Harry and the other Gryffindor students to report Malfoy's disobedience (and dishonesty) to Madame Hooch when she returns. Nothing of consequence turns on stopping Malfoy—Madame Hooch could easily retrieve the Remembrall from the tree herself. If the students report Malfoy, the school authorities could punish Malfoy. Since the teacher involved is Madame Hooch rather than Professor Snape, there is no reason to believe that the rules will be misapplied, so the students undoubtedly would believe that if they report him, Malfoy will receive a just punishment. But this is not what Harry does. Instead, he risks punishment for himself and for Gryffindor in the House Cup competition (as Hermione warns him) and acts on instinct and emotion.

Second, Harry's violation of the rules is rewarded. Not only does he save the Remembrall when Malfoy throws it but he gains stature in the eyes of the other students. Even worse, from a legal point of view, when he is seen breaking the rules by Professor McGonagall, he is given the unprecedented honor, for a first year, of being made the Seeker on the Gryffindor Quidditch team and receives a Nimbus 2000 broom, rather than being punished. Further, in breaking the rules, Harry discovers something important about his true nature ("something he could do without being taught").

More is going on here than Harry becoming a member of the Quidditch team, a key plot development. Rowling could easily have made Harry perform well in class, perhaps catching a falling student in a dramatic dive, to bring his flying skills to Professor McGonagall's attention without breaking rules. Instead, Harry *acts* rather than analyzes, and his actions are in pursuit of natural justice rather than in compliance with formal rules.

In the second of these rule scenes, in a pivotal scene in *The Sorcerer's Stone*, Neville Longbottom chooses to defend the rules (wrongly, as it turns out) against his friends. He is unsuccessful at stopping Harry, Ron, and Hermione (and a good thing too), but it is his stand against them that is the event that puts Gryffindor over the top to win the House Cup. Dumbledore's comment in awarding the points makes it clear that moral choice is the key, not simply the result of the larger battle between good and evil: " 'There are all kinds of courage,' said Dumbledore, smiling. 'It takes a great deal of bravery to stand up to our enemies, but just as much to stand up to our friends.' "[31] Neville was objectively wrong to try to stop the three others—had he succeeded, Voldemort might have gotten the Sorcerer's Stone. What makes Neville's action praiseworthy is his willingness to sacrifice to defend his choice: he is making a hard

---

31. *Sorcerer's Stone* 306.

choice in standing up to his only friends, standing up for himself, as well as for the House and the rules.

What kind of world does Rowling's treatment of rules suggest? Again, keeping in mind the hypothesis that the books are aimed at offering readers the opportunity to calibrate their own moral choices, we see that providing such an opportunity requires a world in which the "real" rules (i.e., those whose violation is morally weighty) are relatively few in number and rooted in a higher moral law. Rowling seems to have nicely, if unintentionally, captured the Hayekian distinction between law and legislation. Once again, the key insight is that moral choice requires freedom, including the freedom to disregard rules that prevent us from making moral choices. Slavishly following rules, even well-intentioned ones, does not lead us to the right choices. Rather, we must listen to our hearts and find the courage to oppose evil.

Conclusions

I have argued that the Harry Potter books are about "calibrating" readers' ideas of the importance of moral choice and that constructing such models requires a world in which the state is largely absent, that individuals must choose the higher law when confronted by a choice between morality and rules, and that it is the moral choices individuals make that matter, not the utilitarian consequences of those choices. There are two lessons about law one can take from this exercise.

First, the state tends to crowd out moral choices. Not entirely, of course— bad government offers plenty of opportunities for individuals to make moral choices—but with some frequency. Perhaps unintentionally, the Harry Potter series makes a case for a minimal state as a necessary condition for individuals to exercise their moral faculties. To see this, simply imagine the outcome if Harry followed the rules rather than flouting them. Not only would he be a far less interesting character and the outcome of the struggle against Voldemort would likely be worse, but the choices would "feel wrong" to most readers.

Second, what Hayek termed legislation, as embodied in the detailed and often ridiculous rules that govern day to day life in the wizarding world, just as they do our own, must give way to law when the two conflict. I don't mean to suggest either that Rowling has been reading Hayek or that her work explicitly embodies a Hayekian notion of law, but merely that the distinction between the higher law and the mere rules in Harry's world is consistent with Hayek's analysis. To the extent we approve of the choices Harry and the others make, that suggests some support for the Hayekian position.

Crimes & Punishments

2

Harry Potter and the Unforgivable Curses

Aaron Schwabach

Introduction

This chapter focuses on a particular inconsistency, or apparent inconsistency, in the legal regime governing the British wizarding world: the Unforgivable Curses, the use of which on humans is absolutely prohibited by wizarding law. The three Unforgivable Curses are the Cruciatus Curse, which causes unbearable pain; the Imperius Curse, which allows the user to control the actions of the victim; and the Killing Curse, which causes instant death. The use of any of these curses on a human being is punishable by life imprisonment in Azkaban, the exceptionally grim wizards' prison. Yet there are inconsistencies both in the application of this law and in the selection of certain curses as Unforgivable.

Why has the wizarding world chosen to outlaw certain spells and not others? What values do these choices reflect, both for Harry's world and for ours? What does it mean for a society to choose to punish some offenses more seriously than others, or not to punish at all? The most extreme penalties wizarding law has to offer—the Dementor's Kiss and life imprisonment in Azkaban—are handed out arbitrarily. In spite of, or perhaps because of, this arbitrariness, the denizens of the wizarding world seem to use the Unforgivable Curses fairly frequently.

This chapter attempts to explore, and perhaps answer, some of these questions. It looks at the Unforgivable Curses and their Forgivable companions, the Dementor's Kiss and the Memory Charm, and examines the legal treatment of these spells under the Ministry's regime as well as under relevant British (Muggle) and international law.

The Unforgivable Curses

Barty Crouch Jr., a Death Eater impersonating former Auror Mad-Eye Moody, explains and demonstrates the nature and illegality of the three Unforgivable Curses to Harry Potter's fourth-year Defense Against the Dark Arts class. Crouch first demonstrates the Curses on three spiders, although one spider would have sufficed.[1]

Crouch comments that the Ministry doesn't want him to demonstrate the curses until the sixth year and implies that Dumbledore has authorized him to demonstrate them to fourth-year students. This is notable for a couple of reasons: It shows that the educational use of these curses, on spiders or perhaps other small animals, is not absolutely prohibited, and it suggests that Dumbledore has authority to override the Ministry's guidelines as to when the Unforgivable Curses should be taught. Crouch might be lying, of course, but it seems more likely that he's telling the truth. He is teaching at Hogwarts in order to carry out an unnecessarily complex plan to revive Lord Voldemort, and his success depends on not being detected as an impostor. If he were to lie about something that could so easily be checked, someone, probably Hermione Granger, might catch him in the lie.

The Cruciatus Curse

As a convicted Death Eater sentenced to life in Azkaban for use of the Cruciatus Curse, Barty Crouch Jr. has first-hand knowledge of the Unforgivable Curses and their legal penalties. He demonstrates this curse for the students:

> Moody raised his wand again, pointed it at the spider, and muttered, "Crucio!"
> At once, the spider's legs bent in upon its body; it rolled over and began to twitch horribly, rocking from side to side. No sound came from it, but Harry was sure that if it could have given voice, it would have been screaming.
> ***
> "Pain," said Moody softly. "You don't need thumbscrews or knives to torture someone if you can perform the Cruciatus Curse ... That one was very popular once too."[2]

---

1. By the time of the movie version of *The Goblet of Fire*, Crouch had apparently realized this, and made do with a single spider.
2. *Goblet of Fire* 214–15.

The Cruciatus Curse presents the easiest case for Unforgivability: torture is universally recognized as a crime, and there is no legitimate use for a curse that does nothing other than cause pain and, in some cases, insanity. Crouch was imprisoned for using the Curse to torture Frank and Alice Longbottom, the parents of Harry's friend Neville. Fifteen years later the Longbottoms remain institutionalized with no hope of recovery. Harry and his friends meet them, in one of the series' most emotionally affecting scenes, while visiting their former professor, Gilderoy Lockhart, who is also institutionalized. Frank and Alice Longbottom are barely able to communicate with, let alone relate to, their son Neville or his grandmother, Frank's mother. Neville's mother attempts to reach out to her son by giving him bubble gum wrappers.

The Cruciatus Curse also provides disturbing insights into Harry's character and his links to the Dark Side. Harry wishes that "he knew how to do the Cruciatus Curse ... he'd have Snape flat on his back like that spider, jerking and twitching...."[3] Later Harry actually uses the curse, or attempts to, on three occasions. After Bellatrix Lestrange kills Sirius Black, Harry pursues her and, catching up with her, uses the curse: "Bellatrix screamed. The spell had knocked her off her feet, but she did not writhe and shriek with pain as Neville had—she was already on her feet again, breathless, no longer laughing."[4] He also attempts to use the curse on Severus Snape after Snape kills Dumbledore. His most successful use of the curse comes near the end of the seventh book; Harry uses it to torture Hogwarts professor (and Death Eater) Amycus Carrow into unconsciousness after Carrow spits in Professor Minerva McGonagall's face:

> As Amycus spun around, Harry shouted, *"Crucio!"*
> The Death Eater was lifted off his feet. He writhed through the air like a drowning man, thrashing and howling in pain, and then, with a crunch and a shattering of glass, he smashed into the front of a bookcase and crumpled, insensible, to the floor.
> "I see what Bellatrix meant," said Harry, the blood thundering through his brain, "you need to really mean it."[5]

Harry's first two uses of the curse, against Bellatrix and Snape, are witnessed only by his intended victims. The third is also witnessed by McGonagall and Luna Lovegood. While Luna would never turn Harry in, McGonagall has been presented throughout the series as a stickler for the rules who will tolerate no

3. *Goblet of Fire* 300.
4. *Order of the Phoenix* 810.
5. *Deathly Hallows* 593.

bending, even from her own side.[6] The event represents a turning point in McGonagall's development as a character, however; she does no more than call Harry's use of the curse "foolish," if "gallant," and proceeds to use another Unforgivable Curse—the Imperius Curse—on Carrow.[7]

It's interesting, and disturbing, that in these three instances Harry chose the Cruciatus Curse rather than one that would have simply immobilized his opponents or, for that matter, killed them. This parallels his reaction to Malfoy's insults after he defeats Malfoy at Quidditch:

> He had completely forgotten the fact that all the teachers were watching: All he wanted to do was cause Malfoy as much pain as possible. With no time to draw out his wand, he merely drew back the fist clutching the Snitch and sank it as hard as he could into Malfoy's stomach....[8]

The Cruciatus Curse presents the easiest case in legal terms, but an especially difficult moral question for young readers: If Harry uses the curse, knowing that it is both wrong and illegal, is Harry still good? And if he's flawed—if he has a touch of evil in his personality—is it still okay to root for him?

The Imperius Curse

The Imperius Curse subordinates the will of its victim to the will of the attacker:

> Moody jerked his wand, and the spider rose onto two of its hind legs and went into what was unmistakably a tap dance.
> Everyone was laughing—everyone except Moody.
> "Think it's funny, do you?" he growled. "You'd like it, would you, if I did it to you?"
> The laughter died away almost instantly.

---

6. It is McGonagall who imposes the disastrous fifty point per person penalty on Harry, Hermione, and the nearly innocent Neville during their first year. *Sorcerer's Stone* 243–44.

7. *Deathly Hallows* 593–95.

8. *Order of the Phoenix* 413. *See also generally* MICHEL FOUCAULT, DISCIPLINE AND PUNISH: THE BIRTH OF THE PRISON 129–131 (Alan Sheridan trans., 2d ed. 1995). In addition to attempting to use the Cruciatus Curse on the fleeing Snape, Harry also tries to kill Snape with Sectumsempra—the first time we see Harry deliberately try to kill someone.

"Total control," said Moody quietly as the spider balled itself up and began to roll over and over. "I could make it jump out of the window, drown itself, throw itself down one of your throats...."[9]

Crouch also subjects each of the students in turn to the Imperius Curse despite the fact that this is a use of an Unforgivable Curse on a fellow human being. Apparently Crouch, as a Hogwarts professor or at least Dumbledore as Hogwarts headmaster, has the authority to authorize this use of the curse for educational purposes, or else Dumbledore has chosen to disregard wizarding law on a fundamental matter:

> "But—but you said it's illegal, Professor," said Hermione uncertainly as Moody cleared away the desks with a sweep of his wand, leaving a large clear space in the middle of the room. "You said—to use it against another human was—"
> "Dumbledore wants you taught what it feels like," said Moody, his magical eye swiveling onto Hermione and fixing her with an eerie, unblinking stare.[10]

Again, Crouch might be lying, but given the danger to his plan such lying would entail, it seems more likely that Dumbledore actually has agreed to Moody's demonstration of the Curse. It becomes clear later, however, that the Ministry was not informed of this in advance and would not have approved had it known: "It is my understanding that my predecessor not only performed illegal curses in front of you, he actually performed them *on* you."[11]

It turns out that the Imperius Curse, unlike the Killing Curse and, presumably, the Cruciatus Curse, can be overcome—but not by everyone. There's a disturbing subtextual message here, too—some wizards' wills may be stronger than others'. The Curse is not completely effective on Harry the first time Crouch uses it, and by the end of a single class session he is able to resist it completely. Later, he successfully resists the Curse when Voldemort uses it

---

9. *Goblet of Fire* 213.

10. *Goblet of Fire* 230. The Ministry's preference, at least while Fudge is Minister, would be to have Defense Against the Dark Arts taught as an entirely theoretical subject. During the year that Dolores Umbridge, a Ministry stooge, teaches the course, her course aims are: (1) Understanding the principles underlying defensive magic; (2) Learning to recognize situations in which defensive magic can legally be used; (3) Placing the use of defensive magic in a context for practical use. *Order of the Phoenix* 240 (Dolores Umbridge). Alas, Professor Umbridge's preferred text, Wilbert Slinkhard's Defensive Magical Theory, is unavailable to Muggles; it would have made this chapter much easier to write.

11. *Order of the Phoenix* 243 (Dolores Umbridge).

against him. Barty Crouch Sr., also placed under the Imperius Curse by Volde-mort, eventually manages to escape. But Broderick Bode, a Ministry employee, struggles unsuccessfully against an Imperius Curse placed on him by Lucius Malfoy. An unsuccessful Imperius Curse may have the potential to do lasting harm: When the brains of a Muggle named Herbert Chorley are addled by "a poorly performed Imperius Curse," the Muggle Prime Minister asks Fudge's replacement as Minister of Magic, Rufus Scrimgeour, "He'll be all right, won't he?" Scrimgeour responds with a shrug.[12]

The moral logic behind the Unforgivability of the Imperius Curse is, as with the Cruciatus Curse, straightforward, but it exposes a moral and legal contra-diction in the Ministry of Magic's legal regime. Although the characters in Harry's universe are often moved by factors beyond their control or knowl-edge, free will is sacred (except, perhaps, in the case of house-elves). Dumb-ledore says, "It is our choices, Harry, that show what we truly are."[13] The Imperius Curse is an offense against free will; it enslaves the victim, and en-slavement is universally recognized as a crime and has been illegal in England for centuries.[14] The Ministry, however, openly tolerates the enslavement of house-elves. Even the benevolent Dumbledore makes either a conscious or un-conscious exception for house-elves: "'Kreacher is what he has been made by wizards, Harry,' said Dumbledore. 'Yes, he is to be pitied. His existence has been as miserable as your friend Dobby's.'"[15] This seems to undermine Dum-bledore's earlier assertion that "our choices … show what we truly are." Dobby, after all, chooses not to harm anyone, while Kreacher initially chooses to ally himself with Death Eaters, to injure Buckbeak, and to betray Sirius to his death. To blame wizarding society for Kreacher's crimes seems to deny the validity of his choices; after all, his and Dobby's ability to work against their masters' in-terests is proof of house-elves' ability to make independent moral choices.[16]

Nor is McGonagall the only good guy to use the Imperius Curse when it is expedient to do so. Harry uses the curse on Bogrod the goblin—twice—and Travers the Death Eater.[17] Hermione may also have used the Curse to convince

---

12. *Half-Blood Prince* 17–18.

13. *Chamber of Secrets* 333.

14. *See* Sommersett v. Stuart, 20 How. St. Tr. 1, 81 (K.B. 1772). The Imperius Curse has been illegal for longer. Along with the other two Unforgivable Curses, it was outlawed in 1717. *Tales of Beedle the Bard* 86 n.6.

15. *Order of the Phoenix* 832.

16. Later Kreacher again demonstrates free will by repudiating his earlier choices and siding with Harry. And Dobby's death—one of the few in the series that can truly be de-scribed as heroic—is stripped of its heroism if Dobby lacks free will.

17. *Deathly Hallows* 531, 535.

her parents to move to Australia, for their own protection, although she only admits to modifying their memories.[18] Harry performs the Curse in front of several unfriendly witnesses—Bogrod, Travers, and the goblin Griphook—but again avoids a life sentence in Azkaban. This may be because, after he has defeated Voldemort, popular opinion makes him untouchable, or it may be because there is a necessity defense: The use of the Curse on Bogrod and Travers is necessary for Harry to retrieve one of the Horcruxes, without which it would have been impossible to defeat Voldemort.

The Killing Curse

The third of the Unforgivable Curses, and the least convincing in its Unforgivability, is the Killing Curse:

> "*Avada Kedavra!*" Moody roared. There was a flash of blinding green light and a rushing sound, as though a vast, invisible something was soaring through the air—instantaneously the spider rolled over onto its back, unmarked, but unmistakably dead.[19]

Less unmistakable is what makes *Avada Kedavra* Unforgivable. The illegality of murder is, of course, even more widely recognized than the illegality of torture and enslavement. But not all killings are murder, and the wizarding world apparently acknowledges the legality of some killings. The lives of house-elves can be arbitrarily terminated at the will of their masters: Sirius Black's "dear Aunt Elladora ... started the family tradition of beheading house-elves when they got too old to carry tea-trays."[20] As discussed below, the Ministry imposes the death penalty on magical beasts and the Dementor's Kiss on wizards. The Ministry's Aurors kill on occasion; their ultimate goal is "to find and kill Voldemort."[21] The real Mad-Eye Moody makes a wry comment to Dumbledore regarding Moody's part in killing a Death Eater named Rosier, and other Aurors apparently rack up an even higher body count than the sinister Moody. Harry's godfather, Sirius Black (an escapee from Azkaban, where he was sent by Barty Crouch Sr. for murder, without a trial), tells Harry that Moody, in apparent contrast to some other Aurors, "never killed if he could help it."[22] In passing, Sirius also mentions another Death Eater, Wilkes, being killed by Au-

---

18. *Deathly Hallows* 96–97.
19. *Goblet of Fire* 215–16.
20. *Order of the Phoenix* 113 (Sirius Black).
21. *Half-Blood Prince* 104.
22. *Goblet of Fire* 532.

rors,[23] and Ron tells Harry that "loads [of giants] got themselves killed by Aurors."[24]

Sirius, Moody and Ron do not explain how the Aurors killed these giants and Death Eaters. Perhaps they are licensed by the Ministry to use the Killing Curse, in an analogue of 007's "license to kill" in the regrettable James Bond fantasies. This seems unlikely, though; if they were permitted to do so, surely the Aurors Kingsley Shacklebolt and Nymphadora Tonks would use the curse in, among other places, the battle at the Department of Mysteries near the end of the fifth volume.

There are many other ways to kill people in the magical world. The Death Eater Peter Pettigrew managed to kill a dozen Muggles with an explosion caused by a single curse. A wizard named Benjy Fenwick "copped it too, we only ever found bits of him...."[25] Whatever killed Benjy Fenwick, it wasn't the Killing Curse, which leaves its victims "unmarked, but unmistakably dead."[26] Giants kill each other by purely physical means, and centaurs use bows and arrows that do not appear to be magical. At the age of thirteen, Harry threatens to kill Sirius Black, a threat that everyone, including Black, seems to find credible. In Harry's first year at Hogwarts Professor Quirrell tries to kill him by casting a spell on his broom, hoping that Harry will fall off. Hermione, as a first-year student, is able to set Snape's clothes on fire. Devil's Snare, a magical plant that strangles its victims, can be used for murder: it endangers Harry, Ron, and Hermione in their first year and, disguised as a gift, is successfully used to murder Broderick Bode in the Closed Ward at St. Mungo's. Magical creatures like Salazar Slytherin's basilisk can also be used to kill. A snake possessed by Voldemort bites and nearly kills Arthur Weasley. Sirius Black is apparently killed when an otherwise non-lethal spell knocks him through the veil of death in the Department of Mysteries. And Harry nearly kills Draco, more or less by accident, with Sectumsempra—and then tries to kill Snape with the same spell.[27]

Harry shows misgivings about the use of lethal force. When he leaves the Dursleys' house at number four, Privet Drive for the last time, he is pursued by Death Eaters. He immobilizes one with a spell—as they are flying high above the ground at the time, the immobilized Death Eater probably dies, although

---

23. *Goblet of Fire* 531.
24. *Goblet of Fire* 430.
25. *Order of the Phoenix* 174 (Mad-Eye Moody).
26. *Goblet of Fire* 216.
27. Harry's first use of Sectumsempra provides an extended pun—Harry-slash-Draco—for the amusement of the fan universe.

this is never made clear. Moments later he uses Expelliarmus, a disarming spell, to avoid killing another of his pursuers.[28] And during the final Battle of Hogwarts, Harry kills no one but Voldemort—and even that is done only by deflecting Voldemort's Killing Curse back at him.[29]

Harry's reluctance to kill may be less admirable than it appears. Several of the people he stuns, or otherwise disables, later kill others, including Harry's friends and allies. Harry's friend and former mentor Remus Lupin, for example, is killed by Antonin Dolohov.[30] Before Lupin's death, Harry had twice defeated Dolohov, immobilizing him with the Body-Bind Curse each time.[31] Harry and Hermione also defeat Dolohov and another Death Eater, Thorfinn; this time Hermione puts the Body-Bind Curse on Dolohov.[32] Had Dolohov been killed any of these times, Lupin would have survived—or, at least, would not have been killed by Dolohov. Dolohov also endangers Harry's classmates Dean Thomas and Parvati Patil; both are last seen fighting Dolohov, and their ultimate fate is unknown.[33] Dolohov belatedly falls "with a scream at Flitwick's hands."[34]

Harry's friends and allies have fewer scruples, apparently. Hagrid deploys a magical brick wall against several Death Eaters in mid-air; one would have died had he not been rescued by a companion.[35] Hermione turns a tapestry to stone so that two Death Eaters slide into it at high speed with "two loud, sickening crunches."[36] Neville uses deadly mandrake plants[37] and Venomous Tentacula,[38] while Professor Trelawney drops a crystal ball on Fenrir Greyback.[39]

---

28. *Deathly Hallows* 58–59. This time the pursuer is Stan Shunpike, wrongly imprisoned by the Ministry of Magic and apparently liberated during the Death Eaters' mass breakout from Azkaban. Whether Stan is, as Harry seems to believe, under the Imperius Curse or whether he became embittered and joined the Death Eaters as a result of his unjust imprisonment is never made clear.

29. *Deathly Hallows* 743–44.

30. J.K. Rowling, Reading at Carnegie Hall, Oct. 19, 2007, *transcript available at* The Leaky Cauldron, *J. K. Rowling at Carnegie Hall Reveals Dumbledore is Gay; Neville Marries Hannah Abbott, and Much More*, post by Edward, http://the-leaky-cauldron.org/2007/10/20/j-k-rowling-at-carnegie-hall-reveals-dumbledore-is-gay-neville-marries-hannah-abbott-and-scores-more (Oct. 19, 2007, 9:17 p.m.).

31. *Order of the Phoenix* 793, 803.

32. *Deathly Hallows* 165–66.

33. *Deathly Hallows* 644–45.

34. *Deathly Hallows* 735.

35. *Deathly Hallows* 57.

36. *Deathly Hallows* 643–44.

37. *Deathly Hallows* 620.

38. *Deathly Hallows* 645.

39. *Deathly Hallows* 646.

It's not clear whether any or all of these attacks are actually lethal, but they are meant to be.

Killings may be excused as self-defense or, when the killer is under the Imperius Curse, as involuntary. While *mens rea* is relevant to determining whether a killing is "murder," the prohibition of the Killing Curse is not based on the *mens rea* of the user, but rather on the method employed. There is some sense to this. At common law and in many jurisdictions today, murder committed in certain ways, such as by the use of bombs or poison, is treated as first-degree murder regardless of intent or *mens rea*. In California, for example, murder committed by explosive device is first-degree murder and carries a mandatory sentence of either death or life without parole.[40] Certain instrumentalities are deemed too dangerous. The Killing Curse may be banned for the same reason bombs are banned: not because it can kill, but because, for those able to use it, it makes killing too easy. However, there is evidence that the Killing Curse is difficult to use. Barty Crouch Jr. tells Harry's class that "*Avada Kedavra*'s a curse that needs a powerful bit of magic behind it—you could all get your wands out now and point them at me and say the words, and I doubt I'd get so much as a nosebleed."[41]

Although there is a not inconsiderable amount of killing and attempted killing in the novels, the Killing Curse is used relatively rarely. Voldemort uses it to kill Harry's parents in a scene often revisited throughout the series. Voldemort also uses it to kill a Muggle named Frank Bryce, and he (or perhaps Wormtail using his wand) uses it to kill Bertha Jorkins. He also uses it in six unsuccessful attempts to kill Harry. Bellatrix Lestrange uses it, unsuccessfully, against Molly Weasley in the Battle of Hogwarts, and is in turn killed by Molly with an unspecified curse.[42] Barty Crouch Jr., posing as Mad-Eye Moody, uses it on a spider. (He also kills his father, although we don't learn how.) Wormtail uses Voldemort's wand and the Killing Curse to kill Cedric Diggory.

The Killing Curse is most often used by Voldemort; Pettigrew performs it with Voldemort's wand, even though he presumably has another wand—the one taken from Bertha Jorkins. In the battle at the Department of Mysteries, the Death Eaters use many spells against Harry's gang, but none uses *Avada Kedavra* except, at the end, Voldemort. (One Death Eater attempts to use the

---

40. Cal. Penal Code §§ 189, 190.2(4) (2008).

41. *Goblet of Fire* 217. Crouch may be overconfident; two of his students might succeed. Harry shows a natural aptitude for the Dark Arts, and Hermione is an exceptionally powerful witch.

42. *Deathly Hallows* 735–37.

Killing Curse on Hermione, but Harry and Neville prevent him from completing the spell.) It may be that the Killing Curse is too difficult, or takes too much out of its user, to make it useful in combat to any but the most skilled wizards.

Fates Worse Than Death:
The Dementor's Kiss and Memory Charms

It's also surprising, even disturbing, that one more spell is not Unforgivable: The innocuous-sounding Memory Charm. The Dementor's Kiss, which is not a spell and can only be performed by a dementor, is also considerably more horrific than the Killing Curse: It sucks out the victim's soul. Nonetheless, it can be carried out on orders from the Ministry of Magic as criminal punishment.

1. Memory Charms

The Memory Charm can erase or modify memories. The Ministry of Magic routinely dispatches Obliviators to modify the memories of Muggles who have witnessed magical events. This rather cavalier attitude toward Muggles is presented without evident disapproval, as part of the ordinary work of the Ministry. The pompous Gilderoy Lockhart's use of Memory Charms against other wizards and witches, however, is presented as skullduggery, and he gets his comeuppance when his own Memory Charm backfires and wipes out his memories. To paraphrase Doctor Who, a Muggle may be the sum of his or her memories, but a wizard is even more so.[43]

A uniquely privileged group of Muggles—relatives of wizards and the Muggle Prime Minister—seem to enjoy some immunity from the Ministry's use of Memory Charms. For example, when Harry blows up his Aunt Marge while she's visiting the Dursleys, Obliviators erase Marge's memory of the event—but not the Dursleys'. The Dursleys already know that Harry is a wizard, and either this knowledge, or their relationship to Harry, or some combination of the two makes their memories less vulnerable to casual Obliviation.

Other Muggles, however, have their memories erased or modified at the whim of the Ministry's Obliviators, or even of ordinary wizards; the right to

---

43. Dr. Who, *The Five Doctors* (BBC television broadcast, Nov. 25, 1983) (The Fifth Doctor (Peter Davison)).

use Memory Charms against Muggles is not limited to the Ministry's Obliviators. Among the memories to be erased are memories of having seen magical creatures:

> When the worst happens and a Muggle sees what he or she is not supposed to see, the Memory Charm is perhaps the most useful repair tool. The Memory Charm may be performed by the owner of the beast in question, but in severe cases of Muggle notice, a team of trained Obliviators may be sent in by the Ministry of Magic.[44]

Sometimes this use of the Memory Charm can be justified as necessary to prevent immediate loss of life: in 1932 a wizarding family used memory charms on beachgoers at Ilfracombe "when a rogue Welsh Green dragon swooped down upon a crowded beach."[45] The Memory Charms prevented a panic that could have cost lives; although other spells might have accomplished the same result, the situation did not allow for sober reflection as to the least intrusive spell to use.

Use of Memory Charms to protect Muggles from immediate harm is rare, however. More often the Charms are used out of what often seems a merely reflexive desire, characteristic of so many governments, for secrecy. The Muggle witnesses to Peter Pettigrew's mass murder have their memories of the event erased after their statements are taken. Perhaps, had their memories been left intact and had the witnesses been questioned at greater length, the Ministry might have discovered that Pettigrew, not Black, was the murderer; instead, it took the statements, erased the memories, and sent Black to Azkaban without a trial. The use of the Memory Charms thus prevents justice from being done and indirectly leads to Voldemort's return, much as Fudge's too-hasty use of the Dementor's Kiss on Barty Crouch Jr. sets the Ministry on the wrong path for a full year and allows Voldemort time to gather strength and unite his followers. When young, Voldemort himself deliberately used Memory Charms to conceal his own guilt and send innocent persons (his uncle Morfin and Hokey the house-elf) to Azkaban.

The Ministry's use of Memory Charms on Muggles also prevents Muggles from participating in the discourse regarding the punishment of their magical assailants. When, for example, Voldemort's uncle Morfin magically assaults Tom Riddle, the Muggle who will later become Voldemort's father, Morfin dismissively tells an investigating Ministry employee, "I expect you've wiped the Muggle's filthy face clean for him, and his memory to boot."[46] By wiping Rid-

---

44. NEWT SCAMANDER, FANTASTIC BEASTS & WHERE TO FIND THEM xx (2001).
45. NEWT SCAMANDER, FANTASTIC BEASTS & WHERE TO FIND THEM xvi (2001).
46. *Half-Blood Prince* 208.

dle's memory, the Ministry has defined Riddle as an object of wizarding law, like a dragon or an enchanted doorknob, with no part in the structuring of the ongoing legal discourse. To Riddle, though, the Ministry's modification of his memory might seem a more serious assault than the hives inflicted on him by Morfin's curse.

The Obliviators are sent in because of their expertise, not because the use of Memory Charms is dangerous. Yet it *is* dangerous. Mr. Roberts, the Muggle owner of the land on which the Quidditch World Cup takes place, cannot help noticing that his tenants are wizards, and his memory is modified repeatedly. Later, Roberts and his family are captured by Death Eaters and tossed high in the air for some time. The next day, as Harry, Hermione and the Weasleys are leaving,

> Mr. Roberts had a strange, dazed look about him, and he waved them off with a vague "Merry Christmas."
> "He'll be all right," said Mr. Weasley quietly as they marched off onto the moor. "Sometimes, when a person's memory's modified, it makes him a bit disorientated[47] for a while ... and that was a big thing they had to make him forget."[48]

We never see Roberts again, so it's not clear whether Mr. Weasley was correct or merely trying to reassure the children. But we know that Memory Charms can cause permanent memory damage: when the witch Bertha Jorkins discovers that Barty Crouch Sr. is concealing his son, the Death Eater Barty Crouch Jr., in his home, Crouch Sr. uses such a powerful Memory Charm that Jorkins' memory is permanently damaged. Breaking Memory Charms, while possible in some cases, is also damaging: Voldemort's extraction of Obliviated memories from Bertha Jorkins left "her mind and body ... both damaged beyond repair."[49]

Memory Charms used against wizards seem to be taken more seriously than Memory Charms used against Muggles. Gilderoy Lockhart is a credit-stealer; he claims credit for the evil-fighting accomplishments of other wizards. To make sure that his thefts remain undiscovered, he uses Memory Charms to erase his victim's knowledge of their own accomplishments. This is wrong on several levels and is presented as evidence of Lockhart's bad character. Not only does Lockhart deprive his victims of memory, wealth and fame, but also

---

47. A disconcerting word for American readers, who are likely to feel a bit disoriented when they see it.
48. *Goblet of Fire* 145 (Arthur Weasley).
49. *Goblet of Fire* 655, 685 (Lord Voldemort).

of the sense of self-worth that comes from having overcome an evil and dangerous opponent for the benefit of the community as a whole.

Later, Lockhart attempts to use Ron Weasley's damaged wand to erase Harry's and Ron's memories; the wand explodes in his hand, and Lockhart's memory is completely erased. He does not recover; two and a half years later Harry, Ron, and Hermione visit him in the Closed Ward at St. Mungo's Hospital for Magical Maladies & Injuries, and he remains an amnesiac. Not only does he not remember events before the Memory Charm, he seems to have difficulty forming new memories. Despite this, the healer in charge of the ward does express the perhaps overly optimistic opinion that "Gilderoy does seem to be getting back some sense of himself,"[50] and he does show slight signs of recognizing Harry. His basic personality is not destroyed, however, as it would have been after a Dementor's Kiss: he remains amiable, conceited and utterly self-centered, as always.

Sharing the closed ward with Lockhart are Frank and Alice Longbottom, Neville's parents, who were severely tortured with the Cruciatus Curse and as a result are in no better mental shape than Lockhart. The parallel seems obvious, yet the Memory Charm, perhaps because of its usefulness to the Ministry, is not Unforgivable. The Cruciatus Curse, on the other hand, is of no use to the Ministry even if it wished to disregard British and international law and use it to extract information from prisoners, as Umbridge attempts to do to Harry. Information extracted under torture is far less reliable than information extracted under Veritaserum. (Interestingly, despite its apparent usefulness, only one effective use of Veritaserum appears in the books: The interrogation of Barty Crouch Jr. by Snape and Dumbledore. Logically, it should be used in all criminal proceedings. But then, as Hermione points out, "A lot of the greatest wizards haven't got an ounce of logic."[51])

Memory Charms are not only useful to the bad guys and the self-serving Ministry; the good guys use Memory Charms, too. Kingsley Shacklebolt, an Auror and member of Dumbledore's secret Order of the Phoenix, surreptitiously modifies the memory of a student, Marietta Edgecombe, to prevent her from incriminating Harry. During the multi-character confrontation in which this takes place, both Shacklebolt and Dumbledore intervene to prevent a teacher, the evil Dolores Umbridge, from shaking Ms. Edgecombe. Yet at the end of the scene Dumbledore speaks approvingly, even admiringly, of Shacklebolt's modification of Ms. Edgecombe's memory and asks Professor McGonagall to thank Shacklebolt. The modification of Ms. Edgecombe's memory is

---

50. *Order of the Phoenix* 511.
51. *Sorcerer's Stone* 285.

not harmless, however. Harry sees her "clutching her robe up to her oddly blank eyes, staring straight ahead of her."[52] She apparently recovers later, although we don't see enough of her to be certain.

Hermione Granger extensively modifies her parents' memories to protect them from Voldemort.[53] She plans to "find Mum and Dad and lift the enchantment" if she survives; we never see the results, however. She also erases the memories of the incapacitated Death Eaters Thorfinn and Dolohov when Harry vetoes Ron's suggestion of killing them.[54]

2. The Dementor's Kiss

The Dementor's Kiss is even worse than the full-erasure Memory Charm performed by Gilderoy Lockhart on himself. It sucks out the victim's soul, leaving an empty shell without memory or personality. It is a punishment worse than the death penalty; there are more than hints of an afterlife, or various sorts of afterlives, in the wizarding world, but not for those whose souls are sucked out by dementors. Yet the Ministry inflicts it without requiring anything resembling due process of law, let alone the intricate process required for the execution of Buckbeak the hippogriff.

The Dementor's Kiss is not a spell, and it can only be performed by dementors, not by wizards. However, dementors perform the Kiss at the direction of wizards: Cornelius Fudge sends dementors to perform the Kiss on Sirius Black, and a dementor accompanying Fudge performs the Kiss on Barty Crouch Jr., with Fudge's apparent consent. Dolores Umbridge sends dementors to Little Whinging to perform the Kiss on Harry; they nearly suck out Dudley's soul, but Harry manages to save himself and his cousin with the Patronus Charm. For this use of magic, Harry undergoes what appears to be a criminal trial before the Wizengamot.

Even before his trial, Harry has no faith in the Ministry's commitment to due process: "I bet you anything Fudge would've told Macnair to murder Sirius on the spot...."[55] When Sirius is later captured, Fudge does, in fact, have Macnair bring dementors to suck out Sirius' soul. As with the Barty Crouch Jr.

---

52. *Order of the Phoenix* 617.

53. *Deathly Hallows* 96–97.

54. *Deathly Hallows* 167. Oddly, Hermione says that she's never done a Memory Charm before, even though she earlier admitted to modifying her parents' memories. Perhaps, in her inexperience, she accidentally damaged her own memory as well.

55. *Prisoner of Azkaban* 404. The use of the Dementor's Kiss on Sirius was pre-authorized by the Ministry, however. *See Prisoner of Azkaban* 247.

affair, Fudge's concern seems to be for appearances rather than justice: "This whole Black affair has been highly embarrassing. I can't tell you how much I'm looking forward to informing the Daily Prophet that we've got him at last."[56]

Apparently the wizarding world, too, has its share of people who agree with Uncle Vernon, and Fudge is pandering to this audience: "'When will they *learn*,' said Uncle Vernon, pounding the table with his large purple fist, 'that hanging's the only way to deal with these people?'"[57]

Later, when the Death Eater, Barty Crouch Jr., is captured, Fudge himself brings a dementor into Hogwarts to suck out Crouch's soul, thus preventing Crouch from giving testimony that might have been politically embarrassing to Fudge.

The Law of the Wizarding World

The wizarding world of Great Britain, and probably Ireland as well, is governed (badly) by the Ministry of Magic. The exact relationship between the Ministry and the Muggle government is not clear, but the Ministers of Magic seem to treat the Muggle Prime Minister not as a superior or even an equal, but as a subordinate. In Harry's first five years at Hogwarts, the Minister of Magic is Cornelius Fudge, a "[b]ungler if there ever was one."[58] The Ministry is apparently part of the British government, although its existence is not publicized: eleven-year-old Harry is surprised to learn of its existence, as is Uncle Vernon, four years later: "*Ministry of Magic?*" bellowed Uncle Vernon. "People like you in *government*? Oh this explains everything, everything, no wonder the country's going to the dogs...."[59]

This secrecy from the Muggle population as a whole appears to be required by Britain's obligations under international law, particularly the International Statute of Wizarding Secrecy of 1692.[60] The maintenance of this secrecy seems to be the primary reason for the Ministry's existence: Hagrid tells Harry that "their main job is to keep it from Muggles that there's still witches an' wizards up an' down the country."[61] When Harry asks why such secrecy is necessary, Ha-

56. *Prisoner of Azkaban* 416–17 (Fudge to Snape).
57. *Prisoner of Azkaban* 17.
58. *Sorcerer's Stone* 65.
59. *Order of the Phoenix* 29.
60. *See Chamber of Secrets* 21.
61. *Sorcerer's Stone* 65.

grid tells him "Blimey, Harry, everyone'd be wantin' magic solutions to their problems. Nah, we're best left alone." This answer is not particularly satisfying; if magic could cure Muggle ills, it seems selfish of the wizarding world to deny the Muggles the benefit of their assistance. Madame Pomfrey, the Hogwarts school healer, can regrow missing bones overnight and could probably save the lives of millions of Muggles. To provide a moral justification for keeping Madame Pomfrey at Hogwarts healing minor Quidditch injuries, rather than in Africa saving Muggle children from malaria and AIDS, something more compelling is needed. A mere desire to be left alone is not enough.

Three more compelling justifications are possible: Secrecy may be necessary to protect wizards from Muggles, to protect Muggles from each other, and to protect Muggles from wizards. The first of these is given little attention. On an individual basis, wizards have little to fear from Muggles. One of Harry's schoolbooks explains that medieval witch-burnings were "completely pointless":

> On the rare occasion that [Muggles] did catch a real witch or wizard, burning had no effect whatsoever. The witch or wizard would perform a basic Flame Freezing Charm and then pretend to shriek with pain while enjoying a gentle, tickling sensation. Indeed, Wendelin the Weird enjoyed being burned so much that she allowed herself to be caught no less than forty-seven times in various disguises.[62]

Wendelin is played strictly for laughs, but there are hints of "the dark days that preceded the wizards' retreat into hiding."[63] While the potential for individual Muggles to harm individual wizards is slight, words like "retreat" and "hiding" suggest a fear for the safety of the wizards rather than of the Muggles. Wizards are not immune to harm from Muggle weapons, and Muggles greatly outnumber wizards, so one reason for the International Statute of Wizarding Secrecy may be fear of persecution.

The consequences of a false accusation of witchcraft, even in today's Britain, can be dangerous and even fatal. In past centuries tens of thousands, perhaps hundreds of thousands, of innocent people, mostly women and girls, died in witch-hunts; the problem has not vanished even today.[64] The wizarding world

---

62. *Prisoner of Azkaban* 2 (quoting BATHILDA BAGSHOT, A HISTORY OF MAGIC (1947)).

63. *See also Chamber of Secrets* 150 (At the time of the founding of Hogwarts, "witches and wizards suffered much persecution." (Professor Binns); *Tales of Beedle the Bard* 12–13 & 12 n.2 ("a number of deaths did occur").

64. *See generally* CHARLES MACKAY, EXTRAORDINARY POPULAR DELUSIONS AND THE MADNESS OF CROWDS 462–564 (2nd ed. 1852) (1932); ALAN C. KORS & EDWARD PETERS,

acknowledges that the Muggle fear of witches is more dangerous to Muggles wrongly suspected of witchcraft than to actual witches:

> If any Muggle is unwise enough to confide in another that he has spotted a Hippogriff winging its way north, he is generally believed to be a drunk or a "loony." Unfair though this may seem on the Muggle in question, it is nevertheless preferable to being burnt at the stake or drowned in the village duckpond.[65]

There is another reason for keeping the two worlds as separate as possible: Wizards have the capability, and many have the inclination, to harm Muggles. With the Unforgivable Curses, they can torture, enslave and kill Muggles, who are powerless to resist. With ordinary, everyday magic they can also torture and kill, as well as steal, play practical jokes, and cheat Muggles in business. And, judging from the number of people of Harry's parents' generation who died violent deaths, the British wizarding world is far more violent than the United Kingdom as Muggles know it. For example, just before the beginning of Harry's fifth year Mad-Eye Moody (the real one) shows Harry a picture of the original Order of the Phoenix. Of the twenty-two people in the photo, eight have already died violent deaths by the time Moody shows the picture to Harry, one has disappeared and is presumed dead, and two have been tortured into insanity. Moody has sustained serious injuries. Six more (Sirius Black, Dumbledore, Remus Lupin, Peter Pettigrew, Emmeline Vance, and Moody himself) die by violence within the next two years. (This count assumes that Fabian Prewett, mentioned by Moody, is actually in the photo. The text is unclear on this point.)

Secrecy may be required by international law and necessary for the good of Muggles as well as wizards, but the Ministry's choice of the Memory Charm as one of its primary tools for maintaining this secrecy may do more harm than good, especially to the Muggles.

The British Wizarding World and International Law

The laws and customs governing the wizarding folk of other countries differ from those of the British wizarding world. Durmstrang teaches the Dark Arts, while Hogwarts only teaches Defense Against the Dark Arts. Different wiz-

---

WITCHCRAFT IN EUROPE 1100–1700: A DOCUMENTARY HISTORY (1972); BBC News, *Congo Witch-hunt's Child Victims*, Dec. 22, 1999, available at http://news.bbc.co.uk/2/hi/africa/575178.stm (visited September 8, 2006).

65. NEWT SCAMANDER, FANTASTIC BEASTS & WHERE TO FIND THEM xvii (2001).

arding cultures produce different laws; flying carpets, for instance, are legal in (at least) Bangladesh, India, Iran, Mongolia and Pakistan,[66] but have apparently been illegal in Britain for several decades, although there is pressure to repeal the ban.

As in the Muggle world, these different legal systems interact, when necessary, through international law. Wizards have their own structures of international law, with rules such as the International Statute of Wizarding Secrecy. International human rights law, however, seems to mean little more to the Ministry of Magic than does British Muggle law. Executions, let alone executions ordered by administrative officials without any judicial determination of guilt, are forbidden by Protocol 6 to the European Convention on Human Rights, to which the United Kingdom became a party in 1999.[67]

Torture has long been outlawed by conventional international law. The United Kingdom has been a party to the European Convention for the Prevention of Torture[68] since it entered into force in 1989, and to the Convention against Torture and Other Cruel, Inhuman or Degrading Treatment or Punishment[69] since 1988. These treaties thus apply to most of the acts described in the text regardless of which chronology is used. While the Ministry of Magic may feel that it has done its bit to comply with Article 4 of the latter treaty by outlawing the use of the Cruciatus Curse,[70] it continues to operate the prison at Azkaban, where the prisoners are subjected to constant mental torment by dementors, driving most mad. This may be torture within the meaning of Article 1 of the treaty, which provides that:

> For the purposes of this Convention, the term "torture" means any act by which severe pain or suffering, whether physical or mental, is intentionally inflicted on a person for such purposes as obtaining from him or a third person information or a confession, punishing him for an act he or a third person has committed or is suspected of having

---

66. KENNILWORTHY WHISP, QUIDDITCH THROUGH THE AGES 46 (2001).

67. Protocol No. 6 to the Convention for the Protection of Human Rights and Fundamental Freedoms concerning the Abolition of the Death Penalty art. 1, Apr. 28, 1983, Europ. T.S. No. 114.

68. European Convention for the Prevention of Torture and Inhuman or Degrading Treatment, Nov. 26, 1987, Europ. T.S. No. 126.

69. Convention against Torture and Other Cruel, Inhuman or Degrading Treatment or Punishment, Dec. 10, 1984, 1465 U.N.T.S. 85.

70. Convention against Torture and Other Cruel, Inhuman or Degrading Treatment or Punishment, art. 4(1), Dec. 10, 1984, 1465 U.N.T.S. 85: "Each State Party shall ensure that all acts of torture are offences under its criminal law...."

committed, or intimidating or coercing him or a third person, or for any reason based on discrimination of any kind, when such pain or suffering is inflicted by or at the instigation of or with the consent or acquiescence of a public official or other person acting in an official capacity. It does not include pain or suffering arising only from, inherent in or incidental to lawful sanctions.[71]

Not only is the United Kingdom a party to various anti-torture treaties that would seem to outlaw the use of dementors at Azkaban, but the prohibition against torture has come to be accepted as a *jus cogens* norm of international law—one from which no derogation is permissible.[72] In other words, even if the United Kingdom were to withdraw from all of the anti-torture treaties to which it is a party, international law would still forbid it to authorize torture.[73]

There is no *jus cogens* norm forbidding the death penalty; if the Ministry is not bound by Britain's treaties, nothing in international law prohibits it from executing prisoners—but only after they have been afforded due process of law, and not by the Dementor's Kiss, which is probably torture. Muggle international law has not had the opportunity to address memory modification and erasure, probably because Muggles lack the ability to do these things.

British Law—Magic and Muggle

If the Ministry is subject to British law, its actions in sending Sirius Black, Stan Shunpike, and especially Hagrid to prison without trial are questionable, and Fudge's de facto summary execution of Barty Crouch Jr. is an extremely serious crime. The British government has some latitude to imprison suspected terrorists for limited periods without a trial, and while the definition of "terrorism" is slippery indeed, Death Eaters certainly fall within it.[74] Hagrid, how-

---

71. Convention against Torture and Other Cruel, Inhuman or Degrading Treatment or Punishment, art. 1, Dec. 10, 1984, 1465 U.N.T.S. 85.

72. *See* Vienna Convention on the Law of Treaties, art. 53, May 22, 1969, 1155 U.N.T.S. 331. Under U.S. law, at least, violation of the *jus cogens* norm against torture does not necessarily create a private right of action, because of sovereign immunity. *See* Saudi Arabia v. Nelson, 507 U.S. 349 (1993).

73. *See, e.g.,* DAVID J. BEDERMAN, INTERNATIONAL LAW FRAMEWORKS 98 (2001); WILLIAM R. SLOMANSON, FUNDAMENTAL PERSPECTIVES ON INTERNATIONAL LAW 12–13, 45–46 (3d ed. 1999) (quoting Committee of U.S. Citizens Living in Nicaragua v. Reagan, 859 F.2d 929 (1988)).

74. *See, e.g.,* CLIVE WALKER, THE PREVENTION OF TERRORISM IN BRITISH LAW 4–6 (1986).

ever, is suspected of an ordinary crime (sending a monster to attack students), not of being a Death Eater.

While the Muggle authorities in Britain can detain suspected terrorists on the authority of the Secretary of State (or, presumably, the Minister of Magic), the period of such detentions is limited to a maximum of five days under the 1984 version of the Prevention of Terrorism (Temporary Provisions) Act of 1974.[75] From 1975 on, the government did not have the power to intern suspects for long periods without trial even in Northern Ireland.[76] Black is detained for over a decade; Shunpike, for at least several months before his escape. The Terrorism Act of 2000,[77] like the various preceding Temporary Provisions Acts, includes no provision for internment without trial. The Anti-terrorism, Crime and Security Act of 2001,[78] however, provides for the possibility of long-term detention of suspected foreign (but not British) terrorists.[79] Under the 2001 Act over a dozen persons, presumably suspected terrorists, have been detained, some for many years, at Belmarsh prison—Britain's Guantánamo. But Stan and Sirius were imprisoned before 2001 and are British, not foreign.

The action of Barty Crouch Sr. in sending Sirius Black to Azkaban without a trial was not exceptional, nor was it peculiar to Crouch. Over a decade later, Cornelius Fudge does the same to Hagrid, even though he does not appear to be convinced of Hagrid's guilt:

> "Look at it from my point of view," said Fudge, fidgeting with his bowler. "I'm under a lot of pressure. Got to be seen to be doing something. If it turns out it wasn't Hagrid, he'll be back and no more said. But I've got to take him …"
> ***
> "Not a punishment, Hagrid, more a precaution. If someone else is caught, you'll be let out with a full apology—"[80]

Although Dumbledore disapproves and disagrees, he seems to believe that Fudge is acting legally, if incorrectly. On the next page Dumbledore himself is suspended as Hogwarts headmaster–a step that seems to require more in the

75. Prevention of Terrorism (Temporary Provisions) Act, 1984, c. 8 §§ 12(4), 12(5) (Eng.).

76. CLIVE WALKER, BLACKSTONE'S GUIDE TO THE ANTI-TERRORISM LEGISLATION 217 (2002).

77. Terrorism Act, 2000 (Eng.).

78. Anti-terrorism, Crime and Security Act, 2001 (Eng.).

79. Anti-terrorism, Crime and Security Act, 2001 §§ 21–23 (Eng.).

80. *Chamber of Secrets* 261.

way of legal formalities than sending someone to prison, possibly for life: "'*Dreadful* thing, Dumbledore,' said Malfoy lazily, taking out a long roll of parchment, 'but the governors feel it's time for you to step aside. This is an Order of Suspension—you'll find all twelve signatures on it.'"[81] Apparently wizarding law provides more protection for Dumbledore's job than for Hagrid's freedom.

Fudge's replacement as Minister of Magic, Rufus Scrimgeour, shows no greater respect for due process: His government arrests Stan Shunpike, a conductor on the Knight Bus, on extremely flimsy evidence and holds him for many months, with no indication of any plan to release him.

Most suspected Death Eaters do receive a trial of sorts, though. In Dumbledore's Pensieve, Harry witnesses the trials of several such suspects, including Barty Crouch Jr., Ludo Bagman, and Igor Karkaroff. To adult readers the McCarthyesque aspect of these proceedings, especially Karkaroff's (Karkaroff is pressured to incriminate others and granted clemency when he does so), provides a protracted political pun: witches and wizards conducting a witch-hunt. Ludo Bagman is acquitted, evidently rightly. Although he passed information to a Death Eater named Rookwood, there seems to be no evidence that he knew that Rookwood was a Death Eater. The main factor in his acquittal, however, is not the lack of evidence but his popularity as an athlete.

Barty Crouch Jr. and his co-conspirators were convicted before the Wizengamot in a trial at which Barty Crouch Sr., despite the glaring conflict of interest, acted as a sort of combination of prosecutor and sentencing judge. Again, the result turned out, in retrospect, to have been correct; the defendants had in fact committed the crime of which they were accused. However, the irregularities in the proceedings are worrisome.

Years later Harry is tried in the same courtroom, before the full Wizengamot, for using a Patronus Charm to protect himself and Dudley from dementors. He sits in the same seat where he has seen the accused Death Eaters sit. The time of the hearing is changed with no effective notice, apparently to prevent the participation of witnesses for Harry's defense. The venue of the trial, and the participation of the full Wizengamot, shock Arthur Weasley. Some of the irregularities in this proceeding disturb even the wizards hearing the case. Dumbledore comments that:

> "In your admirable haste to ensure that the law is upheld, you appear, inadvertently I am sure, to have overlooked a few laws yourself."
> * * *

81. *Chamber of Secrets* 262.

"[Y]ou certainly seem to be making many changes, Cornelius. Why, in the few short weeks since I was asked to leave the Wizengamot, it has already become the practice to hold a full criminal trial to deal with a simple matter of underage magic!"[82]

When Dumbledore says this, "[a] few of the wizards ... shift[] uncomfortably in their seats.[83]

To Muggles, however, even more irregularities appear. Harry is not represented by counsel, and Arthur Weasley is not even permitted to accompany him to the hearing. (Oddly, though, Harry is allowed to retain his wand, going armed to a hearing at which he is the defendant.) Dumbledore shows up as a witness and ends up acting as an advocate for Harry, calling another witness (Arabella Figg) and offering to call a third (Dobby the House-Elf). But this is not because Harry has a right to counsel; it is just something that Dumbledore, very fortunately for Harry, does—despite Fudge's efforts to prevent him. Harry's trial highlights what is evident throughout the series: Without lawyers, there can be no rule of law. Adequate representation makes all the difference for Harry, as it might have for Buckbeak and even, perhaps, Sirius Black–especially if an attorney for Sirius could have prevented or delayed the mind-wiping of the Muggle witnesses.

Conclusion

Harry Potter's story is not just about law, but about a society trying to establish a rule of law. The Ministry of Magic is not a dictatorship, but it is not a democracy, either. It is a sort of muddling misrule that has grown out of the first war against Voldemort's Death Eaters. Under that stress, the Ministry regime adopted an ad hoc and inconsistent approach to justice, just as some Muggle governments have done under similar stress. The Ministry never recovered from that initial stress, or, perhaps, there was never a rule of law in the wizarding world in the first place. In the years of peace after Voldemort's downfall, the wizarding world failed to build working legal structures. When the second wizarding war places the Ministry under stress again, it reverts to type, and even the good guys—Dumbledore's Order of the Phoenix and Harry's school friends—seem to follow personal loyalties rather than rules.

---

82. *Order of the Phoenix* 149.
83. *Order of the Phoenix* 149.

These failings of the Ministry and the Order are not glossed over; they are presented with concern. An entire generation, perhaps many generations, of future lawyers, litigants, lawmakers, judges, jurors and citizens is confronting these questions. What is the rule of law? Should it be absolute? What limits should be placed on government and private power? When is it right to disobey not only unjust laws but just ones? The final volume leaves these questions unanswered. According to the author's post-publication statements, Kingsley Shacklebolt becomes Minister of Magic, albeit apparently by a process as opaque as any in the past. The plight of the house-elves is unresolved.[84] The questions, though, are almost certainly more useful to the reader than any given set of answers might be; we have already seen that the Ministry's regime is not one to emulate, but ultimately each society, and perhaps each generation, must re-create the rule of law for itself.

---

84. *J.K. Rowling Web Chat Transcript,* The Leaky Cauldron, Posted by Melissa, July 30, 2007, 09:09 AM, http://www.the-leaky-cauldron.org/2007/7/30/j-k-rowling-web-chat-transcript. Shacklebolt does "decorrupt" the Ministry and ends one of its worst abuses—the use of dementors to guard Azkaban. Rowling also says that Hermione, working through the Ministry, brought about an "improvement" in the house-elves' situation—but it seems the underlying moral problems they present remain. Sadly, in the end the house-elves are reduced to a narrative device through which the privileged classes—Hermione and Ron, in this case—can impress each other with the depth of their caring. *See Deathly Hallows* 625.

Sirius Black: A Case Study in Actual Innocence

Geoffrey Christopher Rapp

The possibility of wrongful conviction of an innocent person has long haunted American public consciousness. The Fox Channel's recent hit series *Prison Break*, in which hard luck Lincoln Burroughs is framed for the murder of a prominent businessmen, convicted, and sentenced to death, is only the latest example of pop culture attention paid to this "worst case" criminal procedure result. ABC's recent show *Injustice* and the more venerable *Fugitive* franchise (both the TV series and the movie) are others. While the conspiracies behind *Prison Break* and *The Fugitive* may overstate the plight of the accused in American criminal courts, both accurately represent the difficulty those challenging the correctness of their criminal convictions face.

Nor has the problem of wrongful conviction escaped the attention of legal scholars. In his 1932 monograph *Convicting the Innocent: Errors of Criminal Justice*, Yale Law School Professor Edwin M. Borchard wrote:

> Among the most shocking ... injuries and most glaring of injustices are erroneous criminal convictions of innocent people.... In an age when social justice has made such marked advances ... it seems strange that so little attention has been given to one of the most flagrant of all publicly imposed wrongs — conviction in criminal cases.[1]

In the last quarter-century, advances in scientific analysis of bio-genetic evidence have empowered a new generation of activists to confront this problem head-on. Working under the auspices of entities such as Northwestern University's Center on Wrongful Convictions and the Cardozo Law School's Innocence Project, such activists have used DNA testing to reveal a number of cases of

---

1. Edwin M. Borchard, Convicting the Innocent: Errors of Criminal Justice vii & 350 (1932).

clear error, including cases in which the wrong person was sentenced to death. Innocence Project lawyers Barry Scheck and Peter Neufeld, along with journalist Jim Dwyer, chronicled their efforts on the part of the Cardozo Innocence Project in the excellent and readable book *Actual Innocence: Five Days to Execution and Other Dispatches from the Wrongly Convicted*. Whereas in the past, defenders of the American criminal courts could write off exonerations as the work of sneaky lawyers or "Monday-morning quarterbacking," DNA analysis of trial evidence has provided irrefutable *scientific* proof that the American system sends innocent men and women to prison and even to death row. DNA has thus "shaken the foundations of the system."[2] Wrongful conviction is a problem, a problem that is *real*.

Readers of the Harry Potter series are also familiar with this problem, or at least with its parallel problem in the Wizarding World: Wrongful Incarceration of the Actually Innocent in Azkaban. Although the series presents several instances of wrongful incarceration (including that of the Hogwarts gatekeeper, Hagrid, on charges of having "petrified" various Hogwarts residents in *The Chamber of Secrets*), by far the most vivid and well-developed is the story of Sirius Black.

In this chapter, I explore briefly the parallels between Black's story and the American problem of wrongful conviction. I begin by describing the contours of the problem in America, drawing primarily upon *Actual Innocence*. I then recount what we know about the story of Black's incarceration (and the subsequent difficulty he faced in striving to clear his name) from the Harry Potter books. I then explore where the stories of America's wrongly convicted and the story of Black come together, and where they diverge. My aim is to facilitate use of the Black story as a case study in actual innocence. Teachers, students, and fans of the Harry Potter series can use Black's story to reveal some of the sources and challenges posed by the conviction of the innocent in the real ("Muggle") world.

The American Problem of Wrongful Conviction

Actual Innocence and other scholarly work has revealed a troubling number of wrongful convictions. While the number of wrongful convictions is small when compared to the large number of suspects processed and charged in American courts each year, even a small number of wrongfully convicted

---

2. BARRY SCHECK, PETER NEUFELD & JIM DWYER, ACTUAL INNOCENCE: FIVE DAYS TO EXECUTION AND OTHER DISPATCHES FROM THE WRONGLY CONVICTED 248 (2000).

defendants challenges the faith most of us place in our criminal justice institutions. Many suspect that the guilty often "get off" — particularly if, like O.J. or Robert Blake or Michael Jackson, they have the money to afford a "dream team" of lawyers to confuse and confound the truth. But at the same time, public support for the adversarial criminal justice system depends on a belief that while some level of "false negatives" is to be expected, a "false positive" is a virtual impossibility. The language and rhetoric of our criminal justice system — including the well known phrase, "beyond a reasonable doubt" — are keyed into this article of faith.

Yet the reality is very different. While there may never be a precise count of the wrongfully convicted, since some are never exonerated and others are freed on technicalities or clemency grants that do not acknowledge error in the initial criminal conviction, the number of convicted individuals subsequently proven innocent is arrestingly high. Cardozo Law School's Innocence Project alone has obtained 218 exonerations, according to its web site.[3]

Given the degree to which wrongful conviction challenges our core assumptions about the justice system, scholars have sought to explain how that can happen in a country like ours. In his 1932 study, Professor Borchard identified three main causes of error after reviewing 65 cases: mistaken identification, circumstantial evidence ("from which erroneous inferences are drawn"), and perjury.[4] In their 2000 book (which studied 67 people exonerated by DNA analysis), the authors of *Actual Innocence* identify the following factors as explaining the conviction of the innocent:

- *Junk Science*: This was a factor in a substantial number of wrongful convictions. In particular, "hair analysis," in which a prosecution "expert" engaged in "microscopic" analysis of hair left at the scene of a crime and compared it to a suspect's hair, was a factor in 29% of the cases studied.[5]
- *Faulty Witness Identification*: 84% of wrongful convictions studied involved mistaken witness identification.[6] Psychologists have long recognized the limitations of memory and perception (far more severe than the possibility that the witness in *12 Angry Men* couldn't see without her glasses). Yet the criminal justice system has placed an amazing level of power in the hands of witnesses who so often seem to get things wrong.

3. The Innocence Project, http://www.innocenceproject.org/ (last visited Aug. 19, 2008).
4. BORCHARD, *supra* note 1, at viii.
5. SCHECK, NEUFELD & DWYER, *supra* note 2, at 166.
6. SCHECK, NEUFELD & DWYER, *supra* note 2, at 73.

- *Police and Prosecutorial Misconduct*: This factor was present in 63% of the wrongful convictions studied in *Actual Innocence*.[7] Examples of such misconduct included concealing from defense lawyers potentially exonerating evidence (something prosecutors are forbidden to do under U.S. law).
- *Incompetent and Sub-par Legal Representation*: This played a role in 27% of wrongful convictions.[8]
- *False confessions*: Shockingly, 23% of the wrongly convicted individuals studied in *Actual Innocence* confessed to the crime with which they were charged (and ultimately exonerated).[9] While many readers who have never dealt with the criminal justice system may find it hard to believe that innocent people could ever be made to confess to crimes they did not commit, the evidence shows that they do. Suspects may "break" under aggressive police interrogation, may suffer from mental disabilities that impair their ability to understand to what it is they are confessing, or may even see advantages to confessing to capital crimes so as to avoid the possibility of facing the death penalty.[10]
- *Jail-house Snitches*: Motivated by hate or self-interest to fabricate jail-house confessions by innocent cell-mates, such snitches may offer false testimony about criminal defendants. They played a role in 21% of the wrongful convictions studied.[11]
- *Race*: No discussion of wrongful conviction is complete without an acknowledgement of the racial dimensions of the problem. Crimes by black men against white victims (rape and murder) were overrepresented (as opposed to their overall occurrence rates) among the crimes for which *Innocence Project* clients were wrongfully convicted.[12]

These causes operate together—not in isolation—to increase the likelihood that the most disadvantaged defendants are the victims of courtroom travesties. Poor lawyering makes it more likely, for instance, that junk science will find its way into a criminal proceeding unchallenged. These factors interact in what the

---

7. SCHECK, NEUFELD & DWYER, *supra* note 2, at 166.

8. SCHECK, NEUFELD & DWYER, *supra* note 2, at 187.

9. SCHECK, NEUFELD & DWYER, *supra* note 2, at 92.

10. *See* SCHECK, NEUFELD & DWYER, *supra* note 2, at 244 (describing the story of borderline mentally retarded suspect David Vasquez, who pled guilty to rape and murder to avoid the death penalty).

11. SCHECK, NEUFELD & DWYER, *supra* note 2, at 263.

12. SCHECK, NEUFELD & DWYER, *supra* note 2, at 204.

authors call an "echo chamber" to create a high risk of wrongful conviction for the most vulnerable defendants.[13]

Actual Innocence does not end with a description of the problem. It describes the "long, expensive and maddening battles" the Innocence Project faced in convincing prosecutors to allow the introduction of DNA evidence in post-conviction relief proceedings.[14] It describes the "schmoozing, publicity and cajoling" needed to obtain relief for the wrongly convicted.[15] It also suggests avenues for reform, such as administrative screening of jailhouse snitches,[16] prompt DNA testing for all suspects,[17] mandatory videotaping of all police interrogations,[18] and further development of groups like the Innocent Project at the nation's law schools.[19]

While there is much left to learn about the pre-DNA tendency of American courts to convict innocent men and women wrongfully, narratives like those in *Actual Innocence* have sketched the contours of the problem in a sophisticated and meaningful manner.

Sirius Black's Story

Sirius Black is one of, if not the most, tragic and compelling characters in the Harry Potter series. Black is the last scion of a historic Wizarding family, all of the prior members of which were Slytherins (Black was placed in Gryffindor, although his brother, Regulus,[20] was a Slytherin). Physically, Black has shadowed eyes and a sunken face that seems dead. With waxy white skin, he strikes Harry as looking like a vampire (though Harry has never seen a vampire himself). Black is an Animagus, capable of transforming himself into a large black dog.

Black was Harry's father's best friend during their time at school, served as best man at James and Lily Potter's wedding, and was named godfather to new-

---

13. Scheck, Neufeld & Dwyer, *supra* note 2, at 114.
14. Scheck, Neufeld & Dwyer, *supra* note 2, at 219.
15. Scheck, Neufeld & Dwyer, *supra* note 2, at 148.
16. Scheck, Neufeld & Dwyer, *supra* note 2, at 256–57.
17. Scheck, Neufeld & Dwyer, *supra* note 2, at 255.
18. Scheck, Neufeld & Dwyer, *supra* note 2, at 256.
19. Scheck, Neufeld & Dwyer, *supra* note 2, at 260.
20. Regulus Black is the subject of much speculation amongst fans of the series. Although he is supposedly dead, fans speculate he may emerge in subsequent installments (for example, that he may by the mysterious "R.A.B." who made off with the locket Horcrux sought by Harry and Dumbledore at the end of *The Half-Blood Prince. See* http://www.hp-lexicon.org/wizards/regulus.html; http://en.wikipedia.org/wiki/Regulus_Black.)

born Harry. After James and Lily were killed by Voldemort, Black arrived at the scene to find Hagrid there, holding young Harry. Black was "[w]hite an' shakin."[21] Hagrid comforted him, but resisted Black's request to entrust Harry to his care (which contradicted Hagrid's orders from Dumbledore).

We first encounter Black as an escaped and raving murderer described on the network news in the opening pages of *The Prisoner of Azkaban*. Black, we are told by the *Daily Prophet* newspaper, murdered thirteen people twelve years earlier with a single curse. Harry learns from Stan Shunpike, conductor of The Knight Bus, that Black's thirteen-person murder took place in broad daylight in front of witnesses. According to Shunpike, Black was cornered by Ministry of Magic wizards in a street full of Muggles and resisted arrest, using his wand against his would-be arresters. A wizard and a dozen Muggles "got it." Black apparently broke into a laugh, and although he eventually went with his arresters, he remained laughing all the way.

Black was supposedly the target of these wizards because he was believed to be in league with "You-Know-Who," and to have tipped off Voldemort about the location of James and Lily once they had gone into hiding. We later learn from Cornelius Fudge that it was not Ministry wizards but rather Peter Pettigrew who found Black. Pettigrew, according to Fudge, died a hero's death. A "street full"[22] of Muggle witnesses told the Ministry wizards "how Pettigrew cornered Black. They say he was sobbing, 'Lily and James, Sirius! How could you?' And then he went for his wand. Well, of course, Black was quicker. Blew Pettigrew to smithereens...."[23]

Fudge was one of the first on the scene. He saw a crater in the middle of the street, which had penetrated a sewer below. Bodies were everywhere, Muggles were screaming, and Black was standing with "what was left of Pettigrew" in front of him. Pettigrew's mother eventually received her son's posthumous citation (the Order of Merlin, First Class), along with Pettigrew's finger in a box.

As it turned out, Pettigrew, of course, was responsible for giving away the Potters' location to Voldemort. At the denouement of *The Prisoner of Azkaban*, Harry and Sirius engage in the following dialogue:

> "There were witnesses who saw Pettigrew die," [Harry] said. "A whole street full of them...."
>
> "They didn't see what they thought they saw!" said Black savagely....[24]

---

21. *Prisoner of Azkaban* 206.
22. *Prisoner of Azkaban* 392.
23. *Prisoner of Azkaban* 208.
24. *Prisoner of Azkaban* 350–51.

Pettigrew had removed his own finger in a brilliant ploy. Pettigrew yelled for the whole street to hear that Black had betrayed the Potters, then blew apart the street, killing everyone within twenty feet, and transformed himself into a rat before scurrying away.

Black's feelings of guilt at his role in the Potters' death were immeasurable. When Harry confronts him near the end of *The Prisoner of Azkaban*, and accuses Black of having killed his parents, Black responds, "I don't deny it."[25] Later, Black elaborates, "I as good as killed them.... I'm to blame, I know it."[26] Black blamed himself for having encouraged the Potters to confide their location to Peter Pettigrew, who eventually betrayed them to Voldemort.

After his arrest, Black is imprisoned on Azkaban. This most terrible of prisons is set on a tiny island out at sea, guarded by dementors who drain the cheerful thoughts from their prisoners, trapping prisoners inside their own heads. Black, however, is surprisingly unaffected by the dementors, in spite of being one of the most heavily guarded prisoners at Azkaban.

Although Rowling at one point describes Black as having been "convicted,"[27] he was in fact sent to Azkaban on the order of Barty Crouch, Head of the Department of Magical Law Enforcement, without a trial. He served twelve years in Azkaban before escaping. Even after his innocence is revealed to Harry, Dumbledore, and the readers of the series, Black is forced to live on the run, eating mostly rats to avoid drawing attention to himself while he hides in the outskirts of Hogsmeade, keeping watch over Harry. Media attention—in the form of a *Quibbler* article—begins to question the conventional wisdom regarding Black's guilt. While the tabloid's alternative, that he is an "Innocent Singing Sensation," is silly, it is clear that at least some members of the Wizarding World have begun to question his guilt.[28] Still, he is never formally exonerated of the charges against him, and remained on the lam until his death, suspected as the "rallying point" for other Death Eaters, who escape *en masse* from Azkaban in *The Order of the Phoenix*.

After Black's death, Cornelius Fudge is asked about Black by the Muggle prime minister at the outset of *The Half-Blood Prince*. Fudge stammers,

> "Black's dead. Turns out we were—er—mistaken about Black. He was innocent after all. And he wasn't in league with He-Who-Must-Not-Be-Named either. I mean," he added defensively, spinning the

25. *Prisoner of Azkaban* 342.
26. *Prisoner of Azkaban* 365.
27. *Goblet of Fire* 23.
28. *Order of the Phoenix* 191.

bowler hat still faster, "all the evidence pointed—we had more than fifty eyewitnesses—but anyway, as I say, he's dead."[29]

Parallels and Contrasts

Black's story presents an ideal case study of actual innocence for the young reader, because it offers both contrasts and parallels with the experience of the wrongfully incarcerated in the American criminal justice system.

The similarities are worth exploring first. The most striking similarity is the role that mistaken witness identification played in Black's case. As discussed above, *Actual Innocence* found an appalling number of witnesses who *swore* the defendant committed a particular crime (or was seen leaving a particular area at the time the crime was committed). Yet DNA evidence later proved such witnesses were wrong. In many cases, witnesses pick up on cues from investigators: they became more convinced of the correctness of their mistaken identification the more useful it appears to be to investigators. Black's incarceration in Azkaban was also due to mistaken witness identification—although the witnesses were right about Black having been on the street when Pettigrew killed twelve Muggles, the witnesses did not see what they thought they saw. Readers of the Harry Potter series should be able to see how perception is often not as scientific and reliable was we might hope.

Another similarity between Black's story and the story of the wrongly convicted in America is the role that false confessions play. In America's experience, a surprising number of subsequently exonerated inmates confessed to the crimes science later proved they did not commit. Black admitted his guilt to Harry, although he was speaking at a higher level of abstraction (he did not admit to killing Harry's parents, although he viewed himself as ultimately responsible). But his laughter during the time of his arrest was, in some ways, a "confession." He was obviously laughing at the tragic irony of Pettigrew's betrayal and clever escape, not because of happiness at the death of twelve Muggle bystanders. But the same forces that motivated him to laugh (despair, fear, and resignation) may be at work in America motivating false confessions. And the effects of Black's laugh are similar to the effect of an American suspect's confession: It became part of the "lore" of his story, repeated (and modified) as proof of his guilt. Once Black had behaved in what appeared to observers to be an "odd" way (as laughing amidst tragedy surely did), it became very difficult for observers and retellers to understand that he might in fact have been innocent.

---

29. *Half-Blood Prince* 11.

Readers should also appreciate the similarity between the unpleasant circumstances Black faced even after the truth of his innocence was revealed and the plight of the wrongly convicted seeking exoneration in the American criminal courts. Black was forced to remain on the lam, hunted by the Ministry of Magic, even though powerful wizards like Dumbledore and other Order of the Phoenix members knew of his innocence. There was no apparent way for him to clear his name quickly and effectively. In America's courts, post-conviction relief proceedings face severe procedural hurdles. Even where evidence of actual innocence exists, our courts have limited opportunities for presenting that evidence and for obtaining release of wrongly incarcerated individuals. Of course, there are also important differences in the post-incarceration aspects of Black's story. American inmates may actually be in a somewhat more favorable position in that DNA evidence can be used to prove their innocence. The Wizarding World, however, seems to have a deep fear of or aversion to science and engineering. Even though wizards would seem to have available powerful tools for investigation (such as "Legilimency" and "Scrying," in which a wizard reads another's thoughts), for whatever reason, such tools were not deployed to investigate the "truth" of the perception that Black had betrayed the Potters and killed Pettigrew and the innocent Muggle bystanders. Because of their fear of or aversion to science, wizards are unlikely to embrace DNA analysis for evaluating the innocence of those imprisoned at Azkaban; for whatever reason, they have chosen to ignore the tools they might be able to bring to bear. This, of course, is another similarity: Even after DNA analysis became widely available and accepted in America, many prosecutors have resisted its introduction in the context of determining the guilt or innocence of those seeking exoneration.

Another similarity between Black's experience and that of America's wrongly convicted has to do with the severity of the crimes involved. In America, wrongful conviction appears to be most common (or, at a minimum, is most galling) in "serious" or "shocking" crimes like rape and murder. In the face of shocking facts, which are widely covered in the media and threaten the public's sense of safety, police and other investigators may feel pressure to "cut corners." Quick decisions may lead to path-dependent investigations focusing on building a case against an early suspect even if it means ignoring or possibly suppressing contradictory exonerating evidence. Black's supposed crime—the murder of his closest friends as well as a number of innocent Muggle bystanders (all in front of other Muggle witnesses)—were among the most shocking crimes ever in the Wizarding World (which is saying something, given the depravity of a number of J.K. Rowling's "dark" characters). In the face of such shocking and attention-getting facts, Crouch's aggressive approach to Black—

incarcerating him without trial—is, while not acceptable, at least not surprising.

While there are similarities between Black's experience and the American problem of wrongful conviction, there are also many important differences. Most notably, Black hardly fits the "profile" of the typical wrongly convicted American criminal defendant. Black was from an extremely wealthy and respected Wizarding family; many of America's wrongly convicted are from more socioeconomically and racially disfranchised groups. While Black may have suffered from "guilt by association" with a family that had a history of preference for the Dark Arts (and Slytherin membership), his economic circumstances were certainly not to blame for his treatment. Nor was his status as an "unregistered" Animagus—although Animagi seem to be the victims of some discrimination in the Wizarding World (especially werewolves like Professor Lupin), no one other than Black's closest friends appears to have known of his status, and thus it could not have played a role in how and why he was wrongly incarcerated.

Another obvious difference worth emphasizing is that Black had no trial. False evidence and "junk science" cannot play a role at a trial that does not exist. Of course, not all wrongly convicted Americans are convicted at trial (some accept plea agreements in the hopes of avoiding harsher punishments). But as a general matter, America's accused criminals may have procedural protections and constitutional rights that wizards like Black do not possess—who may apparently be and are regularly incarcerated in Azkaban with little or no investigation and adjudication (other times, there appear to be more or less well developed tribunals to address the fate of wizards accused of violating norms or laws of the Wizarding world). However, it may be worth noting that even though America's wrongly accused are afforded a right to a trial, such trials can be rendered meaningless when the accused are represented by ineffective, incompetent, or perhaps even inebriated counsel.

The differences in the psychological effects of imprisonment on Black and the wrongly convicted in America may also be worthy of exploration. One of the effects of America's criminal system on innocent people may be to create the kind of despair that Black seems to have avoided, in spite of the dementors' best efforts. It may be worth emphasizing that Black had something most wrongly convicted Americans do not have: a reason to remain focused and psychologically "alive" in the face of harsh circumstances. Black had Harry of whom to think; most wrongly convicted Americans have few or no family resources and support (or, to the extent they once had such networks, are estranged from them during the process of criminal investigation, conviction, and incarceration).

Conclusion

Because of the threat posed to the American criminal justice system by wrongful convictions, and the simple human injustice of punishing an innocent person, the problem of actual innocence is one worthy of serious consideration at all levels. For young people, the story of Sirius Black may be far easier to understand than a complicated and possibly graphic narrative of a rape or murder trial. Black's story can be used to unlock in young readers' minds some of the dynamics of the problem of wrongful conviction and the difficulties associated with exonerating the innocent. Ultimately, while there may be many things about the Wizarding world that seem radically different from our own, when it comes to occasionally making criminal justice errors of the worst kind, we are not alone.

The Persecution of Tom Riddle:
A Study in Human Rights Law

Geoffrey R. Watson

> *Will ROPER: So, now you give the Devil the benefit of law!*
> *Sir Thomas MORE: Yes! What would you do? Cut a great road through*
> *the law to get after the Devil?*
> *ROPER: Yes, I'd cut down every law in England to do that!*
> *MORE: Oh? And when the last law was down, and the Devil turned*
> *'round on you, where would you hide, Roper, the laws all being flat? This*
> *country is planted thick with laws, from coast to coast, Man's laws, not*
> *God's! And if you cut them down, and you're just the man to do it, do you*
> *really think you could stand upright in the winds that would blow then?*
> *Yes, I'd give the Devil benefit of law, for my own safety's sake!*
> —From the film *A Man for All Seasons*

Fellow witches and wizards, our government has chopped down all our laws to kill a single innocent man: Tom Riddle. Our corrupt Ministry of Magic did this because it believed that Riddle was guilty of multiple sins. Tom was guilty of idealism: he resisted totalitarianism instead of collaborating with it. He was guilty of benevolence: he attempted to bestow upon wizard-kind the gift of eternal life. He was guilty of egalitarianism: he tried to lift wizards and witches up from their low stations in life. He was guilty of courage: "I always value bravery," he once said.[1] Above all, Tom Riddle was guilty of the cardinal sin, the most heinous offense in the eyes of any authoritarian government: he sought to replace that government with one that respected liberty. For that, the Ministry determined that he must die.

To achieve this end, the Ministry was quite happy to deforest our legal landscape. Just as trees supply oxygen for lungs, law supplies the oxygen for free-

---

1. *Sorcerer's Stone* 294.

dom. And so the Ministry hacked away at every great oak of international human rights law: the United Nations Charter, the Universal Declaration of Human Rights, the International Covenant on Civil and Political Rights, the Convention on the Rights of the Child, and the international norms protecting freedom of the press.[2] But while these laws fell, the strongest tree of all—the tree of liberty, embodied by Tom Riddle—refused to bend. The Ministry lacked the courage and strength to cut it down. Instead, it hired a lumberjack. The name of that lumberjack was Harry Potter.

The authoritarianism of our Ministry is a familiar thing to most who will read this parchment. Our Minister of Magic is not popularly elected. (Say what you will about Muggles, at least their Prime Minister is chosen by the people.) There is no separation of powers, no checks and balances. We have no legislature to speak of. There is no accountability, no public record of Ministry proceedings. Our primitive judicial system is presided over by the Minister himself, and it rarely defies his will. And our prison system is a shocking travesty—a rock in the middle of the North Sea, guarded by creatures of unspeakable evil, creatures that impose a penalty worse than death.

But the Ministry's role in the persecution of Tom Riddle, and especially its conspiracy with Harry Potter and Albus Dumbledore, has not been fully documented before now. We cannot know what exactly the Ministry and Dumbledore promised Potter: perhaps gold, or unusual magical power, or even the office of Minister of Magic itself. It may even be that Potter and Dumbledore were driven partly by simple racism, as they seem to have found Tom's leathery visage offensive. What we do know is that Potter and Dumbledore, working in tandem with the Ministry, pursued Tom Riddle relentlessly. Mr. Riddle was defamed, muzzled, assaulted, imprisoned, exiled, stalked, kidnapped, waterboarded, and tortured. Ultimately he was murdered as he stood alone in the middle of the dining hall of the school he loved—murdered at the hand of Harry Potter, murdered as hundreds of Potter's henchmen watched and applauded.

This paper systematically exposes the astonishing breadth of the conspiracy to suppress, defame, torture, and ultimately murder Tom Riddle. The conspiracy grew in scope with every passing year of Harry Potter's tenure at Hogwarts School, and so I have organized my account chronologically, tracking the various evil deeds of Potter and his minions. In this endeavor, I have

2. U.N. Charter, June 26, 1945, 59 Stat. 1031; Universal Declaration of Human Rights, Dec. 19, 1948, U.N.G.A. Res. 217 (III 1948); International Covenant on Civil & Political Rights, Dec. 16, 1966, 999 U.N.T.S. 171; Convention on the Rights of the Child, Nov. 29, 1989, 28 I.L.M. 1448.

been greatly assisted by the renowned journalist Rita Skeeter, who was for a time falsely imprisoned by Potter's thugs, but who has managed to claw her way back to freedom.

It is too late to save Tom Riddle, who lies dead and broken. But perhaps this exposé will encourage witches and wizards to stand up for the ideal Riddle championed: liberty.

* * *

Harry Potter's first attack on Tom Riddle[3] was not his own doing, as it came when Potter was only one year old. It was Potter's mother who was responsible for the assault. She and her husband were members of a state-sponsored terrorist cell known as the Order of the Phoenix, which worked covertly to help the Ministry weed out anti-government freedom-fighters. She used ancient magic to poison Harry Potter's skin, making it lethal to Tom's touch. This magic nearly killed Tom when he ventured too close to Potter during a visit to Potter's home. As Tom once described it: "pain beyond pain, my friends; nothing could have prepared me for it. I was ripped from my body, I was less than spirit, less than the meanest ghost … but still, I was alive…. Nevertheless, I was as powerless as the weakest creature alive."[4]

Tom was still recovering from these injuries ten years later, when Harry Potter matriculated at Hogwarts. Indeed, Tom's disabilities were so severe that he was on emergency life-support, linked directly to the brain of Professor Quirrell. Potter conspired with three others—the addled Albus Dumbledore, the haughty Hermione Granger, and the comically inept Ron Weasley—to deprive Tom of access to life-saving medication called the Sorcerer's Stone. Potter and the homicidal half-Giant Hagrid stole the Stone from its vault in Gringotts bank, regulation of which is clearly below international standards.[5] Then Dumbledore hid the Stone in the Mirror of Erised—a disgusting instrument of self-gratification that should never have been made available to an immature delinquent like Potter.

Thereafter Potter stalked Tom, cornered him in a deserted room at Hogwarts, produced the Stone from the Mirror, and proceeded to taunt him with

---

3. Tom's critics sometimes refer to him as "Lord Voldemort," an unflattering name to say the least. I have chosen to refer to Tom by his given name, in accordance with human rights law, which holds that everyone has "the right from birth to a name." Convention on the Rights of the Child, Art. 7.

4. *Goblet of Fire* 653.

5. For more on the subject of wizard-bank regulation, please see Heidi M. Schooner, *Gringotts: The Role of Banks in Harry Potter's Wizarding World*, and Eric Gouvin, *The Magic of Money and Banking*, both in this volume.

it. Potter then pressed his poisonous skin against that of Quirrell, torturing both Quirrell and Riddle with intense, life-threatening pain. Quirrell did not survive; it's a wonder that Tom Riddle did. It should not be forgotten that Potter was a student in Quirrell's Defense Against the Dark Arts class. What sort of student kills his own teacher?

Potter's conduct plainly violated the Convention Against Torture,[6] Article I of which defines torture as the infliction of "severe pain or suffering" for such purposes as intimidation or coercion—or if the torture is inflicted "based on discrimination of any kind," including Potter's obvious revulsion at Tom Riddle's swarthy physical appearance. In addition, Potter's efforts to deprive Tom of life-saving medication violated Article 6 of the International Covenant on Civil and Political Rights, which provides: "Every human being has the inherent right to life." Potter might try to argue that Mr. Riddle was not a "human being" within the meaning of Article 6 because Tom was a wizard, but this claim is quickly answered by the European Convention of Human Rights,[7] which applies to Hogwarts, a British school. Article 2 of the Convention provides: "*Everyone's* right to life shall be protected by law. No one shall be deprived of his life." (emphasis added). The European Convention, then, is not limited to "human" rights. Indeed, as the Klingon dignitary Azetbur once observed, the very term "human" rights is racist.[8]

Thus Potter's torture and attempted murder were human rights violations of the most serious sort. Of course, these acts were also ordinary crimes, punishable by the most severe penalties in both the Muggle and wizarding worlds. But Potter was shielded from prosecution by his mentor Dumbledore. Instead of punishing Potter, Dumbledore rewarded him. In particular, the Headmaster of Hogwarts awarded Potter's House, Gryffindor, with 170 points in the annual House Cup. Conveniently, that was just ten points more than necessary to overtake the actual winner of the Cup, Slytherin House. What sort of Headmaster manipulates school contests to reward violence by juvenile delinquents against teachers?

It's hardly a surprise, then, that Harry Potter resumed his crime spree in his second year at Hogwarts. Potter and his henchman Weasley began by gathering intelligence on Riddle's whereabouts. To do this, they spied on Draco Malfoy, a decent and hard-working student who was one of Tom's friends. But Potter and Weasley didn't choose merely to eavesdrop on Draco. Instead, they

---

6. Dec. 19, 1984, 23 I.L.M. 1027.

7. Nov. 4, 1950, 312 U.N.T.S. 221.

8. "If only you could hear yourselves. 'Human rights.' Why the very name is racist." STAR TREK VI: THE UNDISCOVERED COUNTRY (Paramount Pictures 1991).

decided to spy by drugging and mutilating Draco's loyal friends Vincent Crabbe and Gregory Goyle. First Potter's accomplice Hermione Granger injected a Sleeping Draught into chocolate cakes. The conspirators then gave the cakes to Vince and Greg, who took one bite and immediately "keeled over backward onto the floor."[9] Next, Potter and Weasley chopped off body parts from each of the stricken students. Granger then used these body parts to brew a Polyjuice Potion, allowing Potter and Weasley to assume the identities of Vince and Greg. Using these disguises, Potter and Weasley infiltrated Slytherin's Common Room and interrogated Draco about his friendship with Tom.

This conduct was a violation of a variety of human-rights norms. Article 7 of the International Covenant on Civil and Political Rights provides in no uncertain terms that "no one shall be subject without his free consent to medical or scientific experimentation." Vince Crabbe and Greg Goyle never consented to have body parts whacked off for the sake of Granger's twisted chemistry experiments. More fundamentally, drugging and disfiguring the two innocent boys was a plain violation of their right to "liberty and security of person," enshrined in Article 9 of the same Covenant. And impersonation of Vince and Greg violated Article 6 of the Universal Declaration of Human Rights, which provides: "Everyone has the right to recognition everywhere as a person before the law." Finally, the interrogation of Malfoy violated the spirit if not the letter of the wiretapping laws. Malfoy did not consent to this intrusion, and no court or magistrate had authorized this invasion of privacy.

In any case, the interrogation seems to have borne fruit. After Potter and Weasley grilled Draco, Potter seized one of Tom Riddle's most cherished and private possessions—his personal diary. Potter had no compunction about stealing it, or about invading Tom's privacy by opening the diary and showing it to his friends. To make matters worse, Tom was still extremely ill, and to keep himself alive, he had placed part of himself inside the diary. When Potter discovered this fact, did he try to help save Tom's life? Did he bring the diary to a medical professional? Hardly! Potter plunged a sharp instrument "straight into the heart of the book. There was a long, dreadful, piercing scream. Ink spurted out of the diary in torrents ... flooding the floor. Riddle was writhing and twisting, screaming and flailing, and then—[h]e had gone."[10]

Miraculously, Mr. Riddle somehow managed to survive this attack. Not surprisingly, Dumbledore again rewarded Potter and his friends for their criminality. Dumbledore acknowledged that he'd earlier pledged to expel Potter,

---

9. *Chamber of Secrets* 214.
10. *Chamber of Secrets* 322.

Granger and Weasley for violations of school rules, but instead of expelling them, Dumbledore gave them Special Awards for Services to the School—plus more points for Gryffindor.

The conspiracy against Mr. Riddle widened in Potter's third year at Hogwarts. A convicted murderer, Sirius Black, escaped from Azkaban and joined forces with Potter and his cronies. At the same time, Dumbledore knowingly hired a *werewolf* to teach Defense Against the Dark Arts to children, and Potter and Dumbledore enlisted the werewolf in their campaign to murder Tom Riddle. This conduct put defenseless children at risk, and ran roughshod over the Convention on the Rights of the Child. Article 3 of the Convention provides that "institutions … responsible for the care or protection of children" shall conform with standards of "safety" and "health." It cannot seriously be argued that deliberately placing students in the care of a werewolf in any way comports with modern safety or health standards.

Nor was a werewolf the only inappropriate choice of teacher. Dumbledore also hired the incompetent and dangerous half-Giant Hagrid to teach Care of Magical Creatures, and Hagrid forced defenseless students to do battle with a violent hippogriff named Buckbeak. Predictably, this monster caused serious injury to a Hogwarts student:

> It happened in a flash of steely talons; Malfoy let out a high-pitched scream and next moment, Hagrid was wrestling Buckbeak back into his collar as he strained to get at Malfoy, who lay curled in the grass, blood blossoming over his robes.
> "I'm dying!" Malfoy yelled as the class panicked. "I'm dying, look at me! It's killed me!"[11]

Not only did this conduct violate the Convention on the Rights of the Child, but it also would seem to entail tort and criminal liability for Hagrid and Dumbledore. But there was no criminal prosecution of either, and young Draco Malfoy was doubtless too scared to risk bringing a tort suit against his own teacher and headmaster.

That academic year culminated in Potter's attempt to kidnap and falsely imprison Peter Pettigrew, a long-time friend of Tom's. Doubtless Potter intended to "interrogate" Peter in order to force him to divulge the whereabouts of Tom, who had understandably gone into hiding to avoid further attacks. But Peter escaped, using a non-violent charm to slip out of the manacles Potter and his friends had jammed around his wrists. Once again Dumbledore shielded Pot-

---

11. *Prisoner of Azkaban* 118.

ter from responsibility, concealing Potter's role in the abduction, and in turn helping Potter to hide Sirius Black. Harboring a fugitive is, of course, a serious offense in both Muggle and wizarding law.

Dumbledore's cavalier attitude toward his students only worsened during the following academic year. Hogwarts hosted the Triwizard Cup, and Dumbledore knowingly placed three school champions—plus Potter, who conveniently managed to become a second "champion" for Hogwarts—in mortal danger. The four underage wizards were first required to confront fire-breathing dragons, imported in violation of the Convention on International Trade in Endangered Species ("CITES").[12] Dumbledore later ordered the four children to fight armed mer-people and to enter a life-sized maze full of lethal enchantments installed by Dumbledore himself. Subjecting children to such dangers is a grave breach of the Rights of the Child Convention. Of course, Dumbledore's favoritism ensured that Potter wasn't ever in real danger, but the same could not be said for the other three champions. One of them, Cedric Diggory, died in the final stage of the competition. Dumbledore ultimately tried to pin this death on Peter Pettigrew, but the only "eyewitness" to support this story was Dumbledore's co-conspirator, Potter.

Dumbledore also hired an unstable former Auror, Mad-Eye Moody, to teach Defense Against the Dark Arts. Moody turned one student into a ferret—a flagrant violation of Hogwarts rules—but was not disciplined in any way. At another juncture, Moody showed his students the three most dangerous Dark Curses: the Imperius Curse, the Cruciatus Curse, and the Killing Curse, *Avada Kedavra*. Use of these Unforgiveable Curses in such circumstances is, as every witch and wizard knows, a serious offense against wizarding law. Moody even demonstrated the use of the Cruciatus Curse and *Avada Kedavra* on a live spider—a clear violation of Article 3 of the European Convention for the Protection of Pet Animals, which provides: "Nobody shall cause a pet animal unnecessary pain, suffering or distress."[13]

Dumbledore later alleged that "Moody" was in fact an impostor, but even if that were true, it wouldn't absolve Dumbledore of responsibility for exposing children to such a dangerous person. If anything, Dumbledore's unproven claim that Moody was an impostor only suggests that Dumbledore was further negligent in not verifying the identity of the teachers charged with safety of young children. Dumbledore also made the completely unsubstantiated allegation that the supposed impostor was somehow tied to Tom Riddle. That's

12. Mar. 3, 1973, 993 U.N.T.S. 243.
13. Nov. 13, 1987, CETS No. 125.

a claim that, conveniently, will never have to be proven. For Dumbledore allowed a dementor to enter Hogwarts and administer the fatal Dementor's Kiss to the person allegedly posing as Moody, and as Dumbledore himself smugly put it, the dead person "cannot now give testimony."[14]

Potter and his accomplices also conspired in another rights violation: denial of freedom of the press. Rita Skeeter, a widely-read reporter for respected publications such as *The Daily Prophet* and *Witch Weekly*, had accurately reported that Potter cried when asked about the death of his parents; that Hagrid had permitted a hippogriff to attack a student, and thereafter exposed students to dangerous Blast-Ended Skrewts; that Potter's Muggle-born girlfriend Hermione Granger was also flirting with Viktor Krum; and, most ominously, that Potter was a Parselmouth—a person capable of speaking with snakes. Parseltongue is, of course, a Dark Art, and this alarming news was well deserving of public attention.

Yet Potter's Muggle-born gal-pal Hermione Granger captured Ms. Skeeter in the form of an insect and imprisoned her in a jar with an Unbreakable Charm, promising to release her only on the condition that "she's to keep her quill to herself for a whole year."[15] This imprisonment was a violation of Article 10 of the European Convention of Human Rights, which protects "freedom of expression," and Article 19 of the International Covenant on Civil and Political Rights, which provides that "Everyone shall have the right to freedom of expression; this right shall include freedom to seek, receive and impart information and ideas of all kinds ... either orally, in writing or in print." These instruments do not confine the right of free speech to cases of "state action," as does the United States Constitution.[16] Under international law, *everyone* has the right of free expression—not just those whose expression is suppressed by the state.

In his fifth year at Hogwarts, Potter's shallowness became obvious even to his fellow thugs. He spent the entire year sulking like the spoiled fifteen-year-old he was. He complained incessantly about his aunt and uncle, who graciously put him up at their house, even after he inflated his Aunt Marge and repeatedly threatened his family with deadly forms of magic. He whined about

---

14. *Goblet of Fire* 703.
15. *Goblet of Fire* 728.
16. *Cf.* U.S. Const. amend. I ("*Congress* shall make no law ... abridging the freedom ... of the press") (emphasis added). Even if international human rights treaties are read narrowly as requiring state action, Hogwarts appears to function as an arm of the wizarding state. *See, e.g.,* Ministry of Magic, Educ. Decree No. 23 of Aug. 30 (*Order of the Phoenix* 306–07) (appointing a "Hogwarts High Inquisitor"). Insofar as Granger was acting on the instructions of the Headmaster, her suppression of freedom of the press can and should be attributed to Hogwarts, an apparatus of the wizarding state.

his cohorts Weasley and Granger. He grumbled when his hatchet-man Sirius Black neglected to praise him for illegally performing a Patronus Charm in the presence of a Muggle. Potter's misbehavior became so intolerable that even his stooges in the government turned on him. The Ministry of Magic ordered him expelled from Hogwarts for unauthorized use of magic—that is, until Dumbledore intervened and "persuaded" the Ministry to reverse itself.

Dumbledore himself faced a measure of accountability during Potter's fifth year. Ministry official Percy Weasley, author of the famous "Thin-bottomed Cauldron" exposé, was instrumental in this effort. Percy helped craft Educational Decree Twenty-Two, which installed Professor Dolores Umbridge as "Hogwarts High Inquisitor." As Percy put it, the High Inquisitor was necessary to address "falling standards" under the reign of Dumbledore.[17] Unfortunately, Dumbledore obstructed the High Inquisitor's diligent efforts at reform, and ultimately the Ministry of Magic had no choice but to remove Dumbledore as Headmaster.[18] At last some modest steps had been taken to protect the innocent children at Hogwarts.

But these measures, while well-intentioned, were not enough to prevent Potter and Granger from renewing their efforts to kill Tom Riddle. Potter and Granger formed a terrorist cabal called "Dumbledore's Army" in violation of a lawfully-promulgated Order of the High Inquisitor.[19] This paramilitary organization consisted of a secret group of Potter's comrades. Their immediate purpose was to teach each other various spells relating to the Dark Arts. In Granger's rather ominous words, "I thought it would be good if we … took matters into our own hands."[20] But the cell's longer-term purpose was nothing less than the destruction of Tom Riddle. Granger put it quite bluntly: she organized the group "[b]ecause Lord Voldemort's back."[21]

It did not take long for Potter and Granger to put their terrorist[22] organization to work. Dumbledore's Army infiltrated the offices of the Ministry of

---

17. *Order of the Phoenix* 307.

18. *See* Order of the High Inquisitor of Hogwarts, promulgated pursuant to Ministry of Magic Educational Decree No. 28, *quoted in Order of the Phoenix* 624.

19. *See* Order of the High Inquisitor of Hogwarts, promulgated pursuant to Ministry of Magic Educational Decree No. 24, *quoted in Order of the Phoenix* 351–52 ("All Student Organizations [such as paramilitary organizations] … are henceforth disbanded.… Any student found to have formed, or belong to, an Organization [such as a terrorist or other paramilitary organization] … that has not been approved by the High Inquisitor shall be expelled").

20. *Order of the Phoenix* 339.

21. *Order of the Phoenix* 340.

22. The U.S. State Department maintains a list of terrorist organizations in its annual publication, *Patterns of Global Terrorism*, but obviously this list is confined to Muggle cells.

Magic and broke into the Ministry's Department of Mysteries. They ran wild in the Department, looting its priceless treasures. One such relic was a dusty glass ball belonging to Professor Cybil Trelawney, a well-respected seer. The crystal ball contained Trelawney's prophecy foretelling Potter's reign of terror, and it bore an inscription describing Potter quite accurately: "Dark Lord ... Harry Potter." Potter seized it and pocketed it. Tom Riddle's friends caught Potter in *flagrante delicto* and accused him of theft, but Potter and his well-trained Army chose to respond with violence. Potter pointed his wand at one of Tom's pals and shouted, *"STUPEFY!"* "A jet of red light" hit the man, and he "fell backward into a grandfather clock and knocked it over."[23] Thereafter Granger used the same spell, and her victim "collapsed backward," his head coming to rest inside a "jar full of glittering wind." His head thereupon shrank until a "baby's head now sat grotesquely on top of" his neck.[24] To make matters worse, Dumbledore and the convicted murderer Sirius Black joined the attack. This left Tom Riddle no choice but to come to the defense of his stricken friends. At that point Sirius Black stumbled through a mysterious archway, and later his co-conspirators suggested that he'd died in the process. A more reasonable inference, however, is that Black faked his own death to set up an insurance-fraud scam.

In any case, Dumbledore wasted no time attacking Riddle. Dumbledore wasn't interested only in murder; he also had in mind torture. "Merely taking your life would not satisfy me, I admit," said Dumbledore to Tom. "Indeed, your failure to understand that there are things much worse than death has always been your greatest weakness." Then Dumbledore proceeded to waterboard Tom Riddle:

> Dumbledore brandished his wand in one, long, fluid movement ... [and] water ... rose up and covered Voldemort like a cocoon of molten glass—
>
> For a few seconds Voldemort was visible only as a dark, rippling, faceless figure, shimmering and indistinct upon the plinth, clearly struggling to throw off the suffocating mass—
>
> Then he was gone.... [25]

See, e.g., OFFICE OF THE COORDINATOR FOR COUNTERTERRORISM, COUNTRY REPORTS ON TERRORISM (2005) *available at* http://www.state.gov/s/ct/rls/crt/c17689.htm.

23. *Order of the Phoenix* 789.
24. *Order of the Phoenix* 790.
25. *Order of the Phoenix* 815.

Dumbledore would probably argue that waterboarding isn't torture, but rather just a "dunk in the water."[26] Human rights groups, however, have almost unanimously condemned waterboarding as torture, and the Obama Administration has renounced this technique. Even former Vice President Cheney has stopped short of endorsing a Water Charm as an acceptable interrogation technique.

Waterboarding simulates death by asphyxiation but doesn't actually cause death. For this reason, Tom Riddle survived Dumbledore's attack, and Tom was able to flee the Ministry. But Tom's survival doesn't absolve Dumbledore of criminal responsibility for the torture. Nor can it be said that the waterboarding didn't qualify as torture because it was not carried out by the state. Even if torture has a "state action" component, there is little doubt that Dumbledore was acting in an "official" capacity, for Cornelius Fudge and other officials of the Ministry of Magic congratulated Dumbledore and otherwise adopted his acts as their own. Indeed, Fudge rewarded Dumbledore's acts by reinstating him as Headmaster of Hogwarts.

During Potter's sixth year at Hogwarts, the conspiracy to murder Tom Riddle transformed itself in an alarming way. Until this point, efforts to kill Tom had been undertaken by individual criminals or small terrorist organizations, like Dumbledore's Army. But, at Dumbledore's urging, the Minister of Magic enlisted the Muggle Prime Minister of the United Kingdom in nothing less than a "war" against Tom and his friends. "[W]e're at war, Prime Minister, and steps must be taken," Cornelius Fudge told his Muggle counterpart.[27] That this declaration of war against an innocent private citizen violates human rights law should be self-evident. But it also runs afoul of an even more profound international legal norm—the prohibition on the use of force in Article 2(4) of the United Nations Charter. The U.N. Security Council has not authorized war in this case, and no plausible case can be made that peaceful Tom Riddle has engaged in an "armed attack" sufficient to trigger a right of "self-defense" under Article 51 of the Charter.

In such circumstances, the initiation of war by Fudge and Dumbledore is nothing short of a "crime of aggression," which is within the jurisdiction of the International Criminal Court. Again, however, we must be mindful of Saint Thomas More's warning that we not stretch the law too far in pursuit of the devil. Otherwise we would be stooping to Dumbledore's level. For while

---

26. Former Vice President Dick Cheney did once endorse a "dunk in the water" for dealing with terrorists, though he later denied that he meant this phrase to include waterboarding. *See* Dan Eggen, *Cheney Defends 'Dunk in the Water' Remark*, WASH. POST, Oct. 28, 2006, at A02.

27. *The Half-Blood Prince* 12.

the International Criminal Court does in theory have jurisdiction over a crime of aggression, the Court has not yet defined the content or elements of this crime,[28] and due process shields the conspirators from prosecution under it— for now.

In any case, Fudge and Dumbledore were hardly alone in their efforts to suppress Tom Riddle during this time period. Harry Potter continued to discover novel ways to violate Riddle's most basic human rights. One technique was to invade Tom's privacy by probing his memories without his consent. Potter and Dumbledore achieved this by use of a Pensieve, a device that permits the user to enter the memories of others—rather like a Vulcan mind-meld, but without the knowledge or permission of the person whose mind is being probed. Potter and Dumbledore had used this voyeuristic technique in previous years, but in Potter's sixth year they elevated it to a science, using it to expose the most intimate details of Tom Riddle's private thoughts. This conduct is plainly inconsistent with Article 12 of the Universal Declaration of Human Rights and Article 17 of the Civil and Political Covenant, both of which provide that "No one shall be subjected" to arbitrary "interference with his privacy."

Dumbledore's supposed demise raises troubling questions. Harry Potter was seen running from the scene of the crime, and yet Potter was never prosecuted or even held for questioning in the matter. Surely it is possible that Potter had tired of sharing the spotlight with Dumbledore, and that Potter wished to enjoy all the credit for murdering Riddle. On the other hand, the reports of the "death" of Dumbledore, and of Sirius Black, turned out to be greatly exaggerated. Both Black and Dumbledore secretly met with Potter during his year-long stint as a truant and fugitive from justice. One can only wonder whether the two men had insurance policies, and whether Potter was named as a beneficiary. Or did Potter manipulate the probate system to take advantage of Dumbledore's mysterious disappearance? After all, Potter inherited two weapons from Dumbledore—a dangerous Deathly Hallow and the Sword of Gryffindor. In any case, each bequest ran afoul of the international regime regulating the arms trade, and the gift of the Sword was doubly problematic because the weapon wasn't Dumbledore's to give.

As the wizarding world knows, Potter's plans reached their climax during his seventh year at Hogwarts—or, more accurately, during his year as an outlaw and truant. Potter was on the run because, for the only year in our his-

---

28. *See* Rome Statute of the Int'l Crim. Court, July 17, 1998, Art. 5(2) ("The Court shall exercise jurisdiction over the crime of aggression once a provision is adopted ...").

tory, we had a government committed to human rights *and* wizard rights. The administration of Pius Thicknesse ended censorship of the news media, which led to a robust marketplace of ideas, in which periodicals like *The Quibbler* and *The Daily Prophet* printed competing versions of events and published articles both favorable to and critical of the government. The Thicknesse administration released political prisoners like Stan Shunpike, who had been wrongly confined in Azkaban by the Ministry in its pro-Potter years. But Thicknesse was not "soft" on crime; he set up a system of rewards for the capture of terrorists, similar to the rewards offered by the United States and other major powers. Finally, Thicknesse made enormous strides toward the goal of universal education of all children, for example by making attendance at school compulsory. Such a rule, of course, is common in the civilized world. The rule is consistent with—and arguably required by—the Convention on the Rights of the Child and the International Covenant on Economic and Social Rights, both of which mandate "compulsory" primary education and universal access to secondary education.[29]

But Potter, Granger and Weasley made no pretense of going back to school. To hide her truancy from her parents, Granger wiped their memories and sent them off to Australia. This was a plain violation of Article 12(1) of the Economic and Social Covenant, which guarantees "the highest attainable standard of … mental health." Indeed, Granger's connection with Australia may mean she is an undocumented alien, which would explain why she ignored her legal obligation to register with the Ministry.

No, instead of going back to school, the triumvirate went for a joyride. To celebrate his 17th birthday, Potter and his friends jumped on broomsticks and dive-bombed Tom Riddle, who had no broom of his own. Potter fired a lethal spell at Tom and later claimed, implausibly, that his wand acted of its own accord. (Even Potter's cronies didn't believe that.)

Shortly thereafter, Potter seized direct control over Kreacher, a slave he "inherited" from Black. It hardly needs mentioning that Potter's "ownership" of Kreacher is a blatant violation of the 1926 Geneva Convention to Suppress the Slave Trade and Slavery.[30] Potter ordered Kreacher to capture Mundungus Fletcher so that Potter could shake Fletcher down for cash and valuables. Potter's order constituted solicitation of kidnapping, and it violated various international instruments on forcible abduction. Potter's subsequent treatment

---

29. Convention on the Rights of the Child, Art. 28(1)(a) & (b); International Covenant on Economic, Social and Cultural Rights, Dec. 16, 1966, 993 U.N.T.S. 3, Art. 13(2)(a) & (b).

30. Sept. 25, 1926, 212 U.N.T.S. 212.

of Fletcher constituted false imprisonment, assault, battery, theft, robbery, and defamation.

No doubt the shakedown of Fletcher was fruitful, for Potter, Granger and Ron Weasley soon had enough funding to set up a terrorist training camp in the English countryside. Using this camp as a secret base, they embarked on a clandestine campaign to steal Riddle's jewelry and then murder him. Their first operation was infiltration of the Ministry. In a chilling reprise of their assault on Vince Crabbe and Greg Goyle, the terrorists assaulted various Ministry officials, lopping off various body parts and assuming their identities. The trio then burglarized the Ministry, stealing eyewear and jewelry from Dolores Umbridge, disrupting a session of open court proceedings, and releasing known criminals from detention. This operation was so shocking that one of the radicals, Ron Weasley, had pangs of remorse. After a heated argument with Potter and Granger, he fled before they could kill him—though he later returned to the fold.

But this was nothing compared to what was to come. For Potter's field operations now became more deadly. He visited Bathilda Bagshot, and after his visit, she was reported to be dead. He visited Xenophilius Lovegood, and after his visit, Lovegood's house was found to be demolished. He visited his former slave, the house-elf Dobby, and after the visit, Dobby turned up dead. What's more, Potter and his accomplices chopped off yet *more* body parts in order to burglarize Gringotts Bank, and in so doing used the Unforgiveable Imperius Curse on a bank employee. Potter also knowingly released a homicidal dragon in downtown London; it ranges free in Britain to this day.

Potter's campaign culminated with his triumphant return to Hogwarts. He linked up with the paramilitary organization known as Dumbledore's Army, and together with this "DA" assaulted two professors. Potter had no compunction about using *another* Unforgiveable Curse—the torture curse, Cruciatus—on Professor Carrow. Potter then incited a riot, encouraging students and teachers to rise up against the duly-appointed Headmaster, and to take up arms and kill Tom Riddle. Potter's followers dutifully shed their own blood on his behalf, and a number of them (including a new mother and a young child) died in battle. But Potter was too cowardly to do his own fighting. Instead, he skulked around the school in order to steal Tom Riddle's last remaining pieces of jewelry. When Greg Goyle, Vince Crabbe and Draco Malfoy stood in his way, he fought them. Vince did not come out alive.

Then Potter cornered the heroic Headmaster, Sev Snape. In short order, Sev was dead. As Sev breathed his last, Potter seized his memories and then watched them with lurid fascination in Dumbledore's Pensieve. Potter learned that Dumbledore had duped Sev into spying on Tom Riddle for Dumbledore and

Potter. Inspired by this example, Potter engaged in a little duplicity of his own, faking his own death in front of Tom Riddle in order to lure Tom into Hogwarts. He also incited Neville Longbottom to murder Tom's pet, a violation of the European Convention for the Protection of Pet Animals, which provides: "Only a veterinarian or another competent person shall kill a pet animal."[31]

Finally, Potter maneuvered Tom into the center of the dining hall at Hogwarts, where Tom was surrounded by hundreds of Potter's supporters. Potter taunted Tom, toying with him. Then at last Potter cast his signature spell, knowing it would kill Tom. And it did. Tom "fell backward, arms splayed ... [He] hit the floor with a mundane finality, his body feeble and shrunken, the white hands empty, the ... face vacant and unknowing."[32] Tom Riddle was dead. Needless to say, the murder of Tom Riddle violated the most fundamental norm of all human rights law, enshrined in Article 6 of the International Covenant on Civil and Political Rights—the "right to life."

* * *

That, dear reader, is but a short summary of a much longer tale of persecution. I would write more, but it's getting late, and I need to stow this parchment someplace safe. If the Ministry finds it, they will confiscate it, or worse. Minister Shacklebolt certainly lives up to his name—he shackles and bolts anyone who dares publish dissent. Potter lives up to his name too: if you criticize him, he'll have the Ministry declare that you are an "Ambulatory Mandrake." Then they turn you upside down into a chamber-pot, and they pour dirt over your body, and you cry a lot.

(Just now, as I was dipping my quill in the ink, I thought I heard something next door. It's probably just Zabini practicing his potion-making again. He was working on a complicated Healing Draught last night.)

I do want to mention the Free Wizards Legal Defense Fund, of which I'm the President and Treasurer. We help provide counsel to freedom fighters who face time in Azkaban for daring to oppose the Shacklebolt regime. Please forward any such donations to me, preferably in cash. Muggle currency only, please.

(I'm not worried about that light. I'm pretty sure an overheated Healing Draught makes a green flash like that. Zabini is still using those flimsy thin-bottomed cauldrons.)

Even if you don't share my high opinion of Tom Riddle, I hope you will pause to consider the dangerous implications of Potter's brand of "law enforcement." In their zeal to "prosecute" Tom Riddle, Potter and his accomplices

---

31. Nov. 13, 1987, Art. 11(1).
32. *Deathly Hallows* 744.

engaged in waterboarding, mutilation, murder, pet-killing, terrorism, war crimes, kidnapping, false imprisonment, forbidden Curses, and other gross violations of human, wizard and animal rights. All this to "prosecute" one man! Have we forgotten the lessons of our own history—the burning of witches at the stake, the show trials of witches in Salem? The Muggles have yet to learn these lessons. It is time for us, wizards and witches of good faith, to show the way.

(Hmm, look at all those black hippogryphs hovering outside Zabini's window. Haha, I suppose that's where Muggles got the idea for their silly helicopters. Well, nothing to worry about. I think I'll grab Zabini and head over to the Hog's Head for a butterbeer. I could use a good... [the text ends abruptly here—Eds.].)

Punishment in the Harry Potter Novels

Joel Fishman

J.K. Rowling depicts punishment both by Hogwarts teachers and, to a lesser extent, by quasi-judicial criminal courts in the Harry Potter novels. The narratives, however, do not explain how or why particular punishments are chosen over others. Given the wide range of philosophical debate concerning punishment (utilitarian vs. nonutilitarian; retribution vs. non-retribution; consequential vs. non-consequential philosophies),[1] one might expect some level of consistency in the books. However, the books are anything but consistent in the use of punishment,[2] which leaves the reader uneasy about punishment in the wizarding world and, perhaps, questioning punishment in contemporary society.

The past two centuries have seen an extensive accumulation of literature discussing punishment theory. The varied literature provides wide ranging justifications for the use of punishment as theorists attempt to answer such fundamental questions as why punish, how to punish, and whether to abandon punishment altogether. Legal punishment offers both censure and sanction to an offending individual. Censure reflects society's condemnation of a person's actions, while sanction imposes various penalties based on the violation of criminal law. In the criminal justice system, sanctions can be grouped together under four categories: deterrence, retribution, incapacitation of the dangerous, and rehabilitation. Throughout the Harry Potter stories, punishment falls under various sanctioning approaches based on the offending criminal or non-criminal action.

---

1. A READER ON PUNISHMENT (R. A. Duff and David Garland eds., 1994); LUCIA ZEDNER, CRIMINAL JUSTICE 70–114 (2004); Richard Frase, *Punishment Purposes*, 58 STAN. L. REV. 67 (2005).

2. Rowling does not explain, in any detail, how criminal sentencing is meted out in the magical world. The one exception is the use of the Unforgivable Curses, which invariably results in lifetime imprisonment. It is also unclear whether wizards other than the Minister of Magic and the Wizengamot impose criminal sentences, how sentences are matched with crimes, and how sentences are enforced.

There are multiple types of punishment portrayed in the Harry Potter series, moving from simple deduction of points for misbehavior in school to capital punishment offered by the dementors of Azkaban Prison. Rowling's presentation of school life for Harry and the students of Hogwarts is a clear departure from traditional children's literature. Rowling takes them out of the traditional family home and places them into a new school that takes on many of the roles that are traditionally reserved for home and family. In the case of Harry Potter, this role-reversal is even more pronounced as the beginning of a new school year heralds a welcome relief from the "home" provided by the Dursleys of Privet Drive.[3] Beginning in *The Sorcerer's Stone,* we are introduced to the abusive living conditions Harry has to face while living, literally, under the Dursleys, i.e., servant status, cramped living conditions, lack of food and clothing, and verbal abuse. In *The Half-Blood Prince* Dumbledore comments to the Dursleys that they have been poor role models and parents to Harry, but they do not appear to understand his comments.

The narratives extensively portray the use of punishment within the school setting. Like most boarding school stories,[4] rewards and punishments play an important role in how Hogwarts students relate to each other as shown in their inter-house rivalries, Quidditch, and the competition for the annual house cup. There appears to be no specific code or guidelines for punishment within Hogwarts School. Teachers are permitted to give or take away points for good work, misbehavior, or for no apparent reason, usually ranging from one to sixty points depending on the seriousness of the infraction or the bias of the teacher. Professor Snape repeatedly takes points away from Harry, Ron, and Hermione although Hermione is always winning points from other teachers for her intelligence. Even Professor McGonagall, as head of Gryffindor House, gives and takes points from the main protagonists as needed.

Detention also played a part in the punishments, such as Ron Weasley's having to polish armor without using magic in *The Chamber of Secrets,* Harry's having to write his sentences in his own blood for Dolores Umbridge in *The Order of the Phoenix,* or James Potter and Sirius Black serving double deten-

---

3. Chantel Lavoie, *Safe as Houses: Sorting and the School Houses at Hogwarts,* in READING HARRY POTTER: CRITICAL ESSAYS 35–49 (Giselle Liza Anatol ed., 2003); Charles Elster, *The Seeker of Secrets: Images of Learning, Knowing and Schooling,* in HARRY POTTER'S WORLD : MULTIDISCIPLINARY CRITICAL PERSPECTIVES 203–221 (Elizabeth E. Heilman, ed. 2003).

4. Deborah De Rosa, *Wizardly Challenges to and Affirmations of the Initiation Paradigm in Harry Potter,* in HARRY POTTER'S WORLD: MULTIDISCIPLINARY CRITICAL PERSPECTIVES 163, 180 (2003).

tion for using an illegal hex upon another student in *The Half-Blood Prince.* Later, in the *Deathly Hallows*, when Ginny, Neville and Luna were caught trying to steal Gryffindor's sword from Headmaster Snape's office, Snape punished them by sending "them into the Forbidden Forest, to do some work for ... Hagrid."[5]

Other schools had a system of punishment as well. For example: "At sixteen years old, even Durmstrang felt it could no longer turn a blind eye to the twisted experiments of Gellert Grindelwald, and he was expelled."[6]

The faculty-student relationship also becomes a major problem for Harry in Book Five when Dolores Umbridge, through a series of educational decrees, eventually replaces Professor Dumbledore as High Inquisitor of Hogwarts. She is an example of a particularly cruel and biased teacher from the standpoint of Harry and his friends. Harry earned Umbridge's enmity and a week's detention for revealing his fight against Voldemort in class; he received another week's detention for his biting criticism of Umbridge's suggestion that Professor Quirrell had taught age-appropriate subjects: " 'Yeah, Quirrell was a great teacher,' said Harry loudly, 'there was just that minor drawback of him having Lord Voldemort sticking out of the back of his head.' "[7] Harry later lost another fifty points after giving an interview to Rita Skeeter that was published in *The Quibbler.*

Umbridge's punishments result in Harry missing his Quidditch matches: "I think it is rather a good thing that you are missing something you really want to do. It ought to reinforce the lesson I am trying to teach you."[8] Her imposition of "writing lines," and forcing students to use a pen that drew blood for its ink, served as a punishment for both Harry and other students who talked back to her. Umbridge's attempt to change Harry's ways through the specific deterrence of a harsh punishment did not affect Harry's attitude toward her or the Ministry. It appears equally ineffective when she inflicts similar punishment on other students. Not knowing the severity of punishment Harry was receiving, Hermione, at one point, said, "At least it's only lines.... It's not as if it's a dreadful punishment, really."[9] Harry knew if he told them he would see a "look[] of horror" upon their faces.[10] Even worse, from Harry's point of view, was when Umbridge declared a lifetime ban on playing Quidditch for

---

5. *Deathly Hallows* 302.
6. *Deathly Hallows* 356.
7. *Order of the Phoenix* 317–18.
8. *Order of the Phoenix* 265–67.
9. *Order of the Phoenix* 269.
10. *Order of the Phoenix* 269.

Harry and the Weasley twins after they were involved in a fight with Malfoy and the Slytherins. Lifetime, however, is in the eyes of the beholder, as Ginny Weasley observes, and once Umbridge is gone, Harry returns as captain of his team in *The Half-Blood Prince*. Even after Umbridge left Hogwarts, she still desired to punish Harry. When Harry broke into her office at the Ministry, he saw a poster of himself hanging on the wall "with the words UNDESIRABLE NO. 1 emblazoned across his chest. A little pink note was stuck to it with a picture of a kitten in the corner. Harry moved across to read it and saw that Umbridge had written, *'To be punished.'*"[11]

Student-to-student punishment was shown in the Harry Potter series when the students learned spells and practiced them on each other. Gryffindors and Slytherins continually used jinxes upon each other at various points in the stories. None of the students can use strong magic. Nonetheless, Ginny Weasley garners Professor Slughorn's approval by her adept use of a Bat-Bogey Jinx on another student. Hermione's jinx of Marietta Edgecombe also went unpunished after Hermione caused the word "SNEAK" to form across Marietta's forehead when Marietta revealed the existence of Dumbledore's Army in *The Order of the Phoenix*. On the other hand, Umbridge's appointment of the Slytherins as an "Inquisitorial Squad," able to deduct points from other students, led Ernie Macmillan to comment: "He can't be allowed to dock points ... that would be ridiculous.... It would completely undermine the prefect system."[12] The system is further broken under the new regime of the Death Eaters in which students are "supposed to practice the Cruciatus Curse on people who've earned detentions."[13]

The imposition of corporal punishment that Argus Filch so desperately desired to use against students in the earlier stories, takes place in *The Deathly Hallows* when the Carrows are instituted as professors at Hogwarts. The Carrows are "in charge of all discipline. They like punishment, the Carrows." Their punishment of Neville, Terry Boot, or Michael Corner, the latter who "got caught releasing a first-year they'd chained up, and they tortured him pretty badly," shows how the Death Eaters had adversely changed the teacher-student relationship through punishment.[14]

Outside of Hogwarts, Rowling provides a less detailed portrayal of the use of punishment in the criminal justice system. The Ministry of Magic can detect the illegal use of magic but cannot always determine the perpetrator. This

---

11. *Deathly Hallows* 252.
12. *Order of the Phoenix* 626.
13. *Deathly Hallows* 573.
14. *Deathly Hallows* 573–75.

leads to the unfair punishment of Harry in two important instances. In *The Cham-ber of Secrets*, Dobby's use of the Hover Charm results in Harry's receiving a warning letter from the Ministry of Magic for his use of underage magic. In *The Order of the Phoenix*, at Harry's trial, Minister Fudge gives no credit to Harry's claim that a house-elf had committed the earlier crime until Dumbledore offered to have Dobby appear as a witness. Nor does the Ministry believe that Harry used magic purely in self-defense to ward of dementors while in the Muggle world, until Dumbledore produces Mrs. Figg as a witness in his successful defense of Harry. We learn in *The Deathly Hallows* that it is a charm called the Trace "that detects magical activity around under-seventeens," but is lost as soon as one becomes seventeen.[15]

On the other hand, Harry is not punished for blowing up his aunt because of the extraordinary circumstances surrounding Sirius Black's escape from Azakban in which it was supposed by all that he desired to kill Harry. Harry fully expected to be punished for breaking the Decree for the Restriction of Underage Wizardy. Fudge responded "Oh, my dear boy, we're not going to punish you for a little thing like that! ... It was an accident! We don't send people to Azkaban for blowing up their aunts!"[16]

Punishment for crimes can lead to prison in the magical world, but only a few examples are portrayed in the novels. Generally, wizards sent to prison go to Azkaban. Morfin Gaunt is given three months for attacking Muggles while Mundungus Fletcher is given a lesser sentence for stealing. On the other hand, Dumbledore's father Percival was sentenced to life in Azkaban for his attack on the three young Muggles. In a capricious effort to show that the Ministry was doing something against Voldemort, Fudge sent Hagrid to Azkaban Prison in *The Chamber of Secrets* and Scrimgeour sends Stan Shunpike in *The Half-Blood Prince*. Even though both Fudge and Scrimgeour knew they did not deserve punishment, there was no recourse for the condemned. Hagrid was eventually released, but Shunpike was still in prison at the end of *The Half-Blood Prince*. In Book Seven, Shunpike is free, but only because the Death Eaters have freed him from Azkaban for their cause. There is a second wizarding prison mentioned in Book Seven: Nurmengard. Hermione explains to Harry that Nurmengard is "[t]he prison Grindelwald had built to hold his opponents. He ended up in there himself, once Dumbledore had caught him."[17]

---

15. *Deathly Hallows* 47. Mad-Eye Moody points out that they had to use non-magical means of travel so as to elude the Trace.

16. *Prisoner of Azkaban* 45.

17. *Deathly Hallows* 360.

Death Eaters, like Bellatrix Lestrange or Barty Crouch, Jr., who were loyal followers of Voldemort, received punishment as a consequence for their past criminal behavior and to prevent them from committing future crimes. Lifetime imprisonment protects the community from their escaping and returning to aid their evil master. Sirius Black was also sentenced to a life sentence as a purported Death Eater. When he escaped from Azkaban, it appeared that he posed a direct danger to Harry, but later we find out that Black was imprisoned wrongly. Harry discovers that Peter Pettigrew actually committed the crimes attributed to Black. However, Black was still wanted by the Ministry. Underage wizards' testimony will not be accepted by the Ministry for proof of his innocence. In our society, the validity of children's testimony is questioned if a child is under a certain age (especially under thirteen), and there have been attempts to change state constitutions to provide for video deposition of children rather than face-to-face confrontation at trial.[18]

The dementors' role as the Azkaban guards magnifies the punitive effect of a prison sentence. Their presence at Azkaban provides a harsh environment for the prisoners, eventually leading to most going insane and dying shortly after their imprisonment. Although there is no equivalent of dementors in the Muggle world, it could be argued that some prisons in existence today would bear a close resemblance to Azkaban. Even in the United States and the United Kingdom, where the actions of guards are limited by law, Azkaban may not be a far stretch from the reality of some maximum security institutions. Attempts to escape from Azkaban result in the "Dementor's Kiss" which leaves the person worse than dead, an empty body without a soul. In *The Prisoner of Azkaban*, Fudge brings the dementors to suck out Black's soul, but with the help of Dumbledore, Harry, and Hermione, he is able to escape. Unfortunately for Barty Crouch Jr., he was not so lucky.

Some crimes have self-executing "punishments" in the magical world. For example, the killing of a unicorn, as Voldemort did to stay alive in *The Sorcerer's Stone*, results in a cursed life:

> Only one who has nothing to lose, and everything to gain, would commit such a crime. The blood of a unicorn will keep you alive, even if you are an inch from death, but at a terrible price. You have slain something pure and defenseless to save yourself, and you will have

---

18. Article V, Section 9 of the current Pennsylvania Constitution of 1968 was amended in 1995 by the electorate to provide for video depositions, but it was later found unconstitutional by the Supreme Court in Bergdoll v. Kane, 694 A.2d 1155 (Pa. Commw. 1997), *aff'd*, 731 A.2d 1261 (Pa. 1999).

but a half-life, a cursed life, from the moment the blood touches your lips.[19]

For Voldemort, who is trying to gain immortality, the killing of the unicorn appears essential to keeping himself alive. Only later do we learn that his use of Horcruxes kept him alive as well. "I was ripped from my body, I was less than spirit, less than the meanest ghost ... but still, I was alive."[20]

A second example of a self-executing punishment is the Unbreakable Vow, as made between Snape and Narcissa Malfoy. It cannot be broken or the person who breaks it suffers death. Another example is the Taboo. As Ron explains: "the name's [Voldemort] been jinxed, Harry, that's how they track people! Using his name breaks protective enchantments, it causes some kind of magical disturbance...."[21]

There also appears to be a system to impose fines for lesser offenses, but how they are determined is unclear. Arthur Weasley was fined 50 galleons for bewitching his flying car in *The Chamber of Secrets*, while Dolores Umbridge was going to fine Mundungus Fletcher for not having a license for trading in magical artifacts in his attempt to sell Regulus Black's locket, but she took the locket instead and dropped the fine in *The Deathly Hallows*.

Lesser crimes, for which punishments are not specified, include failing to register with the Ministry as an Animagus and the use of Veritaserum. The Ministry, however, does not know that James Potter, Black, Lupin, Pettigrew, and Skeeter are unregistered Animagi. This explains how Black escaped from Azkaban and how Skeeter obtained confidential information for many of her stories. Similarly, when Dumbledore uses Veritaserum to get the truth out of Barty Crouch, Jr., and Dolores Umbridge, unsuccessfully, attempts to use it upon Harry, the Ministry seems to have no knowledge of their use and does not bring charges against either.

The role of slavery in the Harry Potter series displays punishment by master towards house-elf and self-imposed punishments by the house-elves who work for wizards and witches.[22] Both Lucius Malfoy and Sirius Black do not treat their house-elves well. As Dobby related to Harry when they first meet: "Dobby is a house elf—bound to serve one house and one family forever."[23] House-elves

---

19. *Sorcerer's Stone* 258.
20. *Goblet of Fire* 653.
21. *Deathly Hallows* 389.
22. Brycchan Carey, *Hermione and the House-Elves: The Literary and Historical Context of J. K. Rowling's Antislavey Campaign, in* READING HARRY POTTER: CRITICAL ESSAYS 103–15 (Giselle Liza Anatol ed., 2003).
23. *Chamber of Secrets* 14.

were forbidden to discuss their families and when Dobby did so, he required immediate punishment, i.e., bashing his head against the wall, cracking a water jug over his head, etc. After gaining his freedom, Dobby worked at Hogwarts, but was looked upon by his fellow house-elves disdainfully for having his freedom and working for money. Winky's failure to keep control of Barty Crouch, Jr. led to her dismissal from her master to her mortification. Kreacher befriended Harry after Harry showed him some kindness and gave him Regulus's locket. Voldemort looked down on house-elves and did not realize the powers they had were different from wizards and witches, i.e., Dobby could disapparate out of Hogwarts which the students could not do. Kreacher led the house-elves' attack upon the Death Eaters in the battle for Hogwarts, crying "Fight! Fight! Fight for my Master, defender of house-elves! Fight the Dark Lord, in the name of brave Regulus! Fight!"[24]

In an interesting twist, animals in the magical works are also subject to punishment by the state. After Buckbeak injured Draco Malfoy, charges were brought. Hagrid tried, unsuccessfully, to defend Buckbeak, but the hearing was limited in scope and the outcome controlled by Lucius Malfoy. The sentence of execution seems too severe in light of Draco's injury; it was only Hermione's ability to go back in time under Dumbledore's direction that saved the hippogriff, as well as Sirius Black.

Rowling's conflict between good and evil as portrayed in the final battle between Voldemort and Harry, Harry chided him to repent for all of his past criminal actions: "But before you try to kill me, I'd advise you to think about what you've done.... Think, and try for some remorse...." " 'It's your last chance,' said Harry, 'it's all you've got left ... I've seen what you'll be otherwise ... Be a man ... try ... Try for some remorse.'"[25] But Harry knew, because Dumbledore and he had seen the repulsive baby in Kings Cross, that Voldemort did not possess such an ability. And so, failing to show remorse that demonstrated some forgiveness for his criminal actions, Voldemort died with the rebounding of his own *Avada Kedavra* curse upon himself.

In conclusion, Rowling portrays an inept, "half-crazed bureaucracy" (Professor Benjamin Barton's term)[26] that is incapable of providing a suitable criminal justice system. It does not allow for equal treatment of those accused of crimes and imposes arbitrary and cruel punishments. Rowling's portrayal of the criminal justice system also omits other possible approaches other than imprisonment that are available in today's society (sentencing guidelines, or al-

---

24. *Deathly Hallows* 734.
25. *Deathly Hallows* 741.
26. *See* Chapter 3, *supra*.

ternative sentencing). Innocent people are punished while the guilty go free. The powerful manipulate the system for swift retribution. This, of course, is partly due to the lack of lawyers to represent those who may not understand how the Ministry of Magic works.[27]

The Minister of Magic can follow or bend the law depending on his whims and how he relates to specific people. Lucius Malfoy influenced Fudge against Dumbledore in *The Chamber of Secrets*. Scrimgeour used the Decree for Justifiable Confiscation to delay carrying out Dumbledore's will, and Hermione criticized him for violating the intentions of the Decree. The improper use of magic may be punished or may be allowed, depending on the identity of the person who commits a particular illegal act. Umbridge gained increasing power within Hogwarts with the Minister's approval. She threatened to use the Cruciatus Curse against Harry to gain information without Fudge's knowledge, while Voldemort gained control of the Ministry first by putting Pius Thicknesse under the Imperius Curse to infiltrate the Ministry and later kill the Minister himself. As Remus tells Harry, "[T]he Death Eaters have got the full might of the Ministry on their side now.... They've got the power to perform brutal spells without fear of identification or arrest."[28] The defeat of Voldemort and his followers allows one of Dumbledore's followers, Kingsley Shacklebolt, to become the new Minister of Magic, for which the reader expects the return of a neutral, better organized, well-received government. Thus, readers come to understand that rule-breaking or criminal behavior may or may not be punished because of an unfair administration of justice by those in charge of the system. Such portrayal leaves the reader open to questioning today's criminal justice system as well.

---

27. Paul R. Joseph & Lynn E. Wolf, *The Law in Harry Potter: A System Not Even a Muggle Could Love*, 34 U. Tol. L. Rev. 193, 201–02 (2002–2003).

28. *Deathly Hallows* 206–07.

Harry Potter

& Identity

PASSPORT

3

Hogwarts, the Family, and the State: Forging Identity and Virtue in Harry Potter

Danaya C. Wright

J.K. Rowling has shown a remarkable aptitude for creating a world of diverse and fluid families in her Harry Potter series. She has rejected the traditional corn-flakes family of two married parents, two children, a family dog, and a station wagon.[1] Instead, she has created a magical world of interracial and intergenerational families that more closely approximates the family demographics of modern England than the fictional Victorian ideal that legal and social forces persistently try to create.

As we consider these different family structures, we should think about how the individual wizard goes from childhood to adulthood forming his moral character through the crucible of family, school, and state. Rowling depicts significant differences in character and sense of self among the different children that people her wildly popular books. The two main characters, Tom Riddle[2] and Harry Potter, are both orphans who grow to adolescence without even knowing there is a wizard world. Yet the two forge very different identities as they develop their magical abilities at Hogwarts. More importantly, their relationship to magic and their understanding of magic's usefulness is significantly different. These differences in character make us think about how the presence of magic influences the formation, continuation, or breakdown of family relationships in Rowling's wizard world and what these different fami-

---

1. *See* KATHERINE O'DONOVAN, FAMILY LAW MATTERS (1993) (Katherine O'Donovan refers to the traditional nuclear family as the "cornflakes family").

2. I use both of Tom's names throughout this chapter in an effort to distinguish the young, still-impressionable boy that was Tom Riddle from the adult Lord Voldemort who completely rejects the norms of wizarding society and adopts a life of violence and warfare.

lies say about her vision of the interplay of family, school, and state in identity formation.

Traditional liberal theory posits the existence of a private realm of the family where individuals develop their identities, forge their moral sensibilities, and build their characters. The private realm of the family is a place where free will and free associations hold sway. It is also a place where intimacy, friendships, and sustainable human bonds give meaning to our inner lives. The private sphere is often contrasted with the public sphere of politics, government, laws, the economic marketplace, and civil society. The public sphere is governed by laws that regulate rights, obligations, and interactions among strangers in arms-length negotiations. It may intrude into the private realm if necessary to protect individuals from harm or perhaps to foster a particular moral character. While some theorists argue there are fundamental connections between the family and the state, others view them as institutions opposed to one another.

The role of the individual in negotiating the family and state as institutions of power is equally complex. Although we may agree that the family is the locus of identity formation in a child's earliest years, no one believes that a child is immune from outside influences, either from peer groups, school curricula, media, or state intervention. Both familial and non-familial institutions are critical in developing individual identity and civic responsibility. Logically, the more a child is dependent on school or other institutional mechanisms for developing moral character the less important family becomes, and vice versa.

In Rowling's magical world of Harry Potter, both Harry and Lord Voldemort emerge from a similar background as orphans, but Harry's fierce loyalty and abiding faith in moral virtue are in stark contrast to Voldemort's hunger for power. For most of the rest of Rowling's young wizards, there are a variety of familial environments depicted within a larger, relatively coherent and homogeneous culture of wizardry and magic. Many of Harry's friends are raised extremely isolated within, but knowledgeable about, the wizarding world; they have their favorite quidditch teams, they know the rules about interfering with or harming Muggles, and they have heard the legend of the boy who survived, even though their family environments may have been quite different from each other.

Draco Malfoy and Ron Weasley both come from pure wizarding families, but they have very different personalities. Harry and Tom Riddle, however, both grew to age eleven before encountering wizard culture. They grew into adolescence believing that their differences and discomfort with their world was a sign of their own faults or deficits. But when they discovered that they were members of a different world, a world that shared and valued their special qualities, Harry fully embraced his new "home" and accepted the limits on magical power that are necessary if wizards and Muggles are to live harmoniously in larger societies. Tom, on the other hand, never stopped viewing himself as isolated and superior, as entitled to break the rules of his new world just as he did his old one, and to use his abilities without regard to the lives or interests of others.

If we consider the interplay of family, school, and state in the molding of identity and moral values, Rowling has given us much food for thought. While one might view the proper role of the state as non-interference in individual development except where individual expression causes harm to others, others might view the state's role as crucial to fostering a sense of civic responsibility and duty to others. Rowling's young characters are perhaps most influenced by their family environments and their crucial period at Hogwarts. The wizard state seems to have little to do with developing any sense of social responsibility. It typically takes a hands-off approach to activities within the family, except that at times it tries to micromanage (disastrously) the education young wizards receive at Hogwarts when it finds itself unable to control the larger conflicts associated with Voldemort's re-emergence. Ironically, while Rowling's families reflect in many ways the diverse and fluid family structures of twenty-first-century England, her state more closely resembles the weak and inept inquisitorial state of the medieval period. In contrasting her depictions of family with her depictions of state institutions, I wish to explore Rowling's wizard families, the interference of the state within those families, the interference of the state in Hogwarts, and, in so doing ponder how wizards are raised to be virtuous rather than evil.

Rowling's Vision of the Family

Consider, first, some of the interesting family structures Rowling has created. Most important is Harry's "foster" home. When his parents were killed by Lord Voldemort, he was delivered by Hagrid to the doorstep of the Dursleys—his mother's sister, her husband, and their son Dudley—who are all Muggles. There was no formal adoption, no court-ordered home visit, no consideration of the best interests of the child, and, ultimately, no love. Instead, Albus Dumbledore wrote them a letter explaining that they would have to provide a home for this orphan if he was to be protected from the vengeance of Lord Voldemort. We presume that the Dursleys took in Harry because they realized that the alternative quite possibly could be Harry's death, and they were not willing to have the death of a child on their consciences, though the neglect of one seemed not to cause a moment's pause. Through book after book, Harry is neglected, emotionally abused, and treated as the quintessential Dickensian orphan by his maternal aunt and her husband. Like Dickens' orphans, and despite the neglect of living in the closet under the stairs and wearing Dudley's old hand-me-downs, Harry somehow emerges a better person than Tom Riddle, another orphan of the book, but one who had three meals a day, a comfortable room, and some semblance of creature comforts in the orphanage from which Dumbledore rescued him.

The Riddle family seems almost cursed compared to that of the Potter/Dursley family. Riddle's mother enchanted his father, a young Muggle scion of a local noble family, into falling in love and marrying her. The love lasted only so long as Merope Gaunt could live with her husband knowing that his affection was produced by deceit. As soon as she removed the enchantment, he deserted her, pregnant with their infant son, and returned to his family estate. She died a lonely death hours after giving birth to Tom, who would be raised in an orphanage. He is later rescued from the orphanage (or perhaps, more appropriately, the orphanage is rescued from Tom) by Dumbledore, many years before Harry is left on the Dursley's doorstep. Neither child received the love and affection we would wish for all children, and both happily left their childhood abodes for the adventures and community of Hogwarts, a place where both Tom and Harry felt most at home.

A third orphan, Neville Longbottom, whose fate is intertwined with the lives of Harry and Tom, lived a different childhood altogether. Neville lives with his batty grandmother who does not think much of his magical powers, who sends him howlers for forgetting his belongings, and who frequently reminds Neville of how he isn't quite up to par with his parents. Despite her autocratic manners, Neville's grandmother takes Neville to see his parents at St. Mungo's Hospital, teaches him the story of Voldemort's torture of his parents and the ensuing wizard war, and indoctrinates him into the wizarding world in a way entirely absent for both Harry and Tom. As Neville begins to show some magical aptitude and helps fight off the death eaters at the Ministry, his grandmother's disappointment diminishes. But who decided Neville would live with his grandmother? Was a guardianship established or did he wind up there with a flick of Dumbledore's wand?

Other families, though also non-traditional, raise their children with an awareness of wizard culture but also without much intervention by the wizard state. Two "interracial" couples separate early in the books, and the effects on their children are as varied as one would expect to see in the Muggle world. Hagrid, who has more magical ability than a squib, is the offspring of a Muggle father and a giant mother who were separated early in his childhood when his mother returned to her people in France. Hagrid grew up with his father who lovingly raised him not to despise his maternal roots but to be humble and kind. Tom Riddle is also the offspring of an interracial marriage, between a witch and a Muggle, which resulted in separation before Tom's mother died and he murdered his father. Tom was an incredibly powerful wizard in part because of magical talent and in part by hard work. Other Hogwarts children are half-breeds as well, with greater or less magical powers. Seamus Finnegan is the child of a Muggle father and a witch, and he has more magical powers than Argus Filch and Mrs. Figg, who both came from magical parents. Oddly, other children sport magical powers completely unrelated to their hereditary roots. Lily Evans (Harry's mother) and Hermione Granger are more powerful witches as daughters of two Muggle parents than Ron Weasley, who is the son of two magical parents. Even with the tremendous amount of death on both sides of the war in the final book, Rowling left it unclear whether the presumably full-blood Harry[3] was stronger because of bloodline or because of the human emotions, like humility and love, that the half-breed Voldemort could not understand.

While bloodlines and genetic ancestry may play an important role in magical development, it certainly is not determinative of the strength of magical powers, which can be honed by practice, nor does it aid in making the difficult decisions young wizards face when opting to use magic in certain situations. Environment plays a role, if not entirely in the magical abilities, certainly in the moral ones. Except for Tom Riddle, Harry Potter, and Hermione Granger, the magical children of Hogwarts were all raised within a culture of magic that was defined in large part by Ministry rules and involved a proper education at Hogwarts. Magical abilities were discussed, acknowledged, and sometimes even celebrated. When Uncle Algie dropped Neville out of a window in his umpteenth effort to extract some magical reaction, and Neville bounced all the way through the garden and down the road, Neville's Gran cried with delight and Uncle Algie was so pleased he bought Neville his toad. Within the wizarding community, there was a collective understanding of the appropriate limits of the uses of magical powers and the relationship between magic and morality. These are concepts that were foreign to Harry and Tom before they reached Hogwarts.

There are noticeable class differences within the wizarding world, similar to the Muggle world, that have a clear impact on wizard character formation.

---

3. I say "presumably" because Hagrid insists that Harry is full-blooded, but his mother was a mudblood. One must wonder if there is a 1/8th or 1/16th rule in the wizard world.

Harry's best friend, Ron Weasley, is the sixth of seven red-headed children of Arthur and Molly Weasley. Though they have little money, the children wear hand-me-down robes, and Ron can only afford a pet rat, the Weasley home is bustling, happy, and full of love. In contrast, the wealthy and pure-blooded family of Sirius Black is obsessed with appearances and bereft of affection. Sirius is ostracized from his home because he consorts with werewolves, half-breeds, and mudbloods. He happily escapes his ancestral home because it is cold and unhappy, spending most of his time at his best friend's house — that of James Potter. Similarly, the Malfoy home does not seem to be much fun although, unlike Sirius, Draco upholds the snobbish culture of prejudice he learned in his home.

Except, perhaps, for Sirius and Tom Riddle, wizard children are extremely loyal — Harry to his parents, Ron to his family, and Draco to his. In the end, however, the stable and functional homes are those with love. Those homes without love are viewed as not to house one's "true family." Both Harry and Sirius remark numerous times that number four, Privet Drive and number twelve, Grimmauld Place are not home — they have found family acceptance and love elsewhere. For Rowling, stable and happy homes are where love is, and they are made more powerful as the love within has lasting impact on the characters and fates of the children formed within them.

The most powerful love is, not surprisingly, the love of a mother for her children. In at least three instances in the books, mothers desperately try to save their children, even at the cost of their own lives. Lily Potter's effort to save Harry by blocking Voldemort's curse is central to the books. A similar sentiment influenced Barty Crouch Jr.'s mother to take polyjuice potion and stand in for him in Azkaban prison, even dying there, so that her son could escape the Dementors. Lastly, Narcissa Malfoy extracts an unbreakable vow from Severus Snape to protect her son, Draco, who she realizes is being sent to his death by Lord Voldemort. The strength of the mother/child bond in these examples is contrasted with the abandonment of Tom Riddle by his mother, even before her death. Though she tried in her weak way to save him, she could not do so when her own self-loathing destroyed her. In contrast, Hagrid found a loving and happy home with his father, even though his mother deserted them.

The strength, importance, and ultimate "naturalness" of the mother/child bond is highlighted by the disturbing image of Sirius' mother blasting off the family tree the names of not only her son but other relatives who held more enlightened views of individual merit. Sirius' curses against his mother's screaming portrait are not fine examples of filial piety, nor is his mother's intolerance a fine example of unconditional maternal love. Sirius' experiences evoke images of the rejection and ostracism that many gay sons experience when they come out to their parents, especially parents who obsess over image and propriety. The visceral wiping out of Sirius' name from the Black Family Tapestry further marks him as an outcast. Certain forms and expressions of love are acceptable, and others are not.

The love that Lily Potter showed Harry, that Narcissa Malfoy showed Draco, and that Barty Crouch's mother showed Barty are all contrasted with the failure of Tom Riddle's mother to love her child enough to survive the breakdown of her marriage. That failure, I suggest, arose because Merope Gaunt inappropriately used magic to generate the love between herself and Voldemort's father. The intervention of magic in that relationship doomed it, as well as its offspring, to a perverse shadow of a normal life. Clearly, it would be unfair and overly simplistic to blame Voldemort's evil on the failure of his mother's love, but it does seem that Rowling is drawing at least one link between the magical and the Muggle world. Human and wizard relationships cannot depend upon magic; they must rest on a base of truth in order to withstand the outside pressures of power-hungry villains and the social norms of an elitist, exclusionary culture. Intimate relationships, with their attendant successes and failures, do not survive if magic rather than true love is at the core.

Rowling's books clearly give life to the popular slogan, "love makes a family," at least certain types of love. In this one respect, the magical world has no real advantage over the Muggle world, though wizards do seem to have better than Muggle-odds of forming lasting, successful marriages. This may be because Rowling's wizarding families do not have to struggle against a state apparatus that privileges certain family structures and hinders others. The state does not intervene in Harry's placement with the Dursleys, nor does it step in to save Tom Riddle. It does not deny Hagrid's parents the legitimacy of marriage despite the inter-racial character of their union. Nor does it particularly support the most traditional of family structures, that of the Weasleys. The state does not facilitate Mrs. Black's casting off of her son, nor does it support Gran Longbottom's decision to care for her grandson Neville. The state has virtually nothing to do with the private lives of these wizard families.

From the perspective of legal analysis, Rowling's families are oddly anachronistic, both in the state's apparent choice not to privilege certain family forms and in its non-interference in what are traditional family-law matters. When we think of family law, we generally think of marriage, divorce, child custody, adoption, and inheritance. Ironically, while all of these terribly important events are occurring in the books, the state intervenes in none of them. It is not family law that governs so much as the law of the individual family. Rowling hearkens back to a pre-industrialized world of kinship arrangements in which marriage and divorce occur without state interference and control. Adoption, fostering, or informal child custody arrangements occur at the flick of Dumbledore's wand. Two marriages were dissolved without any obvious legal intervention, and two estates appear to have been administered without the benefit of probate. Sirius' will is self-executing and the Potter's family wealth was converted into galleons and placed in Gringotts for Harry's use without a guardianship, custodianship, or a trust arrangement monitored by the wizard courts. In fact, the wizard state seems completely unconcerned with family affairs and only interests itself with underage use of magic and condemning wizards to Azkaban for crimes they did not commit. The absence of direct state control in the family does not mean, however, that the responsible use of magic is an inherent trait in fledgling wizards, or that the family teaches all that young wizards need know.

Rowling's Problematic State

Traditional political theory posits two important tenets about social order. One is that the family predates the formal structures and hierarchies of civil society. The head of the household protects the family, provides for its support, makes rules regarding personal interactions, and settles conflicts. The family is the building block of society, and in order for the state to increase in power, familial power must decrease. As the state has grown over the centuries, it has interfered more and more with the family, reducing the power of the large noble families and weakening the control of parents over children. The second is that in contrast to the somewhat inevitable rise of the bureaucratic state, there is believed to exist a certain private realm of the family to be separated from the public world of the state. Certain decisions within the private realm should be left to the family head while decisions within the public world are properly the domain of the state's ruling apparatus. In most people's minds, there is a proper divide between state control of the economy, business relations, and public order, and the improper interference of the state in the intimate realm of the family, the bedroom, and the conscience. This divide supports the constitutional right to privacy, legal protections for religious freedom, speech, and association, and the right to be free from unlawful searches and seizures. To most people, a man's home truly is his castle, to be protected from unauthorized entry by the state at least as much as by predators and evildoers. The last bastion of family control is in the protection from state interference in the private freedoms of conscience and belief.

Rowling's families are no different. Dumbledore does not intervene in Harry's neglect, though he expresses outrage in *Half-Blood Prince* when he learns the extent of deprivation Harry has experienced. No one seemed particularly concerned within the Ministry when the Black family developed the tradition of mounting the heads of house elves on the wall when they could no longer carry loaded tea trays. And although the Ministry sends messengers and investigators to look into apparent mis-deeds (Morfin's torturing the muggle Tom Riddle) or curious circumstances (backed-up plumbing), even Dumbledore approaches a wizard home with caution. In *Half-Blood Prince*, Dumbledore explains to Harry as they are approaching Horace Slughorn's house from blocks away that "it would be quite as rude as kicking down the front door.... Courtesy dictates that we offer fellow wizards the opportunity of denying us entry. In any case, most Wizarding dwellings are magically protected from unwanted Apparators."[4]

Not surprisingly, wizard homes have better alarms and advanced warning systems for intruders than the crude Muggle varieties we use today, so that it is not only impolite to apparate into a wizard home but may be dangerous as well. Harry enters number twelve, Grimmauld Place and even the Burrow, his favorite place, from the street, as Muggles do. Magic appropriately helps draw the line between the privacy and intimacy of the family and the institutional control of the state, but this privacy of the wizard home allows for all sorts of questionable activities to be carried on that are not appropriately controlled by the magical powers of the wizard state. Harry's neglect and the Black family tradition of stuffing and mounting elf heads are just two of many troubling activities hidden from public view. Barty Crouch Jr. was kept imprisoned in his home by his father after his escape from Azkaban through a powerful imperious curse. In *The Chamber of Secrets* we learn that the Malfoy family was harboring powerful items of dark magic which Lucius Malfoy tried to unload at Borgin and Burkes. At the end of the haggling, in which Mr. Malfoy explained that the Ministry is conducting raids and that certain items in his home might "embarrass"[5] him if discovered, Mr. Borgin mutters to himself "Good day yourself, *Mister* Malfoy, and if the stories are true, you haven't sold me half of what's hidden in your *manor* ..."[6] A dungeon to house prisoners is just another of Malfoy's secrets.

The balance between state control and family privacy seems apparently tipped in favor of the private realm. The Ministry of Magic prohibits the possession of dark items, but it also has relatively strict laws on illegal searches of private homes, though the possibility of raids is not outlawed. And though

4. *Half-Blood Prince* 60.
5. *Chamber of Secrets* 51.
6. *Chamber of Secrets* 53.

Ministry officials are dispatched to private homes to investigate underage magic as well as illegal magical interference with Muggles, the rather botched visit of Bob Ogden to the Gaunt House in *The Half-Blood Prince* shows a determined Ministry completely ill-suited to handle the aggression, dark magic, and violence of the Slytherin heirs' home. In the end, there is very little meaningful interference of the state in family matters, despite the numerous opportunities and scenarios in which state interference in the Muggle world would be common-place. Mr. Malfoy's dark objects, Barty Jr's prison, and stuffed elf heads remain undisturbed by Ministry surveillance.

The relative absence of state interference in the family leaves virtually no checks on the family as the primary realm for forging moral identity. This is certainly true for those young first-years who enter Hogwarts for the first time and are sorted into houses by the Sorting Hat. It does not appear that these children have been to mandatory primary school though they apparently know how to read and write. We might imagine that they have been to Muggle schools where they were taught their basics, except that most of these children have virtually no knowledge of Muggle culture and traditions. They can't use the "fellytone," don't understand Muggle currency, and apparently can't even find their way around London on the underground. Wizard children seem extremely isolated until they leave for Hogwarts, even though many have adopted the prejudices and values of their parents. Draco Malfoy has fully adopted his parents' views on race purity and wizard proprieties, while Ron Weasley feels quite comfortable about consorting with mudbloods and maintaining good wizard/Muggle relations.

The apparent lack of state intervention begs the question: is the wizard family so different, perhaps even infallible, that state interference is unnecessary, or is the family so strong that state intervention would not be tolerated? We could easily imagine that wizards and witches, with their supernatural powers, would be less likely to make mistakes in choosing their spouses so that divorce would simply not be an issue, not because it is unavailable, but because it is unnecessary. Similarly, we could imagine that self-executing wills and private letters could adequately and appropriately distribute estates and determine the best adoption options for orphaned wizard children because magic makes individuals less fallible. Nonetheless, there are dysfunctional marriages that end disastrously without, as far as we can tell, court orders distributing property, settling custody, and ordering child support. The informality and ease with which family relationships shift may be surprising, if not unnatural, to most modern liberal thinkers. Magic may make the family more powerful and private, but it does not guarantee that private relationships will always work.

The strength of the family bond is clearly crucial to Rowling's magical world and is, arguably, the locus of true power, not the state, even with its methods of surveillance and countless decrees. One of the most telling scenes of all the books is of Harry and Sirius looking at the tapestry of the Black family tree, linking back to the Malfoys, the Lestranges, and a host of other powerful families. The wizard world is like the European aristocracy of the medieval period —families intermarried to build dynasties, and family relationships were the core of political power and political alliances. Wizards from these families inherit power and assume their own agency in a world that does not question the appropriateness of bloodlines, the patrimony, and political allegiances. Muggles, like the peasantry, are the unwashed masses, and it is the rare, misfit wizard or witch who rises from the masses to become powerful. Lily Evans and Hermione Granger are the obvious unusual witches who rose not from family alliances but from talent and hard work. Harry's mother and his best friend, mudbloods both, are humble, empathetic, altruistic, and incredibly powerful witches. Lily orders James Potter to stop tormenting Severus Snape and Hermione knits hats to free house-elves from the tedium of domestic servitude. The hardworking mudbloods, who pulled themselves up through sheer talent and hard work, are contrasted with the privileged, lazy, egotistical, and frivolous wizard elite like James Potter, Sirius Black, Crabbe, and Goyle. Even the working-class Weasleys have a hard time competing against the truly talented; and Fred, George, and Ron all suffer a severe deficit in their willingness to work hard. Fortunately, the talented and powerful Ginny Weasley emulates Hermione more than her brothers.

Rowling's social commentary is rather typical nineteenth century liberal critique. The hard-working middle class inevitably overcomes the depraved and decadent nobility and outperforms the deprived and down-trodden working class. The ineffectual peasantry will survive but will not save the world; the snobbish aristocrats will die off from the combined effects of elitism and technological ludditism. In rejecting the inevitability of class-based inferiority that is consistent with liberalism, Rowling evokes a world in which the individual can triumph precisely because the state has removed the barriers to success. But also like the modern liberal world, the individual is still marked by the place of his family in the wizard aristocratic state.

The modern welfare state has not yet emerged in the wizard world and neither have wizards entirely transcended their familial roots. The Ministry departments of "Magical Games and Sports," "Magical Transport," "International Magical Cooperation," "Regulation and Control of Magical Creatures," "Magical Accidents and Catastrophes," "Magical Law Enforcement," and the "Department of Mysteries" highlight the priorities of the wizard state. Perhaps most interesting are the departments that do not exist. There is no department of defense or any other indication of a military, nor a department of education, nor a department of child protective services, nor in fact any department offering any social services. The wizard state is highly concerned with international and Muggle relations, the economic marketplace, and transportation and banking. Even the Aurors, comprising a secret MI-5 agency, function in a very individualistic way. In the end, wizard welfare is left to individual ingenuity.

Rowling's strong families and weak state pose some interesting questions for the reader seeking some connection to our twenty-first century Muggle world. The state does not intervene to prevent the mounting of elf heads, child-neglect, or possession of dark magic because it is still held hostage to the interests of powerful families. Until those powerful families adopt the enlightened views of "Muggle-lovers" like the Weasleys, or develop a sense of social good that is separate from their own self-interests, there will be a rift in the social fabric of the wizard world. That rift creates the opportunity for Lord Voldemort to acquire power for himself and inevitably allows for the hijacking of the wizard state. The Ministry's mantra that Voldemort has not returned, that Dumbledore is power-hungry, and that Harry is crazy is a clear attempt to rewrite reality into some pastoral fiction of the kind that has always served to keep the people distracted while the leaders serve their own interests.

This is not to say that the wizard state plays absolutely no role in the forging of young wizard identities. In one sense the incompetence of the wizard state allows for the creation of substitute organizations that serve much the same ends. Thus, the Order of the Phoenix substitutes for a Ministry army and the Dementors provide mercenary guards for enemies of the Ministry. The state is also present through its control of Hogwarts, which gives children their sense of place in the larger wizard universe. No wizard child is fully formed without attending seven years at Hogwarts.

Hogwarts and Wizard Moral Character

Rowling undeniably views Hogwarts as critical in forming wizard identity. At Hogwarts, wizard children hone their magical powers, learn their own limits as well as those set by the Ministry for using magic in the world outside school, acquire membership in the brotherhood and sisterhood of their respective houses, and engage in communal dialogue about their responsibilities in the greater world. But Hogwarts is forced to take the children as they come, complete with prejudices and moral stains. Just as Harry, Hermione, Ron, Tonks, Lupin, Sirius, and the Potters are products of Hogwarts, so too are Voldemort, Lucius Malfoy, Bellatrix Lestrange, Peter Petigrew, and Crabbe and Goyle. Second to the family, Hogwarts is the next most important influence on the development of wizard character, though it is not clear that it can overcome the influences of family or adequately stand in for a relatively non-existent state.

Hogwarts makes a credible effort in teaching children right from wrong. Notably, it does not teach the dark arts, only defense against the dark arts. It does not have any information about Horcruxes anywhere in its library, and the restricted books are available only for teachers, not impressionable students. The average young wizard who leaves Hogwarts after seven years should be adept at magic and will know the Ministry rules about the limits on the use of magic in the Muggle world. Most important, as Dumbledore tells the young first years in their very first banquet, "Hogwarts will be your home for the next seven years." The houses, the prefects, the head boy and head girl, and the teachers will become surrogate parents for these children.

Two characteristics of Hogwarts are important. The first is the fact that Hogwarts is the place both Harry and Tom feel most at home. More than any other children, Harry and Tom found comfort in this institution and did not want to leave it each summer to return to the Dursleys or the orphanage. As such, Hogwarts and the teachers and students represent the closest thing Harry and Tom have to family, and those lessons one usually learns within the four walls of the family home are transmitted to Harry and Tom at Hogwarts. Where the family fails, Hogwarts not only provides the educational ground rules for all wizards, but it serves as a home for those children who have no family. One important difference, though, is that Harry's father-figure at Hogwarts is Dumbledore while Tom's father-figure was Horace Slughorn, a rather vain and insipid aesthete who loved the adoration of kneeling students and the luxuries of sugared pineapple. Dumbledore did not get involved in Riddle's education nor, apparently, did he serve as a moral guide or mentor. To the extent an institutional safeguard is available, Hogwarts is it. Unfortunately, Hogwarts is only as good a safeguard as the teachers and headmaster can make it.

It is not a coincidence that when Draco Malfoy becomes a prefect for Slytherin House his own moral weaknesses rub off on the other children. Draco unjustly takes away points from Gryffindor, he tattles on Harry, Ron, and Hermione, and he orders the younger kids around. Draco's example proves influential to Crabbe, Goyle, and many other Slytherin students. The entire year that Dolores Umbridge is insinuating herself as Hogwarts High Inquisitor we see a decline in the behavior of the students. Thus, just as the family is only as effective as the parents, Hogwarts is only as powerful at forging young minds as the teachers and headmaster can provide the right moral guidance.

The idea that the educational system serves both to instill in all children certain collective values and knowledge and that it should provide safeguards to failing families is nothing new or unusual. Schools today often provide free breakfasts and lunches for families that cannot afford to feed their children. They provide social services for detecting and remedying a variety of problems that families might face. And the educational system that rigorously indoctrinates children into the regimen of knowledge and behavior plays a crucial role in shaping citizens' understanding of truth, power, and knowledge. The collective culture that is shaped and instilled at Hogwarts is the primary way in which young wizards learn to use their magical powers, and we can only hope they are bounded by the necessary limits set by the Ministry.

Hogwarts, ultimately, must be understood as an institutional tool of the state. As much as Dumbledore might wish to teach the children certain magical skills to defend themselves from Voldemort, he is constrained by Ministry rules. They cannot learn to apparate until their sixth year, and they must achieve certain scores on their OWLS in order to move into advanced studies. The students are counseled on career options by Ministry order, and the Ministry provides a board of directors, of which Lucius Malfoy is a member, to oversee operations at Hogwarts. As much as Dumbledore might like to go against Ministry rules, he is bound to allow Dolores Umbridge to teach Defense Against the Dark Arts when he is unable to find a suitable teacher himself. Even with the strength of Dumbledore, Hogwarts did not improve Draco Malfoy, his henchmen Crabbe and Goyle, and it ultimately produced Tom Riddle. Neither Ministry oversight, nor Dumbledore's individual strength of character can guarantee that children will not go wrong. Logically, therefore, it cannot guarantee that any child, even Harry and Hermione, will ultimately turn out right. As a safeguard, it is not perfect. But, of course, no institution can be flawless in responding to the individualized needs and characteristics of all people. We assume that other institutional responses will catch those that elude the educational system; namely, courts, prisons, hospitals, welfare, and other social services.

We generally consider the state the most powerful collective institution, to which the educational system, the penal system, and the medical system are simply arms, each directed at the same ultimate end. In Rowling's magical world, however, Hogwarts and the state seem in constant tension. Where we might assume that schools would be subordinate to the state, they are in contradiction to it in the wizard world. Educators often teach students to be critical of the state, to challenge its authority, and to question its teachings, but they rarely advocate open disregard for state rules. When push comes to shove, the educational system rarely wins a battle with the state. Yet it is not the power of the Ministry that appeals to Voldemort; it is the power of Hogwarts. Moreover, Dumbledore, knowing that the Ministry is rather incompetent, sets Hogwarts against the Ministry whenever the latter proves incapable of handling the threats of Voldemort and his deatheaters. Hogwarts is more strongly protected than the Ministry against Voldemort's attacks. It is protected by its own army, the Order of the Phoenix, and it is probably at least as involved in international relations as the Ministry.

There is also a tension in the struggle for power between Dumbledore and the Minister of Magic; not power in the traditional sense of armies on a battlefield, but power to define and control truth and knowledge. According to Hagrid, Voldemort was "lookin' fer followers.... He was takin' over."[7] As Hagrid explains to Harry, Voldemort had not yet attacked Hogwarts, which remained the only safe haven during those dark days. Hagrid believes it was because Dumbledore was the only wizard that Voldemort was afraid of, at least until his run-in with the infant Harry. Hagrid hints, however, that it was only a matter of time before Voldemort tried to take over Hogwarts. All of this is borne out in *Half-Blood Prince* when Dumbledore explains to Harry that Tom Riddle wanted more than anything to become a professor at Hogwarts. It is unlikely that Riddle sought out the position because he was seeking career satisfaction. Something about Hogwarts drew Voldemort to its hallowed halls. Dumbledore suggests there were three reasons Tom wanted a job at Hogwarts: because it was the only place he felt at home, because there were ancient powers at work there, and because it gave him control and influence over students.[8]

If we think about the magic of family and the role of Hogwarts in forming identity, it is no wonder Voldemort wanted to stay at Hogwarts. Hogwarts is more like a family, with the magical powers of ancient dynasties, than it is a creature of the inept Ministry of Magic. And like the family, it sometimes fails in raising children to be virtuous and civic-minded. With the benevolent presence of Albus Dumbledore, Hogwarts does a pretty good job, especially when he takes the time to play a personal role in Harry's upbringing. However, if Dumbledore were not headmaster, and teachers like Horace Slughorn allowed students to insinuate themselves into positions of privilege to obtain forbidden knowledge, then Hogwarts the institution fails. For this reason Dumbledore stays at Hogwarts, despite being asked three times to take over the position of Minister of Magic. It is for this reason that Voldemort's rise to power so directly implicates Hogwarts. Not only is Dumbledore the only wizard that can stop him, Hogwarts contains the weapon that Tom needs: the opportunity to control Harry and the young minds of the next generation.

---

7. *Chamber of Secrets* 68.
8. *Half-Blood Prince* 442–446.

That the power to control Harry lies personally with Dumbledore and not generally at Hogwarts is attested to by the attempt of the Ministry to position Dolores Umbridge as High Inquisitor. She has the power to post educational decrees every few days to prohibit the students from meeting and discussing anything remotely related to Voldemort's return. The interference with Hogwarts' operations is a clear attempt to regulate behavior and indoctrinate the students into passive conformity. Surprisingly, the greatest challenge to the Ministry's control over Hogwarts is the creation of Dumbledore's Army where the children learn the truth about Voldemort's return and the skills to combat him. In this example, they once again turn their loyalties toward Hogwarts and not the Ministry, they rely on the school's magical powers and the teachers' protection to learn the skills they will need in the brave new world of Voldemort's resurrection, and they test their own mettle in uncovering truth from falsehood.

Instead of the usual hierarchy of all-powerful state with subjugated institutions like schools that serve to safeguard the moral teachings of families, Hogwarts prevails over the Ministry in the important aspects of control over children and the acquisition and dissemination of truth. To the extent Hogwarts represents Harry's home, it is also a place to be challenged and destroyed because it nurtures and strengthens Harry, Voldemort's chosen enemy. But Hogwarts is at least as fallible as the individual families from which the many students are raised. Without Dumbledore, Hogwarts produces quite a few bad wizards, either because it could not defeat the influences of their home-lives or because it offered too great temptations to power-hungry wizards like Tom Riddle. The Ministry not only cannot control the education children receive at Hogwarts, it is profoundly unsuited to doing so. Nevertheless, without Hogwarts or the state as safeguards for failures within the protected sphere of the family, wizard culture is condemned to a constant struggle between good and evil. So long as Hogwarts allows Lucius and Narcissa Malfoy to be elitist, pure-blood snobs, it will allow Draco to follow in his parents' footsteps. So long as it cannot guarantee that Sirius will be better than his mother, it cannot guarantee that Harry will rise to his potential goodness any more than it can prevent Voldemort from rising to his potential evil.

Conclusion

Rowling clearly views the family as central to identity formation for young wizards and witches; it is where one learns the norms and customs of the wizarding world and the limits of appropriate magical power. The formal institutions of the state appear relatively ill-equipped to inculcate the kinds of necessary restraints and responsibilities that are required in a world in which magical abilities have the capacity to wreak great havoc. If children are left alone within the family, however, they have roughly 50–50 odds of turning out virtuous like Harry Potter or evil like Tom Riddle. They may follow family prejudices blindly, like Draco Malfoy, or they may rebel against them like Sirius Black. Without state interference within the family, there is ultimately no control over how wizard children will grow into capable, responsible adults. Good wizards generally produce good offspring, and bad ones generally produce bad offspring, with the Percy Weasley and Barty Crouch Jr. being the exception.

Hogwarts, however, appears to come to the rescue. Without Hogwarts Harry would never have learned to harness his magical powers to defeat Voldemort. Nor would he have faced the moral challenges that have defined his young life. Hogwarts and Dumbledore's mentoring helped Harry to rise above the average child and to excel in virtue, strength, and moral character. But Hogwarts is not all-powerful. It cannot guarantee that strong wizards passing through its doors will always emerge dedicated to doing good rather than evil. Lord Voldemort is just as much a product of Hogwarts as Harry. Even though Voldemort learned more about the dark arts after he left Hogwarts, he never learned the limits to magical power, nor did he learn to make the crucial decision to pursue good rather than evil, a decision that should be fostered at school while children are still young and impressionable. To the extent we rely on schools as the safeguards to failing families, we simply turn to a different institution that succeeds or fails on the strength of the members within. Hogwarts failed with Tom Riddle, just as it succeeds with Harry, without any clear reason except that Dumbledore was headmaster.

Rowling's vision of the interplay of family, school, and state in the formation of young wizards minds is profoundly troubling. The fortuity of Dumbledore's mentorship may have helped Harry turn out right, but it provides no comfort to those who realize that more Tom Riddles may come along and choose to use their magical powers to benefit themselves rather than others. The wizard state is profoundly ill-equipped to fight the war Voldemort is waging for ultimate power, in part because the war is aimed at control within the private sphere of the family, where real power lies. Voldemort is attacking individual families because they, not the state, pose the real threat to his take-over because they are the sites of truth and love. Even Dumbledore's constant reminder that love, not magic, is the ultimate power rings hollow because true love does not exist for all children. The power of the family, for good and for bad, cannot be defeated at Hogwarts despite the efforts of good teachers and noble headmasters. As Rowling ends the series with the deaths of Dumbledore and Voldemort, her readers are left unmoored as to whether we raise wizards and Muggles to do what is right. The reader must put her faith either in institutions to safeguard failing families, or resign herself to the fatalism of birth and family. Ironically, the fall of the Ministry in the final book and the triumph in the battle over Hogwarts leave the reader still trapped in this nihilistic quagmire. Bad wizards live and good wizards die, more orphans are born, and the world goes on, apparently having changed very little in the ultimate struggle of good against evil. Though individual wizards have learned much, especially Harry, Ron, and Hermione, there is always a next generation that will have to learn anew the limits of magic and the seductiveness of power.

Harry Potter and the Development of Moral Judgment in Children

Wendy N. Law & Anna K. Teller

The Harry Potter series opens with murder. Children learn that the evil Lord Voldemort killed James and Lily Potter and attempted to murder their son Harry before being mysteriously vanquished. Murder is the first of many moral and legal issues that both Harry and his child readers face as he grows throughout the books. As Harry strives to survive in the wizarding world, readers witness his struggles with the concepts of good and evil and with questions of justice, law and morality. The child reader sees the impact of these struggles on Harry's judgment and in turn on his moral development. In the novels, author J.K. Rowling exposes Harry to moral lessons involving the legal concepts of battery, false imprisonment, theft, and murder. Rowling believes her books are "profoundly moral books."[1] Indeed, she even introduces the concept of morality tales in the series when she has Ron and Hermione talk about children's stories that convey morality lessons in *The Deathly Hallows*. After Harry, Ron, and Hermione read "The Tale of the Three Brothers" in *The Tales of Beedle the Bard*, Ron says,

> [T]hat story's just one of those things you tell kids to teach them lessons, isn't it? 'Don't go looking for trouble, don't pick fights, don't go messing around with stuff that's best left alone! Just keep your head down, mind your own business, and you'll be okay.'

Hermione agrees, "I think you're right, ... It's just a morality tale ..."[2] Like characters in morality tales, Rowling views Harry and his friends as good peo-

---

1. Neil Midgley, *ITV to Show Moment J.K. Rowling Finished Potter*, Telegraph (u.k.), July 15, 2007, http://www.telegraph.co.uk/news/uknews/1557330/ITV-to-show-moment-JK-Rowling-finished-Potter.html.

2. *Deathly Hallows* 414.

ple who have to make judgments when confronted with moral dilemmas.[3] Children perceive Harry and his friends as role models[4] and are challenged to explore social issues with them. When the characters exert their independence and form moral judgments, readers are asked to do the same. The very structure of the novels—each succeeding book is a year in Harry's life—encourages this kind of development. Under the ideological power of Rowling's words and the power of character association, the readers' concepts of morality, law, and justice develop as Harry and his peers grow up.

The focus of this essay is what the Harry Potter books teach children about morality and the law. Children learn moral lessons in different ways than adults, and the books provide a rich source of material to help them learn. The series also introduces children to concepts of legal offenses and defenses.

Author Ideology and Childhood Moral Development

Children's literature has an important influence on the development of moral reasoning in children. The ideology of the author impacts their moral development, but the effects differ depending on the age of the child. Writing a few years before the Harry Potter series began, Ian Ward examined children's literature in the legal context, focusing specifically on the role of the author's ideology.[5] Ward explains that to critics like Peter Hunt and Peter Hollindale children prove to be a receptive and impressionable audience, establishing a relationship where the author's words contain unquestioned power over the child. Hollindale stresses that it is within this context that children are exposed to explicit and passive ideology such as the social, moral, or political beliefs of the writer.[6]

---

3. *Today* (NBC television broadcast Oct. 14, 1999).

4. ELIZABETH D. SCHAFER, EXPLORING HARRY POTTER 237 (Beacham's Sourcebooks for Teaching Young Adult Fiction Series, 2000).

5. The following discussion, including many of the examples, is a summary of various sources, including IAN WARD, LAW AND LITERATURE: POSSIBILITIES AND PERSPECTIVES 90–118 (1995) and Lana A. Whited with M. Katherine Grimes, *What Would Harry Do? J.K. Rowling and Lawrence Kohlberg's Theories of Moral Development, in* THE IVORY TOWER AND HARRY POTTER: PERSPECTIVES ON A LITERARY PHENOMENON 182–208 (Lana A. Whited ed., 2004). Like all summaries, it is necessarily incomplete, and interested readers should consult these sources directly.

6. WARD, *supra* note 5, at 92; Peter Hollindale, *Ideology and the Children's Book*, 55 SIGNAL 3 (1988), *reprinted in* LITERATURE FOR CHILDREN: CONTEMPORARY CRITICISM 19, 27, 29–30 (Peter Hunt ed., 1992).

Ward gives an example of this power relationship between an author and children in Beatrix Potter's *The Tale of Peter Rabbit*. In the book, children are taught the moral that small rabbits, and by implication small children, should not commit theft and trespass to property. Children see Peter's interaction between the ordered safe world of adults, as represented by his mother's sandbank, and the disordered world of young animals, as represented by Mr. McGregor's garden. Children, identifying with Peter, see that when Peter ignores his mother's warning and disobeys her by going into Mr. McGregor's garden, he leaves a secure adult world and enters one filled with danger.[7] Young readers equate Peter Rabbit's crimes of theft and trespass to property with danger and learn the moral that if you enter someone else's land and take things, you are separated from the safe adult world and set into a more dangerous realm.[8] Beatrix Potter's moral ideology, as expressed in *Peter Rabbit*, therefore teaches young children that theft and trespass to property are wrong.

As children mature, the author's words still contain power, but this power is mediated by development of the child's own moral judgment and sense of justice. Ward's analysis relies on the work of Jean Piaget and Nicholas Tucker.[9] For Piaget (and Tucker, who follows him), there are three periods of development in a child's sense of justice. Until about age eight, the child's sense of justice is "subordinated to adult authority."[10] Justice at this stage is not distinguished from the authority of law. The child is told what is "just" by the adult authority in the text.[11] Thus, in *Peter Rabbit*, justice is indistinguishable from the warnings of the adult authority (Peter's mother)—bad consequences (losing his coat, getting sick) justly result from disobeying authority. Around the age of eight, children reach Piaget's second stage of moral development. They obtain a crude sense of "progressive equalitarianism,"[12] developing a sense that jus-

---

7. WARD, *supra* note 5, at 99–100; *see generally* BEATRIX POTTER, THE TALE OF PETER RABBIT (2002). In the book, Peter is warned not to go into the garden, where his father had apparently met with an unfortunate accident, but does so anyway. He eats some vegetables, is chased and terrified by the farmer, loses his new coat, barely manages to escape, and returns home too ill to enjoy the nice supper his mother made him and is forced to drink camomile tea.

8. WARD, *supra* note 5, at 100; *see generally* POTTER, *supra* note 7.

9. *See* JEAN PIAGET, THE MORAL JUDGMENT OF THE CHILD (Marjorie Gabain trans., 1965); NICHOLAS TUCKER, THE CHILD AND THE BOOK: A PSYCHOLOGICAL AND LITERARY EXPLORATION (1981).

10. WARD, *supra* note 5, at 95; PIAGET, *supra* note 9, at 315.

11. PIAGET, *supra* note 9, at 284, 315.

12. WARD, *supra* note 5, at 95; PIAGET, *supra* note 9, at 315. Equalitarian (or "egalitarian") means "affirming, promoting, or characterized by belief in equal political, eco-

tice has to do with fairness and equality as they gain solidarity among themselves through social bonding and mutual respect.[13] This sense of justice begins to diverge at times from adult authority, although even at this stage children are still prepared to accept parental moral absolutes with little questioning.[14] When children reach adolescence around the age of eleven, they reach Piaget's third stage. Their sense of justice eventually becomes subtler as their equalitarianism is replaced by a concept of justice or "equity," in which children define equality through consideration of how each individual is situated.[15] At this stage, children can characterize justice or equity by establishing shades of equality.[16]

Tucker used Piaget's stages to explore the question of how children respond to literature. Literature for children between seven and eleven reflects growth in a child's moral development away from the influence of adult authority figures and toward equity, because typically child characters in these stories exercise independence from adults and have the capability to form moral judgments. In the "Trial of the Jack of Hearts" and "Alice's Evidence" passages in *Alice's Adventures in Wonderland*,[17] for example, Ward shows that the child Alice has developed this sense of justice when she invokes the importance of and need for rules and declares that the trial and evidence are meaningless despite the authoritative commands of the adult Queen. At Piaget's third stage, Tucker suggests that children can think abstractly and make subjective moral judgments. Literature for this age group reflects this, demanding children to take responsibility for moral judgments and presenting them with moral issues. Within this context, children must develop their own concepts of law and justice based on their literary and social experience. Huck's dilemma in *The Adventures of Huckleberry Finn*[18] is a good example. Children share his

---

nomic, social, and civil rights for all people." THE AMERICAN HERITAGE DICTIONARY OF THE ENGLISH LANGUAGE 588, 621 (3d ed. 1992).

13. WARD, *supra* note 5, at 95, 97; PIAGET, *supra* note 9 at 294.

14. WARD, *supra* note 5, at 97.

15. PIAGET, *supra* note 9, at 285, 317.

16. *Id.*

17. *See generally* LEWIS CARROLL, ALICE'S ADVENTURES IN WONDERLAND (Books of Wonder 1992) (1866) (Ward's references correspond to the trial of the Knave of Hearts in the chapters "Who Stole the Tarts?" and "Alice's Evidence" in this edition).

18. In the book, Huck runs away from home and meets Jim, a runaway slave. To prevent Jim's capture and return to his master, the two decide to raft down the Mississippi. Along the way, Huck confronts a variety of attitudes about slavery and must make decisions about whether to help Jim or turn him in. *See generally* MARK TWAIN, THE ADVENTURES OF HUCKLEBERRY FINN (Bantam Classic ed., Bantam Books 1981) (1884).

journey of self-discovery in which he has to make his own moral and legal decisions as he floats down the river. Huck must decide on his own rules and determine the rightness of his own actions. Both he and the reader confront ideas of racism and equality and must take responsibility for their own moral judgments.

Child learning theorist Lawrence Kohlberg's work has already been explored in the Harry Potter context by Lana A. Whited and M. Katherine Grimes.[19] Kohlberg identified three levels of development and each of his levels has two stages. Whited and Grimes use examples from the Harry Potter books to illustrate them. Kohlberg's first level, for example, is the Preconventional. This level has the stages Punishment and Obedience and Instrumental Exchange, which roughly correspond to "stick" and "carrot." In the first stage, children learn to do what older children and adults expect of them simply to escape punishment. They develop a "might makes right" attitude. Draco Malfoy is an example of someone who routinely operates at this stage. Harry's son James behaves at this stage as well. He taunts his younger brother saying he might be put into Slytherin House, until he "ca[tches] his mother's eye and f[alls] silent."[20]

In the second stage, children's actions are motivated by "carrots" or the benefits they hope to get, and they begin to feel notions of fairness. Dudley Dursley is a good example because his behavior, good and bad, is directed at getting rewards from others. Children under nine are those most likely to be reasoning at the Preconventional level, but older children and even adults (like Wormtail) can and do operate at this level of moral reasoning.

At the Conventional level—around ages nine to eleven—children's awareness of social expectations and morality increase and they comport themselves with the standards surrounding them. In the Harry Potter series, young wizards begin studying at Hogwarts when they are eleven and presumably nearing the Conventional level. Before they begin school at Hogwarts, a young Snape explains the wizarding world to Lily. He says, "the Ministry can punish you if you do magic outside school, you get letters." Lily is worried by his revelation and says, "But I *have* done magic outside school!" Snape comforts her by explaining, "We're all right. We haven't got wands yet. They let you off when you're a kid and you can't help it. But once you're eleven, … and they start training you, then you've got to go careful."[21] Snape is explaining to Lily that

19. Whited & Grimes, *supra* note 5. The description of Kohlberg's work and the examples that follow in the next few paragraphs, excluding *The Deathly Hallows* references, are taken from Whited and Grimes.

20. *Deathly Hallows* 754.

21. *Deathly Hallows* 666.

eleven year old wizards are expected to comport themselves with the standards that will surround them at Hogwarts—behavior demonstrative of Kohlberg's Conventional level.

The Conventional level has two stages: Interpersonal Conformity and Social System and Conscience Maintenance. At the Interpersonal Conformity stage, children discover what actions are praiseworthy (as opposed to those that will get them material rewards) and behave accordingly. They are able to tell differences in motivation, and can understand the difference between intentional and accidental wrongs. They can put themselves in other people's shoes. Interpersonal relationships are very important. Demonstrations of loyalty are often a clear indication that someone is operating in this moral reasoning stage. A young Lily demonstrates the Interpersonal Conformity stage in *The Deathly Hallows*. When her sister Petunia insults a young Snape, he gets angry and makes a tree branch fall on Petunia. Lily confronts Snape and asks, "Did you make that happen?" Snape says no, but Lily doesn't believe him and runs after her sister. Lily is able to differentiate between intentional and accidental wrongs, and she shows her loyalty to her sister by running after her because she was intentionally hurt.[22] Ron Weasley is another good example of a character in this stage of development. Ron's actions are driven by the expectations of, and his loyalty to, his friends and family, together with the general social conventions of wizard society. Ron can show great loyalty to Hermione, for example, but is unable to shake off society's social norms through the majority of the books when she campaigns for house-elf rights. Some adults remain at this stage, like Vernon Dursley, who can never stop worrying about what other people think of him. At the Social System and Conscience Maintenance stage of the Conventional level, children gain a strong belief in citizenship. They internalize the idea that acting according to society's rules and laws will promote order and harmony. People in this stage have moved past dependence on interpersonal relationships and consider social abstractions. Percy Weasley, with his love of rules and his need to protect them throughout the books even against the wishes of his own family, is a good example. At this stage children can also begin to see conflicts between rules and make decisions on which ones apply.

Most adults and some teens will reach the stages of Kohlberg's Postconventional level. At this level, people are disposed to break rules when a higher principle is at stake. In the Prior Rights and Social Contract stage, they see laws and rules as formed by mutual agreement for the common benefit. When rules and laws become unreasonable or unjust, they believe that they do not

---

22. *Deathly Hallows* 668.

need to be followed. Dumbledore is the prime example here. Harry and his friends learn from Dumbledore that rules sometimes should be broken, as when he tells Harry and Hermione to use the Time-Turner to save innocent lives, even though this is strictly against the law. Hermione often operates at this level, too, in her willingness to challenge wizard rules on house-elves and to brew up an illegal Polyjuice Potion to try to find out who is endangering students at Hogwarts. She routinely stands up to ridicule, even from her friends, and in *The Order of the Phoenix* is the only one of the group who treats Kreacher kindly.

Harry, Ron, and Hermione all act at the Postconventional level in *The Deathly Hallows*. When the Ministry of Magic is infiltrated by Death Eaters, they drop out of school to search for Horcruxes even though the Ministry has made attendance at Hogwarts compulsory.[23] Using Polyjuice Potion to impersonate Ministry workers, they break into the Ministry to steal a Horcrux from Dolores Umbridge. During the course of the theft, they Stupefy Umbridge and another examiner, release the accused Muggle-borns, and help them escape, urging them to go into hiding.[24]

Few individuals will reach Kohlberg's final Universal Ethical Principles stage, in which some moral truths are perceived as absolute and inviolable. Harry acts at this stage throughout *The Deathly Hallows*. Early in the book, Stan Shunpike is one of a group of wizards who attack Harry and his friends as they leave the Dursleys, but Harry refuses to do more than disarm Stan once he realizes Stan was Imperiused. Although Harry is warned that failing to kill or stun his attackers may have given him away to them during the escape, Harry says he "won't blast people out of [his] way just because they're there, ... That's Voldemort's job."[25] If Harry had stunned Stan while he was under the Imperius spell, he would have fallen off his broomstick to his death. Harry shows he will not kill because murder is an absolute wrong. Harry also refuses to kill in his final battle with Voldemort. Voldemort uses the *Avada Kedavra* curse on Harry but Harry counters with Expelliarmus, a disarming spell.[26]

Understanding the three levels and six stages of moral development is important to nurturing moral children. Kohlberg argued that to move up the stages, children need the opportunity to talk about moral conflict, look at alternative resolutions, and discuss the consequences of each. They need the opportunity to role-play different perspectives and viewpoints and realize that

---

23. *Deathly Hallows* 210.
24. *Deathly Hallows* 261–267.
25. *Deathly Hallows* 71.
26. *Deathly Hallows* 743.

one does not always operate at the same moral level. Finally, they need a just community around them, since children living in a just community will progress through the moral development stages faster than other children.

As Whited and Grimes show, the Harry Potter books allow young readers to experience all three of these opportunities. Children see examples of moral decision-making when Harry and his friends talk through moral conflicts, and they can talk to their friends about the actions of the characters and examine the moral conflicts. They can role-play different characters and see how the characters' viewpoints influence their own viewpoints. As children read about the reactions of members of the just community of Hogwarts when it is threatened, they see examples of social justice. Through these experiences, children are encouraged to move up the levels of moral development as they associate with Harry and the other characters.

How Harry Potter Teaches Children Moral and Legal Lessons

Ideology and ideas of justice permeate the Harry Potter stories. Children are exposed to Rowling's social and moral beliefs through the explicit and passive ideology expressed in the books. Though the series appeals to both adults and children,[27] it is written mainly for children aged eight and up.[28] As such, the stories impact the development of moral judgment and the concepts of law and justice among readers of this age group. Children identify with Harry and his friends. As they read about their exploits they are exposed to moral lessons, to legal situations, and to the interplay of law and morality. When, for example, Harry and his friends contemplate the potential consequences of stealing Polyjuice Potion ingredients, or when Harry is devastated after witnessing the murders of Cedric, Sirius, and Dumbledore, children see the impact these events have on Harry. Through their association with Harry, children learn lessons about morality and law—and the differences between them—and are helped to develop their own moral sense. Lessons are shown by examples from both tort and criminal law.

27. Stephen McGinty, *Pottermania*, SUN. TIMES (London), Oct. 17, 1999, *available at* LEXIS, News library, TTIMES file; SCHAFER, *supra* note 4, at 13.

28. Michael Winerip, *Harry Potter and the Sorcerer's Stone*, N.Y. TIMES BOOK REV., Feb. 14, 1999, at 26 (book review). All of the books in the series were reviewed in the N.Y. TIMES in the children's books section. The books are recommended for ages 8 and up.

Tort Law

Tort law is that part of the legal system that governs private harm to persons or property caused by another. It includes intentional torts like battery, trespass, false imprisonment, defamation, and fraud, along with unintentional torts like negligence, malpractice, and products liability. The remedy for a tort is not a criminal prosecution, but a civil lawsuit brought by the victim. The Harry Potter books are full of torts. Watching Harry and his friends, children learn that actions that amount to torts are wrong, unless there is a legitimate justification.

Lesson 1: It is wrong to intentionally cause harm to someone.

Intentionally making harmful or offensive contact with another person without consent is the tort of battery.[29] Putting someone in imminent fear of such harm is the tort of assault.[30] Early in the first book, *The Sorcerer's Stone*, Harry encounters the poltergeist Peeves, who swoops down at the first year students with walking sticks, causing them to duck. This is an assault. When ordered away, Peeves vanishes and commits a battery by dropping the walking sticks onto Neville Longbottom's head. Children do not know that all the elements of a "battery" are present, but they can see that this is wrong. Peeves intended to harm Neville and did in fact harm him. Peeves' actions are bad. By age eight children understand that it hurts to be hit with a stick, and bad to throw a stick at someone else. This is reinforced for children because Peeves' actions are not sanctioned by the adult authority figure. When Peeves threatens to hit the students with the walking sticks, Percy the prefect tells him to go away or he'll report Peeves' actions to the Bloody Baron—of whom Peeves is frightened. Both the readers' own understanding and the reaction of the authority figures in the book teach children that such an action is wrong.

In *The Order of the Phoenix* readers encounter battery again when Professor Umbridge gives Harry detention and has him write lines. Umbridge gives Harry a special quill and tells him to write, "*I must not tell lies.*" When Harry asks how many times he should write the line, she says, "Oh, as long as it takes for the message to *sink in.*"[31] Then he asks for ink and she tells him he won't need any. The horrifying reason he doesn't need ink becomes clear when Harry begins writing and the words appear in blood on the parchment and carved into the skin on the back of his hand. Umbridge's "rather special quill" is a blood

---

29. RESTATEMENT (SECOND) OF TORTS §§ 13, 18 (1965).
30. RESTATEMENT (SECOND) OF TORTS § 21 (1965).
31. *Order of the Phoenix* 266.

quill that extracts the writer's blood for ink and carves the written words into the writer's skin. Using the blood quill causes Harry searing pain and Umbridge is aware that it does, yet she has him write lines with it for hours every evening for more than a week. When Harry's detentions with Umbridge are finally over, the words are etched on the back of his hand permanently. Intentionally making harmful or offensive bodily contact with another person without consent is the tort of battery.[32] Umbridge intended for Harry to use the blood quill and his use of the quill causes him harm. The harm did not result from direct bodily contact but since Umbridge intended to inflict bodily harm on Harry and succeeded in doing so, the indirect contact may constitute battery.[33]

To make Umbridge's actions morally, and possibly legally, correct, she must have a reason for her actions that overrides the basic rule against hurting others. Teachers are privileged to apply reasonable force necessary for control, training or education of a child entrusted in their care.[34] Factors used to determine if a punishment is reasonable include whether the punishment is disproportionate to the offense, unnecessarily degrading, or likely to cause serious or permanent harm.[35] Readers know Harry's punishment is excessive and seriously harmful. Harry hides his hand from Ron and Hermione because he does not want to see their looks of horror when they discover his punishment. This signals to the reader that Harry feels degraded by the punishment. When Ron does see Harry's hand he looks sick and urges Harry to go to Professor McGonagall for help. Ron's reaction reinforces that it is wrong for a teacher to cause serious harm to a student even for disciplinary reasons. When Ron urges Harry to ask Professor McGonagall, an adult authority, for help it strengthens the reader's understanding that Umbridge's actions are not moral. Professor Umbridge's actions are not reasonable so she does not have privilege to discipline Harry with a blood quill and her actions may constitute a battery.

In *The Order of the Phoenix*, both Harry and his readers have matured in their sense of justice. In the scene with Peeves from *The Sorcerer's Stone*, Harry and his friends are brand new to Hogwarts. Their experiences with the school and magic compare to that of a young child. Like children at Kohlberg's Precon-

32. RESTATEMENT (SECOND) OF TORTS §§ 13, 18 (1965).
33. DAN B. DOBBS, THE LAW OF TORTS § 28 (2001 & Supp. 2008). Umbridge may also be liable to Harry for intentional infliction of emotional distress. One who by extreme and outrageous conduct intentionally causes severe emotional distress to another is subject to liability for such emotional distress, and if bodily harm to the other results from it, for such bodily harm. *See* RESTATEMENT (SECOND) OF TORTS § 46 (1965).
34. RESTATEMENT (SECOND) OF TORTS § 147 (1965).
35. RESTATEMENT (SECOND) OF TORTS § 150 (1965).

ventional level, Harry and his friends are learning how to behave in accordance with the expectations of the adults and the older students. They are given the rules and are told what is just by the adult authorities. Since Hogwarts is likewise new to the readers, they also are operating at this beginning level of moral maturation. Harry, Ron, and Hermione have all reached Kohlberg's Social System and Conscience Maintenance stage of the Conventional level in *The Order of the Phoenix*. They know that Professor's Umbridge's actions are wrong even though she is an adult authority figure at Hogwarts. By experiencing these scenes and reflecting their differences in resolution and morality, children are encouraged to develop their individual moral senses. Children may also learn a fundamental legal principal—breaking a rule can only be justified if there is a reason to break it that the law considers legitimate.

Lesson 2: It is wrong to lock people up who have not committed crimes.

Confining someone without his or her consent and without a lawful reason is the tort of false imprisonment.[36] Readers encounter false imprisonment in *The Chamber of Secrets* when Uncle Vernon learns that Harry is not permitted to use magic outside of school. To keep Harry from going back to Hogwarts, he tells Harry that he is locking him up, laughs maniacally and drags Harry to his room.

> The following morning, he paid a man to fit bars on Harry's window. He himself fitted a cat-flap in the bedroom door, so that small amounts of food could be pushed inside three times a day. They let Harry out to use the bathroom morning and evening. Otherwise, he was locked in his room around the clock.[37]

Uncle Vernon has committed the tort of false imprisonment. Readers understand that Uncle Vernon intended to confine Harry, that he succeeded, and that Harry was well aware of it. Uncle Vernon has no legitimate excuse.[38] Harry has not committed a crime, does not deserve any punishment, and is no danger to anyone. Child readers may never have heard the phrase "false impris-

---

36. False imprisonment does not require an actual prison—the confinement can by anywhere and can be accomplished by any number of means. The tort is committed when A intends to confine B within some boundaries set by A (thus, one can actually be confined outdoors), succeeds in confining B, and B is aware of the confinement. RESTATEMENT (SECOND) OF TORTS §35(1) (1965).

37. *Chamber of Secrets* 21–22.

38. Uncle Vernon might argue that as Harry's guardian he is privileged to apply reasonable force necessary for control of Harry. However, his claim would fail because his actions are unreasonable and degrading. See *infra* notes 34–35 and accompanying text.

onment," but they can sense that this is wrong through their association with Harry as a role model. Hagrid's reactions to the Dursleys in *The Sorcerer's Stone* strengthens this lesson since child readers already know that adults disapprove of the way Vernon and Petunia treat Harry. When, in *The Half-Blood Prince*, Dumbledore expresses his contempt and disapproval of the way the Dursleys have treated Harry, this lesson is again reinforced. Yet there is a very similar incident in *The Goblet of Fire*, when Hermione catches reporter Rita Skeeter, in her guise of a beetle, on a windowsill, and imprisons her in a jar with an Unbreakable Charm. Readers understand that Hermione deliberately confines Rita and even smiles at her as she buzzes angrily in the jar. Hermione enjoys Rita's confinement just as Uncle Vernon enjoyed locking up Harry. Her purpose is to stop Rita from lying about Harry; she will subsequently blackmail Rita into writing a favorable article about Harry for *The Quibbler*. Here we again have the classic elements of false imprisonment. No adult is around, however, to give readers an authoritative take on whether Hermione has acted morally in imprisoning Rita.

At this point in the books, Hermione is routinely operating at Kohlberg's Prior Rights and Social Contract stage. She thinks abstractly and makes her own moral judgments. She confronts Rita, who, Hermione learns, is an unregistered Animagus. This is illegal—it could send her to Azkaban—and she has also been forbidden by Dumbledore to be on the Hogwarts grounds where she is caught by Hermione. Rita is doing something wrong by eavesdropping on the conversations of others and has also, readers understand, consistently written horrible lies about Harry. This plainly offends Hermione's own moral code, although (as she subsequently confesses to Harry and Ron on the train) she knows she has no legal basis to keep Rita imprisoned in the jar.[39] She also knows she will have to release her, but she apparently is punishing Rita more for her lies and her sneaking than for the actual crime of being an unregistered Animagus—after all, she doesn't express disapproval of the fact that Sirius Black and James Potter were also unregistered Animagi, and she has no intention of turning Rita over to the police.

Readers see the contrast between Uncle Vernon's unjustified imprisonment of Harry and Hermione's treatment of Rita. Hermione's actions may or may not be correct, but readers experience the decision and its consequences through her experiences, and thus are encouraged to develop their own moral senses.

---

39. Hermione would be privileged to arrest Rita in certain circumstances without a warrant if Rita committed a criminal offense. For a list of those circumstances, *see generally* RESTATEMENT (SECOND) OF TORTS § 119 (1965).

Criminal Law

Crimes play a big role in the Harry Potter series, and the way child readers experience them through the books teaches them important lessons about justice.

Lesson 3: It is wrong to steal things.

Taking something that does not belong to you, without permission, and with intent to deprive the owner of it, is the crime of theft.[40] The second book in the series, *The Chamber of Secrets*, offers two examples of children who take things that do not belong to them.

When Harry and Ron miss the Hogwarts Express, they decide to take the Weasleys' enchanted car and fly it to Hogwarts.[41] Ron reasons that this is acceptable, because underage wizards can use magic if it is an emergency and because his parents can Apparate to get home. Yet Ron and Harry have committed theft because they took the car without permission and with intent to deprive the Weasleys of it. Ron may not have intended a permanent deprivation, but they crash the car and abandon it in the Forbidden Forest, which makes it, at best, very difficult to recover.[42] The question is whether Ron and Harry's actions are morally justified in this scene.

When Harry and Ron take the car, they are operating at Kohlberg's Social System and Conscience Maintenance stage. They are able to invoke one rule—that underage wizards may use magic if it is an emergency—to override both the general prohibition on underage magic and the rule against taking other people's property without permission. But the adult authorities quickly disabuse them of this notion. Professor McGonagall is angry, and points out that they could have sent an owl. When they explain things to Dumbledore, Harry is deeply affected by the disappointment in Dumbledore's voice and cannot look him in the eye. Though Ron and Harry get detention instead of being expelled for the theft, Dumbledore stresses that the offense was serious and that they will be expelled if they do something like this again. Mrs. Weasley piles on the adult disapproval with a Howler, and the boys later learn that their theft

---

40. Technically, the crime is committed when one "unlawfully takes, or exercises unlawful control over, movable property of another with purpose to deprive him thereof." MODEL PENAL CODE § 223.2(1) (1962).

41. This example is also used by Whited & Grimes, *supra* note 5.

42. Even if the taking did not amount to theft, Ron and Harry might also be guilty of a misdemeanor for using the car without the consent of the owners under the Model Penal Code's "Unauthorized Use of Automobiles and Other Vehicles." MODEL PENAL CODE § 223.9 (1962).

caused Mr. Weasley to be fined for bewitching the car and that Lucius Malfoy has called for his resignation from the Ministry. From all of this, child readers recognize that stealing other people's property is wrong.

Another theft is treated very differently in *The Chamber of Secrets*, however. Harry and his friends suspect that Draco may be "Slytherin's heir," and the one responsible for terrorizing the school. They decide the best way to find this out is for Harry and Ron to use Polyjuice Potion to assume the identities of Draco's henchmen, Crabbe and Goyle. They lack the ingredients, but they know that Professor Snape keeps them among his private stores in his office. They decide to steal them; Hermione offers to do the actual theft while Ron and Harry cause enough mayhem to keep Professor Snape busy.

Young readers are well aware that a theft has taken place. Indeed, Hermione admits as much when she says that she will "do the actual stealing." So does Harry when he admits that he would "rather face Slytherin's legendary monster than let Snape catch him robbing his office."[43] The ingredients belong to Snape. They have no permission to take them. They intend to deprive Snape of them permanently because they intend to use them, not return them. Children here are watching a straightforward theft. Both Harry and Hermione recognize that their actions are, at least to some extent, wrong. Both of them recognize that they can be expelled from Hogwarts if they are caught.

But the fact that adult authorities would disapprove does not end the matter. Hermione, Harry, and Ron are operating in Piaget's third period or Kohlberg's Prior Rights and Social Contract stage. They understand the social implications of their actions, but they make the subjective moral judgment to break the rules for the greater good of discovering the identity of Slytherin's heir and the location of the Chamber of Secrets in hopes of stopping the horrible attacks on students. They believe that the prevention of future attacks far outweighs the evil of the theft. They feel they are morally justified in breaking the rules by committing the lesser crime of theft to prevent the more serious crimes they fear. Under the law, this need may give Hermione, Ron, and Harry a defense to a prosecution for theft.[44] In the context of the stories, though, readers must use their own moral judgment to decide whether this greater good justifies the theft.

Children are exposed to contrasting moral lessons again in *The Half-Blood Prince* and *The Deathly Hallows*. In *The Half-Blood Prince*, Harry catches Mundungus Fletcher selling a silver goblet that he had taken from Sirius' house.

---

43. *Chamber of Secrets* 186.

44. They may be able to raise a necessity or choice of evils defense. For the parameters of this justification defense, *see generally* MODEL PENAL CODE § 3.02 (1962).

Readers know that a theft has occurred because Harry accuses him of the theft, pointing out the goblet's Black family crest. Harry's anger over the theft leads him to choke Mundungus as he tries to retrieve the goblet.[45] All of the elements for theft are present since Mundungus takes the goblet, depriving Harry of his rightful possession as Sirius' heir. Through their association with Harry, children see that the theft is wrong because Harry reacts angrily to the discovery. No justification is given for the theft. The wrongness of Mundungus' theft is later confirmed by the adult authority Dumbledore when he tells Harry Mundungus will be taking no more of Sirius' possessions. This lesson that it is wrong to steal is further enforced to readers through their association of theft with the evil Voldemort in the story. Children learn of Voldemort's thefts of the orphans' possessions, the locket, the Hufflepuff cup, and Uncle Morfin's ring, and witness the adult Dumbledore tell young Voldemort that "Thieving is not tolerated at Hogwarts."[46]

In contrast, children see again in *The Deathly Hallows* that some thefts may be morally justified. Harry, Ron, and Hermione make subjective moral judgments when they decide to break the rules by stealing Horcruxes. They are stealing to prevent the more violent, serious crimes Voldemort will commit if he is not stopped. Hermione justifies using a Summoning Charm to take the Horcrux books from Dumbledore's office because they need the books to understand the Horcruxes in order to defeat Voldemort. She explains that she did not steal the books, instead she borrowed them since "[t]hey were still library books, even if Dumbledore had taken them off the shelves. Anyway, if he *really* didn't want anyone to get at them, I'm sure he would have made it much harder to —"[47] Ron and Harry demonstrate their acceptance of Hermione's reasoning for the theft through their admiration of her actions. They continue stealing to stop Voldemort when they take the Horcrux locket from Umbridge and the Hufflepuff cup from the Gringotts vault.

If children are still in the early stages of moral development, the adult overtones of the car theft moral lesson, the reactions of Harry and Dumbledore to Mundungus' theft, along with Hermione, Ron, and Harry's own knowledge that taking the potion ingredients is wrong, may overshadow the greater good justification demonstrated by the characters. Readers who have reached the Prior Rights and Social Contract stage may believe Harry, Ron, and Hermione were justified in collecting the books and the Horcruxes. Regardless, children learn to recognize the elements of theft in these scenes. Through their identification with Hermione, Ron,

---

45. *Half-Blood Prince* 245–246.
46. *Half-Blood Prince* 273.
47. *Deathly Hallows* 101–102.

and Harry, readers will make their own moral judgments about the thefts, which will help them to develop their own sense of right and wrong.

Lesson 4: Killing people is wrong.

Under the law, a person commits murder if he or she purposely or knowingly causes the death of another human being.[48] One who tries to commit a crime is guilty of attempt to commit that crime if he or she performs an act in furtherance of the crime (more than mere preparation) with the intent to commit the crime.[49] Children are exposed to murder at the very beginning of *The Sorcerer's Stone*, when they learn that Voldemort killed Harry's parents and tried to kill Harry. Murder surfaces again when Harry tries to rescue the Stone. Voldemort, possessing the body of Professor Quirrell, knocks Harry down, tries to strangle him, and then attempts a killing curse. Here, neither Voldemort nor Quirrell is guilty of murder because Harry does not die. But readers are aware that there was attempted murder.

The adult authority Dumbledore reinforces that attempting to kill another is wrong. Readers see Dumbledore's reaction to Quirrell's attack, and understand that Harry's life is precious and that it would have been evil for Quirrell to take it. The attempted murder of Harry and Dumbledore's reaction to it impacts the child reader's sense of moral judgment, causing the reader to equate attempted murder with an action that is wrong.

There are many other instances of murder and attempted murder in the books. When Voldemort orders Wormtail to kill Cedric Diggory in *The Goblet of Fire*, the child reader is aware that this is wrong. When Wormtail, at Voldemort's direction, purposely casts the *Avada Kedavra* curse at Cedric, all parties, including the readers, know that this will kill him. Their sense that this was wrong is reinforced by the reactions of the good characters at Hogwarts—Harry, Dumbledore, and other role models suffer due to Cedric's death. Harry's reaction to the deaths of Sirius, Fred, and others, along with his refusal to cast deadly spells at Stan and Voldemort in the later books also impacts readers.

Taken together, these scenes send a strong message to children that murder is wrong, thereby impacting their moral development. By distinguishing between the elements of these scenes, children learn how to recognize and prove the elements of these murder offenses and gain a basic knowledge of these legal principles. Exceptions or defenses to murder are also presented in the series.

---

48. MODEL PENAL CODE §§ 210.1, 210.2 (1962).
49. *See generally* MODEL PENAL CODE § 5.01 (1962).

Children are exposed to the defense of others exception to murder[50] in *The Deathly Hallows*. When Bellatrix Lestrange narrowly misses killing Ginny while dueling Hermione, Ginny and Luna, a frightened Mrs. Weasley duels Bellatrix to the death, killing her in defense of her daughter. In the final book it is also revealed that Snape's killing of Dumbledore was potentially justified because Dumbledore requested it. Dumbledore knew he was going to die within the year from a curse. He preferred to die quickly and painlessly. He asked Snape to kill him if the time came so Draco Malfoy would not have to. Dumbledore's plea for a mercy killing, along with Harry's final acceptance of Dumbledore's death at Snape's hands, suggest to the child reader identifying with these characters that Dumbledore's death may be morally justified. Together with Mrs. Weasley's murdering of Bellatrix in defense of Ginny, children learn about potential defenses for the crime of murder.

Conclusion

Through the exploration of complex, fact-based situations, the Harry Potter books influence children's awareness of legal concepts of tort and criminal law. Children are led to make moral distinctions through their association with Harry, the moral development of the characters, and the ideological authority of the novels. Children are exposed to the kinds of actions that can lead to civil and criminal litigation, but they are not merely told authoritatively that such things are good or bad. Rather, they are encouraged to evolve in their sense of justice. Rowling's expression of ideology in the Harry Potter books actually goes far beyond this, imparting complex situations that lead children to consider social issues such as capital punishment, slavery, and racism.

The Harry Potter books help children follow Kohlberg's methods for encouraging moral development. Children can compare the differences in character morality in various scenes to gain insight into the messages that Rowling expresses on these topics. The books allow children a means of developing their own moral senses by their relationship to the characters and those characters' different views. It is not a mere question of good versus evil, since good

---

50. A person who may be justified in using force to protect themselves if threatened may use the same amount of force in protection of others. For the parameters of the defense of others defense, *see generally* MODEL PENAL CODE § 3.05 (1962).

characters often have differing views on important issues. Children recognize this disagreement and are compelled to make their own decisions about the issues. Through these complex situations, children learn important lessons about law, morality, and justice and they learn them by their own engagement and development.

Harry Potter and the Curse of Difference

Benjamin Loffredo

With hundreds of millions of copies already sold worldwide, J.K. Rowling's Harry Potter has become one of the most important cultural events of the late twentieth century. Indeed, looking back, an entire generation of young readers may soon be known as "Gen-HP"—the generation of Harry Potter. So it is not surprising that commentators have begun to think seriously about the books' message and the lessons that Rowling's audience might take from her story.[1] One important message that has not yet received complete attention is Rowling's treatment of "difference," those aspects of a person that set him or her apart from the dominant culture.[2] For Gen-HP, the issue of difference holds particular importance: Gen-HP increasingly must address questions about the role of diversity in a democratic culture. From gender to race, from national identity to disability, difference (and whether to embrace, reject, or ignore it) forms a part of today's political agenda.

How Harry Potter contributes to Gen-HP's understanding of difference is a topic worth exploring. Rowling's characters experience their difference in various ways: some are enslaved, and others are dominated; some try to camouflage their difference, and others seek separation from the dominant culture. Moreover, if at the beginning of the series Rowling explains the characters' differences as resulting exclusively from their birth and blood, by the end, she shows that an individual's decisions and actions can affect, and profoundly

---

1. *See, e.g.*, THE IVORY TOWER AND HARRY POTTER: PERSPECTIVES ON A LITERARY PHE-NOMENON (Lana A. Whited ed., 2002).

2. For example, discussions of race, gender, and class appear in Paul R. Joseph & Lynn E. Wolf, *The Law in* Harry Potter: *A System Not Even a Muggle Could Love*, 34 U. TOL. L. REV. 193, 198–200 (2003); William P. MacNeil, *"Kidlit" as "Law-and-Lit": Harry Potter and the Scales of Justice*, 14 LAW AND LIT. 545, 551–558 (2002).

change, the person. Looking at Rowling's treatment of difference thus offers important lessons that Gen-HP can take from the Harry Potter series.

Treatment of Difference

As in ours, Harry Potter's world is riddled by differences that cause conflict and distress. Wizards confront Muggles, humans confront non-humans (magical beasts including house-elves, giants, centaurs, and merpeople) and pureblood wizards confront the half-bloods and the Mudbloods, who have Muggle ancestry. The significance of these differences varies with the perspective of the viewer and the context in which the characters find themselves. The Dursleys, for example, believe that Harry's wizardry makes him "not normal,"[3] while young Tom Riddle believes that his innate (but not yet fully comprehended) wizardry makes him "special."[4] Many differences among the characters thus are a source of strife. However, as the series unfolds, Rowling emphasizes that differences also can connect individuals in significant and even loving ways.

Domination and Enslavement

For some characters, the fact that they are perceived as different leads to their domination and even enslavement by the dominant wizard culture. Readers of the Harry Potter books learn that the wizard world depends on a system of domination that enslaves diminutive magical creatures known as house-elves. Dobby, the first house-elf we meet, is dressed in nothing but a filthy pillowcase—lack of clothing is the mark of a house-elf's enslavement. House-elves keep their master's secrets; they lack physical or mental independence. In *The Chamber of Secrets*, when Dobby, attached to the Malfoy home, comes to warn Harry Potter of plots on his life—plots presumably emanating from the Malfoy home itself—Dobby punishes himself for this breach of confidence by repeatedly slamming his head against the oven. Later in the series, Kreacher explains to Harry that he was able to escape from the Inferi after Lord Voldemort had used him to test out his Horcrux defenses because Master Regulus had summoned him home:

> Harry: "How did you get away?"
> Kreacher: "Master Regulus told Kreacher to come back."

3. *Chamber of Secrets* 3.
4. *Half-Blood Prince* 276.

Harry: "I know—but how did you escape the Inferi?"
Kreacher did not seem to understand. "Master Regulus told Kreacher
to come back."
Harry: "I know, but—"
...
Kreacher: "The house-elf's highest law is his Master's bidding. Kreacher
was told to come home, so Kreacher came home...."[5]

Initially, Rowling suggests that only upper-class pure-bloods, living in "big old
manors and castles and places like that," own house-elves.[6] Later, however, we
learn that high-ranking Ministry of Magic bureaucrats, including Mr. Crouch,
own them, too. Indeed, all of the students at Hogwarts depend on house-elves
who work without pay or complaint. "I mean, you're not supposed to see them,
are you?" explains Nearly Headless Nick to Hermione. "That's the mark of a
good house-elf, isn't it, that you don't know it's there?"[7] In Rowling's world,
domination through enslavement offers one important way to regulate difference.

Isolation, Exile, and Separation

Differences among the characters also work to set groups apart in Rowling's story. In some instances, the dominant culture isolates those who are different, for example, forcing the giants to flee to the mountains and banishing
criminals to the Prison of Azkaban, which is on an island far out to sea. In
other instances, those who are regarded as different isolate themselves from
the dominant culture; for example, the centaurs live apart from the wizards
and refuse any contact with the human world.

Rowling's depiction of giants illustrates the use of isolation to separate those
who are different from the dominant wizard culture. To wizards, giants are
inferior beings, less than human. "They're just vicious," Ron explains to Harry,
"it's in their natures, they're like trolls ... they just like killing, everyone knows
that."[8] Hagrid's great secret is that he is not, as he pretends, a pure-blood wizard. He is not even pure human. In the wizarding world, giants are not to be
trusted: they worked with Voldemort aiding his rise to power and cannot control their brutal, bloodthirsty natures. Giants are the "other" of wizard society,
deserving to be killed by Aurors or banished into the mountains.

---

5. *Deathly Hallows* 194–95
6. *Chamber of Secrets* 29.
7. *Goblet of Fire* 182.
8. *Goblet of Fire* 430.

Similarly, Rowling shows the dominant wizard culture using the prison of Azkaban to isolate criminal-wizards from the rest of wizard society. Those who are sentenced to Azkaban find themselves exiled with no hope of rehabilitation or possibility of return. Locked up in a prison that is surrounded by "walls and water," the prisoners are also "all trapped inside their own heads, incapable of a single cheerful thought."[9] By the end of the series, Rowling frighteningly depicts the forced separation of Muggle-borns from pure-blood and half-blood wizards. It starts with the "Muggle-born Register," which requires every Muggle-born wizard to present him or herself to the Muggle-born Registration Commission. Muggle-born wizards are allowed a "hearing" in front of the Commission, but it seems they are always sentenced to Azkaban because it is impossible to prove that they did not "steal" their magic.

Some groups, however, such as centaurs, perceive themselves as different — special — and exclude themselves from the wizard world. Centaurs treat wizards as inferior creatures. They regard themselves as a race apart, and are proud of it. Living in the Forbidden Forest on the edge of the Hogwarts grounds, they make up an extremely insular and tightly knit society. They distrust humans and prefer to live without human interference of any kind. Indeed, they believe that if a centaur has contact with humans, he will become degraded, his purity violated. Firenze's decision in *The Order of the Phoenix* to join Hogwarts as a divination teacher threatens to cause his permanent exile from centaur society. In his fellow centaurs' view, there is no return for someone who has suffered such a disgrace. Like certain religious groups that live in isolation from the dominant culture, the dignity of the centaurs depends on their absolute separation from human society. The centaurs eventually join in the fight against Voldemort, but they hold back until the very end of the fray. Unable or unwilling to collaborate with wizards, the centaurs live in self-enforced isolation.

Passing, Covering, and Invisibility

Other characters deal with their difference by trying to pass for what they are not or by trying to make themselves invisible. When a person who would otherwise be perceived as different "passes," he makes an effort to assimilate into the dominant culture. Covering, an aspect of passing, means "to tone down a disfavored identity to fit into the mainstream."[10] Passing and covering

---

9. *Prisoner of Azkaban* 188.
10. Kenji Yoshino, Covering: The Hidden Assault on Our Civil Rights ix (2006).

render differences less visible; a feature that otherwise would define the person negatively in the eyes of the dominant culture is kept out of sight. Hagrid, son of a giant mother, lives in wizard society, but pretends to be a non-giant: Ron believes him to be the victim of a bad Engorgement Charm. Similarly, Madame Maxime refuses to acknowledge, even to Hagrid, that she is "'Alf-giant," claiming instead that she has "big bones."[11]

Harry's life with the Dursleys illustrates the technique of passing. His aunt and uncle, knowing of his magical nature, want to keep it a secret. Their biggest fear is that someone will find out about it. They force Harry to live in the cupboard under the stairs, placing him in the closet (literally and figuratively) to hide the secret that they do not want revealed to society. At the opening of *The Chamber of Secrets*, Harry promises the Dursleys, "I'll be in my room, making no noise and pretending I'm not there."[12] One of the most shocking moments in the books occurs in *The Order of the Phoenix* when dementors appear in Little Whinging and Harry must use magic to protect himself against assault. Not only must Harry reveal his wizardry, but his Muggle guardians must acknowledge its existence: "The furious pretense that Aunt Petunia had maintained all Harry's life—that there was no magic and no world other than the world she inhabited with Uncle Vernon—seemed to have fallen away."[13]

More broadly, wizards make themselves invisible (again, literally and figuratively) when they are physically present in Muggle society. Invisibility through "passing" is critical to wizards while they live in the Muggle world. Indeed, the major point of wizard government seems to be, as Hagrid explains, to "keep it from the Muggles that there's still witches an' wizards up an' down the country."[14] The Decree for the Restriction of Underage Wizardry prohibits all young wizards from performing magic in the Muggle world. The Knight Bus provides emergency transport to wizards who find themselves stranded in the Muggle world. And when wizards need to appear in the Muggle world, they attempt to dress like Muggles and to appear incognito, although (despite the aid of "Twenty-five Ways to Mingle with Muggles") they are sometimes unsuccessful.

Wizards take many other steps to prevent themselves from being seen by the Muggles. Most wizards live in very out of the way places. The Weasleys, for example, live in a huge, run-down house very far away from any Muggles.

---

11. *Goblet of Fire* 429.
12. *Chamber of Secrets* 6.
13. *Order of the Phoenix* 38.
14. *Sorcerer's Stone* 65. The practice seems to have a good deal of help from the Muggles themselves: "Bless them," says Mr. Weasley of the Muggles, "they'll go to any lengths to ignore magic, even if it's staring them in the face." *Chamber of Secrets* 38.

In *The Goblet of Fire*, Mrs. Weasley suggests that Harry send a letter to the Weasley house, but she says that she is not sure the Muggle postman even knows where it is. Similarly, in *The Chamber of Secrets,* when Mrs. Weasley learns that Ron and Harry have flown an illegally bewitched car halfway across the country, she seems as afraid that they might have been observed as that they might have suffered serious harm: "You could have *died*, you could have been *seen*, you could have lost your father his *job*."[15] In addition, many wizard facilities cannot be seen by Muggle eyes. The Hogwarts Express, for example, leaves from the invisible Platform 9¾ at King's Cross Station; the massive Ministry of Magic is entered by a shabby phone booth down an alley; and should any Muggle ever spy the location of Hogwarts, it would appear to be nothing more than a "moldering old ruin with a sign over the entrance saying 'DANGER, DO NOT ENTER, UNSAFE.'"[16] Similarly, every time Harry, Ron, and Hermione change locations while they are in hiding, they set up their tent and perform various charms around it. One of the charms is always *Repello Muggletu*.[17] The need to be invisible in Muggle society is a basic feature of wizard life. Indeed, the price for revealing a person's wizardry is high: when Tom Riddle, Sr., learns of his wife's magical powers, he abandons her and leaves her to shame and destitution.

Just as wizards use invisibility to protect themselves within the Muggle world, so Harry uses invisibility to protect himself within the wizard world. Harry wears the invisibility cloak to move around Hogwarts undetected, away from the eyes of even his fellow wizards. Because of his status as "The Boy Who Lived," Harry, in his way, is just as much an outsider in wizard society as wizards are in Muggle society. His invisibility cloak can be seen as a way of "covering" his differences. Just for a while, he can be not Harry Potter the hero, or the celebrity, or the boy who looks just like his father, but just Harry Potter himself. Conversely, the former followers of Lord Voldemort, now restored to wizard society, "cover" the mark that he had placed on their arms and that reappears as You-Know-Who begins to gather strength. In both instances, the person perceived to be different must disclaim difference in order to move freely within the dominant culture.

Confederation and Joint Action

Finally, the wizard world is itself divided among different wizard cultures: Gryffindor, Hufflepuff, Ravenclaw, and Slytherin are wizards who joined to-

---

15. *Chamber of Secrets* 33.
16. *Goblet of Fire* 166.
17. *Deathly Hallows* 272.

gether to establish the Hogwarts School. Each has a distinct personality and approach to magic. Although these four wizard-types do not seem to correspond to race or ethnicity in the Muggle sense, differences among them, in terms of temperament and skill, are relatively clear, as evidenced by the distinct cultures of the four Hogwarts houses. Students are not randomly assigned to the four houses and no effort is made to create diversity within them. Rather, the students are sorted on the basis of their differences:

> Said Slytherin, "We'll teach just those
> Whose ancestry is purest."
> Said Ravenclaw, "We'll teach those whose
> Intelligence is surest."
> Said Gryffindor, "We'll teach all those
> With brave deeds to their name,"
> Said Hufflepuff, "I'll teach the lot
> And treat them just the same."[18]

As co-founders of Hogwarts, the four wizards coexisted and created a magnificent school—until Lord Voldemort disrupted their cooperative venture. By Harry's fifth year, cooperation began to break down. The Sorting Hat warned that the four houses of Hogwarts "must unite inside her/Or we'll crumble from within."[19] After Voldemort thought he had killed Harry and captured Hogwarts, he told everyone that: "There will be no more Sorting at Hogwarts School. There will be no more Houses. The emblem, shield, and colors of my noble ancestor, Salazar Slytherin, will suffice for everyone."[20] Voldemort wanted to banish difference through terror and fear—all wizards were to conform to his wishes.

Concepts of Difference

Taken as a whole, the Harry Potter series reveals two competing accounts of difference. On the one hand, Rowling depicts a world in which a person's destiny is determined even before birth by "blood" and status. On the other hand, Rowling provides her characters with opportunities to grow and to make choices, especially choices that build on friendship and love. In an important sense, the wizards' world, like our own, reflects a tension between nature and nur-

18. *Order of the Phoenix* 205.
19. *Order of the Phoenix* 207.
20. *Deathly Hallows* 732.

ture: Rowling explores the importance of biological determinism and individual decision-making, ultimately rejecting "blood" as the end-all marker of difference.

At first, the Harry Potter saga may seem to describe a world in which every aspect of life is determined at birth. From the beginning, Harry seems marked by difference. Harry is special because of the family into which he is born, not because of his actions or choices. Harry thus illustrates the importance of genetics to the wizard world. Without the right parentage, a person cannot learn to be a wizard, regardless of how hard he tries. For this reason, the students of Hogwarts do not apply to the school; their names are written down at birth. Sadly, when as a child Petunia writes to Dumbledore to ask if she, like her sister Lily, can be admitted to Hogwarts, he has to reject her.[21]

The importance of genetic heritage does not apply only to humans. House-elves are born into slavery. Each house-elf (or perhaps even line of house-elves) must serve the same family, uphold its honor, and never speak ill of the master. Similarly, giants and centaurs are born into their category of difference—they possess traits that can be acquired only at birth and not through work or culture. Likewise, Harry learns, "Metamorphmagi are really rare, they're born, not made."[22] And as for dementors, it is simply "not in the nature of a dementor to understand pleading or excuses"—a trait that cannot be changed.[23]

Associating difference with biology generates a major narrative conflict: the distinction between pure-bloods and Mudbloods. Draco Malfoy stands for the view that biology denotes not only destiny, but also superiority. In his first meeting with Harry, Draco is certain that Hogwarts should not admit "the other sort," noting, "They're just not the same...."[24] By locating difference in "blood," Rowling gives the impression that an individual's qualities are fixed at birth so that the differences that distinguish individuals are permanent and unchanging.

Yet the major protagonists, including Hermione, Lord Voldemort, and Professor Snape, are not pure-bloods and have had to make choices for themselves about the role each will play in the wizard world. Indeed, human agency plays an increasingly important role in the series, suggesting that individuals have opportunities to change, to develop, and to transform. In Book One, Harry faces significant choices the minute he receives the invitation to attend Hogwarts and enrolls as a student. When Malfoy wants to be Harry's friend, telling him

21. *Deathly Hallows* 669–70.
22. *Order of the Phoenix* 52.
23. *Prisoner of Azkaban* 92.
24. *Sorcerer's Stone* 78.

that he ought to associate with the "right sort of people," Harry declines, favoring the less aristocratic, although pure-blood Ron. Even more significantly, as the Sorting Hat considers the house to which Harry should be assigned, Harry self-consciously rejects Slytherin, the house of those who speak in the tongues of snakes. By making decisions about who he is and what he must do, Harry frequently finds himself in conflict with rules that provide borders and define difference. Professor Snape frequently criticizes Harry for being "a law unto himself."[25] Harry faces detention because he is "out-of-bounds."[26] However, Harry is not alone in crossing boundaries. Hagrid overcomes the "essential" nature of a giant by being a kind and gentle guardian to the students he loves. James and Sirius, not wanting to isolate Lupin during his monthly werewolf transformations, keep him company as animals, undergoing their own transformations. And Tom Riddle "pushe[s] the boundaries of magic further" than any wizard has gone before, driven by his desire "to be different, separate, notorious."[27]

By the end of the series, Rowling provides numerous examples of characters who transform themselves in important ways through their decisions and actions. Neville Longbottom starts the series as a cowardly boy—he embarrasses even his grandmother. By the end, however, he has become a person who can stand up to the Death Eaters at Hogwarts and attack Voldemort head on. Indeed, even house-elves change, as illustrated by Kreacher's transformation after his decision to betray his master, Sirius Black. Dumbledore defends Kreacher against Harry's criticism, arguing that Kreacher "is what he has been made by wizards." Sadly, Dumbledore says, Sirius failed to treat Kreacher with "kindness and respect"—Sirius never "saw Kreacher as a being with feelings as acute as a human's."[28] The suggestion is that elf identity depends not only on birth, but also on social relations; the master's treatment can open up or close possibilities for change. Treated kindly by Harry, Kreacher vividly transforms: "Nothing in the room, however, was more dramatically different than the house-elf who now came hurrying toward Harry, dressed in a snowy-white towel, his ear hair as clean and fluffy as cotton wool, Regulus's locket bouncing on his thin chest."[29]

Ultimately, Rowling shows that an individual's identity does not build exclusively on birth and biology, but rather develops through choices, action,

25. *Prisoner of Azkaban* 284.
26. *Sorcerer's Stone* 242.
27. *Half-Blood Prince* 442, 277.
28. *Order of the Phoenix* 832.
29. *Deathly Hallows* 255.

and the courage to take stands. Albus Dumbledore, headmaster of Hogwarts, is the main character to articulate this view, repeatedly explaining in various ways the lesson that "it matters not what someone is born, but what they grow to be!"[30] Above all, Dumbledore emphasizes, Harry differs from Voldemort because he can act out of love. Harry's ability to love, Dumbledore says, "is a great and remarkable thing," given everything that has happened to him.[31] After Harry is "killed" by Voldemort, he has the choice to come back and fight or to move "on." Even though going back to fight means heading "back to pain and the fear of more loss," Harry chooses to return.[32] During the final confrontation, Harry suggests that Voldemort "try for some remorse" and offers him a chance to change. Voldemort chooses not to be remorseful and tries to kill Harry, but ends up killing himself.[33]

When the series opens, Harry's life seems to be entirely shaped at birth: he is the subject of a great prophecy and survives Voldemort's attack. Only later does Rowling reveal that it is Lily Potter's love and her own decisions as a mother that saved Harry, not his genetic code. Harry, says Dumbledore, is free to turn his back on the prophesy, even though it was carefully lodged and protected in the Ministry of Magic. Indeed, what distinguishes Harry and makes him different is not so much a set of genetic traits but rather actions that have created a relationship with Lord Voldemort. Harry is the Chosen One not because of his innate qualities, but because You-Know-Who deliberately marked him as his equal. Their wands share feathers from the same Phoenix. And in their hex and counter-hexes, they have exchanged power and thoughts. The difference that separates individuals also joins them together and opens up the possibility of shared survival or common death.

Conclusion

Harry Potter offers no classic tale of acceptance and tolerance. Indeed, the series may prove not to be a classic at all. But whatever the long-term fate of the books, Rowling's story provides a current and provocative look at the role of difference in a society that resembles our own in important ways. The wizard's world is not a utopian fantasy: it is a world complete with bigotry, violence, and hatred. Yet Rowling shows that despite our differences, we are

---

30. *Goblet of Fire* 708.
31. *Half-Blood Prince* 509.
32. *Deathly Hallows* 722.
33. *Deathly Hallows* 741–44.

connected in important ways. Regardless of the barriers we erect, the borders we build, and the boundaries we create, we cannot keep others at bay—we are linked together in a shared fate. Muggles lack magic, but they need not be slaves to destiny: like wizards, they can choose to effect positive change in themselves and in their collective life.

When Harry Met Martin: Imagination, Imagery and the Color Line

Benjamin G. Davis

I am a fan of the Harry Potter series, stories full of magic and mystery. I have enjoyed seeing the Harry Potter movies over the years. Yet even as I enjoy these films, I must admit that a shadow, almost like a Dementor, passes across my soul and saddens me.[1]

What Saddens Me?

That shadow is a complex feeling that is part frustration and part resignation with a state of affairs. Part of the difficulty comes from the perennial problem of translating a text into images. In text, the reader's imagination intersects with the author's effort to create a fantasy world. That fantasy world has aspects of what the author sought to do, but also draws on the reader's experiences as it is shaped in the Mind's Eye of the reader. This fantasy world is in large part the work of the reader's imagination.

When a film is made, the filmmakers must make choices, which result in only one version of the imagined story world being presented to us. Many of the aspects of the film may be familiar—hearkening back to what we remember in the written story—but the whole is different from that imagined world of the Mind's Eye. The work on the screen is the work of another (usually collective) imagination, and the choices made by the filmmaker inevitably reduces the ability of the viewer to participate in creating the world.[2]

---

1. This essay is based on the first four Harry Potter films: *The Sorcerer's Stone, The Chamber of Secrets, The Prisoner of Azkaban,* and *The Goblet of Fire.* At the time of this writing, the fifth film, *The Order of the Phoenix,* was still in production.

2. This theme is explored in RUDOLF ARNHEIM, FILM AS ART (Univ. of Calif. Press ed. 2006) (1957).

My sadness is occasioned by the tension between what I imagine the films could be and what the actual films tell me about limits. Put simply, my pleasure in watching the first four Harry Potter movies is tempered somewhat by the perfunctory presence of people of color. None of the Hogwarts professors, none of the principal characters, and none of even the secondary characters are people of color. Now one might think that this is not surprising at an elitist boarding school such as Hogwarts, but it is clear that there are students of color at Hogwarts. They are just passive ciphers in a world where all the action happens among a group of Caucasians.

It seemed to me that in the third film, *The Prisoner of Azkaban*, there was some self-conscious recognition of this curious state of affairs. One black student finally had a couple of lines and a chance to do more than mug and be more than background. This uncomfortable state of affairs appeared to also be addressed in *The Goblet of Fire*, as Harry had a brief love interest with an East Asian looking young lady (Cho Chang), and Harry invites one of two South Asian twins to the dance. Yet, in many ways the stilted and self-conscious nature of these scenes confirms more than goes against the essential whiteness of the film series.

Universal Pretensions, but Old Marginalizing Hierarchies

While being white is not a bad thing, it saddens me that in 2006 I would see a movie with universal pretensions, one that speaks to the imaginations of so many different types of people around the world, and yet wonder again why the people of color are so marginalized. For example, the South Asian twins Parvati and Padma Patil, dressed in saris, walk through the film saying hello to Harry in *The Goblet of Fire*. When Harry and Ron, as a defensive reaction to Hermione's being "taken" by the potent Viktor Krum, reach out to these twins, inviting them to the dance, the question of their acceptance is a foregone conclusion, not even worth filming. They are to be compliant South Asian women—a caricature, really. Yet, at the dance, all the sexual tension in these scenes is among Hermione, Harry, and Ron. Hermione comes down the stairs as some beautiful goddess—as one of the twins, as if to further subjugate herself, is made to state. Hermione also complains about Ron's lack of courage in asking her to the dance. The South Asian twins, meanwhile, sit sexless with Harry and Ron. The boys are passive in reaction to these beautiful twins. They are not even willing to engage with them in the stylized sexual ritual of dancing. The South Asian twins appear as almost servants at the beck and call of these two white males, waiting patiently to humor their masters. One senses that the South Asian twins are being used and, after a time, we realize, along with them, that they *have* been used. But the twins' frustration with Harry and Ron is marginalized; the story goes on without any further reference to them or that date. They were vehicles to advance a plot and not characters—in short, people of color as ciphers.

Another interesting scene in the same movie is Harry's brief flirtation on the parapet with the young East Asian Cho. Her regret at not being able to accept Harry's invitation to dance as well as Harry's frustration at the rejection remind us of largely repressed taboos regarding consorting with people of a different color. On still another color line scene, one of the Weasley brothers' casual invitation to Angelina Johnson, a beautiful black student, and her willing and rapid acceptance evokes white male potency and black female subservience in an almost nineteenth century slave tableau.

I hope that this tableau does not appear too negative towards the Harry Potter films. In one sense, the four films actually demonstrate some racial progress, as they at least show students of diverse backgrounds. Compared to the 1950s English books and films I saw in Nigeria in the late 1960s on television (*Biggles* comes to mind),[3] it is significant that the Harry Potter films show so much integration of an elitist institution like Hogwarts. This progress can be measured in particular when one notes that the ghosts and pictures that talk on the walls (presumably coming from an earlier era) are all images of white people in contrast with the many hues of the students. And, when one compares the Harry Potter series of movies with other recent movies of fantasy such as the trilogy of the Lord of the Rings[4] or Narnia,[5] it still has the distinct virtue of having an integrated cast even if all the people of color are relegated to ciphers. At least people of color are in Harry Potter in virtuous roles as opposed to being dark non-humans (orcs), wordless elephant drivers of some nondescript darker skinned hue, and faceless dark knights.

Harry Potter, Narnia and Lord of the Rings have in common that they are a form of childhood fantasy, each pulled from part of the collective unconscious and projected into the modern world. And in that process of transpo-

---

3. BIGGLES (Granada Television 1960). The series was based on the popular series of adventure novels by Capt. W.E. Johns that featured ace pilot Major James Bigglesworth.

4. The trilogy of films is THE LORD OF THE RINGS: THE FELLOWSHIP OF THE RING (New Line Cinema 2001); THE LORD OF THE RINGS: THE TWO TOWERS (New Line Cinema 2002), THE LORD OF THE RINGS: THE RETURN OF THE KING (New Line Cinema 2003).

5. CHRONICLES OF NARNIA: THE LION, THE WITCH, AND THE WARDROBE (Walt Disney Co. 2005).

sition, as we proceed through the twenty-first century, it pains me that the imagery used in each seems to draw a sharp line on the basis of color. In these areas of fantasy, persons of color cannot either play key roles (as in Harry Potter or a little bit in Narnia) or even exist on the side of the good (Lord of the Rings).

Now, in my Mind's Eye in my imagination, I can do fantasy in Technicolor. I dream the images in ways that reflect my personal history. Taking characters at will, I might say that both *The Wizard of Oz*[6] and *The Wiz*[7] are two sides of the same complex coin—appropriate a story to fit an all-white or an all-black world, the product of a segregated imagination. But, Munchkins do not have to be any particular color, they need only be short. Maybe, when image meets imagination in a future time, we will see a Rainbow Wizard.

In my Mind's Eye, when I read about the Men of the West, the elves, the dwarves, and the hobbits of The Lord of the Rings they are not all white, they are magical in different hues. Bilbo might have South Asian features and Frodo have more Middle-Eastern features. Elves would come in many hues, as would dwarves. Heroic Men of the West can, in my imagination, include not only Viggo Mortensen but also Danny Glover, much as the cowboys in *Silverado*,[8] where Glover and Kevin Costner are both good guys. Battles with evil would not all be scenes where black dragon's heads are lopped off like the ends of protean and dangerous black phalluses. When I read the Harry Potter books, I give the characters features from my own imagination. As I watch the Harry Potter films, I think that while it is nice to have so many people of color get work, it is a shame that none of them has been allowed to have a meaningful role.

We can contrast this with the state of affairs at the time of *Star Wars* in 1977.[9] "A long time ago in a galaxy far away" was nevertheless understood as a film about the future, and one of the outcries was that this was a future with no black people in it. As a result of that outcry, Lando Calrissian (played by Billy Dee Williams) was introduced in the second film to integrate the heroes.[10] While the debate about Jar Jar Binks in *Star Wars Episode I*[11] is something for the ages,[12] we nevertheless see Samuel L. Jackson as a Jedi Knight, and, in

---

6. THE WIZARD OF OZ (Metro-Goldwyn-Mayer 1939).

7. THE WIZ (Universal Pictures 1978).

8. SILVERADO (Columbia Pictures 1985).

9. STAR WARS (20th Century Fox Films 1977).

10. It is interesting that Williams had auditioned for the role of Han Solo in the original film, but was rejected in favor of the largely unknown white actor Harrison Ford.

11. STAR WARS EPISODE I: THE PHANTOM MENACE (20th Century Fox Films 1999).

12. Was he a Jamaican minstrel caricature? George Lucas, please say it ain't so.

Episode III, the Surinamese/Puerto Rican actor Jimmy Smits plays a key role as the adoptive father of the baby Princess Leia.[13]

Outcry of the kind that led to those additions is not the type of reaction one sees today. The absolute silence about the color line in the Lord of the Rings, Narnia, and Harry Potter is perplexing. One must keep in mind that in all of these works, the heroes and heroines may, in the imagination of the reader, resemble the reader whatever his or her color, whatever his or her location. Thus, to then come to the silver screen and see this line of demarcation between people of color and whites is a strange anachronism. Can anyone save us from this state of affairs?

Calling on Martin

Well if not Harry, maybe Dr. Martin Luther King, Jr., can help us re-de-segregate our imagination through non-violent action. For when one goes back and reads Martin, one is struck not only by his focus on non-discrimination (judgment on content of character, not color of skin) but on his insistence on a social vision of integration.[14] One compares the promise of what Martin wanted with these films of childhood fantasy and it becomes clear that Martin's call for civil disobedience gently urges us to go beyond memories of imagery of the civil rights struggles. We are called to integrate more than our workplaces and schools. We must integrate our fantasies and the projections of our fantasies that we see on the silver screen. In the dynamic integration of Martin's vision, all of the children play key roles, not just those of one group. The professors come from diverse backgrounds not just one. In Martin's vision, even the evil is multi-hued, not just dark.

---

13. Star Wars Episode III: Revenge of the Sith (20th Century Fox Films 2005).

14. "Therefore, every Christian is confronted with the basic responsibility of working courageously for a non-segregated society." *For All ... A Non-Segregated Society, A Message for Race Relations Sunday, February 10, 1957, New York, New York, reprinted in* 1 The Papers of Martin Luther King, Jr. 124 (2000). I encourage all to read the papers to see the breadth and depth of the King vision. *See also A Call to Conscience, in* The Landmark Speeches of Dr. Martin Luther King, Jr. 193 (Clayborne Carson & Kris Shepard eds., 2005) ("I want to say to you as I move to my conclusion, as we talk about 'Where do we go from here?' that we must honestly face the fact that the movement must address itself to the question of restructuring the whole of American society."); *We Chose as our Motto: "To save the soul of America," in* The Trumpet of Conscience 24, *reprinted in* The Wisdom of Martin Luther King. Jr. (1993).

Martin calls us to move beyond perfunctory integration in the most elite places and get to a world where each of us can see ourselves played in many roles. If we were to redo the Harry Potter films in line with such a vision, maybe Harry Potter could have Asian features and Dumbledore would be a tall woman and Professor Lupin could be of Hispanic origin. Professor Snape might be being played by Spike Lee. Sirius Black might be seriously black.[15] As to He-Who-Must-Not-Be-Named, would it be too much poetic license to have it be "She"?[16]

As I attempt to imagine these integrated scenes it occurs to me that what is suggested is a willingness to move away from constricted production values to what must be considered a more daring vision. That this lack of daring is the hallmark—at least in regard to the color line—of these childhood fantasy films also suggests to us where we still need to go in integration. Put another way, we must take these works as literature that spurs the imagination of many different persons. These stories encourage us to dream fantasies, and Martin's vision encourages us to believe we are and can be the hero or heroine—no one is relegated by color to the role of a cipher.

But, as I write this I hear a voice saying to me, "Be realistic." The people who write these books and make these films are thinking about what will yield the greatest revenue, and the movies demonstrate that the wisdom tells those who do these movies that when we move into this area of fantasy the people of color should be relegated to minor roles. In this area of fantasy, it seems at least to me that subservient people of color or (put another way) principal characters who are all white people may be seen to sell more books and movie tickets. Woe to him or her who would question that hierarchy.

Yet, the magic of imagination is that imagination is *internal*. Fealty to the hierarchy constricts that imagination. Surely the essence of what Martin wanted for us was to unchain our thoughts and free our minds. And where is it more important to free a mind, than when a child is engaged in fantasy? We must strive to keep children from feeling that their places are in the back of the scene, just as it used to be in the back of the bus. Each child should be able to feel that his or her place is in the front or in the back, depending on the time and the place. It is that freedom to float from center stage out to the far reaches and back that is Martin's freedom. The child can be heroic or craven, brave or fearful. The child should not feel trapped in one of these roles or—even more painfully—made invisible and thus irrelevant to the story line.

15. Though it might raise other issues if Black, the "Prisoner of Azkaban," were black, because of the disproportionate number of black men incarcerated (many just as unjustly as Sirius Black) in the United States.

16. A tip of the hat to RUMPOLE OF THE BAILEY (Thames Television 1978–1992).

Perhaps our key question for this context is whether the story line reinterprets or reinforces the color line. Harry Potter reinterprets reality in a fantasy world, yet the films reinforce a color line, as do the other films mentioned here. As we await new films, we have hope for a breaking of these taboos. There will be something of a Lando Calrissian moment in *The Order of the Phoenix*, when Jamaican actor George Harris plays Kingsley Shacklebolt, a character who at least has some role to play—but he is a much less important character than was Lando.

Yet, even as I call for heeding Martin's energy and urge to action, I find his noble sentiments betrayed by the fact that I find myself needing to write them. Does the reader understand my dilemma? Here I have grown through fifty years of life having been an avid reader of many fantasies and an absolute addict for films that depict fantasy worlds, alternative universes, magic, and so on. Yet, even with all that stimulating diversity of film-making and story writing, I see, like glint on Excalibur, that color may again be made to play its old role. Like an old wound, it gets rubbed every time—a reminder to "remember your place."

In this context, one senses that the kind of dynamic integration vision that Martin stood for is beyond the ken. Heroic Supreme Court decisions today are the modest *Grutter*[17] (it could have been worse) and not something stronger, more emphatic and unanimous. Today, 5–4 votes replace 9–0.[18] Efforts are being made to not merely to turn back the clock, but to break it and, it seems, just turn back time. Harry reflects this vision to some extent. His pedigree within Hogwarts assures him a role that no other student—let alone a student of color—could aspire to. He is of Hogwarts, but one feels that the images of his parents (as in his battle with Lord Voldemort in *The Goblet of Fire*) mark his face much as does his scar, always changing the reactions of those around him. Lupin speaks of seeing in Harry his father's qualities and his mother's eyes in *The Prisoner of Azkaban*. Harry is a child of royalty on his path to take his "rightful" place in a hierarchy that preordains his place at the front. He is an anointed one, like a child Neo of the Matrix trilogy.[19] Ron plays the loyal working class friend, a Pauper to Prince Harry, whose own status is

---

17. Grutter v. Bollinger, 539 U.S. 306 (2003). The U.S. Supreme Court held, by a 5–4 vote, that it was not unconstitutional for the University of Michigan's law school to take race into account when admitting applicants.

18. The most famous desegregation cases, Brown v. Board of Education of Topeka, 347 U.S. 483 (1954), was a 9–0 decision by the U.S. Supreme Court.

19. The Matrix (Warner Bros. 1999); The Matrix Reloaded (Warner Bros. 2003); The Matrix Revolutions (Warner Bros. 2003).

raised simply by being associated with Harry. Hermione's intelligence, like her mane of hair tells us she too is a dominant person to whom all should pay homage—she will be a Queen to Harry or Ron.

Unhobbling Harry Potter

Yet, by mixing Harry and Martin we can actually free Harry's mind. Harry's professors need not only be wizards of one rich tradition, but they can be drawn from multihued traditions. Wizards of Chinese, Indian, Ghanaian, Jamaican, Haitian, Brazilian, Mexican, and Native American traditions could spread the breadth of his knowledge. Lord Voldemort is not simply a British phenomenon, but a vast evil force that has been seen in many places in many times. Surely, Harry's magic would be strengthened in his conflict with Voldemort if he could draw from these many traditions. And, with professors of those diverse traditions, surely Hogwarts becomes something beyond an English boarding school and emerges as an international center where students of traditions around the world would come together and learn all of the arts— dark, light, red, green or yellow.

In this international magic center, the traditions that have made Hogwarts such a wonderful place would be enhanced by the opening of the school to the world. Already, with *The Goblet of Fire*, the French and the Russians[20] appear to have been recognized in an effort to expand the story out from England to the world. Yet, even that is really only a small step; French and Russians are only a very narrow slice of the richness of the world's multihued experience.

Harry is the best of Hogwarts. Just imagine how he would grow if he were exposed to the best of all these traditions of wizardry. But, even in exposing him to this broad world of wizardry, we must guard against a threat. The threat is that with Harry's majestic rise, he would use this knowledge to make Hogwarts dominate all centers as opposed to Hogwarts being a source of inspiration for the work of all centers. One can imagine Harry—like some Robert Clive leaving London for India—sending back riches to Hogwarts from the antipodes, allowing the school to amass wealth and prestige while still maintaining a strict color line internally. However, if Harry were imbued with Martin's social sense of integration, perhaps that expansion of Harry's abilities

---

20. The books are not clear where exactly the Durmstrang Institute lies, but from its name and the description it is most likely in the stretch of Russia that runs north from the Baltic to the Barents Sea.

would be shared with all the students and all would be enhanced. In turn, those riches would be returned to the antipodes.

And, going back to Harry's modest and difficult home situation, maybe instead of taking revenge on inane aunts by turning them into balloons, Harry might open their minds. Bring home a friend other than Ron from a different tradition. Have some of the parents of different children from different traditions spend time together learning each other's ways. Have parents commiserate over the problems of having wizards as children. In other words, have Harry help others to humanize themselves to each other, and by those acts humanize Harry and give him a broader destiny.

Reimagining Harry

One could wonder whether such a Harry is one that J.K. Rowling would want. Yet, the breadth of this vision of Harry is one that I think would change the nature of his battles with Lord Voldemort. We might then think of the Harry Potter series as being a reinforcement of the greatest universal human characteristics—loyalty, faith, courage, friendship, openness, and truth. It would be a story in which the blood that flows in Harry Potter's veins and that brought Lord Voldemort back to life would glow in Lord Voldemort—maybe helping to turn him away from his evil. It would be a story where each of the young wizards gains strength from the other, helping all to progress. A story where those who thrive by division and spite, like the Malfoys, are diminished by their own narrowness, weakened, and constrained to regress to irrelevance—or, perhaps shown a path to inclusion.

This Harry who met Martin—the Martin who transcended color lines and taught us all the power of love—would become a special character. His ideas would be preserved in the institution that is Hogwarts and that institution would have its power used to help humanity progress, rather than stagnate in stale hierarchies. It is a feeling that could be strong in Harry Potter. It is a feeling I have been fortunate to have felt on special occasions, such as a recent conference at my school, such as a day many years ago in honor of a very old man. If Harry and Ron and Hermione can be imagined in this way, then we would see some real power, extraordinary power, for the good and the best in all of us.

That is the image of Harry I see in my Mind's Eye. Harry meeting Martin. Martin teaching him love. Martin helping Hogwarts be a place where all can play all roles. Martin smiling down on Harry. Harry growing and sharing his wizardry for the good of the world—fighting evil as a boy and later as a man. In this vision the color of Harry and the color of Martin blur in my Mind's

Eye, and I see two people, each caring greatly to help the world. In that moment, when soul triumphs over color hierarchies maybe, for once and for some children somewhere, the color line will finally disappear like a bad dream. At that moment, I would believe that the promise of justice and equality that undergirds all that is law would bind them together as they strove towards a peaceful horizon together.[21]

---

21. It is too early to speculate on the impact of the inauguration of President Barack Obama (a product of Harvard—maybe an American Hogwarts?) in the real world on this type of children's fantasy writing and films.

Harry Potter and the Image of God: How House-Elves Can Help Us to Understand the Dignity of the Person

Alison McMorran Sulentic

> *Every economic decision and institution must be judged in light of whether it protects or undermines the dignity of the human person.*
> —U.S. Conference of Catholic Bishops[1]

> *If you want to know what a man's like, take a good look at how he treats his inferiors, not his equals.*
> —Sirius Black[2]

What Does Harry Potter Have to Do with Catholic Social Thought ... and Why Should Lawyers Care?

What does it mean to be a person? And why does it matter?

These questions lie at the heart of Catholic social thought. Sometimes called the "best kept secret" of the Roman Catholic Church,[3] "Catholic social teaching" refers in general to the teachings of the popes and bishops of the Catholic Church on the relationship of the individual to society and, in particular, to a series of papal and episcopal texts addressing moral theology and Christian

---

1. UNITED STATES CONFERENCE OF CATHOLIC BISHOPS, ECONOMIC JUSTICE FOR ALL ¶ 13.

2. *Goblet of Fire* 525.

3. *See* EDWARD P. DEBERRI, JAMES E. HUG, PETER J. HENRIOT & MICHAEL J. SCHULTHEIS, CATHOLIC SOCIAL TEACHING: OUR BEST KEPT SECRET (4th ed. 2003).

social ethics.[4] In the words of the United States Conference of Catholic Bishops, this teaching lays the groundwork for the task of "building a just society and living lives of holiness amidst the challenges of modern society."[5]

Such an immense task—"building a just society and living lives of holiness"—necessarily engages the positive law of a given state at a given time, as well as unwritten and perhaps unconscious assumptions about law and its role in the promotion or destabilization of the common good. In 1986, for example, American Catholic bishops issued a pastoral letter entitled *Economic Justice for All* in order to clarify the central concepts of Catholic social teaching in regard to economic relations. This letter locates the responsibility for safeguarding the dignity of the human person with both private and public institutions.[6] In the words of *Economic Justice for All*, "[s]ociety, as a whole, acting through public and private institutions, has the moral responsibility to enhance human dignity and protect human rights."[7] Such an ambitious project requires engagement in economic, political and jurisprudential discourse.[8] To borrow a phrase from the Ministry of Magic's leaflet on careers in Muggle re-

---

4. *See* Kenneth R. Himes, *Introduction, in* MODERN CATHOLIC SOCIAL TEACHING: COMMENTARIES AND INTERPRETATIONS 3–4 (Kenneth R. Himes, ed., 2005). In contrast to the term "Catholic social teaching," the phrase "Catholic social thought" is generally regarded as a more inclusive term that incorporates not only the official magisterial documents, but also the reflective work of other commentators who do not have the authority to promulgate official Church teaching. *Id.* at 4.

5. UNITED STATES CONFERENCE OF CATHOLIC BISHOPS, SEVEN KEY THEMES OF CATHOLIC SOCIAL TEACHING (1999).

6. The implementation of Catholic social teaching does not easily fit within a liberal/conservative division commonly invoked in political discourse. Catholic anti-war protestors are just as likely as Catholic pro-life activists to see their work as fulfilling the mandates of Catholic social teaching.

7. UNITED STATES CONFERENCE OF CATHOLIC BISHOPS, ECONOMIC JUSTICE FOR ALL ¶ 18. In addition to the precepts mentioned in this paragraph, *Economic Justice for All* identifies the following pivotal requirements for a just society:
- "Every economic decision and institution must be judged in light of whether it protects or undermines the dignity of the human person." *Id.* at ¶ 13.
- "Human dignity can be realized and protected only in community." *Id.* at ¶ 14.
- "All people have a right to participate in the economic life of society." *Id.* at ¶ 15.
- "All members of society have a special obligation to the poor and vulnerable." *Id.* at ¶ 16.
- "Human rights are the minimum conditions for life in community." *Id.* at ¶ 17.

8. While acknowledging pluralism of religious belief among Americans and of political belief among Catholics, the Bishops' 2004 letter on *Faithful Citizenship* calls for an "ongoing participation in the continuing political and legislative process." UNITED STATES CONFERENCE OF CATHOLIC BISHOPS, FAITHFUL CITIZENSHIP: A CATHOLIC CALL TO POLITICAL RESPONSIBILITY (2004).

lations, one might also infer that "enthusiasm, patience, and a good sense of fun" would ease the enormous burden of transforming advocacy of the dignity of the person into workable and sustainable social policy.

This chapter suggests that J.K. Rowling's wizarding world offers a challenging commentary on the role of the person in economic and legal relations. More importantly, playing with the idea of personhood in the wizarding world allows us to imagine new and different ways in which personhood might be acknowledged in our own world. In the preface to *Acts of Hope: Creating Authority in Literature, Law and Politics*, James Boyd White argues that "[t]he management of the competing claims of the world on the self, the self on the world, is a primary human process...."[9] Drawing on his own experience in analyzing texts such as Plato's *Crito* or Jane Austen's *Mansfield Park*, White suggests that the analysis of literature offers a gateway to the examination of issues that bear upon us in the "real" world:

> When and why should we grant authority to particular institutions or social practices and when by contrast, should we insist instead upon our own sense of what is right, or good, or necessary? If we are in doubt, how long should we defer making up our minds, with the aim of educating ourselves into what we are at first inclined to resist? ... What kinds of authorities should we create in our own acts of thought and speech?[10]

Literary texts, whether in the form of fiction, philosophical tracts or other genres, provide the opportunity to "lear[n] from the performances of others, situated in other times and other cultures."[11] Moreover, in the case of philosophical conversations that are not part of everyday discourse, analogy to a well-known literary text provides a neat way to introduce unusual or unfamiliar paradigms for analysis.

The wizarding world provides an opportunity to look more closely at the way in which our own society functions. For the Catholic social thought scholar, in particular, the wizarding world presents a new paradigm of "personhood" that necessarily extends beyond the human being. This chapter therefore examines the wizarding world in order to discern the manner in which Rowling's fictional characters might enrich our understanding of personhood in the "real" world and the ways in which laws might best protect rights associ-

---

9. *See* JAMES BOYD WHITE, ACTS OF HOPE: CREATING AUTHORITY IN LITERATURE, LAW, AND POLITICS ix (1994).

10. *Id.* at xii.

11. *Id.* at xiii.

ated with personhood. Given the extraordinary breadth of the series' appeal, it might not be too much to hope that lessons discerned from the wizarding world could be a gateway to new ways of thinking about the rights of the person in our own world.

Catholic Social Thought and the Concept of the Person

Catholic social teaching functions both as an analytical system and as a prescriptive ideology. The foundational premise of Catholic social teaching is the "transcendent dignity" of the person as a being made in the image and likeness of God (*imago Dei*).[12] This "theocentric" understanding of personhood is also the foundation of the Church's teachings concerning the rights and responsibilities of the person in community with fellow beings.[13] Thus, the central concepts of Catholic social thought—the dignity of the human person, the communitarian nature of human society and the universal destination of goods—may serve as a methodology for examining, organizing and understanding the raw data provided by the observation of social facts. At the same time, however, it would be disingenuous to suggest that Catholic social teaching limits itself to the goal of advancing a methodology for social science research. Instead, Catholic social teaching calls for the transformation of society in order to align the "temporal world" more closely with its ideals.

The concept of the "person" in Catholic social thought derives from the basic Christian belief in Jesus of Nazareth as the incarnation of God, a belief that crosses all denominations of Christian practice.[14] In Catholic moral theology, the image of human beings as "made in the image and likeness of God" (a phrase borrowed from Genesis) is also the starting point for reflection on human dignity and the social rights and responsibilities that flow from that dignity. But what does it mean to say that a person is made in the image and likeness of God?

Modern Catholic social teaching emphasizes both the physical and the spiritual or intellectual dimension of the human person. The *Compendium of the Social Doctrine of the Church* (released in 2004 after many years of study and

---

12. *See* Pontifical Council for Justice and Peace, Compendium of the Social Doctrine of the Church ¶ 4 (2004).

13. *See* John C. Dwyer, *Person, Dignity Of, in* The New Dictionary of Catholic Social Thought 724–25, 734–36 (Judith A. Dwyer, ed., 1994).

14. This idea is also clearly rooted in Genesis, where both accounts of the creation stress that men and women are made "in the image of God."

reflection of Church teaching and commentary) states that "*Man was created by God in unity of body and soul.*"[15] This theme restates both the work of early theologians, such as Thomas Aquinas, and the more modern language of the Second Vatican Council. In *Gaudium et Spes* (also known as the *Pastoral Constitution on the Church in the Modern World*), the Council explained that the human person differs from other animals by virtue of "intellect," "diligent use of ... talents," "attempts to search out the secrets of the material universe and to bring it under their control" and the search for "truths of a higher order."[16] Yet the Council also was very conscious of the unity of the human person's intellect and will and his or her bodily form. The human person "in its very bodily condition" is the synthesis of "the elements of the material world, which through it are thus brought to their highest perfection and are enabled to raise their voice in spontaneous praise of the creator."[17]

The "transcendent qualities" of the human person in body and in soul demand a social response that respects the dignity of each person. The Second Vatican Council admonished "everybody [to] look upon his or her neighbor (without any exception) as another self, bearing in mind especially their neighbor's life and the means needed for a dignified way of life...."[18] In *Gaudium et Spes*, the Council instructed:

> Today, there is an inescapable duty to make ourselves the neighbor of every individual, without exception, and to take positive steps to help a neighbor whom we encounter, whether that neighbor be an elderly person abandoned by everyone, a foreign worker who suffers the injustice of being despised, a refugee, an illegitimate child wrongly suffering for a sin of which the child is innocent, or a starving human being who awakens our conscience....[19]

These rights extend not only to Christian believers but to any human being simply because he or she is a person. As *Gaudium et Spes* explained, "All this holds true not only for Christians but also for all people of good will in whose hearts grace is active invisibly."[20]

---

15. *See* COMPENDIUM, *supra* note 12, at ¶ 127 (emphasis in the original).

16. SECOND VATICAN COUNCIL, GAUDIUM ET SPES: PASTORAL CONSTITUTION ON THE CHURCH IN THE MODERN WORLD (1965) at ¶ 15.

17. *Id.* at ¶ 14.

18. *Id.* at ¶ 27.

19. *Id.*

20. *Id.* at ¶ 22.

If modern Catholic social thought suggests that personhood is the basis for rights, how are we to understand the meaning of personhood? What are the characteristics that allow us to identify a particular embodied being as a person who bears the rights championed by Catholic social thought? The Christian belief in the incarnational knowledge of God goes some way to explaining the answer to this question. Yet, in truth, given that Christians also believe that we cannot see God the Father and we have no authentic painting or sculpture of Jesus, the phrase "*imago Dei*"—made in the image and likeness of God—requires some examination if it is to be anything more than a slogan.

One fundamental difference between human beings and other creatures is the capacity for understanding and rational thought, a quality that traditional Thomistic theology understood to be essential to the human person's relationship to God. Aquinas argued that, "in God to be and to understand are one and the same."[21] In contrast, human beings differentiate between the experience of being and the experience of understanding. Thus, a human being has the capacity to understand, but the act of understanding is relational—it depends upon the existence or concept of something to be understood. Closely linked to human understanding is the ability to organize thoughts in a rational manner and to communicate these ideas to others. The rational or intellectual soul is therefore the unique characteristic "of man as man," as seen in his capacity "to understand; because he thereby surpasses all other animals."[22] The intellectual soul thus enables a relationship with God and, at the same time, distinguishes the human being from other animals.

Yet human life requires more than just both a soul and a corporeal form. How does the human person—who unites soul and body—bear the "image and likeness of God?" Could the term "image of God" possibly be limited to the intellectual component of the human person or is it large enough to include the corporeal element? Aquinas perceived this problem and argued in response that the soul may "subsis[t] to the corporeal matter, out of which and the intellectual soul there results unity of existence; so that the existence of the whole composite is also the existence of the soul."[23] The term "image of God" must therefore incorporate more than the intellectual capacity for understanding.

Aquinas' exposition of the "image of God" clearly does not dismiss the human body. Aquinas believed that irrational creatures may display a "trace" of the image of God, but his own perception of the "image of God" reposed

---

21. THOMAS AQUINAS, SUMMA THEOLOGICA Pt. 1, Q. 34, A.2, Reply Obj. 1. (Fathers of the English Dominican Province, trans. 1948).

22. *Id.* at Pt. 1, Q. 75, A.1.

23. *Id.* at Pt. 1, Q. 75, A.1, Reply Obj. 5.

more comfortably in his appreciation of the intellectual capacity of the human person.[24] However, it would be overly simplistic to assume that the priority that Aquinas places on the human intellect is necessarily dismissive of the corporeal aspect of the human person. He writes:

> Although the image of God in man is not to be found in his bodily shape, yet because the body of man alone among terrestrial animals is not inclined prone to the ground, but is adapted to look upward to heaven, for this reason we may rightly say that it is made to God's image and likeness, rather than the bodies of other animals.... But this is not to be understood as though the image of God were in man's body; but in the sense that the very shape of the human body represents the image of God in the soul by way of a trace.[25]

Thus, during a person's life, the body assists and is necessary to the operation of the intellectual soul and, in its own right, reflects "traces" of the image of God.[26]

Modern Catholic social teaching reflects much of Thomas Aquinas' thought about the nature of the human person. John Paul II wrote, for instance, that a person is "a subjective being capable of acting in a planned and rational way, capable of deciding about himself and with a tendency to self-realization."[27] Yet the late Pope recognized the corporeal aspect of the person when he referred to "the specific nature of man, who has been created by God in his image and likeness" as incorporating both "a bodily and a spiritual nature, symbolized in the second creation account by the two elements: the *earth*, from which God forms man's body, and the *breath of life* which he breathes into man's nostrils."[28]

In recent years, theologians have searched for a way to understand the image of God (*imago Dei*) that acknowledges the breadth of our experience of the

---

24. *Id.* at Pt. 1, Q. 93, A.2.

25. *Id.* at Pt. 1, Q. 93, A.7, Reply Obj. 3.

26. *See, e.g.,* Mary Catherine Hilkert, O.P., *Imago Dei: Does the Symbol Have a Future?*, Santa Clara Lectures, (Apr. 14, 2002), *available at* http://www.scu.edu/ignatiancenter/events/lectures/archives/upload/s02_hilkert.pdf (last visited Aug. 23, 2008). On the general issue of extending traditional notions of *imago Dei*, Hilkert states that "the affirmation that women are created equally in the image of God is explicitly affirmed in the Catholic tradition today," but acknowledges questions concerning the extent to which liturgical leadership and practice reflect this position. *Id.* at 8. *See also* Mary Catherine Hilkert, *God's Word in Women's Words*, 181 AMERICA 14 (Nov. 27, 1999).

27. JOHN PAUL II, LABOREM EXERCENS: ON HUMAN WORK ¶ 6 (1981).

28. JOHN PAUL II, SOLLICITUDO REI SOCIALIS: ON SOCIAL CONCERN ¶ 29 (1987).

person. Critical race theorists and feminists, for example, may find companionship among theologians who enlarge the *imago Dei* to include people of all races, genders and disabilities. Moreover, in recent years, concern for environmental protection and the sustainable development of the Earth's ecological resources engages both theologians and lawyers in the shared task of defining the obligations of human persons to our fellow creatures, as well as to our planet.[29] Mary Catherine Hilkert, a theologian deeply concerned with the anthropological implications of the power of phrases such as "*imago Dei*," argues for an increasingly broad vision of the *imago Dei*. She writes: "Human beings and human communities—including ecclesial communities—have the power to deny, and in that sense, to 'blot out' the image of God in those we consider to be the 'other.'"[30]

Hilkert suggests that "naming one another and fragile human and ecological communities as capable of imaging God—if only in fragments" invites a new "delight in creation" and allows us to "learn to live within limits that respect the common good of the whole community of the living."[31]

This avenue to an expanded understanding of the "image of God" suggests that an exercise in "imaging God—if only in fragments" might similarly enrich our understanding of social rights even if the source of our imagination is decidedly fictional.[32] Like people in the "real world," Rowling's wizards "have the power to deny and ... to 'blot out'" the personhood of those whom they consider to be "other."[33] The wizards' treatment of the "other," whether house-elf or Muggle, permits us to evaluate the consequences of this behavior without the presuppositions that might hamper the recognition of these behaviors in our own world.

Concepts of Personhood in Harry Potter

So, what can a student of Catholic social teaching—a subject primarily concerned with the rights of human persons in society—learn from the "performances of others, situated in other times and other cultures," particularly when

---

29. *See, e.g.,* David J. Bryant, *Imago Dei, Imagination, and Ecological Responsibility,* 57 THEOLOGY TODAY 35 (2000).

30. Hilkert, *Imago Dei, supra* note 26, at 18.

31. *Id.* at 19.

32. *Id.*

33. *Id.* at 18.

those "others" are not necessarily human and do not occupy such a doggedly non-magical world as our own?

The question is not as far-fetched as it seems. The fact that Rowling's immense creativity also draws on mythological and literary traditions is testimony to the willingness of the human imagination to suspend disbelief and rational empiricism in order to meditate upon the potential for other beings to share the very attributes that make us human.[34] In its liberal use of mythology and its appeal to both children and adults, J.K. Rowling's storytelling resembles the work of J.R.R. Tolkien and C.S. Lewis.[35] Like Rowling, both Tolkien and Lewis reinterpreted common mythology while creating new and elaborate histories of creatures and civilizations. Alan Jacobs, C.S. Lewis' biographer, writes:

> The question of myth was one that had much occupied Tolkien for many years.... For Tolkien the problem had several dimensions. In part he wanted simply to understand his own deep attraction to myth.... Only as [his] writings grew in complexity and came to mean more to him did he have to think about *why* they meant so much to him and what he would be communicating through them.[36]

Lewis was at first skeptical of Tolkien's views (or perhaps simply played the devil's advocate), but later came to embrace much of his colleague's thinking on myth. Jacobs continues:

> Tolkien was reaching to the heart of his friend. Lewis had focused all his attention either on what Joy was or how to get it, but Tolkien was forcing him to consider the matter in a wholly different light.... That we dream and wish at all is a powerful element of the case for belief that myths communicate some truth that cannot be communicated in any other way. Lewis would use this argument repeatedly for the rest of his life....[37]

Rowling's work slips easily into the tradition of telling stories in order to make ideas both intelligible and accessible. Her interpretation of mythological creatures such as elves or centaurs emphasizes personality and personhood and,

---

34. *See generally* JOSEPH CAMPBELL, THE HERO WITH A THOUSAND FACES (1949).

35. For a fascinating exposition of the development of Tolkien's and Lewis's theories on the capacity of myth to express truths, *see* ALAN JACOBS, THE NARNIAN: THE LIFE AND IMAGINATION OF C.S. LEWIS 138–150 (2005).

36. *Id.* at 142–43.

37. *Id.* at 145–46.

from the perspective of Catholic social thought, lends itself to communicating significant ideas about the rights of the marginalized in society.

Needless to say, the discussion of social rights and responsibilities in the "real world" is primarily a discussion of human rights. In the thirteenth century, Thomas Aquinas wrote in great detail of angels as "persons," but modern commentary on the idea of the "person" in Catholic social thought is distinctly less imaginative and generally confines itself to the study of the human person in relationship to God, to other human beings and to the environment. When scholars of Catholic social thought refer to persons "made in the image and likeness of God," we are generally speaking of human beings.[38] The discussion of the religious basis for human rights is hardly the only subject to take such an anthropocentric focus. Even the discussion of animal welfare and animal rights is also, at some level, a discussion of the rights of humans in relationship to other animals.[39]

The wizarding world is not nearly as anthropocentric as our own. In the wizarding world, humans—both magical and Muggle—do, of course, occupy a primary role both in the narrative and in the world described by that narrative. But a host of other beings are self-conscious and exercise the powers of rational thought and creativity that we, in the "real world," normally claim as the prerogative of the human person. House-elves, centaurs, hags, giants, poltergeists, ghosts, merpeople, goblins—all of these creatures exercise the capacity to observe the world around them, to reflect upon that world with rational intelligence, to make choices in the face of moral conflict, to communicate with other beings on matters both trivial and profound, and to fashion creative responses in light of their decisions. In the wizarding world, J.K. Rowling offers us a far more complex community of "persons" than the tradition of "human rights" can capture.

Harry Potter himself serves as J.K. Rowling's reason for providing some basic exposition concerning the wizarding world and its inhabitants. Harry's first encounter with a house-elf immediately signifies the moral dilemma concerning the status of the house-elf in wizarding society. Relegated to his room while the Dursleys entertain an important client, Harry discovers Dobby sitting on his bed. Harry's first words to Dobby reflect both the anthropocentric view of the Muggle world in which Harry has been raised and an awareness that

38. For an interesting commentary on the philosophical limitations of such a viewpoint, see ALISDAIR MACINTYRE, DEPENDENT RATIONAL ANIMALS (1998); MARTHA C. NUSSBAUM, FRONTIERS OF JUSTICE: DISABILITY, NATIONALITY, SPECIES MEMBERSHIP (2006).

39. See generally ANIMAL RIGHTS: CURRENT DEBATES AND NEW DIRECTIONS (Cass R. Sunstein and Martha C. Nussbaum, eds., 2004).

Muggle paradigms do not adequately explain magical creatures: "He wanted to ask, 'What are you?' but thought it would sound too rude, so instead he said, 'Who are you?'"[40]

Dobby is patently non-human and Harry's first instinct is therefore to regard him as a thing: "What are you?" At the same time, however, Harry's developing understanding of the wizarding world warns him that the appropriate question might not be "What are you?" but "Who are you?" After a year at Hogwarts, Harry knows that creatures that are not human might nonetheless be rational and able to provide him with information and explanations in a manner that would only be duplicated by humans in the "real" world. Whether the rational powers of non-human creatures entitle them to the rights of human persons is less evident both to Harry and to the other inhabitants of the wizarding world. Are house-elves persons or are they something else?

Rowling's description of the physical characteristics of house-elves leaves no doubt that the elves bear some resemblance to human beings. Rowling draws an obvious parallel, for example, between Dobby and Harry by describing their facial characteristics; both elf and boy have green eyes and thin features. The descriptions of the four house-elves who play significant roles in the story—Dobby, Winky, Kreacher and Hokey—also establish that each house-elf has two eyes, two hands (with an unspecified number of fingers), two legs and two ears. Their bodies are hairless and they walk upright. House-elves are gendered (Dobby and Kreacher are male, while Winky and Hokey are female). Repeated references to "mothers" and "grandmothers" suggest that they reproduce, although the nature of family life and social interaction is ambiguous. We also know that house-elves age and can infer that some physical functions decline with the years. Kreacher, for example, shows signs of deafness and Hokey is described as "old and confused." Sirius' offhand comment that "dear Aunt Elladora ... started the family tradition of beheading house-elves when they got too old to carry tea trays"[41] suggests a decline in physical strength as an accompaniment to advancing age. House-elves are not immortal; we know, for instance, that Kreacher's ancestors are dead and that Dobby dies from a knife wound.

The physical descriptions of house-elves nonetheless make it clear that they are not simply miniature human beings. After two years' acquaintance with Dobby, Harry is able to identify Winky as a house-elf immediately upon spotting her in the top box at the Quidditch World Cup and does not demonstrate

---

40. *Chamber of Secrets* 13.
41. *Order of the Phoenix* 113.

the confusion that accompanied his first encounter with Dobby. The house-elves therefore must share some characteristics that are common to their own species and distinguishable from humans and other creatures, thus enabling Harry and others to recognize and classify them. We know, for example, that house-elves are typically diminutive in stature: Dobby is a "little creature," while Winky is "a tiny creature" with legs "so short they stuck out in front of it on the chair." Kreacher is "bald like all house-elves." Dobby, Winky and Kreacher each have "bat-like ears."

Despite their physical similarities, house-elves also seem to have physical traits that identify them as differentiated individuals. Dobby, for example, has "[t]wo enormous green eyes" and a "long, thin nose," while Winky has "enormous brown eyes and a nose the exact size and shape of a large tomato." Kreacher's eyes are "bloodshot and watery gray." Some characteristics appear to be hereditary and perhaps signal a distinct family identity. Note, for example, the similarity between the "rather snoutlike nose" on each of the stuffed heads of the house-elves mounted in Sirius' corridor and the description of Kreacher's "large and rather snoutlike" nose.

Rowling's description of the physical characteristics of house-elves makes a clear distinction between the human body and that of an elf. The distinction between the house-elf's intellect and that of a human is much less clear. Consider what we know about the intellectual lives of house-elves.

First, house-elves can formulate independent thought and communicate that thought to other beings. While it is not clear that house-elves have their own language, the signs do point in that direction. First, many creatures who can communicate in English or other human languages also have their own particular language, including, for example, giants, goblins or merpeople. While the books do not specifically list a language particular to house-elves, their poor command of English grammar is consistent with the suggestion that English is their second language. Moreover, the idioms that Rowling uses in portraying house-elf speech vary from elf to elf. Dobby, for example, always refers to himself in the third person, while Winky uses the pronoun "I." Kreacher's command of English grammar is quite good, while Winky and Dobby both struggle with agreement between nouns and verbs. These verbal variations suggest that the house-elves have varying degrees of proficiency in English as a second language.

Second, house-elves have the ability to form moral judgments and to make moral choices. Dobby, for example, determines that the Malfoys' plot to kill Harry is morally wrong and defies his master's orders in order to act upon this judgment. Winky is able to differentiate between Dobby's conduct, which she finds unbecoming, and the behavior that is appropriate to a house-elf. Kreacher's assessment of the morality of Sirius' and Mrs. Weasley's cleaning efforts results in his repeated efforts to recover items that he believes have been wrongly removed from the house. In each of these cases, the house-elf has a decided understanding of the difference between right and wrong and the capacity to act in a manner consistent with this understanding. The fact that house-elves are bound to their masters by an enchantment suggests that in the absence of such an enchantment, they would be able to exercise their moral choices in a manner independent of the help or interference of wizards.

Third, house-elves have the skill to perform "powerful magic of their own" which apparently differs from the magic that wizards can perform. Moreover, it is conceivable that the magical skill of the house-elf exceeds that of the wizard, for Dobby can perform charms without a wand and can Apparate and Disapparate in locations where it is impossible for wizards to do either. Although positive wizarding law forbids the use of a wand by a house-elf, the very existence of this law suggests that elves can and would learn how to use wands in a way that might not further the interest of wizards.

Perhaps nowhere is Rowling at greater pains to diminish the apparent differences between humans and house elves than in the shared ability to feel and act on the strength of emotions. Sirius and Dobby, for example, share a love for Harry that ultimately costs each his life at the hands of the same Death-Eater, Bellatrix Lestrange. When Kreacher leads the house-elves into the Battle of Hogwarts, his appeal to the memory of "Master Regulus" echoes Harry's characterization of himself and, ultimately, Snape as "Dumbledore's man." Love and loyalty bind both house-elves and humans.

Social and Political Consequences of Accepting House-Elves as Persons

A reader schooled in the Catholic social thought tradition will find little difficulty in recognizing that an anthropocentric concept of personhood is too narrow a principle to operate with analytical consistency in the wizarding world. House-elves demonstrate exactly the kind of rational, intellectual and creative capacities that go to the heart of "personhood" as that term is understood in Catholic social teaching. Moreover, as embodied beings, they resemble the unity of body and intellect that we, in the real world, understand to be fundamental to the human person. So, if we accept house-elves as persons, what are the consequences for moral choice and legal rights?

Rowling's work repeatedly stresses the individual's duty to make morally defensible choices to advance a social good. At the end of *The Chamber of Se-*

crets, Dumbledore explains to Harry, "It is our choices, Harry, that show what we truly are, far more than our abilities."[42] The importance of the ability to choose and to choose wisely is perhaps best highlighted by the Imperius Curse. The Imperius Curse effectively dehumanizes its victims by removing all ability to choose between right and wrong. Although the imposter Mad-Eye Moody demonstrates the curse to Harry's class in a light-handed manner (skipping on one foot, singing the national anthem, hopping on desks), he openly explains that the Imperius Curse is hardly a laughing matter. The instances in which the Imperius Curse comes into play are graphic reminders of these comments: Ginny Weasley opens the Chamber of Secrets, Viktor Krum tries to kill Cedric Diggory, Mr. Crouch facilitates the imposter Moody's duplicitous place at Hogwarts. Even when there is no direct evidence that a person has been "Imperiused," an apparent absence of moral choice suggests that he or she is not whole. Harry knows, without having witnessed the curse itself, that Stan Shunpike could only have attacked him during the flight from Privet Drive as a result of the Imperius Curse. Not being able to choose is a radical restriction of a person's ability to exercise moral responsibility.

Rowling also portrays moral responsibility and choice as matter of social obligation. The central plot—Harry's mission to end Lord Voldemort's reign of terror—contains both individualist and communitarian elements. Dumbledore explains to Harry that this mission is not the result of predestination (prophecy), but instead of Harry's individual decision to challenge Lord Voldemort and the social evil that he represents. Harry's increasing desire to avenge his parents' deaths does not blind him to the repercussions of Lord Voldemort's actions in the wider wizarding world as well as the Muggle environs. Harry's initial confrontation with Lord Voldemort reached into the ranks of house-elves and, for most, ended the treatment of house-elves as "vermin." This is one small example of the impact that Harry's moral choices will have on a society that is much greater in scope than he can possibly imagine.

The text also gives some indication of the gauge by which moral choice is to be measured. In some sense, The Goblet of Fire and The Order of the Phoenix chronicle the last year of Harry's boyhood, a period when Sirius, Dumbledore and, to a lesser extent, Lupin and Mr. and Mrs. Weasley can still counsel him in their perceptions of morality. The first lesson, reiterated throughout the series, is the difficulty of discerning an ethically correct response. From Sirius, Harry learns that "the world isn't split into good people and Death Eaters."[43]

---

42. Chamber of Secrets 333.
43. Order of the Phoenix 302.

Harry's choices will be made in a realm where good and evil are not clearly labeled. The disastrous consequences of Harry's impulsive decision to use the *Sectumsempra* curse on Malfoy show that even Harry, the "Chosen One," will confuse the two from time to time. A second lesson is that the morality of a particular decision does not always square with the prevailing views of social relations or social hierarchy. An early example is Neville's decision to "stand up to [his] friends" in discouraging Harry, Ron, and Hermione from breaking school rules in a way that might jeopardize the overall well-being of Gryffindor. Sirius makes a similar point about the unreliability of received social hierarchies when he tells the trio, "If you want to know what a man's like, take a good look at how he treats his inferiors, not his equals."[44]

This last comment—the connection between moral goodness and the ability to look beyond social hierarchies—provides a pivotal connection between Catholic social thought and Rowling's implicit critique of the treatment of house-elves. The idea of "person" as the "image of God" is the means by which Catholic social teaching evaluates the moral dimensions of social action. Drawing on Paul VI's encyclical entitled *Populorum Progressio*,[45] John Paul II argued that social conditions "must be measured and oriented according to the reality and vocation of man seen in his totality, namely, according to his interior dimension."[46] Paul VI set forth the following expectations to which any person might aspire:

> Freedom from misery; the greater assurance of finding subsistence, health, and fixed employment; an increased share of responsibility without oppression of any kind and in security from situations that do violence to their dignity as men; better education—in brief, to seek to do more, know more and have more in order to be more ... political freedom [and] a fitting autonomous growth, social as well as economic.[47]

In more recent years, this idea has been captured in the idea of the "preferential option for the poor," a phrase coined by liberation theologians but later emerging as a basic tenet of Catholic teaching on the evaluation of moral choices in economic, legal and social relations. In the world of Harry Potter, Sirius' admonition of the importance of looking to the treatment of marginalized persons and Dumbledore's persistent willingness to give chances to peo-

---

44. *Goblet of Fire* 525.
45. Paul VI, Populorum Progressio: On the Development of Peoples (1967).
46. Sollicitudo Rei Socialis, *supra* note 28, at ¶ 29.
47. Populorum Progressio, *supra* note 45, at ¶ 6.

ple otherwise ostracized in wizarding society illustrate a similar notion of justice.

Harry's world contains many creatures that ours does not and, among these, the house-elves consistently lag behind in social rights. If house-elves are persons, then what should this mean for their rights in the wizarding world?

Hermione offers one simplistic (albeit well-intentioned) analysis of the moral and legal rights of house-elves—as "fellow magical creatures," house-elves should participate in the governance of the wizarding world on equal terms with wizards. Moreover, Hermione's vision of a just society for elves includes access to a panoply of social benefits that sound very similar to the economic expectations of the Muggle world in which she was raised. When Nearly Headless Nick explains that over one hundred house-elves serve as caretakers of the physical needs of Hogwarts and its inhabitants, Hermione responds, "But they get paid? ... They get holidays, don't they? And—and sick leave, and pensions, and everything?"[48]

Hermione's goals—"to secure house-elves fair wages and working conditions"—are in fact the very goals for a just and secure workplace set forth in papal encyclicals from *Rerum Novarum* (1891) to *Centesimus Annus* (1991). Moreover, Catholic workers, activists, business leaders and scholars (including myself) continue to see workplace justice in our "real world" in terms very similar to Hermione's hopes for house-elves. Hermione's proposed recalibration of the wizarding world would prove very inconvenient to wizards in ways that we know to be real obstacles to liberation movements in our own society. Recent appraisals of the history of race relations in the United States reveal the way in which Catholic moral theology teaches that human dignity is to be valued above the inconvenience and cost to existing power structures. While the Catholic Church is certainly not above reproach with regard to its participation in unjust structures, the ideological value that Catholic theology places on human dignity explains why labor activists such as Monsignor Charles Owen Rice marched alongside Martin Luther King during our own country's struggle for civil rights.

While there is no doubt that J.K. Rowling shares Hermione's exuberant defense of the marginalized members of the wizarding world, however, the description of her efforts is quite obviously satirical. Rowling uses some of the characters for whom, as a writer, she shows the greatest deal of affection, to counterbalance Hermione's zeal. Hagrid, the Weasley twins and Mr. Weasley are all appreciative of house-elves as individuals, but do not join in her vision

---

48. *Goblet of Fire* 182.

of justice. Moreover, with the exception of Dobby, house-elves themselves do not embrace freedom in the sense of an individual right to autonomy and leisure. Most house-elves respond to Hermione's clumsy efforts to recognize the personhood with fear or distaste.

In our own world, where human beings claim a monopoly on the complex skill set of rationality, communication, intellect and creativity, it is the idea of the human person as a being created "in the image and likeness of God" that leads directly to the goals of securing equal rights for all human persons and, more specifically, just wages and working conditions. The idea that all human persons are entitled to a full range of rights is integral to the Catholic understanding of justice. Yet, in the wizarding world, this view of human rights would plainly reinforce structures that already diminish the position of creatures that are not human. The idea that human beings alone deserve these rights would, at some level, justify the inhumane treatment of all creatures that the wizarding community regarded as non-human. Rowling's obvious affection and respect for Dobby, the werewolf Remus Lupin, the giant Grawp and the community of centaurs do not sit well with an entirely anthropocentric understanding of the "person" or "rights." The wealth of "persons" in the wizarding world demands a more sensitive appreciation of personhood.

Rowling's resistance to Hermione's simplistic idea of justice captures a more complex idea of the dignity of the person. Hermione's heart may be in the right place, but she does not differentiate between the kinds of rights that are the appropriate and necessary goals of social reform in a world where "persons" are necessarily only humans and the world in which she actually lives. The plain reason why Hermione's schemes do not serve the needs of house-elves is the fact that her world is populated by many more "persons" who are made "in the image of God" than our own. Hagrid, a character who knows few boundaries in his love for creatures of all kinds, points out Hermione's failure to really get to know the special "image of God" that is unique to house-elves. In some sense, the charism of house-elves is to use their intellectual, creative and magical skills to serve others. In the wizarding world, human sin may have subverted the relationship between humans and house-elves in a way that Hermione properly criticizes as unjust. Yet Winky's refusal to accept freedom is essentially a resistance to losing her work and her fiduciary relationship to the Crouches. Even Dobby still wants to work and takes pride in his ability to do so without detection.

Rowling's depiction of the earnest house-elves who fulfill their desires through meaningful work suggests that the "image of God" perceptible in the person of a house-elf must be protected in way that honors their essential being. The fact that this charism is different from that of a human being or a centaur is simply a testimony to an image of God that is different from the form most recognizable to human beings. The house-elves invite us to recognize the image of God in the "other." The re-evaluation of the concept of *imago Dei* by modern theologians has suggested that human persons must consider the potential of all living things to reflect the image of God in a way that requires us to conform our civil laws and economic practices to a standard of justice that values these "images."

Rowling repeatedly ties a character's acknowledgment of the magnificent value of life in all its forms to the fulfillment of his or her own potential. The moment when Ron publicly recognizes that the lives of house-elves are worthy of rescue is also the moment when Hermione finally kisses him. Griphook, the goblin banker, likewise understands that the care that Harry takes in digging Dobby's grave is a public affirmation of the inherent value of Dobby—and, implicitly, other non-wizards—in Harry's eyes. This affirmation moves him to disclose secrets that goblins have never revealed and enables Harry to gain the tools he needs to destroy Voldemort. For Rowling, then, the practice of justice seems inextricably linked to individual and collective fulfillment.

Suggestions for Enlarging the Jurisprudential Imagination of the Real World

My work as an author and yours as a reader is not over. As a legal scholar, I do not believe that it is sufficient to persuade you that house-elves are persons and that the wizarding world would be the better for treating them as such. Instead, I challenge those of us who are Harry Potter fans to find ways to widen our own encounters with the "other" and to search for the *imago Dei* in faces different from the one we see in the mirror. And once we have studied these perceptions, we must take up the task that Hermione has set for herself in studying and advocating for the rights of other persons, even (and perhaps especially) if they find it hard to speak for themselves. Rowling's work opens our eyes to the fragments of the image of God (Mary Catherine Hilkert's phrase) that might be perceptible if we look beyond ourselves and our familiar communities.

More important is the way in which we act in our own world. Suffice it to say that there are many new and creative ways of thinking about justice that complement the concern of Catholic social thought—and, dare I say, J.K. Rowling—for the marginalized members of society. On some profound level, the house-elves teach us that the image of God may be refracted through many different lenses, each of which offers its own valuable glimpse of the moral life. Here, I find Martha Nussbaum's recent book, *Frontiers of Justice: Disability, Nationality, Species Membership*, to be of real help in enlarging our thinking concerning the dignity of the person. Explaining the capabilities theory of justice, which she, together with economist Amartya Sen, has pioneered, Nussbaum writes:

> I ... have used the [capabilities] approach to provide the philosophical underpinning for an account of core human entitlements that should be respected and implemented by the governments of all nations, as a bare minimum of what respect of human dignity requires.... [T]he best approach to this idea of a basic social minimum is provided by an approach that focuses on human capabilities, that is, what people are actually able to do and to be, in a way informed by an intuitive idea of a life that is worthy of the dignity of the human being.[49]

The capabilities approach, which Nussbaum has also explored in connection with non-human animals, offers a promising method for fashioning morally defensible policies that respond to the reality of lived experience.

Read the Harry Potter series for the fun of it. But, as you do so, ask yourself whether the wizarding world can help us to see an image of God that will help us to transform our relationships, as human beings, with the other living creatures in our own world. Unless you are luckier than I, you will never meet a house-elf. But, thanks to Dobby and his fellow elves, you may see a fragment of the image of God in the "other" and find that, like Harry, you will choose to pursue a course that can enrich justice in a much larger community of beings than you had ever contemplated.

---

49. NUSSBAUM, *supra* note 38, at 70.

The Wizard Economy

4

Economic Growth in the Potterian Economy

Avichai Snir & Daniel Levy

For a literary work to succeed, it needs to conform to the expectations and beliefs of its readers. In particular, the text must succeed in convincing the readers that its plot is logical and internally consistent. Otherwise, readers, who judge plots against their own experience, would probably find it difficult to identify with the actions of the heroes and the development of the plot.

Internal logic and consistency are also necessary ingredients of any scientific model. The main differences between scientific models and literary works lie in their goals and in the way their success is judged. A scientific model is judged according to its ability to yield results and generate predictions that are in line with real world data and observations, while a literary text is judged according to its ability to appeal to readers.

For readers to follow and relate to the plot, they must identify with the rules that guide the actions of the book's heroes and the environment in which the heroes live and operate. Thus, for a book to be a best-seller, a large number of people must identify with the norms and the rules that drive the plot. A fictional world that is governed by rules that are not consistent with readers' beliefs and logic is not likely to be popular. And since readers' understandings of the world are based on their own real-life experiences, it seems plausible that models that guide the fictional worlds of best-sellers likely reflect the readers' attitudes and perceptions of their own real-world environment and society. Therefore, understanding the set of rules that drives the plot in a best seller may also assist in studying the readers' beliefs on how the real world functions.

The Harry Potter books enjoy a universal success and they are probably the biggest best-sellers of their time. This popularity suggests that the Harry Potter books offer readers around the world an internally consistent model that appeals to their intuition and expectations, and is in line with the way they view and perceive the world. For example, psychologists and economists such as the Noble Prize winner Daniel Kahneman, often find that people like to think about the world as a place that is governed by regularities, and as a consequence they tend to underestimate the probability of unlikely events.[1] The Harry Potter books, though fantasies, obey this psychological need and follow strict laws of logic as demonstrated in *The Goblet of Fire*, where almost nothing occurs as a result of pure luck or coincidence. In that book, even things that look like pure coincidences, like an elf that is found in an unusual situation, have a sinister and logical significance.

Many readers may not notice that Harry Potter and his friends operate not only in a social world, but in an economic one. They buy, sell, trade, and engage in banking. We are interested in the economic world of Harry Potter because as economists, we build models and use them to obtain insights and predict events in the real world. When we build these models we make assumptions about the way people perceive and act in their economic environments. We are therefore interested in finding out whether our assumptions, and the insights and predictions that our models offer, appeal to laymen as well as to professionals. Otherwise, since the real economy consists of many individual decision-makers who act according to their understandings of the world, we may find that many economic models fail in some of their predictions.

If, as we assume, best sellers are books that reflect the readers' model and perception of reality, then the popularity of the Harry Potter books suggests that the attitudes, the norms and the perspectives the books offer on economic organization of life must appeal to an almost universal audience. By looking at the economic organization of the world described in these books, we may learn something about the attitudes and understandings of their readers.

In this essay, therefore, we take a look at the economic aspects of the life of Harry Potter and his co-actors. Our goal is to study the economy in the Harry Potter books as a model of a real world economy. We use the term "Potterian economy" to refer to this economic model. We compare the Potterian economy with the Solow growth model, which is one of the most important economic models for studying income determination and economic growth. We search the books for what Frank Knight called "social organization of economic activities," and we study the similarities and differences between the Potterian economy and the real world economies.[2]

In many cases, we find that the real and the imaginary worlds are quite similar, which underscores the reality's prominence in the readers' eyes. But there

---

1. *See* Amos Tversky & Daniel Kahneman, *Judgment under Uncertainty: Heuristics and Biases*, 185 SCIENCE, 1,124 (1974).

2. *See* FRANK KNIGHT, THE ECONOMIC ORGANIZATION (1965).

are differences. We take the differences between the real and imaginary worlds to reflect what readers would have *liked* to see. By focusing on the differences while controlling for the similarities, we can make some inferences about the way readers might perceive the economic institutions of the real world.[3]

The Solow Growth Model

Ever since Adam Smith published his book *The Wealth of Nations* in 1776, one of the most important goals of economic science has been to discern and identify the factors that affect the economic growth of countries and the welfare of their citizens. The topic of economic fluctuations and their effects on employment, growth, consumption and income became even more important after the Great Depression in the 1930s, a period during which the average U.S. unemployment rate peaked at twenty-five percent.

In this essay, we rely on the model of growth and development formulated by the Nobel Prize-winning economist Robert Solow as a framework for studying the factors that affect the growth of the Potterian economy.[4] The Solow growth model is a standard textbook workhorse framework for studying economic growth and its determinants. When economists talk about "economic growth," they mean growth in per capita output (or income) and consumption. The Solow growth model focuses on three main ingredients: two factors of production and technological progress. The two factors of production are (i) labor (or population) growth and (ii) investments in physical capital. Technological progress can take one of the two forms. First, technological progress can occur through technological innovations such as improvements in machinery and equipments. Second, technological progress can occur through improvements in the skills and the productive abilities of

---

3. Some might say we are reading too much into the books. After all, the lack of economic growth in the Potterian economy (as we document in this study) might merely serve the author as a simplifying assumption adopted for plot purposes rather than a description of some "ideal" world or the exposition of a particular point of view. But simplifying assumptions only work when they do not stray too far from reality, or else readers are not likely to accept them. That readers accept a fictional economy with these characteristics suggests that they might not be too far from the readers' perceptions and beliefs, regardless of the reason why the author settled on them.

4. *See* Robert Solow, *A Contribution to the Theory of Economic Growth*, 70 Q. J. ECON. 65 (1956); Robert Solow, *Technical Change and the Aggregate Production Function*, 39 REV. ECON. & STAT. 312 (1957).

the work force. The stock of per capita education, training and experience that affect the skills and productiveness of the workers is usually termed "human capital."

Like all models, the Solow model ignores some important aspects of reality that affect welfare and growth, such as inequality in income distribution, productivity differences between workers, and social and political institutions and environments. But its simplicity and elegance make it extremely useful as a benchmark model for analyzing and predicting the long term growth and the performance of economies.

The model assumes that an economy's total output increases when the economy has more workers, more physical and human capital, and better technology. The model also assumes that the returns on investments in physical capital decline as the stock of physical capital per worker increases. This is what economists often call "decreasing marginal product." If, for example, you provide one tractor to a farm where all the workers are using shovels and sickles, production will increase dramatically. Providing a second tractor will also increase production, but not as much as the first one did. Each tractor you add increases the productivity, but the productivity gain of each additional tractor is smaller than the one before.

Similarly, economists also assume that the returns on investments in human capital decline when the stock of human capital per worker increases. As an outcome of these assumptions, the model predicts that an economy's total output increases when the economy has more workers, more physical capital per worker, and more human capital per worker.

It follows that economies with higher birth rates will enjoy greater growth in total output than economies with lower birth rates. However, growth in output does not guarantee economic growth, because economic growth is achieved only when there is growth in the *per capita* output and consumption. Thus, when the population grows, the total output has to grow faster than the population in order for the output per capita to increase. Similarly, when population grows, the stock of physical capital has to grow at least as fast in order to sustain economic growth.

However, when an economy increases its stock of physical capital, it has to spend a larger share of its output on maintaining and operating the larger stock of physical capital. As a consequence, increasing the stock of physical capital is a necessary but not sufficient condition for economic growth. In the Solow model, only constant investments in technology and in human capital lead to long term economic growth, because investments in technology and human capital make workers more productive, and more productive workers earn higher incomes which enable them to increase their consumption and welfare.

Thus, the Solow model predicts that differences in human capital are a major source of differences between economic outcomes across countries. For example, according to the Solow model, a large proportion of the difference between developed and developing economies is an outcome of the differences in the stock of human capital (education, training, and experience), rather than the differences in physical capital.

Another prediction of the Solow model is that investments should flow from rich to poor countries because decreasing marginal product of capital (the tractor example) implies that the return on investments in physical and human capital is greater in countries with lower stock of capital. The same amount of money invested in physical and human capital in a *developing* country should, in theory, give a much bigger return than the same amount invested in a *developed* country where capital stocks are already high.

In the following sections, we study whether these predictions of the Solow model apply to the Potterian economy. To accomplish this, we examine the effects of education, population trends, and capital accumulation on the Potterian economy. In doing so, we also discuss some implications of the findings for real world economies.

Education and Investment in Human Capital

In the Solow model, education improves human capital, improved human capital increases worker productivity, and increased worker productivity contributes to economic growth. Moreover, workers with better education are more likely to invent new technologies or improve existing ones. Thus, economies with a large stock of human capital per capita are also more likely to have a high rate of technological innovations and progress.

Thus, it is not surprising that governments as well as individuals around the world spend a large proportion of their income on education.[5] There is much disagreement, however, on the efficiency with which these investments are made.

Because the Potterian education system receives a special emphasis in the books, we are able to analyze it in detail and assess its likely implications for the Potterian economy.

---

5. *See* Andrew Young, Daniel Levy & Matthew Higgins, *Many Types of Human Capital and Many Roles in US Growth: Evidence from County-Level Educational Attainment Data*, Bar-Ilan University and Emory University Working Paper (2004), available at http://www.economics.emory.edu/Working_Papers/wp/levy_04_02_cover.htm.

Many of the shortcomings of the modern education system, we note, also exist in the Potterian world. Following our assumption that the Harry Potter books appeal to readers because they reflect an environment with which they can identify, we argue that an economic analysis of the Potterian world might offer some insights on readers' beliefs about the current and future state of education.

Harry Potter is a student at Hogwarts School of Witchcraft and Wizardry, a boarding school for underage wizards, and most of the events described in the books take place there. From the first day Harry Potter arrives at the school, and throughout the books, it is clear that at Hogwarts, the curriculum focuses on practical rather than theoretical subjects. Few of the subjects studied are aimed at improving the students' general or theoretical knowledge. Instead, almost all the subjects have practical orientation. The courses in Potions, Herbology, Charms, Care of Magical Creatures, Astrology, Defense Against the Dark Arts, Occlumency, Flying, Apparition, Transfiguration, Enchantments, and Divination all are practically, not theoretically, oriented.

The classes themselves seem to be almost entirely dedicated to practice. At Harry's favorite, Defense against the Dark Arts classes, for example, students are taught to perform various spells and counter jinxes. The class tests consist of putting these skills into action. Similarly, during Charms classes, the students practice casting various useful spells, while at the Transfiguration classes the students study how to change the shapes of various objects and animals. But in none of these classes are the students required to study *why* magic works. Little or no time is devoted to the study of the "Theory of Magic." The wizards adopt a black box approach towards magic. It seems that wizards find it important to know how to *use* magic, but unnecessary to study *how* or *why* the magic works.

It is not surprising, therefore, that Hogwarts' students are good in replicating others' work, in finding facts, and in following instructions precisely. But when it comes to inventing, innovating, or open-mind thinking, Hogwarts' students are less successful. The paragon of Hogwarts students, Hermione Granger, is an example. Hermione does extremely well at the school because she has a remarkable ability to learn facts and use her knowledge at the right moment. When it comes to originality and innovation, however, she does very poorly. For instance, in *The Order of the Phoenix* she tries to establish a secret and secure communication channel between her friends. Despite her contempt for the evil Voldemort and his supporters, the only solution she can come up with is to mimic their communication protocol, even though it has some obvious weaknesses. Her friends, instead of trying to improve her solution, simply accept her authority and praise her for her inventiveness and skill, although she is honest enough to identify the source that inspired her. Another example is given in *The Deathly Hallows* when the Order of the Phoenix continues to use the same protective procedures that failed it in the past because none of its members is able to suggest any alternative procedure, despite the fact that some of its members are among the most able wizards in the world.

While the books focus mostly on Hogwarts, these same shortcomings also seem to apply to other schools in the Potterian world. When students from the three best wizard schools in the world meet for a competition in *The Goblet of Fire*, the reader learns that none of the school champions could have completed their tasks without outside assistance, because they all lack the ability to think originally. Barty Crouch emphasizes this point when he boasts that the schools' champions are fools who cannot work out clues on their own.

The lack of emphasis on a general knowledge in the Potterian education system continues when students graduate from Hogwarts. Nowhere in the books is there any mention of a higher-education system. Wizards do not go to colleges or universities after graduating. Instead, they choose a profession and dedicate their careers to it. Indeed, there is even a fairly sophisticated system of job-matching where students are encouraged to take classes that will be particularly useful for their future careers. None of the students, however, not even Hermione, is advised to study further. This underscores the heavy emphasis that the Potterian education system puts on the narrow goal of obtaining practical knowledge that helps the graduates in finding jobs, but not in advancing further the knowledge of magic.

In the real world, universities, colleges and other research institutes have advantages over other types of learning institutions in that they provide a broader spectrum of knowledge and create what economists sometimes refer to as "non-rivaled" knowledge.[6] Such knowledge, which can be widely shared, serves the entire society in innovation and advancement. When society gives no weight to this type of knowledge and prefers instead that people specialize in one field and dedicate all their energy to serving their workplace—effectively keeping their knowledge as private property—then universities and col-

---

6. In economics, a good is "rivaled" if its possession by one party effectively excludes another from it. Only one person can wear a hat at a time; no one else can wear it so long as the original wearer enjoys it. Goods are "non-rivaled" if a person's enjoyment of them doesn't keep anyone else from enjoying them. For example, a television broadcast or a beautiful day is a non-rivaled good because enjoyment by one person does not exclude anyone else. General knowledge is a "non-rivaled" good because one person's possession of the knowledge does not exclude anyone else from acquiring it.

leges have no competitive advantage over on-the-job training programs, and there is no reason, therefore, for people or governments to finance a university education. Indeed, the government's attitude to formal education is revealed when the ministry of magic first appoints Dolores Umbridge as a schoolmaster and then as a judge, although she has no formal training in either education or law.

The lack of research universities and of professionals who are trained to think and inquire has other implications as well. For example, when in *The Deathly Hallows*, Harry Potter and his friends need help in understanding the relationship between a legend and their current situation, they cannot turn to a scholar who specializes in ancient myth. Instead, they have to find Xenophilius Lovegood, a wizard who is considered a lunatic by his community because he looks for the grains of truth hidden in myth and legends.

Thus, as the students from Hogwarts mature and leave for the job-market, their inability to create and to innovate goes with them. Even the best of Hogwarts students seem to prefer jobs in the public sector or at established institutions. None of the good students try to open a place of their own or try to sell a new product or service.

The only ones who innovate are those who grow outside the system. Professor Dumbledore, Lord Voldemort, Professor Snape, and the Weasley twins are all wizards who disregard the official schooling curriculum. They are the only ones who try and decipher what lies behind the written orders and instructions in textbooks, and come up with new solutions, such as the *Levicorpus* spell invented by Professor Snape as a schoolboy and discussed in *The Half Blood Prince*.

The lack of originality and creative thinking in the Potterian economy is also the source of the Weasley twins' success as entrepreneurs and shop-owners. They are the only students who ignore schooling and prefer the trial-and-error method. But their success only serves to highlight the general state of affairs. We see a public that wants innovations and is willing to pay for them. Yet before the Weasley twins open their shop, no new business has opened in Diagon Alley since Borgin & Burke's, many years before Harry Potter was born.

Thus, the Hogwarts education system, with its emphasis on practice rather than theory, seems to yield poor results. More importantly, it contradicts the goals of scientific education. The Potterian education system seems to belong to a different era, an era when people tended to rely on authorities rather than to look and search for new knowledge on their own initiative. The advantage of the scientific method over other methods for obtaining knowledge is that it emphasizes the systematic, empirical search for answers over various types of "why" and "how" questions. Economists like Fernand Braudel and Joel Mokyr have argued that it was the change in the way people thought about obtaining knowledge that led to the industrial revolution and to the modern world.[7]

The Potterian educational system thus departs sharply from the objectives of the modern education system. It seems to fail in providing its students with the tools that are necessary for inventing new technologies and innovations. As a consequence, the Potterian economy lacks the ability to come up with the constant stream of innovations and new and fresh ideas that is required for sustaining technological progress.

It is therefore intriguing that readers can relate to the Potterian education system and find it appealing. A possible explanation is the gap between the achievements of modern science and the uses of the machinery invented by this science. For example, most education systems view skill at using computers as compulsory, but they do not require students to study how computers function. The same attitude is often found at the workplace as well, where the emphasis is on workers' ability to use rather than understand the machinery they work with. This leads students with future career opportunities in mind to choose more narrow technological studies at the expense of theoretical subjects. This might be a reflection of the recent trends in the Western market economies toward studying more practical and market-oriented subjects such as engineering, business, medicine, law, and computer science.

Further underscoring the emphasis that Hogwarts gives to practical subject matters is the almost complete absence of classes in humanities and general knowledge from its curriculum. The wizards' teaching material includes only two subjects that seem to be purely theoretical, Arithmancy and History of Magic, and of these two, only History of Magic is obligatory. It appears, therefore, that students in the Potterian world do not study arts, philosophy, or other purely theoretical subjects. The fact that wizards do not learn sciences explains why Arithmancy which is Hogwarts' equivalent of mathematics is redundant for most students; when one does not study sciences, it is unnecessary to study the language of the sciences, mathematics. This magnifies the effect of the narrow teaching curriculum, and may further explain why Hogwarts students lack the ability to think for themselves.

If the Potterian model reflects a situation readers are familiar with, then this suggests that readers of Harry Potter do not view the current schooling system as one that encourages creativity and originality. It suggests that the readers expect that new school graduates would focus on maintaining and per-

---

7. *See* FERNAND BRAUDEL, AFTERTHOUGHTS ON MATERIAL CIVILIZATION AND CAPITALISM (1979); Joel Mokyr, *Technological Inertia in Economic History*, 52 J. ECON. HIST. 325 (1992).

haps improving existing knowledge and technologies rather than searching for new inventions and innovations. It also suggests that the readers seem to agree with the view that the education system gives greater emphasis to private job-oriented schooling and less emphasis to general education which yields general and unrivaled knowledge.

Another important question that is related to the issue of investments in human capital is the lack of classes in spoken foreign languages. The Solow model predicts that since investment is most profitable in places where the stock of existing capital is small, investors and entrepreneurs would choose to invest more in developing countries. This process should lead, over time, to a more equal distribution of capital and wealth across nations, a phenomenon often termed "income convergence" in the economic literature. The real world data, however, does not support this prediction. The Potterian model may offer some clues for this "home country bias."[8] In the Potterian economy, more so than in our world, wizards should have little concern for distances when they do business. The books give ample examples of the ease of travel and communication in the wizards' society. Wizards can fly from one place to another on personal broomsticks, or they can use the Floo network, Portkeys, or transportation spells to move instantaneously from place to place. This absence of significant transportation cost should facilitate trade between wizards even from the most remote places. Consider for example the price of eggs: if wizards can travel at zero or low cost between any two points, and if the price of eggs is much lower in one place than another, then every wizard would shop at the place with the lower price.

The situation depicted in the books, however, does not indicate such an open market. Potterian wizards interact with foreign wizards only rarely. Harry Potter and his friends do not meet foreign wizards until they go to the Quidditch World Cup Tournament in *The Goblet of Fire*, when they are almost fifteen years old. This initial interaction with foreigners is also marked with a

---

8. This is the term used by economists to refer to the phenomenon of investors' apparent preference to invest in their home countries rather than investing in other countries even if the latter would yield higher returns on the investment. Possible explanations for the home country bias include lack of information about many aspects of the conditions in foreign countries which include political risks, economic uncertainty, policy uncertainty, exchange rate risks, etc. *See* Daniel Levy, *Investment-Saving Comovement and Capital Mobility: Evidence from Century-Long US Time Series*, 3 Rev. Econ. Dyn. 100 (2000); Daniel Levy, *Investment-Saving Comovement under Endogenous Fiscal Policy*, 6 Open Econ. Rev. 237 (1995); Daniel Levy, *Investment-Saving Comovement, Capital Mobility, and Fiscal Policy*, UC-Irvine Economics Paper No. 90-91-04 (1990); Karen Lewis, *Trying to Explain Home Bias in Equities and Consumption*, 37 J. Econ. Lit. 571 (1999).

series of misunderstandings. Ludo Bagman, who is in charge of the cooperation with official delegations from abroad, does not feel embarrassed to boast
that he cannot communicate with his guests.

In addition to the lack of foreign languages skills, Hogwarts students are
also unfamiliar with other nations' cultures and traditions. When foreign students arrive at Hogwarts in *The Goblet of Fire*, a feast is held in their honor. At
the feast, French dishes are served, but many Hogwarts students pass on them
because they are unfamiliar with the strange flavors, names, and appearances
of the food. A similar kind of disrespect and lack of cultural knowledge is displayed by the visiting foreign students. French champion Fleur Delacour is
keen to show the superiority of her nation's way of doing things, but her remarks in *The Goblet of Fire* that "we 'ad a different way of doing things. I think
eet was better," often irritate her English hosts.

The mistrust between people of different nations is also demonstrated by the
fact that one of the first tasks that Percy Weasley receives in the ministry of
magic is to set regulations to stop the import of cauldrons because imported
cauldrons are of a "low quality."

The same problem of distrust and misunderstandings also exists between wizards and other creatures. For example, when Harry Potter tries to negotiate
with a goblin in *The Deathly Hollows*, he finds that the possibility of reaching
a satisfactory contract is made complicated by his inability to understand the
goblin's traditions and style of negotiations.

Thus, in the Potterian world, negative sentiments towards foreigners are
found both among average people, like the Weasleys, and public officials, like
Bagman. In the Potterian world, young people from different countries are
unable to communicate with each other, and they only meet sporadically. When
they do meet, it is in situations that encourage animosity rather than cooperation, such as the Quidditch World Cup and the Triwizard Tournament. The
Potterian world shows that a lack of both the will and the ability to communicate with foreigners may be an important barrier to international flow of
goods, services, and ideas. This is consistent with recent work by economists
that suggests that trade patterns are often determined not only by objective
characteristics (such as profits and costs) but also by cultural aspects such as
religion, history of conflicts, genetic similarities, and languages.[9] A good example is the trade between Canada and the United States. Despite the fact that

9. *See* Volker Nitsch, *National Borders and International Trade: Evidence from the European Union*, 33 Can. J. Econ. 1091 (2000); Luigi Guiso, Paola Sapienza & Luigi Zingales,
Cultural Biases in Economic Exchange, Nat'l Bureau of Econ. Research Working Paper No.
11005 (2004).

people from these two nations have a strong common heritage and speak the same language, they nevertheless trade with each other much less than the standard economic model would predict.[10]

The implication of the Potterian experience is that lowering the costs of transportation and removing trade barriers such as tariffs might not be enough to promote international trade and investments. Insufficiently broad education and stereotypical beliefs may form barriers to international commerce and trade. The Potterian model suggests that international trade will not reach its full potential as long as people do not invest enough in studying foreign languages, culture and institutions.

Population Trends

Since the baby-boom that followed World War II, the population growth rate in most of the developed world has been on the decline. In some developed countries, the natural growth rate, that is, the difference between the number of births and deaths is already negative. There are fewer children and more old people. In 2005, for example, the population growth rate in Italy was only 0.07 percent, despite a positive immigration rate of over 2.2 new immigrants for every 1,000 Italian citizens. This leads to a decrease in the local labor force and to an increase in the demand for foreign labor, in addition to an increase in the demand for health services and retirement expenditures for the aging population. At the same time, other countries have such a high population growth rate that they cannot produce enough to meet the population's needs and wants. As a consequence, people in these countries suffer from starvation and fight wars over natural resources.

In the Solow model, this is mainly explained as a result of changes in the stock of physical capital per worker. Holding everything else constant, when physical capital in an economy grows at the same rate as the population, the per capita stock of physical capital does not change and the economy's total output grows at the same rate as the labor force. When capital accumulates faster than the population growth, the per-capita stock of capital increases and the economy's total output grows at a faster rate than the population. When the population grows faster than physical capital, then the per capita stock of physical capital decreases and per capita output decreases.

---

10. *See* John McCallum, *National Borders Matter: Canada-US Regional Trade Patterns*, 85 Amer. Econ. Rev. 615 (1995); Charles Engel & John Rogers, *How Wide is the Border*, 86 Amer. Econ. Rev. 1112 (1996).

Thus, developed economies that have low birth rates and large investments in physical capital, enjoy economic growth. Economies such as those of Sub-Saharan Africa which have high birth rates and low investments in physical capital have a low or even negative economic growth.

In the Potterian economy, population trends are similar to the situation in developed countries during the 1990s, and they do not seem to increase even after the conclusion of the war in *The Deathly Hallows*. Thus, the birth rate in the Potterian economy seems to be extremely low. Recall that for the population to remain steady, every married couple must have at least two children. Wizards do not appear to cross that threshold. Almost none of Harry's friends and classmates have siblings. The main exceptions are the Weasleys and the Patil sisters. However, the six Weasley children are such an uncommon phenomenon that other children sometimes ridicule them, and Padma and Parvati Patil are twins, so they do not break the rule of one pregnancy per woman. Since almost all of the wizard children in the United Kingdom study at Hogwarts, this implies a birth rate of no more than 1–1.5 children per woman, which is as low, or even lower, than countries with a negative natural population growth rate. In Italy, for example, where the birth rate is about 1.2 children per woman, it is only about eighty percent of the death rate, leading to a decline in population. The situation does not seem to be very different in the wizard community where the low birth rate leads to the disappearance of some of the old wizard families, such as the Blacks and the Gaunts.

We previously saw that human capital growth in the Potterian world is low, given its lack of innovation. If population growth is negative, and population declines, then the Solow model predicts that total output should reach a standstill. The wizards, however, are used to a high quality of life. To maintain the high standard of living, they must retain their workforce to sustain production. This is particularly true in areas where wizards seem to dislike to work such as factories, manual services, and banking. To satisfy their need for workers, wizards rely on two sources. First, they enslave various humanoid creatures and force them to do some of the most unpleasant work. The house-elves that fill the role of house serfs, for example, do all the unpleasant housework for well-off families and institutions. Another example is the goblins. According to Harry's history books, the goblins fought several wars against the wizards but they were defeated and were forced to give up much of their freedom. In return, the wizards allow them to make their living by operating financial institutions. It seems that the wizards regard those who handle money as avid and as usurers, so they prefer to leave this job to outsiders.

A second source of workers is immigrants. Those are people with magical skills who are born to parents that are not wizards, and immigrate from their communities to the wizard world. They do so in order to win the advantages of living in the wizards' economy, which is still richer and more advanced than the non-wizards' economy, despite its very slow growth rate. For example, wizards control means of production that allow even the poorest wizards to live in a relative comfort. Even the Weasleys—although poor, live in a large house in the countryside, are connected to a quick transport and communication system (the Floo network), receive the newspaper every day by mail, have the wizard equivalent of television, and possess many other useful utensils, such as knives that chop on their own, and stoves that ignite on command. Most importantly, they always have enough to feed both themselves and any number of guests who pay them a visit. Thus, given the wizards' high standards of living, it is not surprising that Justin Finch-Fletchley, for example, gave up prestigious Eton in order to study at Hogwarts.

The dependence on immigrant workers, however, raises many difficulties within the wizard community. The old wizard families are enraged that newcomers compete with them in the job market, and they mock the immigrants for their cultural backwardness. There is also strong racial discrimination against the wizards who come from non-wizards' families. For example, the wizards use the term "Muggles" to refer to people who do not possess magical skills, and they often use the derogatory term "Mudblood" to refer to wizards who were born in families of Muggles. Many wizards from old families, such as Lucius Malfoy and his colleagues, actively act to limit the number and power of the immigrants. For example, Malfoy does not hide his motives for objecting to Professor Dumbeldore's appointment as the headmaster of Hogwarts. In *The Order of the Phoenix* he declares in a newspaper interview that in his opinion Dumbledore is wrong for not discriminating enough against other races and children from non-wizard families.

It seems that many of the wizards who sympathize with Malfoy want to limit the ability of Mudbloods to compete with the pure-blood wizards for prestigious jobs and to move up the social ladder. The hatred of the upper tiers of the wizard society towards the newcomers is so great that the "Death Eaters," a well-funded and well-organized group that supports Lord Voldemort and serves as his private army, go to war against the wizard establishment over the issue of limiting the power of Mudbloods. In the later books this group enjoys so much success that those who oppose it, such as Harry and his friends, consider themselves to be a minority that must hide their activities. This is a testament to the large public support that anti-immigrant feelings and views have in Potterian society. Indeed when the government sets a task force to send all the Mudbloods to prison, it seems that its actions win the support of many of the wizards' middle class.

Even before the outbreak of the violence, however, it seems that efforts to prevent immigration have been successful enough to prevent population growth. The number of immigrants seems to be large enough to prevent an actual decline in the size of the workforce, as indicated by the fact that Hogwarts opens every year with about the same number of students. Hogwarts, however, does not grow, and there is no indication that there is a need to increase the number of schools in the wizard community. But the population balance in the wizard community is not stable. The social schism, the prejudice, the restrictions, and finally the civil war that shakes the Potterian world could seriously impair the society's ability to keep its population from decline.

The population trends in the Potterian world are consistent with the Solow model. Where there is little growth in human capital, population growth is tightly linked with economic growth. As the population in the Potterian world stagnates, so does its economy.

Remember that the Solow model predicts that as gains in physical capital slow down in rich societies, investors from rich economies would invest in poor economies, where they can earn higher returns on their investments. But, as noted above, human capital barriers such as ignorance and a poor education system prevent them from taking advantage of such opportunities. Instead of investments flowing from the Potterian economy to the Muggle world, it is the Muggles who migrate into the Potterian economy. This would in itself be an economic boon, but the assimilation process is difficult and complicated.

Interestingly, the fictional Potterian world closely reflects reality, where differences in capital and wealth between the developed and developing world lead to a flow of immigrants from poor to rich societies, rather than a flow of capital from rich to poor countries. In many countries, massive immigration is necessary to maintain the growth of the population, but the immigration also increases racial discrimination, social unrest and harassment of the foreigners by local populations. This nonproductive activity wastes resources and reduces productivity, as workers devote their efforts to destructive rather than productive use.[11] In the Potterian world, this ultimately leads to a civil war. In the real world, it usually results in racial conflicts, social unrest, and a struggle over jobs between locals and immigrants. Violent riots and the success of anti-immigrant parties in Europe in 2000–2009, offer a modern day example of this type of problem. These types of negative sentiments towards immigrants are more common and more widespread in depressed economies. The

---

11. *See* Gil S. Epstein & Shmuel Nitzan, *The Struggle over Migration Policy*, 19 J. POP. ECON. 703 (2006).

Potterian economy does not grow, it does not expand, and thus the Potterians' negative attitude towards the "foreigners" persists, as expected.

Investment in Physical Capital

As we have seen, improvements in human capital, technology and population growth play an important role in determining the growth path of an economy. Another factor that affects economic growth is the growth rate of the stock of physical capital.[12] Because the term "physical capital" stands for all types of infrastructure, machines, tools, equipment, and other physical factors of production, it would be hard to imagine how a worker's output could grow without improvements in, and additions to, the stock of capital that is at his disposal.

Frequently in history, improvements in human capital occurred hand in hand with additions to the stock of capital. It is often hard to distinguish one type of improvement from another. But even the most able and knowledgeable worker will not be more effective than his or her predecessor without the right tools.

The Solow model predicts that in the long run, the growth rate of physical capital should equal the growth rate of the population plus the growth rate of the human capital plus the rate of technological progress. We have already seen that neither the population nor the human capital grows in the Potterian economy. Thus, the model predicts that there should be little or no growth in the stock of physical capital. Below we assess whether or not this prediction holds for the Potterian economy.

Very broadly, one can divide all products into two types: "consumption goods" and "investment goods." Consumption goods are things produced for end-consumers. Examples include food, clothing, entertainment, transportation services, and medical services. Investment goods are things used as intermediary inputs in the production of other goods, like buildings, production lines, warehouses, machines, and raw materials. These investment goods are used as the "capital input" into the production process. "Investment" is the process by which capital is accumulated in the economy.

In the Potterian economy, it appears that all productive efforts concentrate on producing consumption goods. There are shops that offer clothes, foods,

---

12. *See* Paul M. Romer, *Crazy Explanations for the Productivity Slowdown*, 1987 MACRO-ECON. ANN. 163; Ben S. Bernanke, *Comments on Romer*, 1987 MACROECON. ANN. 202; Daniel Levy, *Output, Capital, and Labor in the Short and Long Run*, 60 S. ECON. J. 946 (1994).

jokes, newspapers, and many other consumer goods and services that wizards value for their daily use. However, the wizards put far less emphasis on adding to their stock of capital. Nowhere in the books is there a description of a new factory. Until the Weasley twins open their shop there are not even any new types of products. And even the Weasley twins do not use any novel production techniques or methods. Instead, they use old methods to produce new types of goods. For example, one of their most important innovations is a type of defensive clothing. Yet they did not invent either the magic or the technique which combines the magic with the clothing. They simply identified the needs of consumers in the marketplace.

Nor does it seem that the Weasleys' new products result in any economic growth, because economic growth occurs when people consume more. The Weasleys' shop, however, only makes people switch from shopping in older shops like Zonko's Joke shop to shopping in the Weasleys' new shop, but it does not enable them to increase their total consumption.

In addition to the lack of advancements in production technologies, there are also no improvements or additions to the infrastructure. There are no new schools, new buildings, or new housing. When a new stadium is built for the Quidditch World Cup tournament it is destroyed after the competition is over. Similarly, the wizards do not try to improve their communication systems. The Floo network, for example, has apparently served the wizards for many years, perhaps hundreds of years, but there are no noticeable attempts to improve or upgrade it. For example, it could have saved Molly Weasley her washing troubles if the Floo network were upgraded to use something other than chimneys.

Thus, it seems that the Potterian economy is one where there are no improvements in human capital, and there are also no or little improvements in existing production technologies. For example, in the Potterian economy there are no new factories that use novel production methods, no new devices that enable better, quicker or more reliable transportation, and no or little addition to existing infrastructures, buildings and services. The only new goods that are produced are consumption goods, and most of these goods are improvements of existing models rather than new products. Thus, it seems that the wizards' economy has reached a high level of technology and welfare, and then stagnates at that level. This stagnation can be seen in the slow growth rate of the population, in the very slow rate of inventions and in the very slow rate of improvements in workers' human capital. For example, although wizards are expected to leave Hogwarts with good knowledge in magic, it seems that the material that they learn there does not evolve over time. For example, in *The Half Blood Prince*,

Harry Potter and his classmates study from the same book as Harry's parents, and he even uses a secondhand copy that belonged to one of his father's classmates.

Thus, because the Solow model predicts that physical capital should accumulate at the same rate as the population growth rate plus the rate of technological progress, the Solow model predicts that the growth rate of physical capital and per capita income of the Potterian economy should be very slow or perhaps even zero. The situation described in the books is consistent with this prediction, and the Potterian economy seems to have a very slow or perhaps even zero growth rate.

The notion that economies tend to stagnate once they reach a high level of welfare is not novel, and it may have its origins in observations regarding the fate of the Roman Empire, which collapsed after it reached a very high standard of living. It seems that modern readers of Harry Potter find it relatively natural to believe that very advanced economies would stagnate once they have reached a high level of welfare. This seems consistent with predictions in the popular press in the beginning of the 2000s which predicted the end of the era in which the Western countries dominated the world. According to people who support this view, people in the highly developed Western economies are not as diligent as people in less developed economies, and as a consequence the growth rate of economies in the western world is very slow relative to the growth rate of some of the emerging economies of South East Asia.

Having described the economy, however, we are not finished. What are the forces that operate within the Potterian economy that make it behave in the way it behaves? Why is the population not growing, capital not accumulating, and education not improving? Is there a causal link between the institutions in the Potterian economy and its failure to grow?[13]

The Potterian Economy as an Economic Model

We have seen that the imaginary Potterian economy behaves in a way that is consistent with the predictions of the Solow growth model. In this section, we try to identify some of the institutional factors that we believe contribute to the lack of growth in the Potterian economy.

---

13. We examine these issues more fully in Daniel Levy & Avichai Snir, *Potterian Economy: Popular Perceptions and Political Economy in the Contrived World of Harry Potter*, Bar-Ilan University and Emory University Working Paper (2005), *available at* http://papers.ssrn.com/sol3/papers.cfm?abstract_id=809465.

One of the limitations of macroeconomic models such as the Solow growth model is that they yield predictions on the macroeconomic level, but they often fail to explain the underlying mechanisms that determine the economy's path. The Solow growth model can tell us that economies that do not accumulate capital will suffer slower growth, but it does not tell us why the economy is not accumulating capital. In this section we want to focus on the behavior of institutions in the Potterian economy to try to answer that question. We think this will also shed some light on the perceptions and attitudes of Harry Potter readers toward the interrelationships between financial, social, political and economic outcomes.

The two institutions we will look at are the two that are the most important to development of economic growth: governments and financial markets. Financial markets are critical for providing the resources that stimulate economic growth. Governments can provide infrastructures and regulations that facilitate economic growth, but they can also act as a powerful barrier to economic growth.

Modern governments are powerful. In well-functioning societies, this power is given voluntarily by the people. In return, governments establish various institutions crucial to the economy, such as a system of laws, a court and legal system, police, and certain infrastructure. They may also be charged with enhancing public welfare by promoting various socio-economic goals such as full employment and price stability. On many occasions, however, government officials abuse the power given to them to obtain personal benefits (in terms of power or money) instead of improving the welfare of their people. Public officials motivated by personal gain may spend public money on inefficient projects rather than making investments in profitable and beneficial projects.

Importantly, the larger the government, the more resources will be lost to inefficiency and corruption. Since inefficiency and corruption wastes resources, economists agree that large governments usually reduce economic growth.[14] This is often known as the "crowding out" effect because when governments supply many services and goods, private entrepreneurs usually cannot compete with the governments and as a consequence they are crowded out of the market. Because governments are often less efficient than private entrepreneurs in

---

14. *See* Arye Hillman, Public Finance and Public Policy, Second Edition (2009); Toke S. Aidt, *Economic Analysis of Corruption: A Survey*, 113 Econ. J. F. 632 (2003); Matthew Higgins, Daniel Levy & Andrew Young, *Growth and Convergence across the United States: Evidence from County-Level Data*, 88 Rev. Econ. Stat. 671 (2006); Matthew Higgins, Andrew Young, & Daniel Levy, *Federal, State and Local Governments: Evaluating their Separate Roles in US Growth*, 139 Public Choice 493 (2009).

inventing new technologies and in supplying goods and services, the crowd-ing out effect usually has negative implications for the growth rates of economies with large governments. For example, it is believed that the crowding out ef-fect is one of the reasons for the collapse of many Communist economies.

In the Potterian world, the government is run by the Minister of Magic, whose role is equivalent to that of a prime minister in a democratic country. But the Minister of Magic is not elected in free elections. Instead, he is ap-pointed by some unspecified process on which the ruling elite seem to have a strong influence. Cornelius Fudge, we learn from the books, was named Min-ister because he does not have the backbone to oppose the rich and powerful.

The Minister of Magic is in charge of a very large public sector which con-trols a substantial portion of the Potterian economy. For example, the gov-ernment is responsible for law-enforcement, international relations, sports, trade regulations, transportation, education, communications, control of non-human races (including the behavior of the goblin bankers), nature preserva-tion, the financial system, and almost every other aspect of the economy. Consequently, almost all the wizards mentioned in the book are employed by the Ministry of Magic. The number of people who work at the government office building is so large that when Harry sees it for the first time in *The Order of the Phoenix* his mouth falls open in astonishment.

The government, therefore, can easily influence the life of almost every-body in the Potterian economy. In *The Half-Blood Prince*, for example, mem-bers of the Weasley family express fear when the Minister of Magic comes to visit them on one chilly Christmas Day. Fear of a conflict with public officials is a barrier to free thought and to private entrepreneurship. In the Potterian world, people must avoid conflict with the government simply to keep their jobs.

Note how this fits with what we saw in the earlier parts of this paper, when we described how Hogwarts produces students who are technically competent but unable to think freely and critically. This deficiency in the school system may be directly related to the risk that adult wizards might face if their free thinking puts them in a conflict with the Ministry. The Ministry appears well aware of the importance of controlling the educational process; to force its view on the population, it does not hesitate to interfere in the teaching curriculum and even appoints a High Inquisitor to monitor the curriculum and to ensure that none of the students express any opinion that differs from the official one.

Another way in which the Potterian government interferes in the market-place is by setting regulations that make it difficult to develop or offer new products. Percy Weasley's attempt in *The Goblet of Fire* to standardize some-thing as trifling as the thickness of a cauldron bottom is an example of government intervention that limits the options and choices that wizard consumers have.

If only few types of cauldrons are authorized, then consumers may not have the option of choosing the one that fits best their needs, tastes, and incomes. In that case, they will be forced to buy only the models that have received official licenses and authorization.

When rules and regulations become excessive it is difficult for entrepreneurs to innovate. They can try to obtain permits from the appropriate government officials, but this opens the door for corrupt bureaucrats to obtain personal benefits in return for the permits.[15] When, in *The Goblet of Fire*, a senior government official, Mr. Crouch, tries to intervene in favor of a certain importer, he does not hide the fact that he has personal interest in the goods that this entrepreneur plans to import. This kind of corruption appears rife in the Potterian world. People like Lucius Malfoy and his friends do not hesitate to use their money to influence politicians. Ministry officials in *The Order of the Phoenix* are well aware that Malfoy is well connected, and that he is entitled to "favors" because he is "giving generously." Such policies have a strong negative effect on economic growth because they increase the costs of investment.[16] At the extreme, government bureaucracies in the real world are sometimes set up for the sole purpose of extracting bribes from entrepreneurs.[17]

Without the ability to get a permit, the only way entrepreneurs can sell new products is by breaking the rules. This is, in fact, the method the Weasley twins use, but their success in avoiding government intervention may be due in large part to the looming war. In *The Goblet of Fire*, Mrs. Weasley predicts that the twins "will end up in front of the Improper Use of Magic Office" for their commercial activities, and if not for the Ministry's preoccupation with more important matters she might have been right.

The Potterian government is large, inefficient, and corrupt, and thus forms a barrier to economic growth. Because it supplies so many goods and services, and because it regulates so many other goods and services, even the few entrepreneurs in the Potterian economy who would have liked to set a new business or offer a new good are prevented from doing so by the bureaucracy. Thus, the crowding out effect in the Potterian economy is very strong, and therefore it might be one of the main reasons for the slow growth rate.

---

15. *See* Daniel Levy, *Price Adjustment under the Table: Evidence on Efficiency-Enhancing Corruption*, 23 EUR. J. POLIT. ECON. 423 (2007).

16. *See* Shang-Jin Wei, *Local Corruption and Global Capital Flow*, 2000 BROOKINGS PAP. ECON. ACT. 303.

17. *See* Alberto Ades & Rafael Di Tella, *Rents, Corruption and Competition*, 89 AM. ECON. REV. 982 (1999).

Another inefficiency of the wizards' government is caused by the fact that it is controlled by incumbent elite of wizard society, it encourages the status quo and discourages change. If entrepreneurs can succeed and climb up the social and economic ladder, the existing elites may lose some of their power and influence. Thus, in *The Order of the Phoenix* we are told explicitly that the rich and powerful wizards buy and control senior officials in order to "delay laws" that they "don't want passed."

Moreover, in *The Deathly Hallows*, the structure of the government allows Voldemort and his supporters to gain control by bringing a few senior officials to support their side. Once they secure their control on these officials, the fear from a conflict with senior ministry officials forces all the other members of society to accept the government's instructions, even when these instructions conflict with their own private opinions and norms.

The Potterian world also offers a perspective on the difficulties of reforming large governments in order to make them more efficient. Because it is so large, the Potterian public sector is able to offer job security to everybody, even to the most inefficient—such as Bertha Jorkins, who in *The Goblet of Fire* disappears for a month without anyone getting worried, because she "got lost plenty of times." The lower- and middle-class wizards have little interest in opposing the government because it provides a job security as well as social, health and entertainment services. The Potterian public sector is also so large and has so much influence over every aspect of life that no individual wizard can realistically oppose it. Even Professor Dumbledore, the most powerful character in the Harry Potter books, has to leave his office and flee in *The Order of the Phoenix* when his opinions bring him into conflict with the Minister of Magic.

Under these circumstances, the government in the Potterian world would oppose actions that would promote economic growth. The rich wizards oppose any change that could promote economic growth because it might erode their power, while the rest of the wizard world—which might be better off with more growth—is too dependent on the system to force the government to change. The result is that the government would consistently oppose entrepreneurial activity, educational reform, and immigration—and will likely stick to those policies no matter how much the economy stagnates.

The second type of institution a society needs for economic growth is some mechanism that facilitates the flow of funds from investors to entrepreneurs. Entrepreneurs who want to improve production need money to invest in buying equipment, hiring workers, and so forth. But it is often the case that entrepreneurs with good investment ideas do not have the money to carry out their plans. In such cases they must look for investors who would agree to put some money in their project, either as a loan or in exchange for profit sharing in the future (for example, by means of issuing and selling stocks or shares), when the project starts to yield profits.

In modern economies, the role of matching entrepreneurs who look for funds with people who are willing to provide funds is filled by banks and stock exchanges. When people buy stocks and bonds, they become investors who transfer their money to entrepreneurs who run the firms that issue those stocks and bonds, and who use the money to invest in the firm. In return, the stock and bond buyers receive dividend and interest payments, respectively. Commercial banks and other credit institutions play a similar role, although in a different guise. Banks collect money from savers and then loan the money to entrepreneurs who pay it back with interest to the bank. The bank pays a portion of these interest receipts to the savers, and keeps the remainder of the interest as a profit.

These types of institutions do not exist in the Potterian economy. There is no stock exchange, and therefore Potterian investors cannot raise funds directly from the public. The monopoly bank, Gringotts, does not offer loans and does not pay interest. It is used by wizards as means for safekeeping their money, but wizards do not deposit money in interest-bearing saving accounts, where it can be lent out, but in vaults. The bank apparently makes its profits from funding gold-hunting expeditions, by recovering money that was already used in the economy. The Potterian banking system does not offer investment funding opportunities, and thus it does not encourage production of new goods and services that would bring about economic growth.

People who are in need of extra gold, therefore, have two main options. First, they can turn to usurers who are willing to give loans in exchange for very high interest, and who use very cruel means to make sure the loans are paid back. For example, when Ludo Bagman cannot pay back a loan that he took, he has to resign his job and flee. Thus, entrepreneurs who may have a plan for a small business might not consider seriously the option of taking a loan. Second, the entrepreneur can find some individual with deep-pockets that is willing to invest or make a loan. The problem is that most of the money in the Potterian economy is held by the ruling elites, and these wizards, as we have seen, are not interested in helping poor entrepreneurs succeed. It is therefore unlikely that an entrepreneur without personal wealth would be able to implement his plans, no matter how good and promising his project is. This is illustrated by the Weasley twins, who in *The Goblet of Fire* even consider gambling as a means of financing their shop. The Weasley twins are, however, lucky, because they have a friend who wins a large sum of money and gives it to them as a gift. That allows them to start their business, but the fact that they are the only people who open a shop in Diagon Alley in many years suggests that most wizards do not have similar luck.

The Potterian economy highlights the importance of political and financial institutions in determining economic growth. The Solow growth model predicts very little growth for Harry Potter's world, and the main reason for that lack of growth is institutional. The government is large and inefficient and the bureaucracy is so cumbersome that it prevents entrepreneurs from offering new products. At the same time, there is a total lack of financial markets in which entrepreneurs can raise funds. The large and inefficient government, combined with the lack of financial markets, brings about stagnation of the Potterian economy.

How is this relevant? It turns out that real-world economies that resemble the world of Harry Potter find themselves developing in much the same way. Societies that do not experience economic growth tend to develop elites whose vested interests may be harmed by change. These elites act to minimize reforms and development that could jeopardize their dominant position. Societies with entrenched elites who oppose change, without financial markets, and without good education systems will see no economic growth.

Conclusions

From the popularity of the Harry Potter books, it seems that the Potterian economy makes perfect sense to readers. That the readers of the series do not find it logically implausible suggests that the Potterian economy can teach us something about the way that these readers perceive their own environment. The stagnation of the Potterian economy may reflect people's perceptions of their own situation in many of the world's leading countries, where government has grown, population growth is shrinking, and economic growth is low. It is interesting that even in a book that describes an economy that uses magic as its main production technology, slow population growth and slow rate of technological progress are associated with slow economic progress. We take this as an indication of the strength of the basic intuition behind the Solow model which seems to appeal to both professionals and layman alike.

The government in the Potterian world offers job-security, health, education and other public services to all. It offers a stable economy, so there are no unexpected macroeconomic shocks. Until the official declaration of the war in *The Half Blood Prince*, the Potterian economy has apparently remained very stable, as there were no noticeable changes in the quantity, quality or prices of the goods offered. This situation seems to be convenient to most middle class wizards. Even Mr. Weasley, who is frequently critical of the Ministry, is proud to be a civil servant and sees his career (and those of his children) as serving the public good.[18] In this respect, the books seem to reflect the favorable attitudes of readers to the role of large governments in managing the economy. The achievements of the Ministry, such as full employment, stability and universal health care are likely to be attractive to many readers, especially to those favoring the model of a welfare state.

At the same time, however, the books are critical of the way that the system interferes with people who want to advance in life. Mudbloods are discriminated against. Elves are enslaved. Even purebloods like Mr. Weasley, who do not have the right connections, are stuck in the bottom of the social ladder and in ordinary circumstances would be unable to advance. Advancement in the Potterian world seems to be based on connections with the ruling elites, not necessarily on one's ability, as seen by the circle of influence that Professor Slughorn in *The Half Blood Prince* tries to cultivate with his student club.

We read the books as suggesting that the price the Potterian economy pays for stable employment, income, and production, is low social mobility, no economic growth and inefficient bureaucracy that interferes with everyday life. Readers seem to empathize with the powerful public sector that takes care of everyone, and at the same time, they object and fear the corruption, cronyism and restrictions on liberty that accompany it. The impression that readers find this conjunction plausible gives us some interesting insights on how they perceive their own world and its possible future.

Before we close, there is a puzzle about the Potterian economy yet to be explored. The reader may have noticed that something important has been omitted in our discussion of government, financial markets, and economic growth. Over the course of seven books there is not a single mention of *taxes* being collected by either the Ministry of Magic or by any local authority—despite the fact that the Ministry is the largest employer in the Potterian economy and it finances many activities that require money. The fact that wizards do not complain about the burden of taxes is a puzzle that deserves further research.

---

18. *See* Josse Delfgaauw & Robert Dur, *Incentives and Workers' Motivation in the Public Sector*, 118 ECON. J. 171 (2008).

The Magic of Money and Banking

Eric J. Gouvin

"I don't know how the Muggles manage without magic."
—Rubeus Hagrid[1]

As a fan of the Harry Potter books and a banking law professor, I wish J.K. Rowling had provided more details about the banking system in the wizarding world. Although banking may strike the casual reader as something quite mundane, it is, in fact, one of the few magical things Muggles can do. Banking magical? Yes, indeed—banking is magic because bankers create money out of thin air.

Money is the sort of useful device that is so much a part of our life that we often forget that it had to be invented. Humans did not always have money, but it is hard to imagine a modern Muggle economy functioning without it. The economy of the wizarding world uses money as well, but there are striking differences between the magical and Muggle worlds on this point. We can only speculate on why these differences exist, but a brief history of money and banking as they evolved among the Muggles[2] may give us some insight on the role played by money and banking in the world of Harry Potter.

A Quick History of Money

Going back to first principles, it is worth noting that primitive economies can exist without money. In these simple economic systems trade occurs through barter. Barter economies suffer from a glaring problem, however, namely, a transaction will not take place unless Party *A* wants what Party *B* has to trade

---

1. *Sorcerer's Stone* 67.

2. For an accessible account of the development of money and banking in the Muggle world, *see* John Kenneth Galbraith, Money: From Whence it Came, Where it Went (1975).

and *B* wants what *A* has to trade. Economists call this dilemma the "double coincidence of wants" problem. Of course, things could get more complex, such as where *B* might trade with *A* because *B* wants something that *C* has and he knows that *C* wants what *A* has to trade, but this can get awfully complicated awfully fast.

Money solves the double coincidence of wants problem by providing a *medium of exchange* that trading parties will accept. Traders don't want money because it is money, but rather because money can be used in trade with other people to obtain other things of value. The system is ingenious and cultures around the world have invented it independently since the dawn of civilization. The range of items that have been used as money is truly impressive, from bags of salt to nails to huge round stones. Today, of course, the government by law can designate pieces of paper as money merely by specifying that, say, Federal Reserve notes are "legal tender for all debts public and private."[3] Historically, however, the first "money" most societies developed derived from a commodity that had wide utility, such as beaver pelts or cattle or, during the colonial period in the United States, tobacco.

People would be willing to take commodities as money because even if they could not convince another trading partner to take the commodity as money, at least they were in possession of a useful commodity. In order for such commodity money to be truly useful, however, it needed to meet three criteria: it had to be (1) durable, (2) not subject to oversupply, and (3) something that people would willingly trade for. Commodities that are not durable do not make good money because we expect money to serve as a *store of value* as well as a medium of exchange (i.e., accumulating money should be a convenient way to stockpile wealth). Commodities that are subject to oversupply are unacceptable as money because they will be devalued if there is an increase in the supply of the commodity/money in the market place. Economists call such an oversupply of money "inflation." Inflation is usually viewed as a bad thing because useful money also needs to serve as a *standard of value,* that is, as a common language people in the market can use to communicate how much things are worth. If the value of the money changes too much, it cannot fulfill that function. Finally, in order to be useful as a medium of exchange, the commodity that serves as money must be something traders can and will accept. So, for example, although cattle have served as money in some rural societies, using cows as money never caught on in urban environments where storage of cattle was a serious problem for active traders.

---

3. *See* Coinage Act of 1965, 31 U.S.C. § 5103 (2000) ("United States coins and currency (including Federal reserve notes and circulating notes of Federal reserve banks and national banks) are legal tender for all debts, public charges, taxes, and dues.").

Clearly, some commodities meet these requirements better than others. Given the practical constraints on the kinds of commodities that will be useful as money, economies the world over and throughout history have reached the same conclusion: precious metals make for good money. Gold, silver, and copper are durable, not subject to wild changes in supply, and in a physical form that traders can accept. In addition, these metals have some intrinsic value as commodities. The Muggle world and the magic world seem to have arrived at the same conclusion regarding money, as the coins in the wizarding world are the gold Galleon, the silver Sickle, and the bronze Knut. We do not know many details about the coins of the wizarding world although we do know that the Knuts are small and bronze and five of them are the appropriate payment for an owl delivery, while the Galleons are quite large, judging from a comment by a Muggle in *The Goblet of Fire* that some people tried to pay him with gold coins the "size of hubcaps."[4]

Shortcomings of Precious Metals as Money

Making Change

While precious metals have much to recommend them as money, they also have some serious drawbacks. For starters, it can be hard to make change. If an item costs less than the face amount of a coin there must be sufficient smaller denomination coins available to make up the difference.[5] In wizarding money, making change must be a nightmare. A Galleon is worth seventeen Sickles, and a Sickle is, in turn, worth 29 Knuts, so a Galleon is worth 493 Knuts. It is a peculiar system, far more so than the old English system in which a shilling was worth 12 pence and a pound was worth twenty shillings (240 pence).[6]

---

4. *Goblet of Fire* 77. As far as the value of the wizard coins, that is a topic beyond the scope of this essay. Others have written about the topic with great cleverness and insight, identifying discrepancies in the various works of Ms. Rowling and formulating both a "high value" and a "low value" theory for the coins. I recommend the discussion in Wikipedia under the heading "Harry Potter Universe — Economy": http://en.wikipedia.org/wiki/Money_in_Harry_Potter#Economy (last visited July 28, 2008).

5. In the history of coinage some coins were designed to be broken apart to make change, the most famous example of which being the Spanish reales, or "pieces of eight," which were scored into eight pie-shaped sections which could be bitten off to make change (i.e., "two bits" was a quarter of the coin and remains our term for a quarter of a dollar).

6. For Americans and the rest of the western world where coinage based on the decimal system is the norm, the old English approach to coinage is odd. The pence was originally the basic unit, though at times in British history coins in denominations of half a penny (ha'penny) and quarter of a penny (farthing) were issued. Although twelve pence made a

Nevertheless, Hagrid tells Harry that wizard coinage is "easy enough" to understand.[7] Even if that is the case, it is hard for a Muggle to understand why the wizards don't coin additional denominations analogous to our nickels, dimes, and quarters to make change easier. At the same time, the lack of five, ten, or twenty Galleon coins means larger purchases must be made by exchanging huge numbers of coins, which is also very inconvenient.

Bank notes would serve well in the role of making change, but the magical world does not seem to have any paper money. We do not know for sure why, but there could be some legal basis for this. It could be that their money system is limited by a legal rule prohibiting the use of paper money altogether. Some modern supporters of the gold standard earnestly argue that the United States is bound by just such a legal regime. Those folks argue that the U.S. Constitution only gives Congress the power to "coin Money," not to print paper money.[8] They believe that prohibiting paper money is an important check on the power of the government since a money supply based on paper currency can be manipulated by the government relatively easily by "running the printing presses," while money based on gold is not as easily manipulable. Perhaps the wizards reached a similar conclusion and decided that restricting their money to coinage was one way to impose some discipline on government spending.

On the other hand, because the wizards seem comfortable with commodity money, it might be an awkward transition to have money made out of paper, which has very little intrinsic value as a commodity. It takes a leap of faith to use paper as money. One could imagine an economy where people would be reluctant to give up the weighty, substantive, reality of gold, silver, and bronze for the flimsy, ephemeral, abstraction of a piece of paper. Perhaps

---

shilling, and twenty shillings a pound, there were coins equal to two shillings (a florin), two and a half shillings (a half crown) and five shillings (a crown) and twenty-one shillings (a guinea). It is possible that the odd wizard money is a way for Rowling to poke fun at the English money system before it was decimalized.

7. *Sorcerer's Stone* 75.

8. The argument against paper money offered by the extreme wing of gold-standard supporters goes something like this: the United States Constitution gives Congress the power to "coin Money, regulate the Value thereof, and of foreign Coin, and fix the Standard of Weights and Measures," U.S. CONST. art. I, § 8, but conspicuously leaves off the power to print paper money. Because the drafters considered, but rejected, the idea of specifically granting to Congress the power to "emit bills of credit" (i.e., small denomination notes against the full faith and credit of the country), some argue that the Congress is prohibited from issuing paper money. Others point out, however, that the Constitution, while not providing an explicit grant of authority, also carries no explicit prohibition on the printing of paper money and that the necessary and proper clause could be employed to justify its issuance.

a combination of law and cultural norms in the wizarding world militates against the use of paper notes as money.

Maintaining Integrity in the Supply of Coins

Regardless of the reason for a money system based solely on coins made of precious metals, the existence of such a system presents some serious systemic challenges. Perhaps most obviously, coins are susceptible to counterfeiting and adulteration, such as by shaving or sweating.[9] Someone needs to police the quality of the coin to make sure that good coin remains in circulation. If no authority keeps an eye on the coinage, a dynamic known as "Gresham's Law" will occur—the bad money (i.e., the debased or counterfeit coins) will drive out the good money (i.e., the unadulterated coinage). In other words, as the coinage becomes debased, people will tend to hoard authentic coins and pass along low quality coins to others. In modern Muggle economies, central banks controlled by the government play an important role in monitoring the quality of the money supply, but there is no evidence that the Ministry of Magic is involved in policing the money supply in the magical world.

Instead, the regulation of coinage seems to be in the hands of a private bank—Gringotts. This could be a case of successful privatization. In modern economies there are many examples of governments spinning off functions to private operators as a way to increase efficiency and reduce the size of government. Born in 1965, Ms. Rowling would have come of age politically during the high-water mark of privatization under Conservative U.K. Prime Ministers Margaret Thatcher and John Major. The important role played by Gringotts could be her literary tribute to privatization schemes. That is, it may very well be that the wizarding community decided it was a better policy choice to harness the private incentives of the Gringotts' goblins (widely reputed to be quite greedy) to run an efficient monetary system than it was to trust the bureaucrats at the Ministry of Magic to perform that task.[10]

---

9. Counterfeiting is the unauthorized production of coins, often of inferior quality, such as "gold" coins which are merely gold-plated. Shaving is a way for a money handler to debase the coins by nicking a little piece of the precious metal off of each coin that passes through his hands. Over the course of many transactions, the shavings add up to a valuable amount of gold dust. Similarly, sweating is a technique where several coins are placed in a leather bag and shaken vigorously so that flecks of gold are dislodged from the coins and retained in the bag. Again, over a large number of transactions, these small debasements could add up.

10. Bill Weasley explains that the goblins recognize they are better bankers than wizards: "there is a belief among some goblins, and those at Gringotts are perhaps most prone

In theory, by aligning incentives correctly the government can design a privatization scheme that will result in a private party like Gringotts serving a socially beneficial function such as policing the money supply. If the Gringotts goblins had a profit incentive to safeguard the money supply, they might engage in that task with enthusiasm. In *The Order of the Phoenix* we learn that the Galleon coins bear a serial number identifying the goblin who minted it. It may very well be that a charm on the coins and this serial number provide a method of monitoring the supply of the coin. But why would the goblins care? Where is the payoff to them? The answer may lie in a concept called seigniorage.

By modern Muggle standards, entrusting the regulation of the money supply to a private bank would be quite unusual. Although Muggles certainly have private banks (and there is historical precedent for those banks issuing money), in most developed countries the government is in charge of managing the money supply through the operation of a central bank. The government has a stake in maintaining a stable and reliable money supply in order to ensure the smooth functioning of the economy and to facilitate the collection of taxes, which is why the British developed the Bank of England—the prototypical central bank—in 1694 and why the United States created the Federal Reserve System in 1913.[11]

More than that, however, governments tend to monopolize the making of money because, quite frankly, it is an easy way for the government to earn a profit. In other words, there is money to be made in making money. The economic windfall that results when new coins are issued is called "seigniorage." Seigniorage is the revenue a money-issuing authority realizes on the difference between the cost of producing the money and its face value when placed in circulation. This can be a significant revenue source for governments. Perhaps this is the private benefit that gives Gringotts the proper incentive to monitor the magical money supply.

Consider the special series of U.S. quarters minted since the late 1990s commemorating the fifty states. That coinage program was designed to appeal to collectors and many of those coins have been taken out of circulation.[12] That

---

to it, that wizards cannot be trusted in matters of gold and treasure ..." *Deathly Hallows* 517.

11. *See* Federal Reserve Act, ch. 6, 38 Stat. 251 (1913) (codified in part at 12 U.S.C. §221 *et seq.* (2000)).

12. The coins were so successful after the first year of the program that demand for quarters shot up by 50 percent. *See* Dean Croushore, *U.S. Coins: Forecasting Change,* FEDERAL RESERVE BANK OF PHILADELPHIA Q2 2003 BUSINESS REVIEW, at 9 (2003), http://www.philadelphiafed.org/files/br/brq203dc.pdf. One might fairly assume that most if not all of that additional demand was due to collectors' interest in the coins.

is good economic news for the U.S. Treasury because it costs the mint less than five cents for each quarter it produces, so the government makes twenty cents whenever a bank "buys" a quarter at face value to put it into circulation. In the ordinary course of a coin's useful life the seigniorage gain is eventually eliminated years later when the government buys back the worn out coins from banks at face value and retires them. For coins which are taken out of circulation by collectors, however, the back end of the seigniorage deal never comes to pass. Based on the total number of state quarters issued since 1999, observers estimate that as of April 2005, the U.S. Treasury had earned about $5 billion in seigniorage from those coins.[13]

So, to a banking policy wonk, one striking difference between the Muggle world and the wizarding world is that it appears that the seigniorage belongs to the goblins who run Gringotts and not to the government. In the Muggle world it is often said that money is power, and one may assume that is at least partly true in the wizarding world as well. If so, it would not be hard to imagine that the Ministry of Magic might want to grab the economic power back from the goblins and nationalize the bank (or re-nationalize it if it was indeed a case of privatization). Just such a move was hinted in a news story that ran in *The Quibbler* under a cartoon captioned: *How Far Will Fudge Go to Gain Gringotts?*[14] The story alleged that Minister of Magic Cornelius Fudge desired to gain control of the bank and the goblin gold supplies therein and that he went as far as to have goblins murdered to attain that end. While stories in *The Quibbler* are usually dismissed as fantastic, they often prove uncannily accurate.

In the wizarding world's political struggles it would seem almost inevitable that if one or the other of the wizard factions did not seek to take control of the bank, they would at least try to get the Goblins on their side. Indeed, in *The Order of the Phoenix* Bill Weasley has used his position at Gringotts' London branch to gain intelligence regarding the political sympathies of the goblins. Of course, in the final book of the series, Gringotts appears to be deeply

---

13. That is, adding up the total production since 1999, about $6.25 billion dollars worth of quarters had been issued. Assuming $0.20 seigniorage on each quarter, that yields total seigniorage of about $5 billion. *See* http://www.usmint.gov/about_the_mint/coin_production/index.cfm?flash=yes&action=production_figures&sqYear=2005 (last visited July 28, 2008) (providing production numbers for the state quarter series). Although it is unlikely that the government will keep the whole $5 billion of seigniorage gains forever, many of these coins are in the hands of collectors and will never be retired from the system. Coins usually stay in circulation for 30 years before they wear out and need to be taken out of circulation, so the government will have the benefit of the seigniorage gains for that period of time regardless of how many quarters are eventually retired.

14. *Order of the Phoenix* 190.

involved in the wizards' political struggles. In that book it appears that the Death Eaters and Voldemort gained control over Gringotts, even as the goblins try not to take sides during the political struggles. At one point in the book Ted Tonks asks two goblins: " 'where do you two fit in? I, er, had the impression the goblins were for You-Know-Who, on the whole.' 'You had a false impression,' said the higher-voiced of the goblins. 'We take no sides. This is a wizards' war.' " Yet even as the goblins aspire to neutrality, the other goblin notes: "Gringotts is no longer under the sole control of my race. I recognize no Wizarding master."[15] This interchange illustrates how the goblins are interested primarily in the well being of the goblins and do not desire entanglements with the wizards. In a world where money and power are inextricably entwined, however, such a position is untenable.

Safekeeping Evolves into Banking

Another problem with money systems that utilize precious metals stems from the fact that people will tend to hoard good money. The operation of Gresham's Law leads us to believe that there will be piles of good money lying around in various hiding places. Where there are piles of valuables lying around there are bound to be robbers who will try to steal those valuables. Indeed, it is the attractiveness of money to thieves that gave rise to what we now call banks.

Early bankers were primarily safe keepers of other people's precious metals. The first bankers were probably goldsmiths, who offered the service of safekeeping gold and other valuables in their strong houses and charged a fee for the service. To keep track of who left what on deposit, the goldsmiths issued receipts to their customers.

The goldsmith's receipts evidenced a certain amount of gold on deposit. When a customer needed the gold to make a payment to another merchant the receipt would be presented to the goldsmith, the customer would be given back the requested amount of gold and either the existing receipt would be modified to reflect the new balance on deposit or a new receipt would be issued. Of course, when the customer withdrew gold to bring to a transaction with another merchant he was extremely vulnerable to robbers and highwaymen. During the trip from the goldsmith to the place where the transaction was to be consummated, there was plenty of opportunity for bandits to intercept the precious metal.

---

15. *Deathly Hallows* 296.

Eventually, it dawned on some clever merchant to convince his trading partner to take the goldsmith's receipt as payment instead of the actual gold that the receipt represented. Perhaps both merchants had accounts with the same goldsmith and both recognized the unnecessary risk involved in taking the gold out of the vault and then bringing it back, when all they really needed to do was to tell the goldsmith to move the gold from one account to another. And so, paper money was born.

In time these receipts were considered to be "as good as gold" and indeed represented a right by the bearer to receive payment in gold from the issuing goldsmith. To make trade more convenient, goldsmiths began issuing these receipts in standard denominations, which made the mechanics of exchange much easier, as people could make change without the necessity of having the goldsmith re-write the receipt every time a transaction took place.

Slowly it began to dawn on the goldsmiths that their customers almost never came to actually get the gold that was on deposit—once it was in the vault, it tended to stay there. That is, it stayed there as long as the customers believed it was safe in the hands of the goldsmith. When customers lost confidence in their goldsmith and believed their gold was not safe they would panic and run to the goldsmith to demand their gold back. From the very beginning, therefore, proto-bankers recognized that the key to a stable money system is confidence. A bedrock principle of banking through the ages is the axiom that as long as customers have confidence that the money remains safe in the bank they will not come to retrieve it. To this day, the concept of "safety and soundness" as a means to instill public confidence in the banking system is the underlying principle that informs all banking regulation.[16]

As it became clear to goldsmiths/bankers that the customers were never going to come get their gold, it also occurred to them that other merchants could use the gold that was just lying around in the vaults collecting dust. For example, a merchant might have a large cargo of goods arriving next week which would generate a large amount of income for the merchant when they were sold two weeks hence, but between now and the time the goods were sold the merchant had some bills to pay and needed gold immediately to make those payments. Enter the goldsmiths/bankers. They began to lend out the gold that was on deposit and charge interest for its use. The merchant could pay off his

---

16. Section 39 of the Federal Deposit Insurance Act, 12 U.S.C. § 1831p-1 (2000), requires the federal banking regulators to establish standards for safety and soundness. The federal regulators have jointly established guidelines for safety and soundness standards. *See* Interagency Guidelines Establishing Standards for Safety and Soundness, 12 C.F.R. § 30, Appendix A (2008).

obligations this week with borrowed gold and then repay the loan (with interest) in two weeks when the shipment of goods was sold.

Because the transportation of gold was dangerous, however, the bankers just issued receipts evidencing a right to the gold instead of relinquishing the gold itself. The receipts functioned as paper money. As bankers developed the practice of lending out receipts to use as "gold" for payment of debts, they again noticed that only very rarely did anyone actually come to collect the gold that the receipts were supposed to represent. In light of this fact, some goldsmiths abused the system by lending out paper receipts representing more gold than they actually had in the vault. Because the receipts were as good as gold, this usually didn't present a problem, as merchants passed the receipts amongst themselves as money. If, however, the holders of the receipts ever actually came to collect the physical gold that the paper was supposed to represent, the goldsmith could be embarrassed by being unable to meet all of the demands. So, although lending out the gold on deposit was a profitable sideline for goldsmiths, it needed to be done carefully. The guild of goldsmiths enforced the norms of behavior that kept the issuance of receipts within a safe limit.[17]

The Magic of Banking

If you take this story about the goldsmiths and substitute "money" for "gold," "bank note" for "receipt," and "banker" for "goldsmith" you get a plausible story about the origins of banking and the money system. This is where the Muggle money magic comes in. Let's consider a very simple economy in which there are three banks and each bank starts with initial capital of $500. Each of these banks would have a balance sheet showing $500 in cash on the asset side and $500 of equity (claims owed to owners) on the liability side. Now let's assume a depositor comes along and deposits $1,000 in Bank A. Bank A's balance sheet will change so that it now has assets equal to $1,500 in cash—the original $500 plus the $1,000 from the depositor. Of course the liability side must match, and it does because we have $500 of equity plus a liability of $1,000 (i.e., the amount

---

17. As an aside, the goldsmiths' self-policing scheme was an early response to the need for some kind of coordinated regulation in the absence of a unified governmental unit capable of serving that function. The legacy of guild rules appears today in the securities industry, which is largely self-policed by a Self-Regulating Organization (SRO) called the Financial Industry Regulatory Authority (FINRA). In the wizarding world, however, regulation seems sparse and self-regulation seems rather meaningless, since Gringotts is the only bank in the economy.

of money owed to the depositor). By virtue of the customer's deposit, Bank *A* now has some extra cash on hand that it can lend out for a profit.

Now let's assume that Bank *A* lends $1,000 to Borrower *X*, who takes the money and deposits it in Bank *B*. The asset side of Bank *B*'s balance sheet changes to reflect that it now has $1,500 in cash—the original $500 of equity plus the $1,000 of cash deposited by *X*—and the liability side changes to reflect $500 in equity plus a $1,000 liability for the deposit owed to *X*. Bank *A*'s balance sheet changes, too. Its assets still equal $1,500, but the composition of those assets has changed to be $500 in cash plus a $1,000 promissory note from *X* (which from the bank's point of view is an asset because it earns the bank money and entitles the bank to repayment). The liability side of Bank *A*'s balance sheet stays the same.

Now repeat the process with Bank *B* making a $1,000 loan to Borrower *Y*, which *Y* then deposits into Bank *C*. Bank *B*'s balance sheet changes to reflect that its assets are not all in cash, but instead consist of cash of $500 and a promissory note of $1,000 from *Y*. Bank *C*'s assets have grown to $1,500 and so have its liabilities. Now assume Bank *C* makes a $1,000 loan to Borrower *Z*....

In case you haven't noticed, there's a little bit of magic going on here, although some critics of banking call it a bit of *léger de main*. By lending out deposits the banks are in fact creating money out of thin air. Consider the amount of money in the system before the series of lending transactions. We had three banks with $500 capital each for a total of $1,500 in capital. One depositor with $1,000 brings the total amount of money in the banking system to $2,500. After the series of loans, however, we still have the same amount of capital, $1,500, and the original deposit, $1,000, but we also have three loans which were used as money by the borrowers. Counting the loans that were made and redeposited in the banking system,[18] we've got an additional $3,000 of money in the system.

This is what I mean by the magic of banking—these banks have created money out of thin air! This is very cool, but it has a downside. Let's now imagine that Bank *A*'s original depositor wants her money back. Bank *A* won't be able to give her the money back because (assume the balance sheet hasn't

---

18. Skeptical readers may be questioning the plausibility of this hypothetical on the grounds that Borrowers *X*, *Y*, and *Z* are unlikely to get a loan and then just leave the loan proceeds on deposit with another bank; they are instead likely to spend the loan proceeds on something. While that is true, the way the dynamic is described is a helpful simplification because we can hypothesize that all of the people receiving payments from Borrowers *X*, *Y*, or *Z* ultimately deposited the payments received in Banks *A*, *B*, or *C*.

changed) the bank only has $500 dollars in cash. That's not to say that the bank is bankrupt—far from it. The bank is not insolvent because it has a second asset—a promissory note from X, which, assuming X is creditworthy and the loan was properly underwritten, should have an economic value of $1,000. Unfortunately, in order to pay off the depositor, Bank A must require X to repay its loan. To do that, X is going to have to withdraw $1,000 from Bank B, but Bank B is in the same situation that Bank A was in—it only has $500 of cash on hand plus a $1,000 note from Y. In order to pay off X, Bank B will have to call in the loan from Y. And so on and so forth. All the money that was created will disappear in the contraction caused by the notes being called in. Growing the money supply this way can create real volatility.[19]

In the modern Muggle world it is well understood that even a conservatively run, "rock solid" bank will not have enough cash on hand at any given time to satisfy all its depositors if they were to withdraw all their funds at the same time. To prevent such liquidity crises, Muggle banks can turn to their central bank as a "lender of last resort" (i.e., to make emergency loans to solvent banks so they can pay off depositors). The magic trick of creating money out of thin air also creates real headaches for the Muggle bankers as the money supply expands and contracts. One must ask whether it is worth the trouble. It is.

Does Money Supply Matter?

American history has shown that the health of the economy is tied in innumerable ways to a stable, but growing, money supply. In colonial times there was not enough gold and silver in British North America. Under the economic thinking of the day most precious metal was siphoned off to England, leaving the colonists to barter and otherwise improvise their way through

---

19. This process is called fractional reserve banking and banks really do create money this way. Modern banks understand, however, they cannot lend out 100 percent of their deposits and they are in fact legally prohibited from doing so. Principles of safety and soundness require that only a fraction of the deposits be lent out with the balance being held as "reserves" for meeting future obligations. In the hypo discussed in the text, if the banks had lent out only 80 percent of the deposits they received, the money supply would have grown in a much less dramatic way. Bank A would have lent X only $800, keeping a reserve of $200; Bank B would have lent Y only $640, keeping a reserve of $160; and Bank C would have lent Z only $512, keeping a reserve of $128. Under this scenario, the money supply would have expanded by $1,952 instead of $3,000. While the expansion would have been more modest, the contraction would have been less dramatic as well.

economic transactions. Foreign coins from many nations circulated freely in the colonies, but they did not serve as a standard of value. A Spanish dollar might be welcome in New York and accorded the equivalence of 81 pence, while that same Spanish dollar might be viewed with some suspicion in Virginia and be given a value of only 60 pence, with merchants in Philadelphia willing to part with 72 pence for a Spanish dollar.[20] Imagine the difficulty of a seller in New York shipping goods to a buyer in Virginia on a vessel out of Philadelphia pursuant to a contract denominated in pounds but actually being settled with whatever coin was available—Spanish dollars, French écu, Portuguese cruzado or Dutch ducatoons.[21] This is the problem of not enough money—it is hard to consummate transactions because the medium of exchange (i.e., acceptable money) is not available in sufficient amounts to pay everyone what they are owed.

Of course, all of this would have been a lot easier if England had just given the colonies enough money, but that didn't happen, so the colonies had to limp along trying to make deals happen without having sufficient coin to facilitate commerce. The colonists, in time, began to establish their own banks and those banks began to issue money, which relieved the money shortage somewhat. But the currency of even well-respected local banks often didn't carry much weight in distant cities where people had never heard of those banks and had no reason to trust their notes. With banks issuing notes that represented claims against the money on deposit, the dynamics discussed above in the context of the goldsmiths came into play. Some banks issued too many notes and the value of those notes declined as the market discounted them in light of the possibility that they would not be honored. If things really got out of hand, holders of those notes would descend on the issuing bank and demand payment, which, of course, the bank would not be able to honor, thereby causing the bank to fail.

So, while too little money was a problem for commerce, too much money was a problem as well. Without a growing money supply, transactions were difficult to execute because there was not enough money to make the deal hap-

---

20. These exchange rates are provided in an online essay at Notre Dame University's Numismatic Endowment website: Louis Jordan, *The Comparative Value of Money between Britain and the Colonies*, Colonial Currency, http://www.coins.nd.edu/ColCurrency/ CurrencyIntros/IntroValue.html (last visited July 28, 2008).

21. Given the confusion of different coins with different values in the various colonies, it is not surprising that the Founders decided to give Congress the power to "coin Money, regulate the Value thereof, and of foreign Coin, and fix the Standard of Weights and Measures." U.S. Const. art. I, §8.

pen. When there was too much money deals didn't happen either because people discounted the money. Finding the right balance between too much and too little required the coordination of a central bank. Historically, Americans have been very skeptical of central banking, although the government did eventually take on the job of issuing all the money—not just the coins. The wizards, with only one bank apparently are more comfortable with a central bank, but in both worlds regulating the money supply has had significant social and political ramifications.

Money Supply in the Wizarding World

A recurring criticism of central banks is that by providing a stable currency they serve the interests of the wealthy without regard to the lower classes. Throughout American history major political battles have been fought over the money supply, generally with poor folks, farmers, and debtors favoring a loose money policy (inflation) and rich folks and creditors favoring a tight money policy. In the days before floating interest rates, the reason for this tension was easy to see: in an inflationary environment debtors could pay back loans with relatively less expensive money. So, for instance, the agrarian regions of the South and West opposed the Bank of the United States in part on "loose money" grounds and in part because its promise of a standard national currency only seemed to be an important benefit for Northern industrialists who were selling their goods on a national scale. Farmers didn't much care about stable money because they only traded locally and the local currency was fine by them. In all regions, people feared that a central bank would concentrate economic (and political) power in the hands of a few.

Throughout our history the regulation of the money supply has fueled political battles that were little more than thinly disguised class warfare. Topics from American History class, like the issuance of continentals during the Revolutionary War (and the decision to redeem them after the formation of the new country), the battles over the first and second banks of the United States, the role of greenbacks in the Civil War, the Free Silver Movement, William Jennings Bryan's "Cross of Gold" speech, the formation of the Federal Reserve System, the tight money policy that precipitated the Great Depression, the Bretton Woods Agreement, and the decision to drop the gold standard, among many other incidents, are internalized as odd trivia facts, known by students across the country but frequently not truly understood because the real story behind those events is a legal, social, political, and economic problem beyond the ken of many high school history teachers.

While the dynamics of the banking system in the wizarding world appear to be quite different from those of the Muggle world, the wizards must wrestle with the same policy issues. There is no evidence in the Harry Potter books that money circulates through intermediaries.[22] From the Muggle perspective, without lending by intermediaries it is difficult to see how the money supply will grow sufficiently to support a robust economy. If Gringotts does not lend out the gold that is on deposit, the money supply would appear to be stagnant. While the wizard economy may work differently, the wizards cannot escape the implications of the economics of the money supply. The wizard economy must suffer the consequences of scarce currency—some deals won't happen or will happen only with great difficulty given the challenges of figuring out how to pay for things when there is no reliable medium of exchange. In addition, the existing money may actually become more valuable as a result of deflation.

When there is too little money in an economy and lots of goods and services that require payment in money, the value of the money goes up in a dynamic that is the opposite of inflation: deflation. In a deflationary environment people who already have money will find their money is even more valuable. Extremely tight money conditions tend to reinforce the status quo—just the sort of thing the Malfoys would love and the Weasleys would suffer from. It would also make it very difficult for entrepreneurs to launch new enterprises, as the cost of capital would be very dear.

When the value of money increases, the cost of attracting capital goes up too, making it especially difficult for new businesses to get off the ground. At the end of *The Goblet of Fire* Harry invests in the Weasley brothers' joke shop. Harry's capital contribution seems like more of a gift than an equity investment or a loan, but in any event it is crucial to financing the start-up business.[23] Had Harry not been keen to rid himself of the tainted money he won in the Tri-Wizard Tournament, it is not clear where Fred and George would have obtained the funds necessary to open their business. It does not appear that there is any other source of capital than the existing piles of old family money.[24]

---

22. *But see* Chapter 16 in this volume by Heidi Mandanis Schooner where she speculates that Gringotts could be engaged in fractional reserve banking. She raises an interesting idea to consider as a thought experiment, but there is precious little in the books themselves to support the idea that Gringotts is a true financial intermediary.

23. Although the Weasley brothers seem to consider Harry's money a loan, in *The Half Blood Prince* Harry seems uninterested in being repaid.

24. This is true even for Voldemort, an orphan whose birth mother died poor. As Harry notes: "I don't know whether [Voldemort] was ever inside Gringotts. He never had gold there when he was younger, because nobody left him anything." *Deathly Hallows* 491.

The various wizard families all start with some initial endowment of wealth. We do not know where the money came from—it is just taken as a given. In a modern capitalist society we expect motivated entrepreneurs like Fred and George Weasley to put resources to work making things others will value. We say these businesspeople are "adding value" or "creating wealth" and they deserve to be paid for it, but if there is only so much money in existence, that money will be subject to revaluation as participants in the market vie for its use.

Without bank lending to expand the money supply it would appear that wizard money exists in a near "steady state." One of the problems of a stagnant money supply is that it reinforces the economic status quo and makes it more difficult for entrepreneurs to attract capital and create wealth. Without a growing money supply, initial endowments of wealth are more persistent over time and tend to perpetuate wealth. Eventually, the society ends up with a world where wizards either have money or they don't. This supports the class warfare theme that pervades the books with countless instances of Malfoy taunting and insulting Weasley for his family's lack of wealth.

Of course, the magical money supply might grow by other means. The most likely source of additional gold is magic itself. Suppose the wizards could just conjure gold out of thin air—that would make managing the money supply an impossible task. It cannot be, however, that wizards possess that power[25] or else gold would be useless as money and, furthermore, there would not be the range of material wealth among various characters that is on display in the books. It appears, therefore, that the power to conjure is not limitless. For instance, when concocting a potion a wizard apparently needs to have the ingredients on hand and cannot merely conjure them into existence.[26] Also, the achievement of Albus Dumbledore and Nicholas Flamel in developing the Sorcerer's Stone would seem quite trivial if wizards generally could conjure gold at will.

We do know, however, that the Sorcerer's Stone was in the custody of Gringotts for some period of time. Perhaps they used it to convert base met-

---

25. Leprechauns can conjure "gold" out of thin air, but as we see in *The Goblet of Fire* it is just a trick—it doesn't last. The Leprechaun "gold" is essentially worthless, as seen in *The Deathly Hallows*, where a goblin is examining a golden coin through an eyeglass, and then tosses it aside when he realizes it is Leprechaun gold. *Deathly Hallows* 530.

26. This may be one of the five Principal Exceptions to Gamp's Law of Elemental Transfiguration. All we know of Gamp's Law is Hermione's explanation to Ron when she tells him why she cannot conjure food out of nothing. "It is impossible to make good food out of nothing! You can Summon it if you know where it is, you can transform it, you can increase the quantity if you've already got some." *Deathly Hallows* 292–93. Of the five Principal Exceptions, Hermione only gets through one: food. Is it possible that gold (or money?) is one of the other four?

als into gold and thereby augment the money supply. Alternatively, there is a reference to the goblins engaging in the exchange of Muggle money, so perhaps they acquire gold in the Muggle world by using the exchanged money as payment. Or maybe the gold supply grows by virtue of mining activity, although the books contain no reference to mineral extraction. Finally, Gringotts might supplement the gold supply by looting ancient graves. We know from *The Prisoner of Azkaban* that Bill Weasley was employed as a curse breaker in Egypt, which makes one wonder if part of the money supply comes from plundering the tombs of the pharaohs.

The short history of Muggle banking provides a context for thinking about the role that Gringotts plays in the wizard economy. Although Gringotts is referred to as a "bank," there is a decidedly child-like quality to the "banking" they provide. In Gringotts the actual coins deposited by the customer are kept in the vault, much the way I believed as a child that the same silver Ben Franklin half-dollars left by the tooth fairy that I deposited in the bank would be returned to me at a later time. At one time in the evolution of Muggle banking in, say, the early Middle Ages, that was exactly how banks worked, but modern Muggle banks treat money as a fungible commodity. The deposits are all mixed together. Gringotts seems more like a storehouse for valuables than a bank in the modern sense, or in contemporary terminology, Gringotts is less a bank than it is a safe deposit company. People leave valuables there for safe keeping and come back to retrieve those exact valuables at a later time—sometimes much later, as apparently some of the vaults have been in the same family for ages.[27]

It is not clear whether the goblins are free to lend those valuables out to others for a price.[28] Of course we can only speculate about how Gringotts really works. Although a customer's money is in the vault when the customer appears, this might be a bit of magic. Who knows what the goblins do with the coins in between visits by the customers? It could be that Gringotts really is a bank, but we have no indication in the books themselves that the goblins are anything but safekeepers of other peoples' valuables.

If Gringotts is not engaged in lending or investing, the economics of their business plan is hard for a Muggle observer of the banking system to under-

---

27. Griphook explains that the Lestrange vault is "one of the most ancient chambers. The oldest Wizarding families store their treasures at the deepest level, where the vaults are largest and best protected." *Deathly Hallows* 509.

28. In *The Goblet of Fire* Ludo Bagman is indebted to "the goblins" for some gambling losses, but it is not clear whether this is the result of a loan from Gringotts or merely a goblin bookie who is owed for lost bets.

stand. In the Muggle world safe deposit box rental is seen as only a marginally profitable business. Yet Gringotts seems to make a profitable business out of it, perhaps because of their monopoly over coinage and other sidelines such as the exchange of Muggle money into wizarding money, and their status as the only "bank" in the wizarding world.[29] It may be that Gringotts' success comes from having the market power to extract monopolist rents[30] from its customers.

Bank Security in the Muggle and Wizarding Worlds

That being said, Gringotts still must deliver the financial services it promises or new competitors will spring up to take away some of those monopolist rents. Given that Gringotts is located on Diagon Alley not far from the intersection with Knockturn Alley (hardly the best neighborhood in the wizarding world), the goblins have to take measures to ensure that the valuables stored with them are indeed safe. This is consistent with legal requirements in the Muggle world where banks are required to take precautions to ensure the security of bank premises and the assets located on those premises.[31]

The level of security at Gringotts has no peer in the Muggle world. Gringotts' main strategy for safeguarding the valuables entrusted to them is to deploy a large number of goblin guards throughout the premises. The goblins are widely feared and may serve a general deterrent function for would-be robbers. The actual vaults are hidden far below the ground, accessible only by special goblin-driven carts. The goblins rely on a hierarchy of authority to ensure that security is enforced—for instance, only certain goblins can ride in the carts down to the vaults.[32]

Having been rumored in earlier books, in *The Deathly Hallows,* it is confirmed that Gringotts does guard some vaults with dragons—a security measure Mug-

---

29. Death Eater Travers laments the Gringotts' monopoly over banking in the wizarding world, when he says: "Gold, filthy gold! We cannot live without it, yet I confess I deplore the necessity of consorting with our long-fingered friends." *Deathly Hallows* 528.

30. A "monopolist rent" is a higher-than-normal profit that a business can make if it has a monopoly over some good or service and is therefore not subject to competitive pressure to keep its prices down.

31. *See* Bank Protection Act, 12 U.S.C. §1882 (2000) ("each Federal supervisory agency shall promulgate rules establishing minimum standards with which each bank or savings and loan association must comply with respect to the installation, maintenance, and operation of security devices and procedures, reasonable in cost, to discourage robberies, burglaries, and larcenies and to assist in the identification and apprehension of persons who commit such acts").

32. *Deathly Hallows* 533.

gle bankers can only dream of. We also find that Gringotts has sophisticated measures in place to detect imposters and to prevent charmed objects entering the premises.[33] The high security vaults are protected by a biometric security system far more advanced than any currently in use in modern Muggle banks. In the Muggle world bankers have been experimenting with security systems based on thumbprints, face recognition and retinal scans, but nothing comes close to the goblins' biometric security system. The goblin system permits the vaults to be opened by a Gringotts goblin passing a finger down the side of the door or pressing a palm against the vault's door.[34] Apparently, the fate of non-goblins who try to open the vault is to be transported into the locked vault with no hope of escape.

Gringotts clearly takes security very seriously and enjoys a reputation as an impregnable stronghold.[35] The security system is so tight and widely acknowledged in the wizarding world that when Quirrell broke into Gringotts trying to get the Sorcerer's Stone, it was a big story in the *Daily Prophet*. Even though the break-in was unsuccessful in that Quirrell did not get what he sought, the mere fact that someone broke into the bank made it newsworthy.

In order to further reinforce a sense of confidence, both Gringotts and Muggle banks use the technique of prominently posting a notice designed to convince customers that their money will be safe in the institution. The Gringotts approach is to post a conspicuous notice that holds out the prospect of painful withdrawal penalty to warn away robbers while at the same time reassuring honest customers that their money is safe.[36] Modern U.S. banking regulation takes a different approach to achieve the same end. The FDIC requires that all insured banks post a notice at each teller window and in advertising informing customers that the bank is FDIC insured.[37] Although the notice is not as scary as the rhyme on the Gringotts door, the goal is to reassure depositors that no matter what happens their money will be there when they come back to get it.

---

33. When Harry, Ron, Hermione and Griphook break into Gringotts, they end up triggering these defenses, including a kind of waterfall that can strip away all magic, at which time Griphook exclaims: "The Thief's Downfall! It washes away all enchantment, all magical concealment! They know there are imposters in Gringotts, they have set off defenses against us!" *Deathly Hallows* 534.

34. *Sorcerer's Stone* 75; *Deathly Hallows* 536

35. Gringotts, according to Hagrid, is the "safest place in the world fer anything yeh want ter keep safe—'cept maybe Hogwarts." *Sorcerer's Stone* 63.

36. The Gringotts notice is reprinted at the beginning of Chapter 16 in this volume by Heidi Mandanis Schooner.

37. 12 U.S.C. 1828(a) (2000); 12 C.F.R. §328 (2008).

It appears that Gringotts' enthusiasm for security might, however, go above and beyond the legal standards required of them. In the Anglo-American tradition, safe deposit companies are considered bailees and must exercise due care with the valuables entrusted to them. A typical statutory standard can be found in Washington state law:

> Whenever any safe deposit company shall let or lease any vault, safe, box or other receptacle for the keeping or storage of personal property such safe deposit company shall be bound to exercise due care to prevent the opening of such vault, safe, box or receptacle by any person other than the lessee thereof, or his or her duly authorized agent, and the parties may provide in writing the terms, conditions, and liabilities in the lease.[38]

The legal standard of a bailee in the Muggle world is "ordinary" or "due" care, which in simple terms means that the safe deposit company must exercise the level of care which a prudent and diligent person would take of goods belonging to those with whom she transacts business. While this requires taking more care than one would with one's own goods, it does not mean that the bailee becomes an insurer of the entrusted goods. The exact duty owed varies according to the type of goods bailed and the extent of the contractual promise to look after the goods. Ordinarily, if the entrusted goods are very valuable and easily damaged, lost, or stolen, then the standard is higher. A Muggle would expect, however, to find a disclaimer of liability in the contract defining the bailment relationship. We are not privy to the account documentation that established the Potter account at Gringotts, but there is no mention of the goblins seeking to get out from any responsibility to take anything but the utmost care of the entrusted goods. Indeed, it appears that the goblins have their own code for dealing with the bailment relationship which covers, among other things, confidentiality of client information.[39]

In addition to the security program sketched out above, Gringotts has special protocols to make sure that customers who seek access to the vaults are authorized to do so. For instance, in the *Deathly Hallows* we find that one way for a Gringotts customer to access his or her vault is with their unique wand.[40] Ordinarily, however, access is permitted only upon the presentation of a special key. In the first book, for instance, when Harry goes to get his money he

---

38. WASH. REV. CODE ANN. §22.28.030 (West 2008).

39. As the goblin Griphook explains the rules: "It is against our code to speak of the secrets of Gringotts. We are the guardians of fabulous treasures. We have a duty to the objects placed in our care." *Deathly Hallows* 489–90.

40. *Deathly Hallows* 530–31.

does so by presenting the goblins with a golden key that fits his vault. Special keys have long been a part of private banking where bankers provide the discreet service permitting customers to hide assets in accounts that cannot be accessed by anyone but the bearer of the key. Holding a key serves the function of both allowing access to the vault and signaling a certain status to others and especially the goblins, of the bearer's place in the wizarding world. Harry Potter inherited a Gringott's vault key and therefore a place in the wizard social order, yet he is humble enough to have empathy for poor Tom Riddle. Harry hypothesizes that the young Voldemort "would have envied anyone who had a key to a Gringotts vault." Harry thinks that Riddle would "have seen it as a real symbol of belonging to the Wizarding world."[41]

In the modern Muggle world these kinds of banking relationships where access is provided solely by a person bearing a key or passbook or document without also establishing the bearer's identity as an account holder are becoming increasingly rare. International police efforts to track down terrorist financing and drug profits are forcing banks to be more aggressive with customer information and to produce that information for law enforcement officials upon request. Nevertheless, in the wizarding world, whether it is Harry with a special key, Hagrid with a special letter, or Bellatrix with her wand, access is provided on a "no questions asked" basis unless the goblins are somehow on notice that the person with the key, letter or wand is an imposter.

During times of crisis, however, financial institutions must make changes in security to address the threat. For example, as evidence of Voldemort's return grew more persuasive, the goblins increased security at Gringotts so that it was taking five hours for patrons to get their gold. In *The Half Blood Prince*, one customer, Arkie Philpott, suffered the added indignity of having a Probity Probe inserted in an unnamed part of his person apparently as part of the goblin security protocol. Like the magical equivalent of a metal detector, the probes are designed to detect spells of concealment and hidden magical objects. Also like metal detectors, the effectiveness of the device is limited by the skill and attentiveness of its operator, as demonstrated by Harry putting a *Confundo* spell on the administrators of the Probity Probes.[42]

41. *Deathly Hallows* 491.

42. "'Ah, Probity Probes,' sighed Travers theatrically, 'so crude—but effective!'
And he set off up the steps, nodding left and right to the wizards, who raised the golden rods and passed them up and down his body. The Probes, Harry knew, detected spells of concealment and hidden magical objects. Knowing that he had only seconds, Harry pointed Draco's wand at each of the guards in turn and murmured, '*Confundo*' twice." *Deathly Hallows* 529.

If the Probity Probe is designed to determine the true identity of people coming to the bank to conduct business, the Muggle equivalent is a set of rules covering financial institutions called the "Know Your Customer" regulations.[43] The regulations require financial institutions to establish a "Customer Identification Program" designed to (i) verify the identity of new accountholders, (ii) ensure that the institution has a reasonable belief that it knows each customer's identity, and (iii) compare the names of new customers against government lists of known or suspected terrorists or terrorist organizations.[44] These rules apply even if the "account" that the financial institution maintains is a safe deposit box or a safe-keeping arrangement.[45]

In addition to keeping tabs on the customers at the time an account is opened, U.S. banking law conscripts bankers into a spy network so that the government must be informed whenever the customer engages in a "suspicious activity."[46] In connection with safe deposit accounts, federal banking guidelines indicate that Suspicious Activity Reports should be filed where:

- The customer visits a safe deposit box or uses a safe custody account on an unusually frequent basis.
- Safe deposit boxes or safe custody accounts are opened by individuals who do not reside or work in the institution's service area despite the availability of such services at an institution closer to them.
- A customer exhibits unusual traffic patterns in the safe deposit box area or unusual use of safe custody accounts. For example, several individuals arrive together, enter frequently, or carry bags or other containers

43. The statutory authority for these rules is section 326 of the USA Patriot Act, codified at 31 U.S.C. §5318(*l*) (Supp. III 2003).

44. The actual regulations appear in several places throughout the *Code of Federal Regulation* because they have been adopted by the several federal banking agencies: Office of the Comptroller of the Currency, 12 C.F.R. §21.21(2) (2008); Federal Reserve System, 12 C.F.R. §208.63(2) (2008); Federal Deposit Insurance Corporation, 12 C.F.R. §326.8(2) (2008); Office of Thrift Supervision, 12 C.F.R. §563.177(2) (2008); National Credit Union Administration, 12 C.F.R. §748.2(2) (2008); and the Department of the Treasury, 31 C.F.R. §103.121 (2008).

45. 31 C.F.R. §103.121(a)(1)(i) (2008).

46. The Annunzio-Wylie Anti-Money Laundering Act of 1992, 102 Pub. L. No. 550, 106 Stat. 3672 (1992) (codified in various section of 12, 18, 31 and 42 U.S.C.A.), amended the Bank Secrecy Act to require the filing of "Suspicious Activity Reports" (known in the industry as SARs). 31 U.S.C. §5318(g)(1) (Supp. III 2003). If a transaction is "suspicious" (i.e., "relevant to a possible violation of law or regulation") it must be reported if in the aggregate $5000 in funds or other assets is involved. *See, e.g.*, 12 C.F.R. §208.62 (2008).

that could conceal large amounts of currency, monetary instruments, or small valuable items.

- A customer rents multiple safe deposit boxes to store large amounts of currency, monetary instruments, or high-value assets awaiting conversion to currency, for placement into the banking system.[47]

These regulations would not cause problems for Harry, as he apparently accesses his Gringotts vault only at the beginning of the school year, but the strategic value to the government of having the bank reporting this information should be clear. As the only wizard bank, Gringotts could keep tabs on almost everyone in the wizarding world and could use that information to aid the Order of the Phoenix, the Ministry of Magic, or Lord Voldemort. Most likely, however, whatever the goblins do will be designed to help the goblins themselves.

Conclusion

So, in the end, Muggle banking and wizard banking are not the same things, but they share some important characteristics. Banking in the wizard world seems to have stopped evolving in the Middle Ages, when bankers were really just trusted keepers of valuables. Apparently, wizards do not manage their money supply the way Muggles do by using the slight of hand of fractional reserve banking to create money out of thin air. Instead, the money supply in the wizard world seems stagnant, creating social problems that emphasize disparities in wealth. Even so, the money that does exist is subject to security measures in both worlds that are designed to instill confidence in the banking system.

Perhaps the most interesting aspect of banking in both the magical and the Muggle worlds is the crucial place in the balance of power occupied by those who control the money supply, be they the goblins who run Gringotts or the MBAs who run the Federal Reserve. Political power and economic power often go hand in hand. The United States took a long time to adopt a system of central banking and when the Federal Reserve Act was finally passed, the structure of the system was intentionally diffuse so that it would be difficult for the central bankers to exercise too much power over the economy.

Nevertheless, bankers still wield a great deal of power, as shown by the influence the remarks of an Alan Greenspan or a Ben Bernanke can have on

---

47. FEDERAL FINANCIAL INSTITUTIONS EXAMINATION COUNCIL, BANK SECRECY ACT, ANTI-MONEY LAUNDERING EXAMINATION MANUAL (2005), http://www.ffiec.gov/bsa_aml_infobase/documents/BSA_AML_Man_2007.pdf.

world markets and the role the Fed has played in the financial crisis of 2008. Policymakers know that economic power and political power are closely related and that economic turmoil can lead to political unrest. That dynamic is likely true in the magical world as well.

The economic/political power struggle in the magical world is, however, much less insulated than in the United States. The battle to gain control over or an alliance with the goblins seems very much out in the open in Book Seven. We learn that Gringotts has fallen under wizard control, although the goblins themselves seem unhappy with that development. Nevertheless, the goblins remain dutiful guardians of the wizard treasure. In that effort they appear to reveal themselves as sympathizers with the Death Eaters, given the enthusiasm with which they seek to thwart Harry, Hermione and Ron from breaking into the Lestrange vault. At the same time, however, Gornuk (a goblin) remarks that the goblins are not for Voldemort and take no sides in a wizards' war.

In the end, the goblin bankers of the magical world are in it for themselves, as Harry's interaction with Griphook illustrates nicely. Griphook was essential to the plan that Harry, Hermione and Ron cobbled together to get the Hufflepuff Horcrux, but Griphook promised to help only in exchange for the Gryffindor Sword. Oddly, Griphook was not very much help in alerting Harry and the others to the various security measures in place at Gringotts, perhaps because he was hoping they would get caught and the sword would be back in goblin hands. When the intruders' presence in the Lestrange vault was discovered by the goblins, Griphook abandoned Harry and the others, shouting "thief" and joining the other goblins so he wouldn't get caught. Oddly though, Griphook was the one who retrieved the Hufflepuff cup and flipped it to Harry. Without Griphook's help, the Horcrux would have been lost in the vault.

So, the goblins—perhaps like bankers generally—may appear to be helpful where it serves their own interests, but they show their true colors when their interests are on the line. In the end, the goblins are in it for the goblins. Ironically, the Gryffindor sword ultimately ends up in the hands of a "true Gryffindor," Neville Longbottom, when during the Battle of Hogwarts he drew the sword from the Sorting Hat to kill Nagini. Perhaps it's a lesson that no one can truly hold and control wealth. Ultimately it is all fleeting—whether it's Leprechaun gold, money created from fractional reserve banking or the Sword of Gryffindor.

Gringotts: The Role of Banks in Harry Potter's Wizarding World

Heidi Mandanis Schooner

> *Enter, stranger, but take heed*
> *Of what awaits the sin of greed,*
> *For those who take, but do not earn,*
> *Must pay most dearly in their turn.*
> *So if you seek beneath our floors*
> *A treasure that was never yours,*
> *Thief, you have been warned, beware*
> *Of finding more than treasure there.*[1]

Deep underground, miles beneath London, goblins run the wizards' one bank, Gringotts.[2] Hagrid explains that "yeh'd be mad ter try an' rob it.... Never mess with goblins, Harry. Gringotts is the safest place in the world fer anything yeh want ter keep safe — 'cept maybe Hogwarts."[3]

Money and wealth are featured prominently in the Harry Potter novels. Harry, raised by stingy Uncle Vernon and Aunt Petunia, becomes owner of a vault full of gold[4] in the depths of Gringotts. Harry's wealth stands in sharp contrast to Ron Weasley's modest means which saddle him with tattered robes and a hand-me-down wand. Harry's nemesis, Draco Malfoy never misses an opportunity to flaunt his family's affluence and consequent influence. Moreover, Gringotts and the goblins that run it are key elements in the Harry Potter novels. In *The Sorcerer's Stone*, Quirrell blunders an attempt to steal the sorcerer's

---

1. *Sorcerer's Stone* 72–73. These words are etched on the doors of Gringotts Bank.

2. The name "Gringotts" might derive from the word "ingot" which is a mold used to cast metals such as gold. The goblin Gringott was founder of Gringotts, the bank.

3. J.K. Rowling, Harry Potter and the Sorcerer's Stone 63 (1997).

4. Wizard coins include Galleons (gold), Sickles (silver) and Knuts (bronze). There are 17 Sickles to one Galleon and 25 Knuts to one Sickle.

stone from Gringotts' vault number 713. Hagrid got there first. In *The Order of the Phoenix*, the wizards fear that the goblins' loyalties might be swayed toward the dark side. In *The Deathly Hallows* Harry retrieves a Horcrux, Helga Hufflepuff's cup, from a "swelling mass of red-hot objects" in Bellatrix Lestrange's Gringott's vault.[5]

In our real, Muggle, world, banks not only play a prominent role, but are also subject to intensive regulation. Bank regulation is justified on the basis of two observations. First, banks are important to the macro-economy. Second, banks are financially fragile. Banks are important to the macro-economy because they dominate the payment system, they serve as a source of liquidity for individuals and firms, and because they are a means for the central bank to transmit monetary policy. Banks are financially fragile because their assets (primarily loans) are typically illiquid and their liabilities (primarily deposits) are payable on demand. This mismatch of assets and liabilities, coupled with the fact that banks maintain only fractional reserves (i.e., they keep on hand only a small percentage of the money deposited by customers), makes banks acutely vulnerable to insolvency. Moreover, banks suffer from contagious insolvency, i.e., the insolvency of one bank can lead to the insolvency of other banks. This form of contagion occurs when the news of the insolvency of one bank causes panicking depositors to lose confidence in all banks—even healthy ones. Therefore, the recognition of the special place that banks occupy in the economy and their inherent fragility creates a strong incentive for the government to regulate their solvency.

This chapter explores the extent to which observations regarding real-world banks translate into the world of Harry Potter. First, this chapter will examine the role of money and wealth in the wizarding world. Second, this chapter will explore the nature of the business of banking in the wizarding world; in particular, Gringotts' offering of traditional banking services, i.e., deposit taking and lending. Third, this chapter will examine the regulation of Gingotts and compare that system of regulation to real-world regulatory regimes. Finally, this chapter will demonstrate how the image of banks and bankers in the Harry Potter novels is reflected in the regulation of banks.

Poor Wizards

Why does Ron Weasley wear second-hand robes? It seems that uber-mom Molly Weasley could whip him up a new set of robes with the flick of a wand.

---

5. *Deathly Hallows* 540.

Yet, Rowling's wizards do not appear to use spells to enrich themselves tangibly. Do wizards lack the power to create matter? Perhaps, for example, in *The Half-Blood Prince*, when Dumbledore produces — out of thin air — a bottle of Madam Rosmerta's finest oak-matured mead, Dumbledore is not creating the mead, but is merely transporting it from his personal stock. In fact, it seems that many of the spells that produce objects out of thin air involve mere transport, e.g., "Accio, broom!"[6] But, there is some suggestion that magic can create things. In *The Goblet of Fire*, wand-maker Ollivander produces a bouquet of flowers and a flock of birds as he tests the wands of Fleur Delacour and Victor Krum at the start of the Tri-Wizard Tournament. Moreover, in *The Half Blood Price*, Dumbledore relates to Harry the story of Voldemort's destitute, witch mother, Merope:

> " … Merope was alone in London and in desperate need of gold, desperate enough to sell her one and only valuable possession, the locket that was one of Marvolo's [her father's] treasured family heirlooms."
>
> "But she could do magic! said Harry impatiently. "She could have got food and everything for herself by magic, couldn't she?"
>
> "Ah," said Dumbledore, "perhaps she could. But it is my belief — I am guessing again, but I am sure I am right — that when her husband abandoned her, Merope stopped using magic. I do not think that she wanted to be a witch any longer."[7]

While this passage suggests that some witches and wizards can use magic to create "food and everything," we learn in *The Deathly Hallows* that the ability to create food, in particular, has limitations. Hermione tells us that food is the first of the five Principle Exceptions to Gamp's Law of Elemental Transfigurations. She explains: "It's impossible to make good food out of nothing! You can Summon it if you know where it is, you can transform it, you can increase the quantity if you've already got some —"[8] This might explain why the Weasleys, despite their limited means, enjoy such hearty meals at the Burrow. Molly must be proficient at spells that increase the quantity of food.

In addition to actual limitations on magic as reflected in laws of science like Gamp's Laws of Elemental Transfiguration, wizards and witches might choose not to use their magic in ways that would enrich themselves. The wizards do

---

6. Similarly, elves do all the cooking at Hogwarts. Yet, food appears, dramatically, on the once empty plates placed before the students.

7. *Half-Blood Prince* 262.

8. *Deathly Hallows* 292–93.

impose all sorts of restrictions on the free use of their magical powers. For example, underage wizards are not permitted to use magic outside of school.[9] Harry would likely violate wizard law if he used the Accio charm to summon Malfoy's broom instead of his own. Most likely, this constraint on the scope of magical power just makes for a better story—consistent with thousands of years of story telling.[10] Recall the fairy tale genie who grants three wishes and warns that none can be used to gain more wishes.

Of course, money does more than just buy things.[11] Wizards might need money even though they have the power to fulfill all their needs and wants. First, magic is work and so wizards might not want to spend their days casting spells just to put food on the table. Money facilitates the division of labor and specialization (money works better than barter). So, the wizards who are good at spells that produce food spend their time doing just that, thereby earning Galleons to buy services and goods from wizards who are good at other sorts of spells. Second, money allows for the accumulation of wealth. Without money, it would have been much harder for James and Lily Potter to not only store, but pass on their wealth to Harry. Without money, James and Lily Potter would have needed a much bigger vault at Gringotts to store their riches. And, Harry would be stuck bartering those riches for the things that he wants (the latest, fastest broom technology) or needs (a home for the summer far away from the Dursleys).

For all these reasons, it seems that magic does not replace the need for money. Moreover, magic is not even an enduring form of alchemy. The gold that rains over the Quidditch World Cup in *The Goblet of Fire* disappears the next day. Leprechauns!

The Business of Gringotts

While modern banks offer a wide range of financial products and services, traditionally a bank's business centered on taking deposits and lending money.

---

9. Decree for the Reasonable Restriction of Underage Sorcery, 1875, Paragraph C. This law, and others like it, is enforced by the Improper Use of Magic Office in the Ministry of Magic.

10. Somehow, supernatural characters are more interesting if they share some human problems or weaknesses. The ancient Greeks knew this and gave their gods some human flaws. Hera, Zeus' wife, is famously and intensely jealous of her husband's roving eye.

11. For a complete discussion of the role of money in history and in the Harry Potter novels, *see* Eric Gouvin's chapter, *The Magic of Banking*.

Banks made their money, and still do, on the "spread," i.e., the difference between the interest paid to customers on their deposits and charged to customers on their loans. What is the nature of the business of Gringotts?

One might conclude that Gringotts is not a bank in the traditional sense, but merely an elaborate vault run by fierce guards (the goblins) who have secured Gringotts with an assortment of spells, enchantments and … dragons (for the high security vaults). Gringotts provides its customers with vaults for safekeeping their gold or other treasures.[12] This service is much like the safe deposit boxes available at your local Muggle bank—only much bigger. Rowling does not tell us whether Harry pays a fee to Gringotts. One might imagine that periodically the goblins take a Sickle or two out of Harry's piles as a fee for their safekeeping service.

On closer inspection, however, it appears that Gringotts might actually provide other banking services, not just safe keeping. Gringotts provides foreign currency exchange: In *The Chamber of Secrets*, Hermione's Muggle father exchanges pound notes for wizard money at Gringotts. Most important, however, is the question of lending. If Gringotts is a true bank, then it not only takes deposits, but it also lends out a portion of those deposits to other customers. The image of Harry and his vault full of money suggests that all of Harry's money remains in the vault at all times. This would mean that Gringotts does not operate on the basis of fractional reserves, i.e., it does not lend out a percentage of the money deposited by its customers. It is also quite possible that Gringotts does not pay interest by periodically adding to Harry's mounds of galleons. Yet, the goblins are also lenders.[13]

In *The Goblet of Fire*, Ludo Bagman,[14] a former Quidditch star whose luck has played out, owes money to Fred and George Weasley, Lee Jordan's dad, and the goblins. While Fred and George wrote Bagman a letter asking for repayment, the goblins took an entirely different approach. A gang of goblins cornered Bagman in the woods and took all his gold. Since the gold on him was insufficient to cover the debt, the goblins tailed Bagman to Hogwarts to keep him under surveillance. Bill Weasley explains that "[g]oblin notions of own-

---

12. When the goblin Griphook unlocks the door to Harry's vault, green smoke floats out the door and reveals mounds of gold Galleons, silver Sickles, and bronze Knuts.

13. Of course, the fact that the goblins might lend money does not necessarily mean that Gringotts itself (as a firm) is engaged in lending. Furthermore, a few loans do not create a market for credit. For a discussion of the problems associated with the lack of credit markets, *see* Eric Gouvin's chapter, *The Magic of Banking*.

14. While "bagman" may refer more commonly to a traveling salesman, a bagman is also an extortionist. A "ludo" is a person who plays.

ership, payment, and repayment are not the same as human ones.... It would be less dangerous to break into Gringotts than to renege on a promise to a goblin."[15] With these sorts of credit collection practices, it is no wonder that, in *The Goblet of Fire*, the Weasley twins did not, apparently, seek a loan from the goblins to start up their joke shop. Borrowing (or, perhaps, accepting) money from Harry was a much less costly option. All that Harry required in return was that the twins buy Ron some new dress robes.

Regulating Gringotts

The regulation of banking has its origins in antiquity. The Babylonian Code of Hammurabi decreed that if the crops failed, the farmer's lender must suspend interest for that year.[16] Since the time of Hammurabi, both the business and the regulation of banking have grown more sophisticated and diverse. As discussed above, the regulation of banks is grounded in the observation that banks are special (i.e., worth protecting) and fragile (i.e., prone to insolvency). Regulation of banks comes in many forms and what follows are only some of the highlights.

First, governments often place entry restrictions on banking—meaning that the bank owners and managers must go through a lengthy and intensive application process before they may open a bank.[17] Entry restrictions are meant to ensure that a bank is formed and run with sufficient capital and management expertise. In the United Kingdom, for example, the Financial Services Authority (FSA), the agency responsible for regulating banks, must assess the "fitness and propriety" of bank managers. In making such an assessment, the FSA must determine the person's (1) honest, integrity, and reputation; (2) competence and capability; and (3) financial soundness.

Second, banks are subject, often, to restrictions on their activities and investments. For example, generally in the United States a bank cannot engage in activities that are non-financial, e.g., a bank cannot own and run an oil company or a become a real estate developer. Activity restrictions prevent the

---

15. *Deathly Hallows* 516–17.

16. "If a man owe a debt and Adad [the storm god] inundate the field or the flood carry the produce away, or, through lack of water, grain have not grown in the field, in that year he shall not make any return of grain to the creditor, he shall alter his contract-tablet and he need not pay the interest for that year." Law: A Treasury of Art and Literature 21 (Sara Robbins, ed., 1990).

17. However, there have been periods in history of "free banking" during which there were few entry restrictions.

over-accumulation of market power (as would be the case, arguably, if a bank owned an oil company) and also restrict banks from engaging in certain risky activities (e.g., real estate development).

Third, and perhaps the most remarkable feature of bank regulation, is a governments' provision of deposit insurance. Through deposit insurance, the government protects depositors from the risk of bank insolvency. The government promises to pay depositors a portion of their deposits in the event of a bank insolvency. While deposit insurance may eliminate much of the negative effects of bank insolvency, deposit insurance itself creates a need for regulation because the government must protect the solvency of the banks it insures (so that the deposit insurance fund does not become insolvent and cause taxpayers to foot the bill for insured deposits).

If, as argued above, Gringotts is a traditional bank engaged in both deposit taking and lending, then the justification for regulating Gringotts would be the same as it is for regulating Citibank. And, sure enough, it appears that Gringotts is regulated. The entry restrictions are perhaps the most powerful form of regulation imposed on wizard banks. Hagrid tells us that there is only one wizard bank, Gringotts. One might conclude that Gringotts is not a private bank at all, but is government owned. However, it appears that the Gringotts is privately owned, by the goblins, but has been granted a government-sponsored monopoly.[18] After all, insulating Gringotts from competition would be one way to protect its solvency. Furthermore, the goblins (and only the goblins) run Gringotts. Yes, some wizards work for Gringotts—Bill Weasley works at a branch in Egypt. Yet, Goblins are in charge until the denouement of the seventh book in which the goblin Griphook is on the run because "Gringotts is no longer under the sole control of [his] race" and he refuses to recognize a wizarding master.[19]

Borrowing from English law—a reasonable approach since Gringotts is in London—are the goblins "fit and proper" bank managers? First, with regard to their honesty, integrity and reputation, the goblins certainly have a reputation for greed.[20] Avarice is actually quite compatible with the qualities one

---

18. In *The Order of the Phoenix*, the wizards' tabloid, *The Quibbler*, reports that the Minister of Magic, Cornelius Fudge, wants to wrest control of the gold supply from the goblins and is willing to use force to do it. This either means that Gringotts is a private bank or a government sponsored entity with considerable independence from the executive branch of the government.

19. *Deathly Hallows* 296.

20. Ron, Hermione, and Harry pass a group of goblins deep in the woods, "who were cackling over a sack of gold they had undoubtedly won betting on the [Quidditch] match, and who seemed quite unperturbed by the trouble on the campsite." *Goblet of Fire* 125.

might expect in a good banker. We do not want people with generous instincts to be bankers. We want individuals who count and account for every Knut and Sickle.[21] Second, the competence and capability of the goblins are their strong suit—never mess with a goblin, Hagrid warns. Goblins have a particular knack for the kinds of spells and enchantments that would protect the bank from thievery. Finally, the financial soundness of the goblins appears well established in their apparent control of all monetary reserves. How Gringott, the founder of Gringotts, accumulated his wealth at the outset is a question apparently best left unanswered.

Further regulation of banking is evidenced by the wizards' restriction of the goblins activities much like our banks are required to engage only in banking and other financial activities. In the *Order of the Phoenix*, Arthur and Bill Weasley discuss with Remus Lupin whether the goblins would ever join Voldemort. Lupin opines: "I think it depends what they're offered.... And I'm not talking about gold; if they're offered freedoms we've been denying them for centuries they're going to be tempted."[22] The potential conflict that faced the goblins, i.e., stay with the forces of good and remain stuck in a highly regulated business, or join Voldemort and enjoy the freedom to do other things,[23] reflects the current federal versus state conflict in the United States. Banks with federal charters (called "national banks") currently enjoy the freedom from various onerous state laws because such laws are, arguably, preempted by federal law. State chartered banks lack such freedoms. Not surprisingly, some state banks have decided to convert to federal charters and enjoy the freedoms associated with the federal system.[24] Does this suggest that such chartering-switching banks have cast off the yoke of regulation to join the dark, chaotic side of the federal banking system? Not seriously.

Rowling gives no indication that the Ministry of Magic administers a deposit insurance program akin to the U.S. Federal Deposit Insurance Corporation. With the myriad of departments within the Ministry, however, it is not hard to imagine a deposit insurance program tucked away behind a bureaucratic signpost. Even in the absence of an explicit deposit insurance scheme, history proves

---

21. Of course, if we were serious about honesty and integrity in wizard bank managers, we would probably choose someone like Dumbledore. But, alas, he is simply too busy.

22. *Order of the Phoenix* 85.

23. Lupin's prediction that Voldemort would gain access to Gringotts by offering the goblins some sort of sweet deal seems, by the final book, naive. While it does appear in the seventh book that Gringotts has fallen to the Death Eaters, it does not appear that the goblins have been offered anything in return for this change of control.

24. *See* Diana Taylor, Superintendent, State of New York Banking Department, Remarks on the Current Issues in the Banking Industry (Oct. 6, 2005) *available at* http://www.banking.state.ny.us/sp051006.htm.

that democratic governments respond to the inevitable public outcry over bank failures by bailing out insolvent banks despite the fact that the government has made no prior promise (e.g., in the form of explicit deposit insurance) to do so.[25] Thus, if Gringotts were to fail under Voldemort's reign of terror, the Minister of Magic would quite likely succumb to public pressure to do something, e.g., provide relief to Gringotts depositors. One can only imagine the headlines: In the *Daily Prophet*: "Gringotts Bankrupt: Ministry Blamed for Failed Goblin Oversight." Or, better yet, in *The Quibbler*: "Minister of Magic Empties Personal Vault on Eve of Gringotts Insolvency: Where's *Your* Gold?"

Reflections of Gringotts

The Harry Potter novels are certainly not the first source of literary or pop-culture images of banks and bankers. Images of bankers in film and literature abound.[26] The nature of such images is, or should be, important to lawyers and lawmakers because the law reflects the attitudes toward and perceptions of the world around us. So, if banks and bankers are viewed as possessing certain talents and flaws, those characteristics will inform the regulation of banks.

Rowling perpetuates literary and cultural images of bankers and moneylenders as not just greedy, but downright unpleasant. Mark Twain described the banker as "a fellow who lends you his umbrella when the sun is shining and wants it back the minute it begins to rain." Ezra Pound displayed his disdain for bankers (and, perhaps, his infamous anti-Semitism[27]) by relegating all bankers to hell in his epic poem *The Cantos*. Bankers, he said, encourage people to incur debt beyond their means and then squeeze them with usurious interest.[28] Accordingly, Rowling's goblins are no rays of sunshine. The goblins,

---

25. *See* Jonathan R. Macey, *Commercial Banking and Democracy: The Illusive Quest for Deregulation*, 23 YALE J. ON REG. 1 (2006). Recent history shows that government bailouts extend well beyond commercial banks. In 2008, the United States government rescued Bear Stearns, an investment bank, and AIG, an insurance company, despite the fact that the government had no legal obligation to do so.

26. *See* Heidi Mandanis Schooner, *Popular Images of Bankers Reflected in Regulation*, 5 GREEN BAG 2D 27 (2001).

27. It is not unlikely that Pound held the stereotypical view that equates bankers with Jews. The existence of famous Jewish bankers, like the Rothschilds, has fueled this stereotype.

28. EZRA POUND, CANTOS, The Fragments: "The evils is usury. The burning hell without let-up. The canker corrupting all things." EZRA POUND, CANTOS, Number 45: "Usura rusteth the chisel. With usura hath no man a house of good stone."

by nature aloof and intimidating, collect their debts like organized criminals—with threats, coercion, and force. Moreover, Gringotts security protocol could be described as a bit over the top. The goblin Griphook explains that if anyone other than a goblin tries to open a vault door they would be instantly sucked into the vault and trapped inside. Eleven-year-old Harry asks how often the goblins check to see if anyone has made such a foolhardy attempt. Griphook responds, with a nasty grin, "About once every ten years."[29] Griphook is further described as "unexpectedly bloodthirsty," laughing "at the idea of pain in lesser creatures."[30] Consistent with their nasty image, goblins are aesthetically challenged. The first goblin Harry meets is short with a "swarthy, clever face, a pointed beard and ... very long fingers and feet."[31] Later, Harry describes the goblin language as "a rough and unmelodious tongue, a string of rattling, guttural noises...."[32] Rowling even christens the goblins with savage names. Would you share a butter beer with someone named Griphook, Ragnok or Gornuk?

Rowling also perpetuates the image of the banker as conservative. Her goblins are portrayed as number crunching drones: "About a hundred more goblins were sitting on high stools behind a long counter, scribbling in large ledgers, weighing coins in brass scales, examining precious stones through eyeglasses."[33] Goblins stand in sharp contrast to flamboyant wizards like the egomaniacal wizard Gilderoy Lockhart who "was immaculate in sweeping robes of turquoise, his golden hair shining under a perfectly positioned turquoise hat with gold trimming."[34] In the Harry Potter films, the goblins wear suits, not robes, and work in a building that resembles an ancient Greek temple—a classical symbol of endurance frequently adopted by Muggle bankers. This image mirrors that of the British bankers parodied in Walt Disney's *Mary Poppins*.[35] George Banks, father of Jane and Michael, is so stiff that only a crafty, magical nanny can break through his British restraint. He and his partners are the epitome of conservatism in their dark suits and matching red carnation boutonnieres.[36]

The popular image (if not reality) of the greedy, mean, and conservative banker is reflected in the law and regulation of banks. With regard to the greed

---

29. *Sorcerer's Stone* 76.

30. *Deathly Hallows* 509–10.

31. *Sorcerer's Stone* 72.

32. *Deathly Hallows* 294.

33. *Sorcerer's Stone* 73.

34. *Chamber of Secrets* 89.

35. Mary Poppins (Walt Disney Productions 1964).

36. For further discussion of the image of bankers in *Mary Poppins*, see Heidi Mandanis Schooner, *Popular Images of Bankers Reflected in Regulation*, 5 Green Bag 2d 27, 30–33 (2001).

and general nastiness, the regulation of lending reflects this perception. Since Hammurabi's time, lenders have been regulated by both religious and secular regimes. Usurious interest is deemed unacceptable and, therefore, prohibited. In recent years, a number of states have enacted "predatory lending laws" which seek to rein in the evil practices of the most unscrupulous lenders.[37] With regard to conservatism, restrictions on banking activities reflect the image of the banker as risk adverse. Bankers are prohibited from engaging in certain risky activities. The clear regulatory purpose for such restrictions is the desire to protect the bank from insolvency. Yet, such restrictions may also reflect our cultural expectation that bankers remain cautious, if not boring.[38]

Conclusion

For those who scoff at the notion that practical significance can be drawn from wizard banking, be advised that Gringotts thrives in our Muggle world. Gringotts encryption software is available[39] and a virtual Gringotts allows you to purchase your Galleons and go shopping.[40] More importantly, the role and regulation of banks in the wizarding world asks us to reconsider the very foundations of an important regulatory system. As regulatory regimes grow and mature, they often lose sight of their fundamental regulatory goals, leaving them open to criticism and calls for reform. The idea that a magical bank would require regulation is an important reminder that regulatory regimes often serve, while imperfectly, important purposes. And, those purposes persist even in a more perfect world where, when hungry, one simply waves a wand and utters the simple incantation "Accio, sandwich."

---

37. *See e.g.*, Predatory Lending Act, 1999 N.C. Sess. Laws 332 (1999); N.C. Gen. Stat. 24-1.1A (2002).

38. This is despite the fact that banking is actually a very risky business. After all, one of the fundamental justifications for the regulation of banks is that banks are financially fragile. The recent failures of two banks, IndyMac and Washington Mutual, provide stark evidence of the riskiness of banking particularly for those banks that were heavily invested in subprime mortgage markets.

39. Free Software Directory, http://directory.fsf.org/gringotts.html (last visited Aug. 16, 2008).

40. Kylie's Virtual Hogwarts, http://kylieshogwarts.com/gringotts_bank.htm (last visited Aug. 16, 2008).

Harry Potter as an Archetype

5

Harry Potter Goes to Law School

Lenora Ledwon

> *"It is our choices, Harry, that show us what we truly are, far more than our abilities."*
> —Professor Dumbledore[1]

Law students read Harry Potter.[2] They read about him in between reading cases, statutes, codes, and other texts filled with magical words. (Sometimes they read about him *instead* of reading cases, statutes and codes.) Hogwarts School of Witchcraft and Wizardry looks very much like a Harvard Law School for wizards, a school where students learn the secrets of magic words of power. Both types of schools offer explicit and implicit lessons about power, its acquisition, and its uses. Education offers student wizards and student lawyers alike the tools to become forces for evil or good in the world.

Like all great novels of development, the Harry Potter stories ask one central question, "How shall I live in the world, for good or for ill?" This is an often unspoken question in law school, where concerns about grades, jobs and salaries can all too easily take precedence. Yet, it is one law students must face. What kind of practitioner will I become? Where will I seek the kind of "fierce joy" that Harry finds in his Seeker role? And, most importantly, what will I choose to do with this power I am acquiring?

This chapter explores the implications of the similarities between law school and wizard school by focusing on the topics of: (1) students; (2) professors; (3) studying and exams; and (4) academic culture. I conclude that the series of Harry Potter books can be read collectively as one overarching bildungsroman (or novel of development) and that this process of development is very simi-

---

1. *Chamber of Secrets* 333.

2. *The Chronicle of Higher Education*, in its periodic surveys of the top ten books being read on college campuses, consistently lists Harry Potter books. My own informal polls of students in my *Law and Literature* courses confirm that Rowling's books are quite popular among law students.

lar to the process law students follow in learning to "think like a lawyer" during their three years of law school.[3] Knowledge is power in the most literal sense in the world of Hogwarts, and in the world of law school, as well. Students at Hogwarts are selected for an elite education (although the acceptance letter arrives by owl, rather than ordinary mail). They face a tough curriculum, grueling examinations, and terrifying and/or boring teachers. (Snape is the frighteningly cruel Socratic teacher who lives to humiliate students. Professor McGonagall is that favorite teacher who is firm but fair.) Harry and his friends must negotiate the process of becoming more and more powerful at the same time they are feeling powerless as "lowly" students within the hierarchy of the educational institution. For law students in particular, there is a profound resonance to the Harry Potter stories.

Student Lawyers and Student Wizards

Sorting Out Ordinary and Extraordinary
Students—Am I Supposed to Be Here?

Rowling's books follow in the popular literary tradition of the 19th-century British school story.[4] (Traditionally, such stories follow the social, educational, and moral progress of a young boy at a British "public" boarding school.) But there is another, more recent type of school story which also is pertinent to understanding the Harry Potter series: the law school story. Whether it is told as a novel (John Jay Osborn, Jr.'s *The Paper Chase*) or as a memoir (Scott Turrow's *One L*), the law school story explores law student life and the challenges of legal education.[5] In law school stories, just as in the British public school story,

---

3. A bildungsroman is a novel of development, a story tracing the formation of a hero or heroine through childhood to adolescence to young adulthood. Famous examples include Goethe's *Wilhelm Meister* and Dickens' *David Copperfield*. CHRIS BALDICK, OXFORD CONCISE DICTIONARY OF LITERARY TERMS 27 (2004). *See generally* JEROME BUCKLEY, SEASON OF YOUTH: THE BILDUNGSROMAN FROM DICKENS TO GOLDING (1974).

4. The most famous example is Thomas Hughes' 1857 novel, *Tom Brown's Schooldays*. *See generally* BEVERLY LYON CLARK, REGENDERING THE SCHOOL STORY: SASSY SISSIES AND TATTLING TOMBOYS (1996); ISABEL QUIGLY, THE HEIRS OF TOM BROWN (1982). For an excellent discussion of how the Harry Potter stories fit into the school story genre, *see* Karen Manners Smith, *Harry Potter's Schooldays: J.K. Rowling and the British Boarding School Novel*, *in* READING HARRY POTTER: CRITICAL ESSAYS 69 (Giselle Liza Anatol ed., 2003).

5. *See, e.g.*, JOHN JAY OSBORN, JR., THE PAPER CHASE (1971); SCOTT TURROW, ONE L (1977). These two are the most well-known law school stories, but the genre continues.

the reader follows the development of the protagonist as he (and the protagonist typically has been a "he") encounters terrifyingly strict teachers, takes part in exhilarating school competitions, works through massive amounts of homework, and makes friends and foes among his classmates. Harry's epic story, spread across a course of intensive study lasting years, reflects many of the same fears, hardships and triumphs that law students face during their time in law school. Law school and wizard school alike are process-oriented. Students move through a process of early self-doubts and anxieties, to a growing knowledge that not all the answers are in books, and to a confidence not only in their abilities to think like lawyers/think like wizards but also a self-confidence in trusting themselves to make the right choices.

When Harry first learns that he has been accepted into Hogwarts, he worries, like many a new law student, that there has been a horrible mistake. "A wizard? Him? How could he possibly be?"[6] He also frequently wonders if the Sorting Hat put him in the correct house—should he be in Slytherin instead of Gryffindor? Similarly, many law students secretly worry that they will be uncovered as imposters—could they really be good enough to compete with all the other obviously bright and talented students?

While the Sorting Hat sorts students into one of four houses based on abilities (Gryffindor for the brave, Ravenclaw for the bright, Slytherin for the ambitious and Hufflepuff for the hard-working), law schools sort students in many ways. We sort our students before they are accepted into law school (on the basis of undergraduate grades, L.S.A.T. scores, applicant essays, etc.) and also once they are in law school (on the basis of course grades, class rank, membership in the Law Review, Moot Court competitions, and the like). Law school admissions committees sometimes can be philosophically more like Helga Hufflepuff (depending on the school's mission statement and commitment to hard work and diversity) or more like Rowena Ravenclaw (totally focused on grades and L.S.A.T. scores). The sorting process in law schools is not unproblematic, for grades are not perfect reflections of ability. Additionally, too much sorting and emphasis on grades can create a debilitating, cut-throat atmosphere on campus. The Sorting Hat warns of the divisive dangers of unbridled rivalry, in the song it sings in *The Order of the Phoenix* (which could be re-titled, "Lament of the Admissions Committee"):

See, e.g., RICHARD KAHLENBERG, BROKEN CONTRACT: A MEMOIR OF HARVARD LAW SCHOOL (1992).

6. *Sorcerer's Stone* 57.

Listen closely to my song:
Though condemned I am to split you
Still I worry that it's wrong.
Though I must fulfill my duty
And must quarter every year
Still I wonder whether sorting
May not bring the end I fear.[7]

Law students are already a pretty competitive bunch, and the sorting process that starts with law school admissions and continues throughout all three years of law school can provoke as intense rivalries among students jostling for top positions as any of those we see between Gryffindor and Slytherin.

Of Gunners and Gut Courses

Harry and Ron begin as rather average students. (Harry's growing skill in Defense Against the Dark Arts seems more innate than gained by studying, and Ron frequently relies on copying Hermione's notes.) Hermione, however, is clearly a gunner from day one. "Gunners," in law student parlance, are those partly despised and partly feared students who constantly raise their hands to every question the teacher asks and who have over-prepared for each and every class. (This is the kind of student who, in a Contracts class, asks, "Professor, in this 19th-century case about sheep-shearing cited in footnote 23, what effect did the exchange rate have on the breach of the wool delivery?")

Interestingly, Hermione seems to be the *only* gunner in the school. (She rarely has any competition in her classes, and she clearly is the most hard-working student.) This is quite different from law schools, where any given class might have any number of gunners shooting their hands up into the air at every opportunity. As a result of the prevalence of gunners, one popular game we used to play in law school was "Gunner Bingo." You would fill out a bingo card with the names of the gunners in your class, and each time one spoke you checked off his or her name. Then, you had to raise your own hand and work the word "bingo" into your answer to the professor. ("Professor, once you prove offer, acceptance, and consideration, then Bingo, you have an enforceable contract!") Gunner Bingo required a large class with a good number of gunners, but we never had a shortage. Hermione appears to be the solitary gunner at Hogwarts.

Hermione would do well in law school. Unlike Harry and Ron, she lives and breathes her studies. Hermione is completely focused on learning, and very

---

7. *Order of the Phoenix* 206.

well-organized. She draws up strict study schedules and color codes her notes. (I remember being completely intimidated by seeing a friend's color-coded looseleaf binder of notes taken during our Civil Procedure class in law school. Her notes were almost as lengthy as our casebook.) We learn in *The Prisoner of Azkaban* that Hermione even studies on vacation. And to top it off, she takes "Muggle Studies" as a course, despite being Muggle-born, because she thinks it will be interesting to study Muggles from the wizarding point of view.

Hogwarts students consider Muggle Studies an easy course (a "gut" course), as compared to a difficult course such as Potions. Perhaps the law school equivalent of Muggle Studies would be a course on Harry Potter and the Law—at least, that is, until the students realized what they were getting into. Taxation might be the equivalent of Potions, as far as legendarily difficult courses go.

The first year students at Hogwarts don't have much choice in their courses, just as first year law students usually have to take a required schedule. While Hogwarts students will be taking such courses as Potions, Transfiguration, and Defense Against the Dark Arts, first year law students will be taking Contracts, Civil Procedure, Legal Writing, Torts, and the like. It is not until after their first year that law students get some choice in their courses, and even then they still have a number of required courses to take.

Friendships

Law school education is a form of initiation (into the mysteries of the law), and a rite of passage (perilous and exhilarating). Strong bonds are forged under such conditions, not unlike the bond formed between Harry, Ron, and Hermione: "There are some things you can't share without ending up liking each other, and knocking out a twelve-foot mountain troll is one of them."[8] Similarly, law student friendships, formed in the camaraderie of late-night studying and tough classes, can be deep and long-lasting. Some friendships ripen into marriage, and some into that other close relationship, the law partnership.

Professors

Socratic Teaching and Learning by Doing

In a famous scene from the film version of *The Paper Chase*, the intimidating Professor Kingsfield (played by John Houseman) humiliates a law student

---

8. *Sorcerer's Stone* 179.

by handing him a dime in front of the whole class and telling him "Call your mother. Tell her there is serious doubt about your becoming a lawyer."[9] Snape would give Kingsfield a run for his money in the "Humiliating Your Students Olympics." He frequently insults and embarrasses students in front of their peers. While some teachers are encouraging (Professor Sprout, for example, is happy to award points for good answers), Snape displays a sadistic delight in taking points away and in teaching through intimidation. Snape is perhaps the nightmare version of the Socratic professor. The Socratic Method is legendary as the traditional technique for law school teaching. Under this method, the professor (like Socrates) engages in a line of directed questioning with the students, hoping to encourage them to think through difficult problems analytically. In its worst form, it can be a tool for humiliation, where a teacher with a great deal of knowledge hides the ball from a student with lesser knowledge. Snape plays such a game with a vengeance. He constantly asks Harry questions to which Harry can't possibly know the answer. Snape abuses the Socratic Method. For example, he brings Neville near tears, criticizing his efforts at potion making: "Tell me, boy, does anything penetrate that thick skull of yours? Didn't you hear me say, quite clearly, that only one rat spleen was needed?"[10] Such behavior would clearly be beyond the pale in today's law school classroom, and would probably result in student protests to the dean.

But what teacher hasn't secretly wished at some time or another to behave as Professor Moody does in turning Draco into a ferret and bouncing him about (to punish him for attacking Harry when Harry's back was turned)? When Professor McGonagall asks Moody what exactly he is doing, Moody answers tersely, "Teaching."[11] It's not Socratic, but it is indeed a priceless teaching moment. (You can bet Malfoy will never forget it.)

Significantly, almost all of the teachers at Hogwarts use some form of practical application in their teaching. The one exception seems to be the History of Magic teacher, whose sole technique is the lecture. He is so boring and his routine is so set, he actually died but didn't notice, and his ghost simply got up to teach one day. Rowling's description of a typical History of Magic class must sound familiar to many a weary law student: "Professor Binns opened his notes and began to read in a flat drone like an old vacuum cleaner until nearly everyone in the class was in a deep stupor, occasionally coming to long enough to copy down a name or date, then falling asleep again."[12]

---

9. THE PAPER CHASE (Twentieth Century Fox Film Corp. 1973).

10. *Prisoner of Azkaban* 125–26.

11. *Goblet of Fire* 206.

12. *Chamber of Secrets* 148.

Aside from Professor Binns, everyone else teaches by having the students actually put the lesson into practice. Thus, Professor Trelawney has the students interpret the patterns in tea leaves. Professor Lupin has the students put away their books and use their wands to face a boggart. Professor McGonagall has them transfigure objects (a beetle into a button, or a mouse into a snuffbox, for example).

The use of practical applications of knowledge is something law students do in clinical courses. Most law schools offer opportunities for second or third year law students to work in a legal clinic under the supervision of an attorney. (Examples of possible clinics might include a child advocacy clinic, a domestic violence clinic, an immigration clinic, a taxation or bankruptcy clinic, an environmental law clinic, a poverty law clinic, and the like.)

The infamous McCrate Report, published by the American Bar Association in 1992, heavily criticized law schools for placing too much emphasis on theory and too little on skills training.[13] (Undoubtedly, any course that focused on something like Harry Potter and the Law would be the first to go, under the Report.) In the world of Hogwarts, all the weights are on the McCrate side of the balance scale. That is, it is only evil teachers (such as the despicable Professor Umbridge) who want to focus on theory at the expense of practice. Indeed, the students are greatly outraged in *The Order of the Phoenix* when Umbridge writes her course aims on the board for Defense Against the Dark Arts, and the aims are purely theoretical.

Hogwarts students, just like law students, show a great enthusiasm for teachers who have been practitioners. There is nothing that beats the mystique of real life experience. Consider the following remarks in response to Harry's question about what Professor Moody is like as a teacher:

"Fred, George, and Lee exchanged looks full of meaning.
'Never had a lesson like it,' said Fred.
'He *knows*, man,' said Lee.
'Knows what?' said Ron, leaning forward.
'Knows what it's like to be out there *doing* it,' said George impressively.
'Doing what?' said Harry.
'Fighting the Dark Arts,' said Fred.
'He's seen it all,' said George."[14]

---

13. Am. Bar Ass'n, Section on Legal Educ. and Admission to the Bar, Legal Education and Professional Development—An Educational Continuum: Report of the Task Force on Law Schools and the Profession: Narrowing the Gap (1992).

14. *Goblet of Fire* 208.

A very special type of practitioner is the celebrity lawyer. (Celebrity professors, alas, are far less common.) The celebrity lawyer is a type seen at many law schools. This is someone who typically comes in to teach a specialized seminar for a semester or two. The administration hopes to add a certain cachet to the school (and possibly give a bounce to the school's reputation). Celebrity lawyers are a mixed lot, but one thing they have in common—they will always assign their own books. Thus, Gilderoy Lockhart is no exception in assigning all seven of his books (everything from *Break with a Banshee* to *Year with the Yeti*) in *The Chamber of Secrets*.

Finally, one of the most interesting teachers Harry has is not even a human, but a centaur. Firenze seems to be a very postmodern teacher (and perhaps a bit of a Critical Legal Studies person at heart in his disavowal of any transcendent system of knowledge):

> It was the most unusual lesson Harry had ever attended. They did indeed burn sage and mallowsweet there on the classroom floor, and Firenze told them to look for certain shapes and symbols in the pungent fumes, but he seemed perfectly unconcerned that not one of them could see any of the signs he described, telling them that humans were hardly ever good at this, that it took centaurs years and years to become competent, and finished by telling them that it was foolish to put too much faith in such things anyway, because even centaurs sometimes read them wrongly. He was nothing like any human teacher Harry had ever had. His priority did not seem to be to teach them what he knew, but rather to impress upon them that nothing, not even centaurs' knowledge, was foolproof.[15]

Studying and Exams

Books and Other Sources of Knowledge

Scott Turrow famously described the process of reading cases during law school studies as "like stirring concrete with my eyelashes."[16] Grinding away at studies is one of the givens of law school education, and of a wizard's education, too. Trying to master the infamously difficult Rule Against Perpetuities (from Property class in law school) is on a par with mastering the fiendishly difficult recipe for Polyjuice Potion.

---

15. *Order of the Phoenix* 603–04.
16. TURROW, *supra* note 5, at 31.

Books are sources of power, both in law school and in wizard school. But because they are powerful, books also can be dangerous. In *The Prisoner of Azkaban*, Harry's *The Monster Book of Monsters* actually bites him. Ron tells Harry just how dangerous books can be: "Some of the books the Ministry's confiscated —Dad's told me—there was one that burned your eyes out. And everyone who read *Sonnets of a Sorcerer* spoke in limericks for the rest of their lives. And some old witch in Bath had a book that you could *never stop reading*! You just had to wander around with your nose in it, trying to do everything one-handed."[17] Tom Riddle's diary, of course, proves especially dangerous, particularly to Ginny and Harry. Similarly, cases and statutes, too, can be used for good or ill.

Law students often prefer used textbooks, not only because they are cheaper than new ones, but because sometimes they are marked-up with good notations made by the previous student owner. Similarly, Harry enjoys his used (and very marked-up) copy of *Advanced Potion-Making* in *The Half-Blood Prince*, amazing Professor Slughorn with his skill in Potions.

Books, law books and magical books alike, are filled with secrets. Part of the process of education is learning how to decipher the words of power in books. Another part of the educational process is recognizing just exactly how far books will take you, and the extent of their limitations. Hermione, through several of the early Harry Potter stories, clearly believes that all the answers are in books. In *The Chamber of Secrets*, when Harry asks why Hermione has to go to the library, Ron replies, "Because that's what Hermione does," adding, "When in doubt, go to the library."[18] Hermione is clearly startled when Professor Trelawney tells them in Divination class, "Books can take you only so far in this field."[19] But by the time of the events of *The Order of the Phoenix*, she is ready to take the plunge and helps form Dumbledore's Army to practice Defense Against the Dark Arts by themselves. Hermione tells Ron, "No, I agree, we've gone past the stage where we can just learn things out of books...."[20] Law students, too, must face that challenging and difficult moment when they realize that there may be no clear-cut answer in the books.

Study Aids and Anti-Cheating Spells

Law students have a wide variety of study aids available to them, based on how much money they are willing to spend and on the depth of their desper-

---

17. *Chamber of Secrets* 230–31.
18. *Chamber of Secrets* 255.
19. *Prisoner of Azkaban* 103.
20. *Order of the Phoenix* 325.

ation as exams approach. Course outlines, flashcards, computer programs, tutors, all these and more tempt students to lay out hard-earned cash. Other chemical substances purporting to aid in concentration also may make the rounds. However, at least law students are not tempted by bottles of Baruffio's Brain Elixir, which Ron and Harry consider buying in *The Order of the Phoenix* until Hermione tells them the real ingredients (dried doxy droppings). And what hapless law student, pulling another all-nighter while studying for a final exam, wouldn't love to have a Time-Turner such as Hermione has? Every student needs more of that most precious commodity, time.

But before exams, Professor McGonagall sternly tells the students, "Now, I must warn you that the most stringent Anti-Cheating Charms have been applied to your examination papers. Auto-Answer Quills are banned from the examination hall, as are Remembralls, Detachable Cribbing Cuffs, and Self-Correcting Ink."[21] While law students undoubtedly are intrigued by the sound of some of these cheating tools, they are also fully aware that law schools use their own computer magic to ensure that students typing exams are unable to log on the Internet, or to access any files or notes.

Examinations

Hogwarts exams often are a combination of written tests and practical tests. Students have to be prepared to write long essay answers explaining the history of the Goblin Rebellion, but also be able to make a pineapple tap dance across a table. (The incentive to study for the Potions test is especially high, when the professor threatens to poison one of the students to see if their antidotes work, as Snape does in *The Goblet of Fire*.)

Exams loom large for law students, too (although law school exams overwhelmingly consist of written essay questions rather than practical applications). First year exams are particularly stressful, with the grade for the entire course resting on one examination. The results of first year exams often become the basis for receiving an invitation to be on the editorial board of the school's law review (a very prestigious position). Many a law student has felt the same pressures Harry feels in his History of Magic exam: "*Think*, he told himself, his face in his hands, while all around him quills scratched out never-ending answers, and the sand trickled through the hourglass at the front...."[22]

---

21. *Order of the Phoenix* 708–09.
22. *Order of the Phoenix* 726.

Grades and Future Careers

There is an old saw about law school grades that goes something like this: "The 'A' students become the law professors; the 'B' students become the lawyers; and the 'C' students become the judges." The comforting idea behind this somewhat ironic saying is that the grade-obsessed gunners who truly "love the law" will find their niche in teaching. The solid students will become practitioners and make piles of money, and those with other skills (such as political skills) will be able to lord it over all as decision-makers in the judicial system. There seems to be some similarity here to the Hogwarts denizens. For example, Dumbledore was one of the smartest wizards of all time and yet he only wanted to be Headmaster. (He was offered the post of Minister of Magic, but was not interested.) Similarly, the equally brilliant Lord Voldemort was one of the brightest students Hogwarts had ever seen, and he wanted to be the Defense Against the Dark Arts teacher. The scholastically average Weasley twins, Fred and George, leave school early to make a mint of money in their Joke Shop. Mediocrities such as Fudge end up as Minister of Magic.

For most of the students, grades are integral to career paths. Thus, it is Book Five, where the students take their O.W.L. exams, that illustrates most clearly the stress and strain of exams. O.W.L.s are similar in importance to the Bar Exam for law students, for like the Bar, O.W.L.s are essential to proceed on with your career.

Perhaps the only thing more excruciating than taking exams is waiting for the results. In addition to final exams in courses, law students have to pass their state bar examination before they are qualified to practice law. The test is usually taken in July, and the results take several months. (Unfortunately, the results are not delivered by owl.) The bar examination score has both an essay component and a multiple choice component and the results are not always capable of being taken in at a glance. One of my friends, out of town on a document review when his letter arrived, had his mother open it for him. He asked her on the phone, "Did I pass?" There was a long, agonizing silence as she opened the letter and read it, and finally she said, "I just don't know!" (He had passed, as it turned out.) Similarly, Harry and his friends have to decipher a complicated grading system where "O" stands for "Outstanding," "E" means "Exceeds Expectations," "A" only means "Acceptable," and the failing grades are "P" for "Poor," "D" for "Dreadful," and of course, the appropriately named bottom grade, "T" for "Troll."[23]

23. *Half-Blood Prince* 102.

However, career planning is perhaps more creative for Hogwarts students than for the typical law student. Our law school placement office rarely has such interesting pamphlets as, "Have You Got What It Takes To Train Security Trolls?" and "Make A Bang At The Department of Magical Accidents and Catastrophes."[24]

Academic Culture

Rankings and School Competitions

Hogwarts seems to be the Harvard of wizarding schools. In *The Goblet of Fire*, Harry first learns of the existence of other wizarding schools. The three largest European schools are Hogwarts, Beauxbatons and Durmstrang. (It's interesting to speculate what the law school equivalent of the other schools would be.) But Hermione tells Harry that Durmstrang's got a horrible reputation. She says, "According to *An Appraisal of Magical Education in Europe*, it puts a lot of emphasis on the Dark Arts."[25] This *Appraisal* seems to be the wizard's equivalent of the annual (and notorious) *U.S. News and World Report* ranking of law schools. (The rankings are notorious because law schools bitterly complain about the relevancy of the rankings, but spend an inordinate amount of time and energy hoping to move up in the rankings.)

The rivalry between schools in the Triwizard Tournament is fierce. Similarly, moot court competitions between teams representing different law schools can be very competitive.

Formalities of Dress and Address

In the type of public boarding school setting of Rowling's novels, the academic culture is quite a bit more formal than at many law schools. For one thing, students and faculty at Hogwarts dress formally for classes. (They wear black robes over their regular clothes.) Law students, in contrast, no longer wear suits and ties to classes (unless they have an interview scheduled for right after class). I remember my grandmother being appalled when she saw me heading out to one of my law school classes in blue jeans and a t-shirt. She was even more shocked when I told her some of my professors also wore jeans.

As for forms of address, Hogwarts teachers address students by last names. In law school classes, this is pretty much a matter of teaching style for the pro-

---

24. *Order of the Phoenix* 657.
25. *Goblet of Fire* 166.

fessor. Some law professors address students as "Mr. Smith" or "Ms. Jones," while other professors use first names. (The choice is also influenced by class size—the larger the class, the more likely that the professor will go by last names.) However, in both Hogwarts and law school, teachers are addressed as "Professor." (It is the rare law professor who feels secure enough to ask students to address her by her first name.)

Setting

Hogwarts School of Witchcraft and Wizardry is a 1,000 year old institution housed in a medieval castle. Many law schools, even the more recently established ones, opt for the ancient medieval look in their buildings (particularly the library). Such a setting suggests a sacred place (a cathedral of learning), a place filled with power, a strong and entrenched institution. The majestic architecture of Hogwarts (and of many law schools) metonymically represents the power and privilege of the place.

Book 7 or Is There Life after Law School?

The well-schooled Rowling begins the concluding book in her Harry Potter series with two epigraphs: a quote from Aeschylus' ancient and bloody Greek tragedy, *The Libation Bearers*, and a quote from the Quaker William Penn's *More Fruits of Solitude*. This is the only book out of the seven in which Rowling includes any prefatory quotes, and it is worth while considering her selection in some depth, particularly for their insights into the rule of law. "Bless the children, give them triumph now," the Chorus prays in the quote from *The Libation Bearers* and Electra and Orestes dutifully plot matricide in their vengeance-based society. The selection from William Penn, on the other hand, offers consolation in the face of death: "For they must needs be present, that love and live in that which is omnipresent." For Penn, love and friendship can never perish, being part of the divine. The two quotations, while dealing with death and love, could hardly be more apt for their resonances with the rule of law.

The Libation Bearers is the second play in Aeschylus' *Oresteia* trilogy, the story of a blood feud that destroys the ill-fated family of the House of Atreus.[26]

---

26. For an excellent version of the trilogy, *see* ROBERT FAGLES, THE ORESTEIA: AGAMEMNON, THE LIBATION BEARERS & THE EUMENIDES (1984).

The trilogy is often taught in "Law & Literature" courses, and broadly features a movement from a revenge society to a rule of law society. It is (among many other things) a study in jurisprudence. In the first play, Queen Clytemnestra kills her husband, Agamemnon, as revenge for his killing of their daughter, Iphigenia. (Agamemnon has sacrificed Iphigenia in order to get fair winds for his war ships heading to Troy.) In the second play, *The Libation Bearers*, the remaining children plot the death of Queen Clytemnestra and her new husband. Electra urges her brother, Orestes, to avenge their father's death by killing their mother. Orestes kills his mother, but then he is tormented by the Furies for his crime of matricide. The third play is the trial of Orestes. Does Orestes deserve continued torment by the Furies for killing his mother, when it was his duty to avenge the death of his father? A jury of Athenians hears the case, presided over by Athena as judge. Apollo acts as Orestes' attorney and the Furies appear on behalf of the murdered Clytemnestra. The result is a hung jury, with Athena casting the deciding vote for mercy. The spiral of vengeance comes to an end.

At first blush, there could hardly be a greater contrast than that between the violent, bloody story of the *Oresteia* and the gentle consolation of the William Penn excerpt. However, for students of legal history William Penn is far more than just the benevolent Quaker founder of Pennsylvania.[27] Penn studied law at Lincoln's Inn and drafted the legal framework for the government of Pennsylvania. But perhaps most significantly, Penn was responsible for protecting the early right to trial by jury in England. Penn, a defender of Quakerism, was accused of preaching in public in violation of an Act to suppress religious dissent. At Penn's trial, the judge directed the jury to come to a verdict without hearing any defense. As an additional outrage, the government refused to present an official indictment (probably over concern that the Act itself might be overturned). Despite enormous pressure from the judge, the jury returned a verdict of "not guilty." The judge then sent the jury to jail. Great political pressures were involved in the case; the Lord Mayor of London even became involved in trying to strong-arm the jury. However, the jury held fast and eventually won their freedom, protecting the right to trial by jury.

Both opening excerpts resonate with the idea of a systemic change, a breathtakingly different world view. The blood vengeance of *The Libation Bearers* must give way to a legal system of reason tempered by mercy. The dark human fear that death is a final end gives way to the divine light of Penn's vision of undy-

---

27. For a good discussion of Penn's life and work, *see* HANS FANTEL, WILLIAM PENN: APOSTLE OF DISSENT (1974).

ing love. (And for legal history fans, Penn's most famous trial created a sea-change by truly democratizing the British jury system, and evidencing the truth that pacifism is not for sissies.)

So what do these two epigraphs have to do with Harry, Ron, and Hermione, or, for that matter, with law students? They are key to understanding the children's quest, and key to understanding the transformative goals as well as the limits of a formal law school education. A new world view, a transformation that comes from within, can change the very idea of "victory" for Harry as well as for young lawyers.

> "If the Deathly Hallows really existed, and Dumbledore knew about them, knew that the person who possessed all three of them would be master of Death—Harry, why wouldn't he have told you? Why?"
> He had his answer ready.
> "But you said it, Hermione! You've got to find out about them for yourself! It's a Quest!"[28]

There is a sea change at work in Book Seven. Of all seven books in the Harry Potter series, *The Deathly Hallows* is the only one not set at Hogwarts. The new setting itself marks a great seismic shift, presaging the coming transformation of world view. Harry, Ron, and Hermione have dropped out of school to fight against Voldemort. Like the children in *The Libation Bearers*, their goal is a death: essentially, they are on a mission to kill Voldemort. No longer for them are the familiar school-year rituals of the Hogwarts Express, school robes, Quidditch matches, House rivalries and final exams. All that is familiar and comforting, including Hogwarts itself (a place Harry views as home), is now dangerous and perverse. At Hogwarts, students practice torture skills on other students. (They use the Cruciatus Curse on those who've earned detention.[29]) Only pure blood witches and wizards are entitled to education. Death Eaters are teachers now. Education is literally upside down (consider the opening scene to the book, where the professor of Muggle Studies is hung upside down and tormented and killed by Voldemort). We are in Big Brother land, Nazi Germany, the place of our living nightmares. The perversion of education is that it can become indoctrination.

Harry as questing hero will himself be transformed by his journey, but only after great suffering. On his quest, Harry finds that one by one he is being stripped of his all sources of power and comfort. His wand is broken, his best

---

28. *The Deathly Hallows* 433.
29. *Deathly Hallows* 573.

friend Ron deserts him, and Harry's core belief in Dumbledore is severely shaken. Why couldn't Dumbledore have told him what to do? Why doesn't Harry just have a magical list of instructions to follow? Has his Hogwarts education failed him? Harry comes to understand that in order to make the greatest paradigm shift of all, the move from childhood to adulthood, "you've got to find out … for yourself." Thinking for yourself, like "thinking like a lawyer," is a leap into a new world, a transformation into a newer self. "Why doesn't my law professor just give us the answers?" is a frequent complaint of first year law students. We want students to think for themselves, to be ready to face new factual situations. And sometimes, like Dumbledore, we don't have the answers—all we have is a good hunch concerning what we think the courts might do.

Harry has learned his lessons at Hogwarts, but Hogwarts cannot teach him everything. His most difficult lesson comes when he decides not to act. In not racing Voldemort to the Elder Wand,[30] Harry does something that is out of character for him—he sits still. As a Seeker in Quidditch, and as a very active hero in the first six books, Harry has been in near-constant motion. But outward physical activity is not always the right decision. Harry suffers through his own sea change when he makes the conscious decision to do nothing about retrieving the Elder Wand. Law students as well may come to the point where they reach the limits of wisdom from formal legal education. Often such moments are ethical dilemmas which arise during summer clerkships or first year jobs. At such points, the young lawyer's decisions shape the type of person, both professionally and personally, she becomes. She is not without power—her legal education will serve her in good stead. But the answer to a quest is not something to be learned in school, but rather something to be found within.

Conclusion

Dumbledore makes it clear that with great power comes great responsibility. When he talks to the young Tom Riddle for the first time, Dumbledore says that at Hogwarts, "[W]e teach you not only to use magic, but to control it.… All new wizards must accept that, in entering our world, they abide by our laws."[31] One of the dangers of acquiring power is starting to believe you are better than those without power. This is Voldemort's mistake, but it also is a common mistake for anyone entering a specialized profession, including the

---

30. *Deathly Hallows* 302.
31. *Half-Blood Prince* 273.

law. Hermione, speaking of elf rights and wizard prejudices, tells Lupin, "It all stems from this horrible thing wizards have of thinking they're superior to other creatures...."[32] Coming to terms with power, whether you are a lawyer or a wizard, means finding the right balance between pride in expertise and humility in good service. How you come to define "good" should be an integral part of the individual lifelong educational journey.

Of course, there is not just one ur-story of legal education, or of a magical education, for that matter. Feminists and Critical Race scholars, among others, have long noted that the structure of legal education still serves to reinforce a power and privilege that all too often is white, male, and not working class.[33] This is one of the reasons I so enjoy Hermione as a character (and why I secretly wish Rowling had made her the main character, despite Harry's charms). Perhaps Rowling will give us further adventures at Hogwarts, featuring Ron and Hermione's daughter, or other diverse wizard students.

At the end of *The Half-Blood Prince*, Harry determines not to return to Hogwarts. (He has to set out on a quest to find and destroy first the Horcruxes, and then Lord Voldemort himself.) After all, one can't stay in school forever (sad as that thought will be to Rowling's fans.) Harry leaves Hogwarts ready for this last quest because Hogwarts has taught Harry to "think like a wizard" the way that law schools teach students to "think like lawyers." This type of thinking means not simply memorizing rules (magical words of power), but also knowing how to apply old rules to new cases, and perhaps even envisioning a re-shaping of the law (or a re-shaping of the rules of magic) as it affects the material conditions of our lives. "There was a lot more to magic, as Harry quickly found out, than waving your wand and saying a few funny words."[34]

32. *Order of the Phoenix* 171.

33. *See, e.g.,* Lani Guinier et al., *Becoming Gentlewomen: Women's Experience at One Ivy League Law School*, 143 U. Pa. L. Rev. 1 (1994). For an example of some of the limits of trying to universalize the law student story, *see* Brian Owsley, *Black Ivy: An African-American Perspective on Law School*, 28 Colum. Hum. Rts. L. Rev. 501 (1997).

34. *Sorcerer's Stone* 133.

Which Spell: Learning to Think Like a Wizard

Mary Beth Beazley

When I started to write this chapter about teaching methods at Hogwarts, I expected to conclude that Hogwarts does a much better job than law schools do. After all, Hogwarts famously requires its students to practice magical technique in almost all of its courses, and law schools famously restrict almost all of its first-year study to *thinking* like a lawyer rather than doing things that lawyers do. And yet, when I analyzed what each type of school does in its quest to train practitioners, I realized that law schools were doing a lot of things right, and that Hogwarts needs to take a couple of pages from *our* book and create some skills courses.

In skills courses, students learn to apply the theory they have learned in other courses to the kinds of situations lawyers encounter in practice. In basic and advanced research and writing courses, for example, law students write legal memoranda, briefs, contracts, and other documents for fictional clients. In trial practice courses, students try fictional cases before mock judges. In legal clinics, students under faculty supervision represent actual clients with real legal problems. Finally, in externships, students work in the field with practicing lawyers.

Skills courses came to the fore during the twentieth century, as American law schools realized that they provided a vital counterpoint to casebook courses. Although Hogwarts has been in existence many more centuries than the average law school, it has not yet recognized this crucial need. Just as law school skills courses allow law students to have guided practice in "thinking like a lawyer," Harry's classmates need to learn how to "think like a wizard" through magical skills courses.

Admittedly, skills courses might seem redundant at Hogwarts. Hogwarts students appear to do nothing but skills: they are constantly swishing, flicking, cursing, and hexing. But there is more to a skills course than performance. The effectiveness of those skills must be honed through practice and instruction, and students must learn to decide which skills are needed in which situations. In law school skills courses, students receive opportunities for supervised decision-making not limited to one subject area. All Hogwarts courses, in contrast, are subject-focused, and thus Hogwarts students have a harder time learning to think like witches and wizards.

Magical and legal educators are both training practitioners—one of magic, the other of law.[1] Practitioners must master three fundamental elements of the trade. First, the practitioner must have book learning: the knowledge necessary to solve the problem at hand, or the ability to get that knowledge. Second, he or she must have mastered the technique, must be able to perform in specific situations. Finally, and perhaps most importantly, the practitioner must have the wit to know *when and whether* to use the powers gained in professional school, and *which* of the many rules or spells available could best be applied to the given situation. In each of these three areas, Hogwarts and American law schools could learn from each other.

Book Learning

Law schools offer varying elective courses, but most students take several "bar courses" on subjects tested by state bar examinations. Accordingly, law students study Criminal Law and Constitutional Law to learn about rights and responsibilities of governments and people. They study Torts to learn about the laws that define duties that people owe to each other, and Contract Law to learn about how people may assume duties to each other in business relationships.

No law school, however, requires that students learn *all* of the law. Doing so would be impossible: new legislation and precedential decisions are constantly being issued, and knowledge gained may quickly be outdated. In practice, lawyers conduct research to learn or verify answers to all but the most basic questions. Thus, first-year law students take Legal Research, and they practice research skills in legal writing courses, seminars, clinics, externships, and summer jobs. Lawyers know that their profession requires lifelong learning, and that their legal research skills must carry them through.

Hogwarts students face O.W.L.s and N.E.W.T.s rather than the bar examination, but like law students, they have their requirements and their electives. They take Transfiguration to learn how to transform both objects and themselves. They take Charms and Defense Against the Dark Arts to learn how to

---

1. For more on the connection between law and magic, see Chapter 20 by Mark Edwin Burge in this volume.

use spells, charms, hexes, and jinxes. They take Potions, Herbology, and Care of Magical Creatures to learn how to make magic with more than just their wands. By taking a full curriculum, they give themselves background information that they can consult when they are faced with magical problems.

Hogwarts does a fine job of acquainting students with magical theory and fundamental knowledge. But no school of magic can teach students *all* the magic they will need to know for a lifetime of magical practice. Snape admits as much in his first Defense Against the Dark Arts lesson. If not for the unfortunate references to death and destruction, his description sounds strikingly similar to some descriptions of the law:

> The Dark Arts ... are many, varied, ever-changing, and eternal. Fighting them is like fighting a many-headed monster, which, each time a neck is severed, sprouts a head even fiercer and cleverer than before. You are fighting that which is unfixed, mutating, indestructible.[2]

Because both law and magic are "unfixed [and] mutating," their practitioners need direct instruction in how to conduct effective research. But the Hogwarts curriculum apparently has no such course. Students use the library occasionally to complete their homework, but Madam Pince (with her competing moods of suspicion and hostility) hardly fits the muggle stereotype of the helpful librarian whose goal is to promote use of the library's materials. If students were going to obtain a complete magical education at Hogwarts—in other words, if they were going to be taught all the magic in the world—there would be no need for research skills. But that is obviously not the case.

Fully qualified witches and wizards conduct research when they confront magical problems that are difficult or unfamiliar. In *The Order of the Phoenix*, Molly Weasley consults *Gilderoy Lockhart's Guide to Household Pests* while cleaning out 12 Grimmauld Place,[3] and in *The Half-Blood Prince*, she reviews *The Healer's Helpmate* to try to find a way to get rid of Hermione's black eye.[4] When Hermione's jinx causes the word "sneak" to appear on Marietta Edgecombe's face after she betrays Dumbledore's Army, Professor Umbridge apparently does some research to try to find a way to undo the damage:

> "Haven't we got a counterjinx for this?" Fudge asked Umbridge impatiently, gesturing at Marietta's face. "So she can speak freely?"

---

2. *Half-Blood Prince* 177.
3. *Order of the Phoenix* 103.
4. *Half-Blood Prince* 99–100.

"I have not yet managed to find one," Umbridge admitted grudgingly, and Harry felt a surge of pride in Hermione's jinxing ability.[5]

Alas, magical research has even benefitted He-Who-Must-Not-Be-Named. In Book Seven, Hermione shows Harry and Ron a book that Dumbledore had confiscated from the library, and that Hermione had liberated from Dumbledore's office, noting "[t]his is the one that gives explicit instructions on how to make a Horcrux. *Secrets of the Darkest Art*—it's a horrible book, really awful, full of evil magic.... I bet Voldemort got all the instruction he needed from here."[6] In fact, when the threesome begin to consider what steps they must take to destroy the Horcruxes, Hermione saves the day, noting "Well ... I've been researching that."[7]

Harry conducts research frequently while he is at Hogwarts, but he is searching for answers to problems presented by his battle with Voldemort, not by his professors. When he uses the library, it is usually the result of a suggestion by library-obsessed Hermione. In *The Chamber of Secrets*, for example, when she has a sudden brainstorm about the source of the voice that Harry is hearing from the walls, Hermione reacts typically: "'Harry—I think I've just understood something! I've got to go to the library!' And she sprint[s] away, up the stairs." As Ron explains to Harry, "that's what Hermione does.... When in doubt, go to the library."[8]

Indeed, Hermione decides that she must bring a library with her when she, Harry, and Ron skip their seventh year at Hogwarts to go searching for Horcruxes. While the threesome are still at the Burrow, Harry and Ron come upon Hermione in Ron's bedroom, "sitting in the far corner ... sorting books, some of which Harry recognized as his own, into two enormous piles."[9] It takes them a while to realize what she is planning:

> "What are you doing with all those books anyway?" Ron asked, limping back to his bed.
> "Just trying to decide which ones to take with us," said Hermione.
> "When we're looking for the Horcruxes."
> "Oh, of course," said Ron, clapping a hand to his forehead. "I forgot we'll be hunting down Voldemort in a mobile library."

---

5. *Order of the Phoenix* 613.
6. *Deathly Hallows* 102.
7. *Deathly Hallows* 101.
8. *Chamber of Secrets* 255.
9. *Deathly Hallows* 93.

"Ha ha," said Hermione, looking down at *Spellman's Syllabary*. "I wonder ... will we need to translate runes? It's possible.... I think we'd better take it, to be safe."[10]

Indeed, shortly after this decision, she receives a runic copy of *The Tales of Beedle the Bard*. Understanding one of the stories in this book is crucial to Harry's understanding of Voldemort's actions.

In *The Goblet of Fire*, on the other hand, Hermione does not succeed when she tries to help Harry find the appropriate magical solutions for the tasks he will face in the Tri-Wizard Tournament.[11] Despite hours of library research, they cannot discover how to "get past a dragon," nor can they find out how Harry can survive underwater for an hour. Perhaps if Hogwarts had offered a research course, Harry would not have needed the help of Barty Crouch Jr. (in the guise of Professor Moody) to survive the Tri-Wizard Tournament.

Hermione's knowledge of how to find and use the printed word would make her a perfect professor of magical research. Unfortunately, her impatience with all those who have not read *Hogwarts, A History* would doom her to a life of frustration as a teacher. Thus, the better path might be for her to pursue a financially rewarding career and then endow a professorship. "The Hermione Granger Chair in Magical Research" has quite a nice ring to it.

Developing Technical Skill

The second aspect of a practitioner's education is gaining expertise in *using* the theoretical knowledge. In both law and magic, book learning will get you only so far. In the film *The Paper Chase*, Professor Kingsfield derides the first-year law student who notes his photographic memory, because knowing what the cases say is not as important as knowing what to *do* with the rules within those cases.[12] For this reason, law professors balance the goals of *coverage* and

---

10. *Deathly Hallows* 95.

11. During a 2006 appearance at Radio City Music Hall in New York City, J.K. Rowling apologized to librarians and admitted that the unfriendly Madam Pince is a plot device: "[I]f [Harry, Ron, and Hermione] had a pleasant, helpful librarian, half my plots would be gone. 'Cause the answer invariably is in a book but Hermione has to go and find it. If they'd had a good librarian, that would have been problem solved." Transcript available at http://www.accio-quote.org/articles/2006/0802-radiocityreading2.html (last visited October 20, 2008) (copy of transcript on file with author). Perhaps Ms. Rowling let Madam Pince retire after *The Deathly Hallows*.

12. THE PAPER CHASE (Twentieth Century Fox Film Corp. 1973).

skills. They strive to cover the fundamentals of the course subject, but many see the development of skills as equally important.

Developing technical skills is where Hogwarts shines. In the best Hogwarts classes, the professors give students theoretical background and practical instruction before the students attempt the magical tasks. For example, on the first day of Transfiguration, Professor McGonagall talks briefly about theory and then sets the students to work on transfiguring a matchstick into a needle.[13] In their second year, Herbology students re-pot Mandrakes after discussing their properties with Professor Sprout.[14] In their third year, Defense Against the Dark Arts students learn about boggarts from Professor Lupin.[15] After telling the students what each must do to prepare for a turn with the boggart, he lets them try their hands at the magic under his supervision, ready to step in when needed.

Practice without expert guidance does not work as well. Professor Lockhart gives his students "hands-on experience," (to use Hermione's charitable term) by releasing a cageful of "freshly caught Cornish pixies," saying simply, "Let's see what you make of them!"[16] Because the class has no apparent knowledge about pixies or how to deal with them, and because Lockhart has even less, pandemonium ensues:

> The pixies shot in every direction like rockets. Two of them seized Neville by the ears and lifted him into the air. Several shot straight through the window, showering the back row with broken glass. The rest proceeded to wreck the classroom more effectively than a rampaging rhino.[17]

Professor Umbridge represents the nadir of Hogwarts teaching when she refuses to allow her students to practice at all. She restricts her Defense Against the Dark Arts students to book-learning and does not let them attempt any spells. This restriction is a bad idea not only because the students may need to defend themselves someday, but also because the O.W.L. test is based in large part on practical expertise. Parvati Patil engages in a heated debate with Professor Umbridge about her refusal to allow them to practice magical technique:

> "[I]sn't there a practical bit in our Defense Against the Dark Arts O.W.L.? Aren't we supposed to show that we can actually do the countercurses and things?"

---

13. *Sorcerer's Stone* 134.
14. *Chamber of Secrets* 94.
15. *Prisoner of Azkaban* 135.
16. *Chamber of Secrets* 101–03.
17. *Chamber of Secrets* 102.

"As long as you have studied the theory hard enough, there is no reason why you should not be able to perform the spells under carefully controlled examination conditions," said Professor Umbridge dismissively.

"Without ever practicing them before?" said Parvati incredulously. "Are you telling us that the first time we'll get to do the spells will be during our exam?"[18]

Like Parvati, Harry also takes umbrage at Professor Umbridge, asking "what good's theory going to be in the real world?" Harry dismisses book-learning, not recognizing that he must learn both theory and technique to practice magic effectively. In *The Half-Blood Prince*, for example, Professor Dumbledore teaches Harry to fight the inferi by reminding him that "like many creatures that dwell in cold and darkness, they fear light and warmth, which we shall therefore call to our aid should need arise." When Harry cannot apply the theory to his situation, Dumbledore provides the answer: "Fire, Harry."[19]

Magic is more than just knowing the words to say; spells take practice and skill to get right. The faculty recognizes the expertise of Madam Pomfrey to perform healing spells, and of Professor Snape to concoct potions. In *The Prisoner of Azkaban*, it is only Snape who can create the Wolfsbane potion that Lupin needs to keep his inner werewolf at bay. In *The Order of the Phoenix*, when the Order comes to rescue Harry from the Dursleys, Tonks has limited success when she tries to help him pack his trunk: "I've never quite got the hang of these sort of householdy spells," she confesses.[20]

Like Hogwarts students, law students need practice in the skills and decision-making that they will use after graduation. In the casebook classroom, law faculty use the Socratic method and problem-based teaching to give students practice in the legal decision-making vital to the practice of law. Unlike Hogwarts students, however, law students often do not get the chance to practice the skills that they will be tested on. For example, in most casebook courses, faculty use only lecture and Socratic discussion in the classroom, with a written final at the end of the semester as the only test. In many courses, students spend the entire semester taking apart previously decided cases, and then are presented with an exam made up of fact patterns, not cases. Further, students spend the semester using the spoken word, and then are tested on the written word, often with little practice in how to perform the "spell" of written legal

---

18. *Order of the Phoenix* 244.
19. *Half-Blood Prince* 566.
20. *Order of the Phoenix* at 53.

analysis. Many law students could say, along with Parvati, "Are you telling us that the first time we'll get to do the spells will be during our exam?" While some professors may believe that simply announcing the expectations for the examination will be sufficient, the Hogwarts example illustrates the importance of theory combined with supervised practice.

Learning to Think Like a Wizard

The thinking skills practiced in the casebook classroom are vital. But law schools have long recognized that real and simulated skills courses provide an advantage that did not exist in Langdell's curriculum. A Socratic dialogue in a torts class is not the same thing as writing a brief to a court, or deciding whether or how to pursue litigation for a client. These aspects of practice require another layer of decision-making, and they are part of the doctrine of skills that law students acquire in the practical courses of legal research and writing, trial practice, externships, and law clinics.

To practice their arts, Hogwarts students must learn to think like wizards. Admittedly, they get significant practical experience under the watchful eyes of their teachers. Unfortunately, however, unlike law students, Hogwarts students are almost never presented with simulated or real-life situations in which they must decide how or whether to use magic. While they must sometimes exercise decision-making skills in examination settings, these exams—even the O.W.L. exams—are always subject-focused. That is, the students prepare for the "Charms exam" or the "Transfiguration final." It is much easier to identify the proper potion for a situation when you are taking a "Potions final" than to identify the proper potion when you are given no hints that a potion is what is needed. Professor Lupin's exam probably comes the closest to requiring independent decision-making. It is described as an "obstacle course," where students cross paths with many of the creatures that they had learned about, including a grindylow, red caps, a hinkypunk, and a boggart.[21] While this exam is effective at testing defense against the dark arts skills and decision-making under pressure, the subject matter is still limited to the information covered during one course.

Law students, in contrast, have opportunities for both subject-focused and open-ended challenges. The subject-focused challenges are a useful tool for gaining both skills and knowledge, but they have their limits. Law students

---

21. *Prisoner of Azkaban* 318.

who take a Torts examination, for example, read over a fact scenario and know that their answer must be based on tort law. They can ignore all other possibilities, even though many torts exams could also present criminal law or contract law questions. In real life, not every case can be so neatly divided into subject areas. A murder, for example, could result in both a criminal action brought by the State and a wrongful death lawsuit brought by the victim's family.

Students in law school skills courses have, however, opportunities for a more open-ended experience that teaches valuable decision-making lessons. In Research and Writing courses, students are presented with fact scenarios that can require knowledge of any subject in the law school curriculum—and even subjects not part of the curriculum. With their teacher's guidance, they must evaluate facts and conduct research to recommend or argue solutions to the problems that the facts present. Similarly, students in trial practice courses, clinical courses, and externships must face the problems that their clients—real or fictional—present, and must craft solutions to those problems from the whole universe of the law, rather than from the topics in the textbook.

These opportunities give students crucial preparation for the practice of law without the neat boundaries of the course outline. Clients rarely walk into a lawyer's office and announce, "I want to file a tort lawsuit for intentional infliction of emotional distress." Instead, clients walk in with a problem and tell the lawyer a story. The lawyer's job is to figure out how to solve that problem or to clean up the mess it has made. Is this a criminal or civil case, or both? Is a lawsuit the appropriate tool, or can a phone call or letter take care of the situation? Who are the appropriate defendants, if a lawsuit is necessary? Does the client need non-legal help? Legal research helps a lawyer to clarify an appropriate course of action; a good legal education, however, teaches the lawyer to analyze the situation and determine what paths of legal research are likely to be most fruitful.

The Voldemort Magical Clinic

Like lawyers, witches and wizards will face problems that require a variety of solutions. Currently, the Hogwarts curriculum does not give them an opportunity to evaluate situations and decide whether or how to use magic. But all is not lost. In fact, Harry, Ron, and Hermione received excellent preparation in learning how to think like a witch or wizard, courtesy of Lord Voldemort.

Professor Moody (Barty Crouch, Jr.), when justifying his decision to demonstrate the unforgivable curses, does a good job of explaining why witches and wizards need to be prepared to use their magical education in real-life settings:

> I say, the sooner you know what you're up against, the better. How are you supposed to defend yourself against something you've never seen? A wizard who's about to put an illegal curse on you isn't going to tell you what he's about to do. He's not going to do it nice and polite to your face. You need to be prepared.[22]

Harry's encounters with Voldemort prepare him and his friends well. As the books progress, we see them evolve from neophytes who often forget their magical powers to skilled professionals who can easily call the right spell to mind.

For example, in *The Sorcerer's Stone*, Peeves chases Harry, Ron, and Hermione down a hallway that ends in a locked door. Trapped, the three "paw helplessly" at the door, while Ron moans, "We're done for! This is the end!"[23] Only Hermione has the presence of mind to realize that they have the magical skills to escape from their situation. "Oh, move over," she snarls, grabbing Harry's wand and whispering "*Alohomora!*" to open the door and make good their escape—from Peeves, at least.[24]

When Harry, Ron, and Hermione decide to go through the trapdoor to rescue the Sorcerer's Stone, Hermione prepares by conducting some research. But knowledge of spells combined with the wit to know when to use them is what is needed. When the boys are trapped in devil's snare, Hermione remembers what she has learned from Professor Sprout about the plant: "[i]t likes the dark and damp." When Harry tells her to light a fire, however, she seems to forget about her powers, crying, "there's no wood!" She is brought to her senses by Ron, who bellows, "Are you a witch or not?" The three of them seem to acknowledge the combination of skills that a good practitioner needs. Harry says, "[l]ucky you pay attention in Herbology, Hermione," while Ron notes snarkily, "lucky Harry doesn't lose his head in a crisis—'there's no wood,' *honestly*."[25]

It is in the Tri-Wizard Tournament that the best magical education takes place, if only for the four champions. The Tournament is the first time that the educational establishment (rather than Voldemort) has presented Harry with a problem outside a subject-focused classroom. Each task presents the cham-

---

22. *Goblet of Fire* 212.
23. *Sorcerer's Stone* 159.
24. *Sorcerer's Stone* 160.
25. *Sorcerer's Stone* 278.

pions with a magical problem, and they have to figure out how to solve it. They cannot compartmentalize the dilemma as a Defense Against the Dark Arts problem, or a Charms problem, or a Potions problem. Instead, they must face the situation, consider all of their magical and non-magical abilities, and identify the best solution.

When Barty Crouch, Sr. tells the champions about the first task, he describes it as a test of "daring," explaining that he will not tell the champions what it is because "[c]ourage in the face of the unknown is an important quality in a wizard."[26] And yet, it is not courage that is most important to Harry when he faces the dragon; rather, it is his ability to figure out how best to use his magical powers:

> He was going to be armed with his wand—which, just now, felt like nothing more than a narrow strip of wood—against a fifty-foot-high, scaly, spike-ridden, fire-breathing dragon. And he had to get past it. With everyone watching. *How*?[27]

Ironically, Moody/Crouch proves to be a good skills teacher, engaging Harry in some supervised decision-making. Moody does not tell Harry what to do, and he asks him only two questions. But their conversation, in true Socratic style, leads Harry to figure out for himself the answer to his dilemma:

> "So … got any ideas how you're going to get past your dragon yet?" said Moody.
> "No," said Harry.
> "Well, I'm not going to tell you," said Moody gruffly.... I'm just going to give you some good, general advice. And the first bit is— *play to your strengths.*"
> "I haven't got any," said Harry, before he could stop himself.
> "Excuse me," growled Moody, "you've got strengths if I say you've got them. Think now. What are you best at?"
> Harry tried hard to concentrate. What *was* he best at? Well, that was easy, really—
> "Quidditch," he said dully. "And a fat lot of help—"
> "That's right," said Moody, staring at him very hard, his magical eye barely moving at all. "You're a damn good flier from what I've heard."
> "Yeah, but …" Harry stared at him. "I'm not allowed a broom, I've only got my wand—"

26. *Goblet of Fire* 281.
27. *Goblet of Fire* 329.

"My second piece of general advice," said Moody loudly, interrupting him, "is to use a nice, simple spell that will enable you to *get what you need.*"

Harry looked at him blankly. What did he need?

"Come on, boy ..." whispered Moody. "Put them together ... it's not that difficult...."

And it clicked. He was best at flying. He needed to pass the dragon in the air. For that, he needed his Firebolt. And for his Firebolt, he needed—[28]

Thanks to Moody/Crouch's excellent teaching, Harry realizes that he needs to use a summoning charm (*Accio*) to get his broom.[29] Interestingly, the other champions use magic from various subject areas to confront the dragon: Cedric transfigures a rock into a distracting dog; Fleur uses a charm to put the dragon into a trance, and Viktor hits the dragon "with a spell right in the eye."[30]

When Harry learns that for his second task he must rescue something from the bottom of the lake, he, Ron, and Hermione head to the library. Hermione, after considering transfiguring Harry into a submarine, decides that his "best chance" is "some sort of a charm."[31] By limiting herself to charms, she neglects the possibilities presented by books on magical herbology, and Moody/Crouch must use Dobby to give Harry the gillyweed he will need to survive. Once again, Harry's opponents use different forms of magic to tackle the task: Cedric and Fleur use the "bubble head charm," and Viktor uses an incomplete form of transfiguration.

The final task is the most demanding—Harry must walk through a maze of magical obstacles. Before the task, Harry, Ron, and Hermione haunt the library and spend hours practicing hexes and curses, combining book learning and technical skill to prepare Harry to be able to think like a wizard under pressure.

By the time Harry and his friends battle the death eaters at the Ministry in Book Five, and within Hogwarts in Books Six and Seven, they are so well-versed in practicing their arts that they react instinctively, confident both in their knowledge of the spells they have at their disposal, and in their skill at deciding how best to use them. In *The Order of the Phoenix*, when Harry asks Ron

---

28. *Goblet of Fire* 344–45.

29. Moody's advice to use a "nice, simple spell" comes in handy when Harry faces Voldemort in the graveyard, where *Expelliarmus* and *Accio* save his life.

30. *Goblet of Fire* at 359.

31. *Goblet of Fire* at 482.

how the members of the DA escaped from Malfoy and the Inquisitorial Squad, Ron's reply is nonchalant: "Couple of Stunners, a Disarming Charm, Neville brought off a really nice little Impediment Jinx.... But Ginny was best, she got Malfoy—Bat-Bogey Hex—it was superb, his whole face was covered in the great flapping things."[32]

Harry discusses the importance of thinking like a wizard when Hermione first asks him to teach Defense Against the Dark Arts to his classmates. When Harry explains what it's like to face the unknown challenges that Voldemort presents, he specifically notes that knowledge of spells is not enough, and that his class work has not prepared him for such a challenge:

> *You don't know what it's like!* You—neither of you—you've never had to face him, have you? You think it's just memorizing a bunch of spells and throwing them at him, like you're in class or something? The whole time you're sure you know there's nothing between you and dying except your own—your own brain or guts or whatever—like you can think straight when you know you're about a second from being murdered, or tortured, or watching your friends die—they've never taught us that in their classes, what it's like to deal with things like that.[33]

Although Harry has learned a lot from it, I do not recommend the Voldemort Magical Clinic to Hogwarts. Regular skills courses will work just fine because, unlike Harry, most wizards, like lawyers, will seldom have to make a life or death decision without being able to take the time to do some research. But professors who give students supervised opportunities for open-ended decision-making are training their students' "brains or their guts or whatever" to make those decisions without supervision in the future.

Conclusion

Practitioners of both law and magic have a lot to learn. Although both kinds of schools do a good job teaching the books, Hogwarts probably does a better job giving students guided practice in technical skills. Only law schools, however, teach the research skills necessary for the lifelong education that is part of any practitioner's career. Further, only law schools provide opportunities for the budding practitioner to make decisions without the clues of a subject-

---

32. *Order of the Phoenix* 760.
33. *Order of the Phoenix* 327–28.

focused task. Law students get guided practice in applied legal theory—in legal research and writing courses, in trial practice, in clinics, and in externships. Hogwarts students need non-life-threatening chances to practice applied magical theory while still in school.

If their schools lay a good foundation, both law students and Hogwarts students will become well-qualified practitioners. Let us hope that they use their powers for good and not evil.

Harry Potter as Client in a Lawsuit: Utilizing the Archetypal Hero's Journey as Part of Case Strategy

Ruth Anne Robbins

Introduction

What can Harry Potter teach us about how attorneys represent clients? Potentially, quite a lot. Although it might seem odd to imagine the bright young wizard flying his Firebolt to a lawyer's office for advice about his numerous guardianship issues, Harry's story nevertheless instructs lawyers about how to invoke more effective characterizations of lawsuit clients and the role of the lawsuit in our clients' stories.[1] There is a reason why Harry Potter novels topped the fiction bestseller lists for so many months, just as there is a reason why so many high-earning movies share a common plot development.[2] Memorable pop culture protagonists such as Harry Potter, Dorothy Gale, Luke Skywalker and Frodo Baggins all share commonalities in their personalities and quests. And, as storytellers in the law, lawyers should understand and appropriately uti-

---

1. Issues that have been casually raised in various discussions included (while he was still underage): did Harry's parents appoint a back-up guardian to the incarcerated Sirius Black? In the magical world, do incarcerated prisoners lose all legal rights, including guardianship appointments? Even if there were no loss of legal rights, what were the guardianship ramifications of Sirius's death? And, after Harry came of age, legal questions arose too. Did he accrue property taxes on 12 Grimmauld Place when its location was a secret? Given the secret nature of that house, what address should Harry have given if he registered to vote? Not to mention all of those other times J.K. Rowling denied Harry access to a lawyer for actual legal hearings. *See, e.g., Order of the Phoenix* (forcing a minor to appear *pro se* in front of an en banc court in order to defend himself against criminal charges).

2. STUART VOYTILLA, MYTH AND THE MOVIES: DISCOVERING THE MYTHIC STRUCTURE OF 50 UNFORGETTABLE FILMS (Michael Wiese Prod. 1999).

lize that phenomenon. In essence, each time an attorney represents an individual, she is representing a Harry Potter. Likewise, the role of a favorable court decision is more often akin to a talisman, such as Harry's wand, than to the slaying of a dragon.

This theory of "applied legal storytelling" shows how everyday lawyers can utilize elements of mythology as a persuasive technique in stories told directly to judges—either via bench trials or via legal writing documents such as briefs—on behalf of individual clients in everyday litigation. Because people respond, instinctively and intuitively, to certain recurring story patterns and character archetypes, lawyers may want to systematically and deliberately integrate into their storytelling the larger picture of their client's goals by subtly portraying their individual clients as heroes on a particular life path. This strategy is not merely a device to make the story more interesting but provides a scaffold to influence the judge at the unconscious level by providing a metaphor for universal themes of struggle and growth.

Folklore and mythology are already part of the doctrine in other disciplines that rely on persuasive techniques. Marketing, in particular, is a very close analogy, and books have been written about the connection of persuasive theory to product branding.[3] Other disciplines also use heroic imagery for purposes such as screenplay writing and political campaigning. All of those disciplines have capitalized on heroes because we respond viscerally to certain story patterns without being aware that we are doing so or even that we are learning moral behaviors through storytelling.[4]

Summoning the imagery of a hero employs metaphoric reasoning, which is effective because metaphors allow us to "understand one domain of experience in terms of another," and the understanding takes place in the gestalt of universal experience.[5] Consequently, use of epic storytelling can influence a jury or a legally trained judge. As Professor Steven Winter wrote, "[t]he attraction of narrative is that it corresponds more closely to the manner in which the human mind makes sense of experience than does the conventional, abstracted

---

3. *See* Margaret Mark & Carol S. Pearson, The Hero and The Outlaw: Building Extraordinary Brands Through the Power of Archetypes (McGraw Hill 2001). In this book the authors urge advertising specialists to pay attention to archetypal patterns that have been successfully employed by a variety of companies. It is a fascinating read. You will never look at Nike or Pepsi advertisements in the same way.

4. Bruno Bettelheim, The Uses of Enchantment: The Meaning and Importance of Fairy Tales 5–6 (Alfred A. Knopf 1976).

5. George Lakoff & Mark Johnson, Metaphors We Live By 115–19 (U. Chicago Press 2003).

rhetoric of law."[6] Story is not a parlor trick used to draw attention away from the logic of law. Story is part of the logic itself.

Basic Legal Storytelling Building Blocks

From the first year of law school and continuing in practice, lawyers are exhorted to "tell a good story" when they write briefs or argue in court. This is good advice. In fact, any experienced trial lawyer already knows that storytelling is a critical part of effective advocacy. Although not included in all textbooks, the basic rubric of story telling is often included in lawyering courses. Within the legal framework, a story should include several key elements: character, point of view, conflict, resolution, organization, and description.[7] The story must contain a cast of characters and the author must choose to tell the story from someone's point of view. Each character has needs and goals. The author controls how much the audience knows about those needs and goals. Skilled lawyers understand, of course, that their client is the protagonist of the story and that the story must be told from the protagonist's point of view.

The next step that lawyers must take in persuasive storytelling is learning to develop the narrative of the client's character, and to describe the lawsuit in terms of where it fits into the framework of the client's needs and goals. Here is where lawyers should consider the concept of "hero." Framing the client's narrative as heroic provides a possible avenue for the lawyer to develop a strategy for character development as well as, possibly, a meaningful type of conflict such as Person vs. Person or Person vs. Self, Person vs. Institution, or Person vs. Powerful Entity.

Heroic archetype, the myth of the hero, has been introduced to everyday culture through the interdisciplinary studies of many individuals but most famously by mythologist Joseph Campbell.[8] Campbell made his hypotheses and reached many of his conclusions by combining the psychological work of Carl Jung with the earlier publications of nineteenth century anthropologists such as Adolph

---

6. Steven L. Winter, *The Cognitive Dimension of the Agony Between Legal Power and Narrative Meaning*, 87 MICH. L. REV. 2225, 2228 (1989).

7. Brian J. Foley & Ruth Anne Robbins, *Fiction 101: A Primer for Lawyers On How To Use Fiction Writing Techniques To Write Persuasive Facts Sections*, 32, No. 2, RUTGERS L.J. 459 (2001), *citing*, ROBERT MCKEE, STORY: SUBSTANCE, STRUCTURE, STYLE AND THE PRINCIPLES OF SCREENWRITING 11–28 (1997) (chapter entitled "The Story Problem").

8. JOSEPH CAMPBELL, THE HERO WITH A THOUSAND FACES (Princeton Univ. Press 1990).

Bastian. Jung believed that individual and social behavior and thought have their roots in a common pattern of characters.[9] It is these common recurring patterns that Jung saw as manifestations of what he called "the collective unconscious."[10] Anthropologist Adolph Bastian first proposed that myths from all over the world seem to be built from the same "elementary ideas." Subsequently, Sir James Frazer similarly observed a pattern of similarity to certain rituals in tribes so separate that no contact had ever taken place. He concluded that the rituals encapsulated the imaginative story of human connection to the universe. More recently, the prolific psychologist and writer, James Hillman, opined that the study of basic human nature necessarily includes learning about a society's mythology.

Joseph Campbell coalesced these related psychological and anthropological theories into an analysis of human religion and spirituality. His tome, *The Hero With a Thousand Faces*,[11] is considered a seminal publication in the field. Campbell believed that within all of the world's mythologies there are heroes whose journeys follow a predictable pattern. He suggests that the storytellers of the different eras and cultures were trying to tell us, through symbolism and metaphor, of our own journeys towards individuation.

According to Campbell, myths can serve a pedagogical function, informing us how to live in our society under any circumstances.[12] Humans learn lessons from storytelling because it is a more experiential type of learning. We use narrative to understand what would otherwise be only abstract concepts. We understand narrative because we join the story and see ourselves as part of it: we place ourselves into the story and walk with the characters. In terms of persuasion, we walk in the shoes of the protagonist. Thus, when lawyers combine storytelling with the "collective conscious," they can increase the persuasiveness of their arguments in a subtle way.

Any hero, no matter the specific type, follows a similar path, symbolizing a journey we each take to transform ourselves as individuals. The journey, then, changes the hero and, potentially, the hero's society as well. Each of us embodies some form of the heroic archetype, and our journeys mirror that of the hero. The noble deeds that make us heroes can be physical in nature, but they can also be psychological or spiritual. The three main stages of the journey include the departure, the initiation, and the return.

---

9. According to a traditional definition, archetypes are the "primary form that governs the psyche." JAMES HILLMAN, ARCHETYPAL PSYCHOLOGY: A BRIEF ACCOUNT 1 (Spring Pub. 1985).

10. THE PORTABLE JUNG 59–60 (Joseph Campbell ed., Penguin Books 1976).

11. *See supra* note 8.

12. JOSEPH CAMPBELL ON MYTH & MYTHOLOGY 5 (Richard L. Sartore ed., 1994).

During the departure stage, the hero may be born to royalty or placed in danger soon after birth. Harry's scarring encounter, at age one, with Voldemort clearly falls into this category. More important to the eventual transformation, the hero will be called to start the quest at some point early in the story. In *The Sorcerer's Stone*, Harry was delighted to embark on the journey, but not all heroes are so willing, initially, to heed the call. Often, a spiritual or magical guide or mentor will herald the call to the quest. That guide will not travel with the hero but will appear at key points during the adventure. Dumbledore is the most obvious example of the mentor figure in the Harry Potter books, and it is his letter accepting Harry into Hogwarts that starts the journey. Further, in the departure stage and after an initial test of commitment, the hero will also receive the gift of a protective amulet or magical talisman. The hero then enters the proverbial "belly of the whale," or road of trials. Those trials are the start of the true lessons and tests. The belly of the whale may be a journey into a cave. It may include a first battle of sorts. It represents the individual going into the abyss to start his or her journey and to begin the confrontation that will ultimately lead the hero to individuation.

In the second phase of the journey, "initiation," the hero encounters a series of challenges or "road of trials" during which the hero learns lessons that he or she will need in order to reach the ultimate goal. Along the way, the hero generally meets companions who will journey with and aid the hero until the final confrontation. The road of trials can be something as simple as taking classes or joining the school Quidditch team or learning how to duel with wands. A companion can be anyone who brings comfort to the hero along the way including peers, animals, or even machines. Hermione Granger, Ron Weasley, Hagrid, Hedwig, and Buckbeak are some of Harry's companions. His broomsticks could also fit into that category.

During the Initiation phase of the journey, the hero will also have a meeting with both mother and father symbolic figures in the form of goddess or damsel-in-distress. These characters could also be shape-shifters masquerading as the mother or father figure. Meeting these characters help the hero reflect upon himself and, thus, recognize what has been missing or holding him back from accomplishing his desires. It is a moment of rebirth. The whole purpose for the journey is revealed. Moreover, the hero also understands that he or she has the tools to complete the quest. Harry has had several of these moments throughout the books, via the Mirror of Erised in *The Sorcerer's Stone*, through the Pensieve in *The Prisoner of Azkaban* and *The Order of the Phoenix*, and by virtue of the wand-duel with Voldemort in *The Goblet of Fire*. It came as no surprise that Harry saw his parents in the final book. Moreover, some of his other quasi-parental figures made a comeback at the end of *The*

Deathly Hallows, namely Sirius and Lupin. Their encouragement and words of pride and love gave Harry some of the final strength he needed just before the final confrontation with Voldemort.[13]

As part of the movement towards the ultimate test or "showdown," the hero may suffer a ritual injury or dismemberment. Harry received several injuries throughout the early books, as each of those books represented a micro-journey of sorts. For example, the basilisk bite in *The Chamber of Secrets* represents one of these sorts of ritual dismemberments. Another, highly ritualized injury happened when he was cut during the Voldemort resurrection scene in *The Goblet of Fire*. The activation of his scar during the latter parts of the series could be seen through the same lens. Finally, Harry suffered a series of dismemberments during *The Deathly Hallows*—the branding by the blistering locket during his fight with Nagini at Bathilda Bagshot's house; and, of course, his near-death experience in the Forbidden Forest outside of Hogwarts. This phase of the journey serves to remind the hero that we are all human or mortal and that there are still risks involved with the ultimate boon. The hero will not die, however, because he or she has faced and conquered those fears.

The final part of the Initiation phase includes slaying the dragon and receiving "the ultimate boon." Slaying the dragon is of course what the hero is best remembered for. In the end, Harry will be remembered by all for stopping Voldemort, an external dragon. In life, however, a dragon can be something that is intangible and internal to the hero. Allowing himself to become truly part of the wizarding society is also Harry's successful end to his quest. He spent the last year of the series alone, separated from the society that had welcomed him back. Harry could not have ended Voldemort's reign unless and until Harry was willing and able to return to Hogwarts. This is all very consistent with his "orphan hero" archetype.

The journey doesn't end with the dragon slaying because the hero still needs to return, transform and reach his bliss.[14] With all of the lessons learned during the Initiation stage, the hero now has tools that will aid the transformation of the hero's former or new society. The hero may go on to mentor others or to merely serve as a role model. And so the hero, by accomplishing individuation, transforms not just himself, but also his culture. We see Harry transform throughout the seven books. His culture changes as well, as evidenced in the

---

13. *Deathly Hallows* 698–701.

14. Joseph Campbell defined bliss as going where your body and soul want to take you; your rapture. Joseph Campbell & Bill Moyers, The Power of Myth 147, 149 (Random House 1999).

peeks we have after Harry defeats Voldemort. Starting on the morning after the final battle, the news comes back to Hogwarts, "as the morning drew on; that the Imperiused up and down the country had come back to themselves, that Death Eaters were fleeing or being captured, that the innocent of Azkaban were being released at that very moment, and that Kingsley Shacklebolt had been named temporary Minister of Magic...."[15] Harry also strives to keep the transformations permanent, i.e., by hiding the Resurrection Stone and the Elder Wand, Never again will someone have the opportunity to become the powerful Master of Death.[16] At the end of the series, with what we are permitted to know in the epilogue, all is still well. In theory, if Harry was charged with theft of the Resurrection Stone (which arguably belongs to someone in the Gaunt line of succession), Harry's attorney could argue that the public policy of allowing society to remain free from the curse of private ownership of that stone outweighs any incidental crime.

Part of deciding how to cast the client necessarily involves the lawyer understanding what role the lawsuit itself plays in the client's overall heroic journey. Is winning the lawsuit the same as obtaining the ultimate boon? In reality, probably only rarely. Those lawsuits are the "Erin Brokovich" situations that are the stuff of Hollywood movies, but are few and far between in litigation. It is more likely that the lawsuit represents one test the client must face along the road of trials. The litigation may be an attempt to keep the hero from her transformation. Or, the lawsuit may be the client's chance to start a new journey by first obtaining some sort of financial recovery or freedom from a destructive relationship.

The Lawsuit Casting Call: One Story, One Hero

Joseph Campbell's words ring true in lawsuits just as in other ritualistic aspects of life. Rituals mimic myths. The rituals of each society give form to our lives, to connect us as individuals to a larger whole. The act of rising when a judge walks into the courtroom demonstrates the modern ritual of legal process. We stand to acknowledge judges in their role as wise and venerable figures; a character known to us through myth. Similarly, when lawyers address a court in writing, they sign documents with "Respectfully...."

The lawsuit, like the hero's journey, necessarily includes a predictable cast of characters. The strategic lawyer should assign a particular role to each character in the lawsuit. Although, in theory, a particular person in the story may

15. *Deathly Hallows* 744–45.
16. *Deathly Hallows* 748–49.

wear more than one mask during the course of the journey. A short story, such as a lawsuit, will necessitate that the lawyer keep the various players in one primary role. The story of the lawsuit, especially when told in the short form of a brief, does not have the space or reader attention span to develop with any complexity the characters of the many different players. This is very different from epic journeys that span seven books or so, such as the Harry Potter series.

The most important casting decisions, undoubtedly, are those of the client and the judge. All else becomes secondary. With rare exception, then, a lawyer can assign only one real hero to an individual lawsuit's story. Though many other characters in the Harry Potter books are heroic, only Harry is the main hero to the series. The lawyer must assign different roles to the lawsuit's other characters. The other possible roles available in a heroic journey include mentor, companion, gatekeeper, dragon, goddess and father. The lawyer, herself, may play only the role of an outsider narrator; if anything, the lawyer may consider herself as a narrator or Greek chorus.

The lawyer faces this task at somewhat of a unique disadvantage, in comparison to an author or playwright, because other narrators are also trying to tell heroic tales of their own. The opposing party is a hero in his own right. Perhaps a greater challenge, however, is the fact finder. Judges are schooled to consider themselves the heroes of the American legal system. Although there may be truth to that notion in the global sense, the careful lawyer should gently shift that mindset for the purposes of telling the particular client's story.

Hero: The Client's Role

Heroes are people who transform themselves or their societies through a search for identity and wholeness. They can do that through internal reflection or through outward action. Heroes are termed such because they all similarly embark on some sort of transformative journey. That journey can take place externally or internally. A hero's journey, for example, may be more inwards and involve transforming herself and, consequently, her culture rather than the other way around. Harry Potter's journey is one of inward transformation just as much as it is an outward journey towards ridding the world of Voldemort.

Because the hero is the person in the story to whom the reader most closely identifies, the writer must grant the hero universal qualities and emotions that most readers have either experienced or will understand. Just as Harry has grown up during the course of the books, so too any hero grows and changes through the course of the journey. The hero starts out as somehow flawed at a fundamental level that affects her daily life and/or prevents her from living up to her potential. Emotions and motivators at both ends of the spectrum are available to the hero; everything from love and joy, to anger and a thirst for revenge, to the middle-range emotions of loneliness, despair and the feelings of oppression. Harry experiences many of those emotions throughout the course of the books. Harry is imperfect, and as we see most clearly in *The Order of Phoenix*, particularly, he can be prone to sullenness or rage in response to his circumstances. He shows his anger towards Dumbledore on several occasions. He also chooses to ignore certain imperfections in his society. For example, he has no patience for Hermione's campaign on behalf of the house-elves. He also experiences jealousy about Ginny's other boyfriends and anger that he was not chosen as a prefect. The last books show similar faults in Harry. He is mad at Ron for leaving during *The Deathly Hallows*; and, frankly, we can't really assign all of the blame on Ron for that decision. At other times in the series Harry experiences self-doubt, whether it is with respect to first crushes or with respect to completing the task of stopping Voldemort. He bares his grief during his many, many losses of friends and family. We love and forgive Harry for his darker emotions and we ache for him as he shows us his growing pains. This is natural; a hero is imperfect by definition, and audiences admire the hero all the more for striving to overcome flaws and crippling sadnesses.

Casting the client as the main character to the lawsuit story similarly gives the client permission to be imperfect. In fact, the hero must be imperfect in order to have the audience identify with that hero and in order to understand the hero's need to embark on or continue on a transformative journey. In a legal story, that flaw could take the form of a weakness, such as a fear, a vice, such as addiction, or any other idiosyncrasy not usually acceptable in the hero's everyday world.[17] The character flaw does not ultimately define a hero, assuming the hero can overcome it, but the hero is allowed to have that flaw, at least at the outset. In this way, the hero is somewhat unique amongst the different roles in the journey. In the abbreviated lawsuit story, the lawyer-storyteller has time to develop only one character with that sort of depth. If the lawyer casts someone else—say the judge—as the hero, then only the judge has been granted permission to be imperfect while also remaining a "good guy." In short stories, supporting characters are often defined by their displayed weaknesses. Thus, a lawyer's decision to place the client in a supporting role may prove disastrous if the client's inevitable flaws are revealed during the course of the proceeding.

---

17. CAROL S. PEARSON, AWAKENING THE HERO WITHIN: TWELVE ARCHETYPES TO HELP US FIND OURSELVES AND TRANSFORM OUR WORLD 4, 15–18 (HarperCollins 1991).

The word "hero" depicts not merely scenarios in which males overcome an external foe, but rather describes a gender-neutral and racially blind category of persons who have undergone or are undergoing a transformative process. Thus, I have departed from the typical "hero" versus "heroine" language and used "hero" to mean the broad class. (One satirist has suggested the word "she-ro" as an alternative designation for heroes who are also females).[18] A character does not have to engage in a physical confrontation in order to earn his or her "hero" status. Heroes are not just warriors but in different story modules can appear as creators, scholars, pioneers, lovers, caregivers, or wise prophets.[19] Harry, in fact, is more than just a warrior hero. He is primarily an orphan, trying to regain the society lost to him when his parents were murdered. His hero type explains to the reader why, although Harry is Voldemort's conqueror, Harry does not directly slay Voldemort in the end.

In modern application there are several authors who have proffered a variety of heroic archetypes.[20] Each of these archetypes, though pursuing different goals and possessing different character traits and flaws, nevertheless share some significant commonalities. Each different type of hero has its own quest and fear. Each has its own proverbial dragon that the hero must metaphorically or literally slay.

Dr. Carol Pearson's work, perhaps best known in the area, proffers twelve different hero types. The list appears below along with some quick examples to help the reader based on what I hope are common experiences. The examples from Harry Potter are the types of heroes that each character would represent if each character was the star of his or her own story (rather than a supporting character in the Harry Potter books).

---

18. James Finn Garner, Once Upon a More Enlightened Time (MacMillan 1995) (referring to the protagonist in *The Little Mer-Persun* as "she-roic" for saving a Greenpeace member from freezing waters after a whaling boat attacked his rubber raft).

19. *Id.* at xvii.

20. Campbell himself suggested six different archetypes, based on world mythology. Campbell, The Hero With a Thousand Faces, *supra* note 9, at 315–354. While originally adopting those six for her earlier work, Dr. Carol Pearson fleshed out those initial six into twelve archetypes. Carol S. Pearson, The Hero Within: Six Archetypes We Live By (Harper & Row 1989); Pearson, *supra* note 13. Fiction and screenwriters have expanded the list further still. *See also* Tami D. Cowden, et al., The Complete Writers Guide to Heroes and Heroines: Sixteen Master Archetypes (Lone Eagle 2000). Moreover, at least one author writing for a screenwriting audience concludes that there are sixteen character types that can be used for story development purposes and that each of these sixteen have a flip aspect to them (for a total of 32). Victoria Schmidt, 45 Master Characters: Mythic Models for Creating Original Characters (Writer's Digest Books 2001). The other thirteen characters are the supporting roles of friends, mentors, and rivals.

Hero type	Illustrative example
Warrior	Prototypical Hollywood hero such as Luke Skywalker from Star Wars. Some may argue that Harry is a warrior hero. He acted like one at least in both The Sorcerer's Stone and The Chamber of Secrets.
Creator	Writer or artist struggling to succeed. J.K. Rowling is a creator hero.
Caregiver/Martyr[21]	Mother taking care of her family against odds. Lily Potter's story is that of a caregiver/martyr hero.
Every person/Orphan	Harry Potter the orphan looking for his birthright, a sense of family, a community and an identity beyond his orphan status. Neville Longbottom is another orphan hero on a related quest for a proper place in his society.
Outlaw/Destroyer	Robin Hood. Sirius Black is also something of an outlaw hero. James Potter had the makings of an outlaw hero (at least in school).
Sage/Scholar	Student trying to do well in school or a professor trying to get tenure. Hermione's sage/scholar story is that of a hero striving for O.W.L.s and all N.E.W.T.s. One could argue that Neville Longbottom has some sage hero characteristics, though we don't necessarily realize that until the very end of the story, when we learn that he eventually becomes a Hogwarts professor.
Explorer/Wanderer/ Seeker	Early colonists and pioneers such as Davy Crockett or Daniel Boone; astronauts.
Magician	In his own life story, Dumbledore is a magician hero —as we learn in The Deathly Hallows, he has his own back story before becoming Harry's mentor.

---

21. Multiple hero entries show differences in terms used by Dr. Carol S. Pearson in her psychological self-help book versus her advertising collaboration book. *See* PEARSON, *supra* note 13; MARGARET MARK & CAROL S. PEARSON, THE HERO AND THE OUTLAW: BUILDING EXTRAORDINARY BRANDS THROUGH THE POWER OF ARCHETYPES (McGraw Hill 2001).

Ruler	King Arthur or Queen Elizabeth I of England. Though some consider Harry Potter a ruler hero his ending doesn't fit this archetype because he is neither headmaster at Hogwarts nor Minister of Magic.
Lover	Cinderella variations.
Jester / Fool	Leads in comic movies are most often jester-heroes. Dobby's life story/heroic journey might be something like a jester-hero, though tragic at the end.
Innocent	Young, happy and well-cared for child who wishes to remain so; Dorothy from *The Wizard of Oz*. Colin McGreevey is a sort of Innocent archetype. Winky, the Crouch family house-elf who ends up a butterbeer addict at Hogwarts after being dismissed by Barty Crouch, Sr., shows us what can happen to an Innocent archetype when taken away from her home environment.

Just as there is more than one story module, there are multiple hero types. According to archetypal psychologists, we are each on different heroic quests throughout our lives as we mature and transform ourselves. The process is not linear or absolute. Instead, we may ourselves be more than one type of hero at any given point in time. This is good news for lawyers working with their clients. The lawyer is not limited to casting her client in the role of Harry Potter-as-warrior-boy. Instead, there are many other options.

Because there are different choices, the lawyer must also carefully construct the story around the correct type of hero that the client embodies. To do that effectively, the lawyer must carefully employ all of the client-centered skills that are the stuff of clinical education and scholarship. Factual investigation of one's own client becomes even more crucial as the lawyer develops the story's theme. Is a client really a warrior hero who is on a quest to slay an external dragon? Or is the journey one of internal transformation?

This line of questions intertwines with considerations of the case's thematic conflict type. For example, consider the case of a domestic violence plaintiff seeking a protective order from the courts. How do we make the domestic violence plaintiff look like a hero, especially if she acted imperfectly herself, either by acting with aggression or by returning to the abuser on more than one occasion? Since a hero cannot be passive, how do we make our client look active? This situation occurs more frequently than one might suppose. By thinking and placing the plaintiff in a "victim" role, the lawyer has essentially cast the client as the damsel-in-distress rather than as the hero of her own story. Too easily, the lawyer in a domestic violence case instead awards the role of hero to the judge, whose job it becomes to save the damsel from her distress. But a hero will save only a true and pure damsel and not one who shows herself to have impurities.

Think about it this way. Suppose in *The Half-Blood Prince* we learned that Tom Riddle, Sr. had turned on the pregnant Merope Gaunt before eventually abandoning her. Suppose she needed a family court's help, whether for a restraining order as in the posed hypothetical, or for spousal support to which she was entitled per the story in *The Half Blood Prince*. Could an attorney make Merope Gaunt a sympathetic plaintiff? Possibly: though she shows us that she is imperfect and flawed, she is still worthy of compassion. But the trick would be to make her look like something other than a damsel in distress because she cannot live up to the perfection that role demands. A judge cast in the role of hero may conclude that the client is no true damsel and does not deserve saving. Alternatively, if the lawyer is cast as hero, the client remains in the role of damsel-in-distress. Setting up the story that way then leaves the judge little choice but to become a threshold guardian. The judge's job becomes one of testing the lawyer-hero. Potentially, the test may include stopping the lawyer-hero from completing the journey of saving the client from the distress. The only other option forces the judge to agree to become a companion—impossible for someone who is supposed to remain a neutral fact-finder. An attorney representing Merope Gaunt would have to think very carefully about how to tell that story.

Hero is the option that allows the client to have flaws. One choice, the lover hero, presents as an obvious option for the legal storyteller. A person seeking a domestic violence protective order is, in a very real way, seeking freedom from her circumstances of a lethal form of love. The legal system, by protecting domestic violence victims, grants these people the renewed opportunity to find bliss. The hero returned to the path. In the typical "lover" story, a beautiful maiden seeks safety and security away from the sad life she currently lives. She is deserving of love but through circumstances beyond her control she is not being loved. Accordingly, her journey is towards the freedom to be herself in a safer place, where she can receive the love that she deserves. The danger with defaulting to the lover hero, however, is the cliché of the Cinderella fairytale. Such romanticized notions of "the maiden" help account for the unfortunate misconception that a woman who "fights back" or who otherwise appears to have economic or educational advantages cannot truly be the victim of domestic violence.[22]

Commonly, Cinderella characters come too close to being one-dimensional or flawless; in other words, the damsel-in-distress. Because Rowling, in *The Half Blood Prince*, describes Merope in a decidedly un-beautiful way, "a plain, pale, rather heavy face," the lover hero presents serious challenges for her legal team. The lawyer must proceed cautiously. The best strategy for the domestic violence lawyer may be to move the storyline far away from one in which the client appears to play the ill-fitting role of damsel-in-distress. The very fact, however, that the domestic violence client is never a perfect damsel-in-distress (or Cinderella) makes it that much more important for the lawyer to consciously consider heroic role casting in this type of lawsuit. The very terminology in common usage—domestic violence victim—suggests anything but a heroic protagonist. A "victim" is someone more like a damsel-in-distress. In the hero's story, this means the victim cannot play the hero but rather plays the person whom the hero might save so long as the victim/damsel doesn't reveal herself to be merely a shape-shifting femme fatale.

Lawyers can delve further into the universe of potential heroes to consider other alternatives, assuming that the client has lifetime goals beyond those of love. A person seeking a protective order or child or spousal support may be on a caregiver's journey. She may be seeking protection not only for herself but for her children or other family members. She may be on a creator's journey, seeking protection so that she may go to work without the fear of being harassed or stalked. Or, she may be an every person or orphan hero who is looking to find her place in society. Think about what spousal support could have done to help Merope and her unborn child find a more stable home and comfort. The lawyer is not locked into one archetype but should feel free to explore other options that are tailored to the individual client.

Further, by carefully casting the client as the story's hero, we are then able to select and use the conflict type that is thematic to the client's journey and goal. For example, a caregiver hero seeking a protective order may have, as a conflict type, person versus nature/environment. The hero is trying to raise

---

22. Statistically, domestic violence victims come from every socio-economic class, from every racial and social group. *See, e.g.,* Department of Justice, Office of Justice Programs, Extent, Nature, and Consequences of Intimate Partner Violence (2000), *available at* http://www.ncjrs.gov/pdffiles1/nij/181867.pdf (last visited Aug. 23, 2008); Jill Davies, Safety Planning With Battered Women (1988). Moreover, contrary to the Hollywood version of a helpless maiden, many domestic violence victims will fight back to some degree yet are still, ultimately, victims.

her children in safety, but first she has to get out of the locked building where she has been trapped.[23] Someone needs to toss her the key. Once she has the key, she will be able to walk out and get back to her caregiver duties. This is a very different story than saving the damsel-in-distress from the evil villain. Alternatively, a caregiver hero's story may involve a "person versus self" theme if the client's struggle is, ultimately, internal.

Mentor: The Judge

If the judge cannot be the hero of the client's story, the next best role that an attorney can award the judge is as the hero's mentor. The mentor is a former hero who now serves as the sage advice-giver to the next hero. In the Harry Potter books, Albus Dumbledore represents the most obvious example of a mentor figure for Harry. Harry has several other mentors, however. Minerva McGonagall, Remus Lupin, and Sirius Black all serve mentor roles as well. In each case, the mentor teaches and tests Harry and offers the gift of an amulet or talisman needed to help him along his journey. Harry has quite a collection of these gifts including his wand, his broomsticks, his Invisibility Cloak and the Patronus Charm. He eventually gains the Resurrection Stone and the Elder Wand, though he chooses to give those up. In a similar vein, a lawyer who has cast the client as hero should strive to place the judge as the hero's mentor. In storyboard terms, the judge, through wise decision-making, provides the hero with the lessons needed to allow the hero to move forward. Further, casting the judge as mentor allows the judge to symbolically and literally deliver a talisman to the client in the form of a judgment and opinion. In myth and story, the symbolic gifts must be earned by the hero by demonstrating the learned lesson of commitment. For example, in *The Sorcerer's Stone*, Dumbledore sends Harry the Invisibility Cloak but only after Harry has spent a few months at Hogwarts learning about magic and his own history. Similarly, Dumbledore protected certain facts until Harry was ready to know them or until Dumbledore was ready to divulge them. In one instance, towards the end of the story, Harry quite literally must unlock a golden snitch in order to obtain the Resurrection Stone. Likewise, in a lawsuit scenario, so too the hero client earns the judge's favorable opinion only after going through the commitment of legal process. And so too, the judge's favorable ruling gives the client something that will help the client as she continues on her journey of transformation.

---

23. *See* VICTORIA LYNN SCHMIDT, STORY STRUCTURE ARCHITECTURE 15–19 (Writer Digest Books 2005) (providing wonderfully useful examples as to what sorts of situations heroes might be facing in each of the six different conflict categories).

Finally, by casting the judge in the role of mentor, we are also acknowledging the judge's own heroism. Mentors in myth may be heroes themselves from a different quest and who now impart the knowledge they have gained onto the next generation of hero.

In *The Order of the Phoenix*, Harry appears, pro se, in front of an en banc court— the Wizengamot—that seems predisposed to convict him of illegally using underage magic. Necessity does not appear to be a viable defense available to Harry. If convicted, he stands to lose not only his ability to do magic, but also his ability to complete his schooling at Hogwarts. The scene is thus presented as one of a scholar hero being challenged by the judges and possibly thrown off the journey. Luckily, Harry's mentor, Professor Dumbledore, appears at the hearing to help explain the story to the judges in a manner that convinces the judges to pardon Harry and, in turn, to allow Harry to return to Hogwarts. The hero, having been tested, is allowed to continue on his journey towards knowledge.

The judges in the scene from *The Order of the Phoenix* are portrayed mostly as gatekeepers. An attorney can learn much from that scene in order to prevent it from happening to the client. A judicial opinion chastising an attorney for his failure to provide effective assistance to a (Muggle) juvenile client provides an excellent opportunity to analyze a successful example of how lawyers cast judges in the role of mentor to a juvenile offender-hero.

The New Jersey mid-level court, its Appellate Division, in a pair of decisions, demonstrated their acceptance of the mentor role and used it to release a juvenile convicted of murder, confident that he would be a productive and educated member of society. In the particular case, the juvenile, James Ferguson, was convicted of the knowing and purposeful murder of a fellow high school student.[24] Tried as an adult, he was sentenced to a thirty-year term without the possibility of parole. At the time of the transfer of the case from juvenile court to the adult criminal division, Ferguson was fourteen years old and his attorney was handling this kind of case for the first time. At the transfer hearing, the lawyer relied completely on the testimony of a psychologist. The trial judge made a ruling based on psychological theory and knowing only that Ferguson had carried a knife on him for a year before the homicide.

The pro bono lawyers representing Ferguson in his appeal told a much more detailed and compelling story, one that they argued the initial lawyer should have told at the transfer hearing. In the legal arena they asked the court to become Ferguson's mentors. The attorneys portrayed Ferguson as a "sage" hero;

---

24. State v. Ferguson, 605 A.2d 765 (N.J. Ct. App. 1992), *opinion on remand*, 642 A.2d 1008 (N.J. Ct. App.), *cert. denied*, 649 A.2d 1285 (N.J. 1994).

a high school student with good grades,[25] with a future ahead of him, and who exercised poor judgment by carrying a knife for protection. At the time of the "sad incident," the victim was two years older, much larger than James Ferguson, and perhaps the initial aggressor. There were possibly racial overtones to the incident. Ferguson had no criminal record at all and, in fact, had previously attended the prestigious Newark Boys Chorus School and Science High School before moving to Edison, New Jersey. Ferguson carried the knife with him because of racial episodes in school and around town and because he sometimes walked home at night, three miles from a friend's house, after his grandmother returned from her evening shift at work. Because of Ferguson's prior racial victimization during some of those walks, his friend had given him a sheathed knife that the friend had received from his own mother as a souvenir from Mexico. Because the initial lawyer did not have Ferguson testify on his own behalf, he was not able to tell the judge any of this when the court decided whether to have him tried as a juvenile or as an adult.

The appellate lawyers for Ferguson were masterful in casting those people involved with the prison system as his sympathetic companions. While in the correctional facility, the Chief of the Division of Juvenile Services wrote an evaluation report on behalf of an experienced group of correctional officers, each of whom had interviewed Ferguson. The report concluded that the correctional officers "were unanimous in our opinion that this youngster represents one of the most appropriate candidates for being treated as a juvenile of any that we have seen. I cannot recall another juvenile offender who had the potential for being rehabilitated that James does in my over 20 years with the Department of Corrections." Not surprisingly, the appellate court reversed the transfer of the case from juvenile court based on ineffective assistance of counsel.

After reversing the case, the appellate court remanded the matter to the trial court for sentencing in accordance with the higher court's opinion. The trial court sentenced Ferguson to an indeterminate term of up to eighteen years. Ferguson again appealed and the same appellate court stepped in to help him.[26] This time the appellate court came right out and used Ferguson's commitment to education as one of mitigating factors outweighing any aggravating factors of the case. Specifically, the reviewing court pointed to the facts that while incarcerated, Ferguson had earned his high school diploma, as well as twelve

25. Brief of Defendant-Appellant at 3–4, State v. James Ferguson, No. A-327-90T2 at 10 (N.J. Ct. App. 1991).
26. State v. Ferguson, 642 A.2d 1008 (N.J. Ct. App. 1994), *cert. denied*, 649 A.2d 1285 (N.J. 1994).

college credits. More correctional officers provided letters praising Ferguson's character and his work at the facility. The appellate court reversed the trial court's penalty, with instructions to sentence Ferguson for exactly as long as he had already been incarcerated, and with credit for time served. The New Jersey Appellate Division acted just as the Wizengamot did for Harry, they sent their juvenile defendant back on his way to school, agreeing that this was a boy who should be set back on his sage path. After being released, Ferguson went on to college.[27]

The appellate court demonstrated the hallmarks of a mentor figure. The opinion represented the talisman, used by the hero to protect himself and to return him to his quest for education. Further, by the very nature of the schooling required to become a judge, the appellate panel fulfilled the mentor role of former-hero-turned-teacher. In contrast, the lawyers handling the appeal played the role of storyteller rather than hero or mentor. The decision was strategically flawless.

Villain or Dragon: Not Necessarily the Opposing Party's Role

Villains or dragons, also called shadows, represent darkness and suppression. The hero must confront the villain in order to complete the transformation. Depending on the type of journey, the villain may be an internal dragon. Joseph Campbell believed that the "ultimate dragon" is within ourselves; the binding of oneself to one's ego. Potentially, this bond could prevent us from following our bliss.[28] Internal struggles include an addiction or perhaps a character trait that the hero needs to overcome such as blaming others, manipulating people's emotions, laziness or diminished self-esteem. Of course, the villain can also be an external source.

Generally, however, when we think of "villains" we think of individuals rather than character traits. In myth, an external villain is often related to the hero by blood.[29] Think of Hamlet and his uncle, the usurper of the throne; Luke Skywalker and his father, Darth Vader; and Moses and the Pharaohs. Even Harry Potter is related, biologically, to the villain Voldemort. Voldemort transferred some of his powers to Harry during the first attempt on his life.

---

27. E-mail from Barry Albin, Esquire of Wilentz, Goldman & Spitzer, to Ruth Anne Robbins, Professor, Rutgers School of Law—Camden (February 19, 2001, 19:03:46 EST) (on file with author).

28. CAMPBELL & MOYERS, *supra* note 13, at 183–84.

29. M. Katherine Grimes, *Harry Potter: Fairy Tale Prince, Real Boy, and Archetypal Hero*, *in* THE IVORY TOWER AND HARRY POTTER 89, 109 (Lana A. Whited ed., Univ. of Mo. Press 2002). Grimes points out other examples from Roman, Greek, and Christian mythology.

In *The Goblet of Fire,* Harry and Voldemort became more biologically connected when Voldemort used Harry's blood as a key resurrection ingredient—something that eventually saves Harry's life when Voldemort tries to kill Harry in the last book. The two are also related through their wands, which both have, as their core, tail feathers from Fawkes, Albus Dumbledore's phoenix.

Because the relationship of villain to hero implicates a familial tie that may or may not actually exist or that the client may not wish to exist, the lawyer should be careful about default casting the opposing party as the dragon. Dragons are also potentially heroes, if viewed from the opposite point of view. Campbell hypothesized that a hero might be a local god to some but to others in the community, the new god might be the enemy. A tyrant is a hero who has gone astray. As a consequence, automatically casting the opposing party as "villain" risks giving the opposing party an opening to reverse the logic and to make the hero look like the actual villain.

Pigeonholing the opposing party as villain may also risk the lawyer entering the world of damaging hyperbole. Part of the lawyer's *ethos* depends on that lawyer displaying good will in her advocacy demeanor. Thus, a lawyer may end up unwittingly giving the opposing party a persuasive opportunity to present himself favorably to the judge. Many writers have earned a lot of money simply by reversing a traditional story's perspective.[30] The wise lawyer, then, refrains from alluding to the other side as He-Who-Must-Not-Be-Named.

Threshold Guardians: A Potential Role for the Opposing Party

A better choice for the opposing party lies in the role of threshold guardian: the minor villains of the story. Threshold guardians, or gatekeepers, are sometimes lesser antagonists to the hero. Draco Malfoy and Professor Snape represent this type of character in the Harry Potter books. Yes, Professor Snape is a threshold guardian even if he was on the right side of the war. He still made Harry's life a misery during Potions class and he still gave Harry detention every chance he had. An ally who makes your life difficult is still a threshold guardian.

Threshold guardians may also be neutral characters that are part of the environment. In the story, they function to test the hero before the hero can progress to the next stage of the journey. The Harry Potter series also contains

---

30. *See, e.g.,* MARION ZIMMER BRADLEY, THE MISTS OF AVALON (Ballantine 1982) (retelling the Arthurian legend from the point of view of the traditionally-wicked Morgan Le Fay); GREGORY MAGUIRE, WICKED: THE LIFE AND TIMES OF THE WICKED WITCH OF THE WEST (Regan Books 1995) (inventing a sympathetic story about the traditional WIZARD OF OZ villain).

an example of a neutral threshold guardian in the form of the Sorting Hat. Presumably, a student would not be permitted to matriculate at Hogwarts if the hat did not sort him. Threshold guardians can even be literal dragons, as was the case in both *The Chamber of Secrets* and *The Deathly Hallows* (if we interpret "dragon" to include, besides the Gringotts dragon, all large reptiles, i.e., also the basilisk and Nagini the snake). Of those three beasts, none was the actual foe, but merely a challenge that Harry had to move past. Ironically, the true dragon in the bank's bowels of Gringotts was the least of the three dragons that he faced.

In a lawsuit, the opposing party may represent a threshold guardian more than a true dragon. Going back to our family law example, the defendant in a domestic violence action may represent more of an initial barrier to the hero starting her journey rather than representing the villain himself. Tom Riddle, Sr. wasn't Merope's ultimate "dragon" but was merely the threshold guardian who broke her heart and abandoned her. Her true villain, as we learned in *The Half-Blood Prince*, was the wizarding community—that knew about her family's abuse but turned a blind eye, that saw she was starving and destitute while pregnant but did nothing, and that tossed her newborn son into a muggle orphanage after she died in childbirth. A lawyer who understands the difference between villains and threshold guardians can make this sort of casting decision most clearly if she has already concluded that her client's quest is larger than the lawsuit; rather, that the lawsuit is merely one early test either along the road of trials or at the threshold to the new world. The dragon, then, is something that will be faced outside the context of the legal system or, at least, outside the context of the current litigation.

Poetically, in terms of the title of this chapter, one of the most accessible examples of an "every person" hero getting past threshold guardians is J.K. Rowling herself, i.e., the author of the quintessentially Campbellian[31] Harry Potter series. Her story and her litigation against someone claiming copyright infringement help demonstrate the power of heroic archetypes in modern and real-life stories. Rowling is a creator hero whose journey—the stuff of Horatio Alger novels—moves her towards contributing unique and lasting work that goes well beyond her own writing and has become the theme of countless interdisciplinary books and conferences.

When J.K. Rowling found herself embroiled in a copyright infringement lawsuit, she had completed *The Goblet of Fire* but had three books left in the promised seven book series. As she was still on her journey, she was confronted

---

31. *See supra* note 9.

with an inevitable test by a minor villain: a threshold guardian. An author by the name of Nancy Stouffer threatened Rowling with a lawsuit, claiming that Rowling stole ideas from Stouffer's book *The Legend of Rah and the Muggles*. J.K. Rowling refused to settle the matter and instead chose to litigate for vindication. Through her American publisher, Scholastic, Inc., she sought declaratory judgment from the federal courts.[32]

Stouffer's claims began with an allegation that Rowling took her word for non-magical humans, "muggle," from Stouffer's books. The Southern District of New York disagreed, stating that Stouffer's usage of the terms differed from Rowling's usage, and that, in any case, it was not a trademark. In Stouffer's works, the court noted that, "Muggles are tiny, hairless creatures with elongated heads that live in a fictional, post-apocalyptic world called Aura." Rowling's "Muggles" are ordinary human beings who lack magic powers. Furthermore, research into the terms shows that the terms are not recently created words by any stretch of the imagination. *A Dictionary of Slang and Unconventional English*, which predates the Harry Potter books, states that the word "mug" had been used in the 1930s and 1940s to mean "anyone not of the Underworld," providing an example from W. Buchanan-Taylor, author of the 1943 work *Shake it Again*: "There is a whole range of talk which cannot be understood by the 'mug,' a word which describes *all* members of the public who attend fairs."[33]

The court also rejected Stouffer's allegations that readers had confused Rowling's Harry Potter with a character, Larry Potter, in one of Stouffer's publications. The federal court, in an excoriating part of the opinion, rejected this argument as well. First, the court stated that evidence did not show that "Larry Potter" was even used in a published work prior to the litigation. The paragraphs that contained "Larry Potter" in the work produced by Stouffer, supposedly during the 1980s, were printed with technology that could not have existed at that time. The court also analyzed and rejected Stouffer's other claims that there was a likelihood of confusion with various aspects of the two publications. The Southern District of New York thus ruled in favor of Rowling, granting Scholastic, Inc. summary judgment. The court also penalized Stouffer with $50,000 in sanctions because it concluded that Stouffer had committed fraud on the court. The Second Circuit affirmed both issues on appeal.[34]

---

32. Scholastic, Inc. v. Stouffer, 124 F. Supp. 2d 826 (S.D.N.Y. 2000).

33. A DICTIONARY OF SLANG AND UNCONVENTIONAL ENGLISH (Partridge & Beale eds., Macmillan Publishing Co. 1984) (1961) (emphasis in original).

34. Scholastic, Inc. v. Stouffer, 221 F. Supp. 2d 425 (S.D.N.Y. 2002); *aff'd*, 81 Fed. Appx. 396 (2d Cir. 2003) (agreeing that Stouffer should pay $50,000 sanctions for submitting to the court falsified evidence).

Not surprisingly, Rowling suffered no real loss at the hands of the lawsuit in terms of her or her books' popularity. The fifth book, *The Order of the Phoenix*, was released several months after the federal district court handed down its ruling. That book had a record first printing of 8.5 million copies in the United States alone. Barnes & Noble reported selling one million copies during the first forty-eight hours after its release. One explanation is that J.K. Rowling's history has always been accessible to the public, and we have identified her as a hero from early on. We want her to become the anointed queen of fiction that she is already moving towards. If you ask a Harry Potter fan what the world would be like without completion of the series you would undoubtedly hear an unhappy response.

In heroic terms, the victory Rowling achieved in the lawsuit represented a "road of trials" victory over a foe trying to stop the hero from reaching her goal and receiving her boon. Stouffer did not, however, play the role of villain but, rather, merely the role of a threshold guardian; a Draco Malfoy. As a creator hero, Rowling's ultimate villain is more societal in nature, i.e., whether or not her entire series would be published and read. Rowling's attorneys actually employed heroic imagery, whether deliberate or not. In their legal brief, the attorneys recognized their client's larger goals and journey when they wrote, as a topic sentence very early in the counterstatement of the case's story, "Rowling conceived of the *Harry Potter* Books in 1990, while on a train between Manchester and London, England."[35] The sentence literally conjures the image of someone beginning a long journey, much as Harry Potter travels each year by train to and from school.

In contrast, a lawyer who has miscast the roles of hero and mentor by assigning those parts to other lawsuit characters is a lawyer who leaves the judge little choice but to become a threshold guardian or gatekeeper. Moreover, a judge may cast himself into the role of gatekeeper when that judge defines the client by her flaws.

Shape-Shifter: Another Potential Role for the Opposing Party

By their very nature, shape-shifters are elusive and unstable characters. Often they appear in stories as potential love interests for the hero. The shape-shifter's fickle or mood-changing personality can make him a negative influence rather than a positive one. Peter Pettigrew and Fenrir Greyback are

---

35. Brief of Plaintiff-Appellees at 5, Scholastic, Inc. v. Stouffer, No. 02-9405 (2d Cir. April 17, 2003).

good examples of this kind of shape-shifter who challenges the hero. The role of shape-shifter, thus, provides the lawyer with a useful casting choice for the opposing party. A lawyer may strategically avoid caricaturing the opposing party as a villain by, instead, merely referring to that party as changeable. Of course, the Harry Potter books also contain examples of positive shape shifter characters, such as Professor McGonagall, Professor Lupin, and Sirius Black.

In more recent history, and after she had completed the last book in the series, J.K. Rowling again found herself in a lawsuit with a shape-shifter. This time she filed a copyright infringement suit over the proposed publication of the online fan site, the Harry Potter Lexicon.[36] Before filing the suit, Rowling's agents had contacted the company that was rushing the Lexicon to print, asking for a copy of the manuscript and voicing concerns about copyright infringement. The Lexicon publisher did not provide substantive responses, and for that reason Rowling felt that she had to file suit.[37] Rowling, in fact, was a supporter of the Lexicon in its free online format and had publicly lauded it as a reference cite. The federal court took note that Rowling has posted praise on her own website, "[t]his is such a great site that I have been known to sneak into an internet café while out writing and check a fact rather than go into a bookshop and buy a copy of Harry Potter (which is embarrassing). A website for the dangerously obsessive: my natural home."[38] It was, then, not an easy decision for Rowling when the Lexicon decided to literally change its skin from online to printed version. Nevertheless, because Rowling herself intends to write an encyclopedia—donating the proceeds—she felt the need to stop the printing of the Lexicon for profit. The federal district court after hearing the case in a bench trial agreed that the proposed Lexicon publication would be a copyright infringement and awarded Rowling the fairly nominal sum of $6,750.[39]

The Lexicon litigation demonstrates that Rowling has chosen to become a mentor. Rowling has always been very tolerant of the fan websites including the "fanfic" that her series has generated.[40] She has only rarely stepped in, mostly

---

36. Warner Bros. Entertainment Inc. v. RDR Books, 575 F. Supp.2d 513 (S.D.N.Y. 2008).

37. *Id.* at 522–25.

38. *Id.* at 521.

39. *Id.* at 554.

40. Aaron Schwabach, *The Harry Potter Lexicon and the World of Fandom: Fan Fiction, Outsider Works, and Copyright*, 70 U. Pitt. L. Rev. 387 (2009) (explaining that fanfic involves characters from the Harry Potter books that are used in stories written by the amateur authors).

to stop NC-17 rated writings.[41] The end of her own heroic journey has presented Rowling with a choice of whether to become a mentor or threshold guardian. The recitation of facts in the recent federal court's opinion seem to demonstrate that Rowling has treated the Lexicon very gently—there was no inclusion of the website as part of the copyright action and the quote about the Lexicon appeared on her website throughout the litigation.[42] There is even a hint that in different circumstances she might not have reacted to another encyclopedia. For example, her attorneys questioned defendant's expert during the trial about whether the Lexicon might simply include shorter descriptions in its proposed publication, i.e., descriptions that did not lift whole passages from the Harry Potter books.[43]

Companions and Minor Characters

The hero's companions are there to accompany the hero and to provide invaluable help at crucial times. The companions also teach the hero about the new world into which the hero has entered. Hermione Granger and Ron Weasley both fulfill the roles of companions. Each of them offers Harry valuable information about the wizarding world, and each of them simultaneously teaches Harry how that he can use that information to reach his goal of finding his own place in society. Hermione, raised in the humdrum Muggle world, as was Harry, demonstrates the importance of research and study to learn and fit into magical society. Ron teaches Harry the ins and outs, the joys, and the importance of having a family to rely upon—critical lessons for any orphan to learn. If a lawyer chooses to cast a lawsuit character as a companion, the most likely candidates would be the witnesses, both lay and expert.

Conclusion

These concepts of hero and journey illustrated in the Harry Potter books provide lawyers with a framework for presenting the client's case. By tapping into our common mythology and ancient hero archetypes, lawyers can tell

---

41. *Id. See also* Joyce Millman, *To Sir, With Love: How Fan Fiction Transformed Professor Snape From a Greasy Git to a Byronic Hero ... Who's Really Really Into S/M*, in MAPPING THE WORLD OF THE SORCERER'S APPRENTICE 39, 49 (Mercedes Lackey ed., 2005).

42. Schwabach, *supra*, n. 36 at 420.

43. *Warner Bros.*, 575 F. Supp.2d. at 546–48.

their clients' stories using powerful persuasive techniques that are deeply ingrained in their human audience. Since humans are each on quests during any stage of our lives, lawyers can use this premise as a foundation or scaffold for starting to strategize a theory of the case.

Who Wants to Be a Muggle? The Diminished Legitimacy of Law as Magic

Mark Edwin Burge

In the Harry Potter books, J.K. Rowling has fashioned a parallel world based on our own, but with a fundamental difference: a separate magical society is grafted onto it. In Rowling's fictional version, the magical population lives among the non-magical Muggle population, but we Muggles are largely unaware of them. This secrecy is by elaborate design and is necessitated by centuries-old hostility to wizards by the non-magical majority. The reasons behind this hostility, when combined with the similarities between Harry Potter-style magic and American law, make Rowling's novels into a cautionary tale for the legal profession.

Lawyers as Wizards

Law has long been compared to magic.[1] This state of affairs originated, in substantial part, in the formalist era that gave rise to our modern system of legal education. As most law professors are aware, today's American law school curriculum traces its origins back to Christopher Columbus Langdell, the dean of the Harvard Law School who famously hypothesized in the 1870s that law is a science that, when correctly applied, should lead to an objectively "correct" resolution of a legal dispute. The postulates of Langdell's science were to be derived from judicial opinions. Langdell's principal method of legal training, accordingly, was to direct students to plow through judicial opinions that

---

1. *See, e.g.,* JEROME FRANK, COURTS ON TRIAL 37–79 (1949) (discussing "Modern Legal Magic" and "Wizards and Lawyers").

they may independently and rigorously derive proper legal rules and reasoning.[2] The process of questioning students rather than lecturing to them remains dubbed the "Socratic method," despite numerous protestations that Socrates himself would have scorned the method.[3]

Langdell's idea of legal science is no longer widely held, but his education system is widespread today, in large part because of its effectiveness in teaching critical thinking.[4] The process of legal education has in fact developed an initiation mystique that exceeds the boundaries of the law school and has found its way into popular culture. Many law students now come to task fully immersed in what we might style "Law School Apocalyptic Literature," a genre that includes Scott Turow's *One L* and John Jay Osborn's *The Paper Chase*.[5] In the popular mind—both within and outside the law student population—Osborn's novel has perhaps been eclipsed by the 1973 film version of *The Paper Chase*, where John Houseman portrayed the archetype of a harsh Socratic instructor, Professor Kingsfield.[6] The sense of initiation, even borderline hazing, is common to these stories. The intensity and hostility of Kingsfield's questioning is thus such that he provokes the hapless "Mr. Hart" into after-class vomiting a scant few minutes into the film version. Socratic questioning of law students by their professors, albeit substantially toned down from the Kingsfield model, is still the most popular method of legal instruction.

As students, future lawyers are, in a sense, "initiated" into a realm of knowledge and skills of which it is implicitly understood that the world-at-large has no part. So are students at Hogwarts. In this arena, Professor Snape could be more than an adequate substitute for Professor Kingsfield. Consider Harry's first Potions class:

> "You are here to learn the subtle science and exact art of potion-making," he began. He spoke in barely more than a whisper, but they caught every word—like Professor McGonagall, Snape had the gift

2. *See generally* M. H. Hoeflich, *Law & Geometry: Legal Science from Leibniz to Langdell*, 30 Am. J. Legal Hist. 95, 119–21 (1986).

3. *See, e.g.*, Richard K. Neumann, Jr., *A Preliminary Inquiry into the Art of Critique*, 40 Hastings L.J. 725, 729 (1989); William C. Hefferman, *Not Socrates but Protagoras: The Sophistic Basis of Legal Education*, 29 Buff. L. Rev. 399, 415 (1980).

4. *See* David S. Romantz, *The Truth About Cats and Dogs: Legal Writing Courses and the Law School Curriculum*, 52 U. Kan. L. Rev. 105, 118–20 (2003); Michael Vitiello, *Professor Kingsfield: The Most Misunderstood Character in Literature*, 33 Hofstra L. Rev. 955, 979–86 (2005).

5. Scott Turow, One L (1977); John Jay Osborn, Jr., The Paper Chase (1971).

6. The Paper Chase (Twentieth Century Fox Film Corp. 1973).

of keeping a class silent without effort. "As there is little foolish wand-waving here, many of you will hardly believe this is magic. I don't ex-pect you will really understand the beauty of the softly simmering cauldron with its shimmering fumes, the delicate power of liquids that creep through human veins, bewitching the mind, ensnaring the senses.... I can teach you how to bottle fame, brew glory, even stop-per death—if you aren't as big a bunch of dunderheads as I usually have to teach."

More silence followed this little speech. Harry and Ron exchanged looks with raised eyebrows. Hermione Granger was on the edge of her seat and looked desperate to start proving she wasn't a dunderhead.[7]

This momentous (and to the student, somewhat frightening) sense of ini-tiation conveyed by Snape is more than a little like law school. Each year, as a new One-L class begins its studies, a law school crackles with excitement. The initiation is underway. The culture, history, and even mystery of law school cre-ate a mixture of terror and wonder for the initiates. When a few hundred Hermione Grangers roam the halls, eager to prove to themselves and their peers that they, too, are not "dunderheads," the experience can be mind-alter-ing, or at least worldview-altering.

The methods of instruction and concepts taught add to the mix, reinforc-ing the sense that the law student is being initiated into an ancient and elite order. This order is somewhat Gnostic, in the sense that the general public does not share in the *gnosis*, the special knowledge being imparted. Though all people must live within and deal with the law, members of the order perceive them-selves as understanding the *real* functioning of the law in a way that the rest of the world does not. Thus begins the process, the student becoming a wizard while those outside of the Gnostic order remain Muggles.

Beyond the methods of their training, however, lawyers are also wizards as to their practices, specifically in their use of words. Law has its specialized vo-cabulary, and these words are magical in more than a figurative sense. In the world of Harry Potter, certain words properly spoken by a wizard can, in and of themselves, change the surrounding world. Consider a few examples from the novels: *Wingardium Leviosa* causes an object to levitate; *Expelliarmus* dis-arms an opponent; *Expecto Patronum* creates a patronus, a temporary guardian; *Morsmordre* invokes the "Dark Mark," Voldemort's evil wizarding sign.

Throughout the series words like these cause events. Only a minor stretch of imagination is necessary to substitute legal terms as magic words.

---

7. *Sorcerer's Stone* 136–37.

> "*Res judicata!*" shouted Malfoy, shooting a blast of sparks towards Harry's Amended Complaint.
>
> But Harry responded almost instinctively. "Waiver!" he cried, deflecting Malfoy's spell harmlessly to the floor of the courtroom.[8]

Or again:

> "We're doomed," said Ron, as Harry glumly looked on. "We have absolutely no direct evidence of causation."
>
> Hermione simply glared at them. "Oh, honestly! Am I the only person to have read *Torts: A History?*" She deftly flicked her wand. "*Res ipsa loquitur*," she said, and the causation gap in the summary judgment response appeared to mend itself.[9]

Indeed, some magic words in American law have even made the jump into being taught as a dark art against which to defend:

> "*Lochner!*" cried Voldemort, striking the bakery workers with a bolt of green light. The gag stifled Harry's gasp as he remained tied to the tombstone. Harry had seen Professor Moody demonstrate the Unforgivable Doctrines, but nothing in the classroom prepared him to see substantive due process used on human beings.[10]

The wizard-like practices of lawyers are not confined to magic words, which seem to fit most closely in the context of litigation. Transactional lawyers—those who in popular parlance are in the business of "doing deals"—are more akin to the potion-brewing wizards Snape alluded to in Harry's first year. Consider Hermione Granger's research in *The Chamber of Secrets* on how to brew Polyjuice

---

8. The doctrine of *res judicata* (i.e., "the thing has already been decided") prevents someone who has lost on a particular issue in court from raising it in a subsequent claim. The doctrine can be waived, however, if the other party fails to raise it in a timely manner.

9. The doctrine of *res ipsa loquitur* (i.e., "the thing speaks for itself") is a doctrine of tort law under which a plaintiff need not prove that someone was negligent if the facts are such that the harm suffered could only have been the result of someone's negligence, as when a passer-by is hit in the head by a safe that someone has dropped out a window, or a surgeon accidentally amputates the wrong leg.

10. This is a reference to the line of cases exemplified by Lochner v. New York, 198 U.S. 45 (1905), in which the U.S. Supreme Court struck down a law limiting the number of hours bakers could work on grounds that it interfered with the constitutional rights of employers and employees to freely agree about hours worked. The *Lochner* variety of "substantive due process" was subsequently repudiated by the Court. *See, e.g.*, West Coast Hotel Co. v. Parrish, 300 U.S. 379 (1937) (affirming the constitutionality of a state minimum wage law).

Potion. Our imaginations will not be taxed[11] if we imagine Hermione as a driven associate at a transactional law firm:

> "I've never seen a deal this complex before!" gasped Hermione as she reviewed the proposal. "It will take at least a month to scratch the surface on due diligence alone."
>
> "A month?" said Ron darkly. "Mr. Malfoy will be sure we've each clocked 300 billable hours by then." But Hermione's eyes narrowed dangerously, and he added swiftly, "But it's our best chance for making partner, so full steam ahead, I say."

With an "initiation" system of education and practices that involve magic words and transactional brewing, lawyers may quite reasonably be viewed as wizards. This may be amusing, but, as the Harry Potter books can teach us, there are potential problems when a small group in society has exclusive access to the magic.

The Separate World

Wizarding separateness and secrecy in the Harry Potter narrative establish the background for the uneasy Muggle-wizard relationship. The lengths to which the magical community has gone to achieve secrecy are almost epic. The worldwide wizarding community requires secrecy far more elaborate than any immense conspiracy that Senator Joseph McCarthy ever alleged in the United States government.[12] Wizards and magical creatures have a documented existence at least as far back as ancient Egypt, but, due to wizard efforts, that history is largely unknown to Muggles.

In the world where Harry lives today,[13] wizards have developed a complete society with institutions helping to ensure that regular interaction with Muggles is largely unnecessary. The magical population certainly has its own system of schools. Though Hogwarts is the most prominent wizarding school in

---

11. And rightly so. Good transactional lawyers always seek to avoid taxation.

12. *See generally* DAVID M. OSHINSKY, A CONSPIRACY SO IMMENSE: THE WORLD OF JOE MCCARTHY (1983).

13. I mean "today" in only a very general sense, as the events recounted in Rowling's novels actually occurred several years ago. Harry's first year at Hogwarts seems to have been 1991–92, and his final confrontation with Voldemort in *The Deathly Hallows* would have occurred in 1998. A timeline of Harry's history can be found at the *Harry Potter Lexicon*, available at http://www.hp-lexicon.org/timelines/essays/timeline-facts.html (last visited July 22, 2008).

the novels, there are others, like Beauxbatons Academy, the Durmstrang Institute, and the Salem Witches Institute. Although Harry and Muggle-born
wizards like Hermione attended ordinary English Muggle schools prior to age
eleven, the wizard-born must go somewhere else, because they seem to have
only the haziest idea of Muggle ways. Nor do the novels suggest that a wizard
would ever re-enter the Muggle educational system once leaving Hogwarts.
Indeed, Professor McGonagall's career-counseling session with Harry in *The
Order of the Phoenix* strongly suggests otherwise, as does Hermione's observation on reading a Muggle Relations recruiting pamphlet: "You don't seem
to need many qualifications to liaise with Muggles."[14] The idea that a properly
trained wizard might go on to attend Oxford or Cambridge is apparently unknown. The wizarding educational system is quite self-contained, and quite
separate from non-magical education.

Wizarding government is also a separate enterprise. The Ministry of Magic
has its own bureaucracy and is not subject to the Muggle Prime Minister's government. In *The Half-Blood Prince* we learn that in dire situations the Minister of Magic will confer with his Muggle counterpart, the Prime Minister, who
does not dare tell anyone lest his sanity be questioned.[15] Though both the Minister of Magic and the Prime Minister are British, governing British subjects,
their spheres of authority clearly do not overlap. Even communication between them is rare. Most wizards can accordingly avoid dealing with Muggles
completely. Government officials like Fudge and lower-level minions like Arthur
Weasley take care of that work. Notably, even the Muggle-loving Mr. Weasley's
interactions with the Muggle population are rare enough that he has great difficulty even using and calculating the value of "Muggle money"—British
pounds.

Another area in which the wizarding world is separate from the Muggle
world is that of public infrastructure. The magical world has its own currency
and banking system—run by goblins, no less—and therefore has no need to

---

14. *Order of the Phoenix* 656–57.
15. Shortly after the July 2005 release of *The Half-Blood Prince*, then-Prime Minister
Tony Blair refused to admit to any conversations with the Minister of Magic, when he told
the House of Commons:
> The Harry Potter brief in my file is somewhat thin, which only shows that my of-
> ficials' sense of importance is not what it should be. I was told by someone, how-
> ever, that in the first chapter of the new book the Minister of Magic comes out
> of a picture to confront the Prime Minister. I am still searching for the Minister.

The United Kingdom Parliament, House of Commons Debates for 20 July 2005, reprinted at
http://www.publications.parliament.uk/ pa/cm200506/cmhansrd/cm050720/debtext/50720-
03.htm (last visited July 22, 2008).

use our Muggle banks and Muggle money.[16] They have their own transit system. Many wizards can magically "apparate" from place to place. If this is uncomfortable or impractical, they may solicit (and pay for) a ride to certain destinations on the Knight Bus, as Harry does in *The Prisoner of Azkaban*, or make use of the Floo Network, a system allowing for travel and communication through fireplaces, or use a Portkey. Wizard shopping also appears to be completely separate from Muggle shopping. A wizard purchasing goods or services in Diagon Alley (or the more sinister Knockturn Alley) has no need ever to visit Harrods, only a very few wizards visiting the famous department store would have any idea how to make a purchase there anyway.

With separate schools, a separate government, and a separate public infrastructure, the magical community in Rowling's novels is able to avoid interaction with most of the non-magical population, and they do precisely that. The Muggles, being the vast majority of the world, constitute a population from whom the very existence of wizards is a carefully guarded secret. The existence of a separate community, elaborately kept secret from the world-at-large, makes us wonder, Why all the secrecy? The separateness and secrecy are symptoms of a problematic instability inherent in Muggle interactions with wizards and magic. The nature of the wizard-Muggle relationship is instructive for the legal profession.

Causes of Conflict

"Are you planning to follow a career in Magical Law, Miss Granger?" asked Scrimgeor.

"No, I'm not," retorted Hermione. "I'm hoping to do some good in the world!"[17]

If difficult-to-comprehend law can be like incomprehensible magic—with lawyers as wizards applying it—and if Muggles have fear and disdain for wizards and their craft, we can quite reasonably view Harry Potter as a cautionary tale for the legal profession. The warning to the legal profession is one regarding comprehensibility—the capability for legal texts to be understood by the general population. If legal texts are not understandable by those who are subject to them, legitimate law risks descent into the illegitimacy of law as

---

16. For discussions of these topics, see Chapters 15 and 16 by Eric Gouvin and Heidi Mandanis Schooner and Eric Gouvin in this volume.

17. *Deathly Hallows* 123–24.

magic. The statement above by Hermione Granger suggesting that lawyers are distrusted even within the wizarding world strengthens the parallel. Even wizards disdain a mysterious magician class within their own ranks.

The backstory for Rowling's novels, some of which the author disclosed in the two "Harry's Books" paperbacks released for charity in 2001, includes history establishing that things do not go well for wizards when Muggles learn of their nature and existence. Harry's miserable life with the Dursleys is the most vivid example of the relational problem, but the Muggle-wizard chasm is far larger than that. Despite their powers, wizards apparently cannot in the end defeat a hostile and much larger Muggle population. Consider the following passage from one of the charity books:

> Imperfect understanding is often more dangerous than ignorance, and the Muggles' fear of magic was undoubtedly increased by their dread of what might be lurking in their herb gardens. Muggle persecution of wizards at this time was reaching a pitch hitherto unknown and sightings of such beasts as dragons and Hippogriffs were contributing to Muggle hysteria.
>
> It is not the aim of this work to discuss the dark days that preceded the wizards retreat into hiding.[18]

The Muggle persecution, we are told in the same text, was a "particularly bloody period of wizarding history," and it ultimately culminated in the International Statute of Wizarding Secrecy of 1692. An excerpt from Bathilda Bagshot's *A History of Magic* likewise recounts how "wizards went into hiding for good" at about this time and "formed their own small communities within a community" following enactment of "the International Statute of Secrecy in 1689."[19] By the time of Harry's story, secrecy has been the law for some three hundred years, and the wizard population has largely mastered the task of secrecy. Harry himself falls victim to the harsh (and in his cases, unjust) enforcement of wizard secrecy in both *The Chamber of Secrets* and *The Order of the Phoenix*.

Fear of magic, only partially understood, seems to be the basis for the intense dislike of wizards by Muggles. Human history is rife with prejudices—whether justified or not—that arise from fear of something that those living

---

18. NEWT SCAMANDER, FANTASTIC BEASTS AND WHERE TO FIND THEM xv (2001).

19. *Deathly Hallows* 318. Do the 1689 and 1692 dates reflect disagreement between esteemed textbook authors Newt Scamander and Bathilda Bagshot? Perhaps each is referring to separate but related pieces of wizarding legislation. Maybe one of the two is wrong. Alas, resolution of such intriguing minutiae is beyond the scope of this essay—not that it wouldn't be fun, though.

in the fear do not understand. In the case of magic, fear of the unknown is especially acute. Not only do Muggles have an "imperfect" understanding of magic, but most aspects of magic are entirely unknowable to them. Harry's Aunt Petunia learned of this exclusivity to great dismay in her youth, first begging for admission into Hogwarts, but then disparaging it as a "special school for freaks" following Dumbledore's "very kind" letter denying her admission.[20] In the Harry Potter universe, it matters not how much study or effort a Muggle might put into the effort to learn magic, the knowledge cannot be learned unless one has the genetic gift. A non-magical Squib (one who has wizard parents yet cannot perform magic) like Hogwarts caretaker Argus Filch can live in the very center of magical education, but magic is unknowable even to him, who instead lives with futile hope of learning magic through a "Kwikspell" correspondence course. For Muggles, garden-variety fear of the unknown is greatly exacerbated in the case of magic. Magic is not only unknown, but it is unknowable. While the young protagonist of a Horatio Alger story might, by effort and determination, ascend from mailroom-boy poverty to the executive echelons of wealth, the same character with the same character traits in the world of Harry Potter can never be more than a Muggle.

Lack of understanding and—far worse—the *impossibility* of understanding lie at the root of Muggle disdain for wizards where Muggles are aware of the magical population. However, the wizards also do themselves no favors by the approach many of them take to Muggle-relations. By this statement, I do not refer to the obvious fact that dark wizards are unlikely to win Muggle friends by perpetrating violence upon them, such as where the villain of *The Prisoner of Azkaban* is said to have murdered thirteen Muggles with a single curse. Rather, the more widespread and subtle problem is the condescending attitude of wizards who deal with Muggles. The most detailed example of wizard condescension Rowling provides is in her telling of meetings between Minister of Magic Cornelius Fudge and the British Prime Minister. The Muggle leader's reaction when Fudge has suddenly and inconveniently appeared in his office is telling:

> "Ah ... Prime Minister," said Cornelius Fudge, striding forward with his hand outstretched. "Good to see you again."
>
> The Prime Minister could not honestly return this compliment, so said nothing at all. He was not remotely pleased to see Fudge, whose occasional appearances, apart from being downright alarming in themselves, generally meant that he was about to hear some very bad news.[21]

---

20. *Deathly Hallows* 669–70.
21. *Half-Blood Prince* 4.

On this particular visit, the Prime Minster is surprised to learn that Fudge has been dealing with the very same disasters and debacles that have plagued his own government over the past week:

> "You—er—your—I mean to say, some of your people were—were involved in those—those things, were they?"
>
> Fudge fixed the Prime Minister with a rather stern look. "Of course they were," he said. "Surely you've realized what's going on?"
>
> "I ..." hesitated the Prime Minister.
>
> It was precisely this sort of behavior that made him dislike Fudge's visits so much. He was, after all, the Prime Minister and did not appreciate being made to feel like an ignorant schoolboy. But of course, it had been like this from his very first meeting with Fudge on his very first evening as Prime Minister.[22]

The put-upon Prime Minister is surely not alone in disdaining "being made to feel like an ignorant schoolboy." No person, even one fully aware of his ignorance, appreciates having a lack of knowledge thrown in his face. The magical world that Fudge represents is, to a large extent, outside the realm of the Prime Minister's understanding. Still, that fact does not require Fudge to make the situation worse by his condescension, yet the tendency is one that even the nobler wizards in Rowling's world cannot avoid. Albus Dumbledore is derided in his old age as a "friend of Muggles," but he shared the superiority complex of a would-be ruling class in his youth. Writing to villain-in-the-making Gellert Grindelwald, young Dumbledore muses:

> Your point about Wizard dominance being FOR THE MUGGLES' OWN GOOD—this, I think, is the crucial point. Yes, we have been given power and yes, that power gives us the right to rule, but it also gives us responsibilities over the ruled.... We seize control FOR THE GREATER GOOD.[23]

Dumbledore thus illustrates a troubling ultimate outcome of wizard condescension, a trait that was arguably a mere boorish annoyance in the hands of Cornelius Fudge.

The Muggles in Rowling's novels fear wizards first because they are intrinsically incapable of understanding them and their magic, a fact which is regrettably immutable. The magical community makes the situation worse, even in its limited interaction with Muggles by condescending words and actions. The Mug-

---

22. *Half-Blood Prince* 4–5.
23. *Deathly Hallows* 357.

5791

gle fear, despite its roots in prejudice, is unfortunately justified. A Grindelwald, a Voldemort, or—disturbingly—even a well-meaning Dumbledore represent a very real danger to Muggles of having a magical ruling class imposed upon them.

The Undervalued Value: Who Wants to Be a Muggle?

Fudge's interaction with the Prime Minister forcibly reminds those of us who have practiced law of the interaction between some lawyers and their clients. Clients, like the Prime Minister, do not and perhaps cannot understand the intricacies. Their fate may hinge on what the wizards or the lawyers do. Yet even the most intelligent and experienced lay person may be entirely unable even to read the statutes they are asked to comply with or the contracts they are asked to sign. And too often they are patronized by those lawyers, the vast majority of whom I would credit as being in the well-meaning category with Dumbledore.

From its founding documents, American democracy is based on an assumption of a general competence of the populace to govern itself,[24] albeit within systems designed to temper the will and whims of the majority.[25] The system further assumes a general submission by that populace to a legal system based on the premise that the system is—on balance—just.[26] Understanding of the legal system among the population-at-large is not only normatively preferable, but it is prudentially critical to the political health of a democracy. Absent public comprehension of the law and how it operates, democracy risks turning into oligarchy—with lawyers as the hated oligarchs.

Comprehensibility—as a self-contained, normative value in the enactment, interpretation, and practice of law—is given short shrift by the legal profession. It deserves a far higher place of honor in the law of a liberal republic than it holds today, and lawyers above all ought not to underestimate the importance of this value.

---

24. *See, e.g.,* U.S. CONST. pmbl. ("We the People of the United States ... do ordain and establish this Constitution...."); THE DECLARATION OF INDEPENDENCE para. 2 ("We hold these Truths to be self-evident, that ... it is the Right of the People ... to institute new Government, laying its Foundation on such Principles and organizing its Powers in such Form, as to them shall seem most likely to effect their Safety and Happiness."); THE FEDERALIST No. 55, at 346 (James Madison) (Clinton Rossiter ed., 1961) (stating that despite the existence of "a degree of depravity in mankind," a republican system "presupposes the existence" of qualities making humans capable of self-government).

25. THE FEDERALIST No. 10 (James Madison).

26. *See, e.g.,* THE FEDERALIST No. 51 (James Madison) ("Justice is the end of government. It is the end of civil society.").

Comprehensibility is an essential value in law because law and the legal profession are fundamentally different from other fields requiring technical expertise, such as engineering, medicine, or physics. The difference arises from the fact that positive law (setting aside any theories of "natural law") is a human construct. All of us must live within the laws of physics, and it is not offensive to learn that there are formulas and reasons for physical phenomena that a solid majority of us will not understand. Likewise, no one is truly offended by the proposition that only a skilled surgeon might understand the nuances of a heart transplant procedure. Some of us cross suspension bridges and work in tall skyscrapers without giving serious thought to the idea that we need to understand structural engineering. But contrast these laws of science with the enacted laws of society. Imagine a moderately educated member of the public being told any of the following things: (1) "You are not capable of understanding the reason for the Supreme Court's ruling." (2) "Do not bother to read what the legislature has enacted; it is quite beyond you." (3) "The court of appeals has reversed your $50,000 judgment, but the reasons why are unfathomable." Such statements—even if actually true—would be condescending at best, and patently offensive at worst, in a way that would not occur if the subject of the discussion were chemistry. Why?

Law is different.

In a republican democracy, law is supposed to be made and changed by the will of the public. All are supposed to have available a participatory role in building and operating the machinery of law, even if that role never becomes more than theoretical. Perhaps the best analogy here is to voting rights. Is the mere *right* to vote of any value to one who never or seldom votes? Certainly. The widespread ability to participate in the political arena has value independent of actual participation. This ability is what makes an election fairly determined by ten percent voter turnout of equal legitimacy with an election determined by ninety percent of the voters. The ten percent did not engage in a *coup d'état*; they merely availed themselves of the voting right as the ninety percent might likewise have done. Law that can be understood by the Muggle population-at-large gains similar legitimacy. Incomprehensibility of a governing legal text to the public at large is ultimately offensive to democracy.

Fortunately, the analogy between law and magic breaks down on a major point. While Muggles can never truly understand and be a part of magical society—and wizards cannot help them to do so—non-lawyers are not genetically barred from understanding legal text. Lawyers have both an ethical and a prudential obligation to bridge this gap in understanding. While one possible "solution" to the increased illegitimacy of law-as-magic would be to send all of the Muggles to law school, the questionable utility of such a proposal is obvious, I suspect.

Short of that, the legal profession has tools at its disposal provided by what is usually called the plain language (or plain English) movement in law. Richard Wydick, author of one of the best-known texts on the subject, describes the premise of plain language legal writing as being "that good legal writing should not differ, without good reason, from ordinary well-written English."[27] Put another way, "Plain English does mean that legal documents should be intelligible to nonlawyers, with exceptions for legitimate terms of art and justifiable technical terms...."[28] The movement has already had some successes, with greater clarity in consumer documents, such as warranties and leases. Comprehensibility, as I advocate it here, is certainly a value championed by the plain language movement.[29] But far more is at stake than a mere question of style. Comprehensibility of governing legal texts—drafting that further removes such texts from being "magic" in their application—has a legitimizing function that extends beyond even immediate readership.

Some of the greatest reluctance to accept the role of plain language has been in the area where I contend that comprehensibility is systemically the most important—in legislation and judicial opinions. The legal profession does not fully appreciate the value of comprehensibility because of a flawed fundamental premise that the comprehensibility of a legal text matters only to those who will actually read it. Dru Stevenson has argued, for example, what others in the profession assume: that although statutory "obfuscation, anachronisms, or unrestrained prolixity" are indefensible, an effort to rewrite any set of statutes in plain language (as the plain English movement seeks to do) is futile.[30] The reason for the futility is that the statutory law "is not addressed to the citizenry as a whole," but rather to "agency officials, judges, law enforcement officers, and perhaps lawyers." Stevenson does not defend cumbersome language and unnecessary technical terms as such, but he concludes that it "does not harm our democracy" for technical vocabulary to outstrip the abilities of the intelligent layman. Brian Hunt, of the Irish Office of Parliamentary Counsel to the Government, makes a similar point, dismissing the importance of the use of plain language in legislation:

---

27. RICHARD C. WYDICK, PLAIN ENGLISH FOR LAWYERS 4 (5th ed. 2005).

28. Wayne Schiess, *What Plain English Really Is*, 9 SCRIBES J. LEGAL WRITING 43, 66 (2004).

29. *See, e.g.*, BRYAN GARNER, LEGAL WRITING IN PLAIN ENGLISH 91 (2001) (advocating clear drafting of statutes, but not asserting increased legitimacy as a reason for such drafting).

30. Drury Stevenson, *To Whom is the Law Addressed?*, 21 YALE L. & POL'Y REV. 105, 149 (2003).

> If it were shown that legislation was widely read by ordinary citizens, I have no doubt that the style of drafting would be altered so as to take account of that audience.... Those who advocate the use of plain language in legislative drafting are making one very large, and I suggest, unwise assumption. That assumption is that members of the public are interested in reading raw legislation.... In the absence of substantive evidence that such public interest in legislation exists, I believe that the arguments in favour of plain language legislative drafting are very weak indeed.[31]

This logic appears unassailable on the surface. Why, after all, should the comprehensibility of a statute or a court opinion matter to a person who will never read either of them, and indeed generally has no interest in so doing?

Yet general comprehensibility to Jane Q. Public matters a great deal, and it matters regardless of whether she ever reads the particular statute or opinion. Comprehensibility does not require that the law actually *be* comprehended, but instead that it be *capable* of comprehension by those who want to know. The issue is one of legitimacy, as legal comprehensibility promotes legal legitimacy. By my use of the term "promotes," please note that I do not suggest the existence of a bright dividing line between legitimacy and illegitimacy of a governing text, though the concept of comprehensibility is clearest at the extremes. In a nation where—to use Lincoln's terms—government is conceived as "of the people, by the people, for the people,"[32] no one would dispute that a governing legal text capable of being understood by only one person is illegitimate. Expanding that number to nine people—the number of Supreme Court justices—does not greatly ameliorate the situation, though that is a separate issue I will not address here. At the other extreme, a governing legal text capable of being understood by all has, if duly enacted, a far greater claim to legitimacy. Ancient civilizations had good reason to post their codes in public places like markets, even though few of their subjects could actually read them.

The comprehensibility value, then, runs along a continuum. The more who are capable of reading and understanding a legal text in a republican democracy, the greater is the claim of the text to legitimacy. The smaller the audience that is capable of understanding such a text, the more diminished is the legal text's legitimacy.

---

31. Brian Hunt, *Plain Language in Legislative Drafting: An Achievable Objective or a Laudable Ideal?* 24 Statute L. Rev. 112, 115 (2003).

32. Abraham Lincoln, *Address Delivered at the Dedication of the Cemetery at Gettysburg on November 19, 1863* (quoted in Garry Wills, Lincoln at Gettysburg 263 (1992)).

Lest there be misunderstanding: I do *not* suggest that comprehensibility is the only or even highest value in ascribing legitimacy to law; I argue only that comprehensibility of a governing text is important, that comprehensibility is today an undervalued value, and that the importance of comprehensibility extends to those who will never read it. To adapt an ancient metaphor: It matters to the ninety-nine sheep whether the one who is lost has at least the fair opportunity to find its way.[33]

Unlike the Harry Potter world, where magic and its machinations are permanently beyond the capacity of the non-magical, lawyers can make governing legal texts such that they can be understood by a sizable majority of non-lawyers. Most non-lawyers will never read most texts. But some will. The cumulative effect of non-lawyer interactions with comprehensible legal texts will be to enhance the legitimacy of those texts and of the legal system as a whole. Representative democracy ultimately requires no less. Law becomes more "magical" in appearance as its incomprehensibility to the non-lawyer increases. Law as magic will ultimately degrade within the imagination of society, and legitimacy—both actual and perceived—will suffer accordingly.

In the end, it behooves all in the legal wizards' craft to make more concerted efforts in writing and in drafting of governing legal texts to aid the non-lawyer public in understanding them. The ease with which such understanding can occur—comprehensibility—is an important and underestimated value. Who wants to be a Muggle? No one, really. The ongoing and critical task of the legal profession is to ensure that governing legal texts and lawyers' treatment of them do not suffer the vices that "make" people into Muggles.

---

33. *Cf. Luke* 15:4–7.

Agents of the Good, Servants of Evil: Harry Potter and the Law of Agency

Daniel S. Kleinberger

Like many works of literature, the Harry Potter novels concern the conflict between good and evil. As is often the case in novels and life, some characters are active in defense of the good while others act to serve and advance evil. In the Harry Potter novels, good and evil are each clearly personified: Dumbledore is the foremost representative of the former, and Voldemort is the unsurpassable embodiment of the latter.[1]

The Potter novels are, among other things, a saga of the almost neverending battle between the minions of Voldemort and the adherents of Dumbledore. Every Death Eater acts on behalf and under the control of Voldemort, and the Order of the Phoenix seemingly acted under Dumbledore's commands until his death. Even Harry Potter was "Dumbledore's man through and through."[2]

The Harry Potter novels are thus replete with examples of agency "relationship[s] in which one person, to one degree or another or respect or another, acts as a representative of or otherwise acts on behalf of another person."[3] As a result, concepts from the law of agency can help explicate these novels, and the novels can in turn furnish appealing illustrations of agency law concepts.

"Agency is the fiduciary relationship that arises when one person (a 'principal') manifests assent to another person (an 'agent') that the agent shall act on the principal's behalf and subject to the principal's control, and the agent

---

1. While respecting the fears that lead many to eschew this name and substitute euphemisms such as "He Who Must Not be Named," this essay follows the Dumbledore-Potter approach and calls a spade a spade.

2. *Half-Blood Prince* 348, 649.

3. Restatement (Third) of Agency § 1.01, comment c (2006) (describing the agency relationship).

manifests assent or otherwise consents so to act."[4] Agency relations are ubiquitous in our society (as well as in the Potter novels), and the study of Agency Law is almost as interesting and important as the study of Potions.

This essay will consider the following eight topics, which arise from the overlap of Harry Potter and the law of agency:

- The Essence of Agency: Interfacing for the Principal
- Why the Labels Matter: Categories and Consequences
- Formation of an Agency Relationship: The Consent Requirement, House-Elves, the Imperius Curse, and Dementors
- Ending the Agency Relationship: Potteresque Variations on the Notion of Termination by Express Will
- The Agent's Duties to the Principal: Loyalty, Obedience, Good Conduct, House-Elves, and Snape
- An Agent's Good Faith Struggles with the Duty of Loyalty
- Dumbledore: Agent or Principal and, if Agent, Agent for Whom?
- Servants of Evil?

The Essence of Agency: Interfacing for the Principal

An agency relationship necessarily involves an agent and a principal and typically implicates one or more others (third parties). In one way or another, an agent's function is to stand between the principal and the world and to "act[] as a representative of or otherwise ... on behalf of [the principal] with power to affect the legal rights and duties of [the principal]" toward the world.[5]

For example:

- A bank, understanding that not all customers like dealing with ATM machines, hires tellers to handle customer deposits, withdrawals, and similar transactions. The tellers are agents of the bank.
- A landowner, preparing to leave for an around-the-world tour and wishing to sell Greenacre as soon as possible, gives a real estate broker "power of attorney." This credential authorizes the broker to sell Greenacre on the owner's behalf and to sign all documents necessary to form a binding contract and to close the deal. The broker is the owner's agent.
- A corporate shareholder, unable to attend the corporation's annual meeting, signs a "proxy" that authorizes another individual to cast the share-

---

4. RESTATEMENT (THIRD) OF AGENCY § 1.01 (2006).
5. RESTATEMENT (THIRD) OF AGENCY § 1.01, comment c (2006).

holder's votes at the meeting. By accepting the appointment, the proxy holder becomes the shareholder's agent.[6]

In the Harry Potter novels, the Death Eaters are the most notorious agents, and Voldemort is emphatically the principal. Acting "on behalf of" another does not fit Voldemort's character, although in his youth Tom Riddle does work briefly as an agent. His first job after leaving Hogwarts is as an employee of the Borgin and Burke partnership. In that role, the Dark-Lord-To-Be is the classic intermediary. According to Dumbledore, "Voldemort was sent to persuade people to part with their treasures for sale by the partners, and he was, by all accounts, unusually gifted at doing this."[7]

Hagrid is likewise an intermediary (and an agent) when he leaves his job at Hogwarts to reestablish diplomatic relations with the giants.[8] And Mr. Weasley is a dedicated, hardworking, and often poorly treated agent for the Ministry of Magic.

In contrast, Hermione is never Harry's or Ron's agent, even though she often does them the favor of "assisting" with their homework.[9] "[A] person does not become the agent of another simply by offering help or making a suggestion."[10]

Thus, the Dursleys are not Dumbledore's agents, even though Mrs. Dursley agrees to take Harry in only because Dumbledore urges her to do so. There is no indication that Dumbledore asks that Harry be harbored on *Dumbledore's behalf*, and certainly the Dursleys manifest no consent to act subject to Dumbledore's control.

For the same reason, the members of "Dumbledore's Army" are not Dumbledore's agents, despite Dumbledore's assertion to the Minister of Magic that it is "Dumbledore's Army, Cornelius.... Not Potter's Army. *Dumbledore's Army.*"[11] This assertion cannot serve as the necessary manifestation by a principal that another act on the principal's behalf, because Dumbledore makes the assertion long after the students have formed the organization.

For related reasons, Draco Malfoy's cronies, Vincent Crabbe and Gregory Goyle, are not Draco's agents. In an agency relationship, the agent has the

---

6. DANIEL S.KLEINBERGER, AGENCY, PARTNERSHIPS, AND LLCS: EXAMPLES AND EXPLANATIONS (Aspen 2002) ("Kleinberger, APLLC-2ND") § 1.2 at 4.

7. *Half-Blood Prince* 432–33 (Dumbledore to Harry as they are about to view a memory in the Pensieve).

8. Identifying Hagrid's principal in this endeavor is complicated and is discussed below.

9. Because Hermione is undoubtedly a "straight arrow," rules on plagiarism and related forms of cheating must be different at Hogwarts than in the Muggle world.

10. Violette v. Shoup, 20 Cal. Rptr. 2d 358, 363 (Ca. Ct. App. 1993).

11. *Order of the Phoenix* 618 (emphasis in original).

power "to affect the legal rights and duties of" the principal,[12] and Draco never reposes that amount of trust and confidence in either of his beefy henchmen.

Why the Labels Matter: Categories and Consequences

Regardless of whether the categories of principal and agent are interesting in the abstract,[13] these labels have serious practical importance. Law often reasons through a process of "categories and consequences—analyzing situations by defining categories of behavior and then attaching consequences to those categories."[14] Such high-powered pigeonholing is characteristic of agency law, and any agency relationship "thus entails inward-looking consequences, operative as between the agent and the principal, as well as outward-looking consequences, operative as among the agent, the principal, and third parties with whom the agent interacts."[15]

Formation of an Agency Relationship: The Consent Requirement, House-Elves, The Imperius Curse, and Dementors

Agency is a consensual relationship. No agency is formed until the would-be agent "manifests assent or otherwise consents to act" for the would-be principal.[16] In most circumstances, the consent is obvious and clear cut. For example:

Employer: You're hired. [principal, "manifest[ing] assent to another person … that the agent shall act on the principal's behalf and subject to the principal's control"]

Employee: Great! [agent, "manifesting assent or otherwise consent[ing] to act"]

---

12. Restatement (Third) of Agency § 1.01, comment c (2006).

13. A person who enjoys Arithmancy will likely find Agency interesting even in the abstract. In contrast, a person who thrills to Divination as "taught" by Professor Trelawney will likely consider too confining the intellectual discipline inherent in agency law concepts.

14. Kleinberger, *supra* note 5, at xxiv.

15. Restatement (Third) of Agency § 1.01, comment c (2006).

16. Restatement (Third) of Agency § 1.01 (2006).

Sometimes, however, consent is at best debatable. For example, house-elves might seem the model of faithful agents, but Hermione would assert (vehemently) that the consent element is completely missing.[17]

At least one house-elf appears to agree. As Dobby explains to Harry Potter in *The Chamber of Secrets*, status rather than consent engenders the relationship between a house-elf and the family of the house: "Dobby is a house-elf— *bound* to serve one house and one family forever."[18] Indeed, after Dobby's "liberation by sock," he describes the house-elf's role as "enslavement."[19]

Even more obedient and seemingly acquiescent are persons subject to the Imperius Curse. However, although such unfortunates may be Voldemort's helpless instruments, they are not his agents. Although an agent's assent is typically inferred "when the agent performs the service requested by the principal following the principal's manifestation,"[20] whether conduct signifies assent depends on all the surrounding circumstances. Agency law applies an "objective" test—that is, the law asks whether, in light of the would-be agent's outward manifestations and the surrounding circumstances, a reasonable person would believe that the would-be agent has genuinely consented to act on behalf of the principal. No reasonable person could view a victim's subservience to the Imperius Curse as a manifestation of genuine consent.

A fortiori,[21] a person *possessed* by Voldemort does not act as Voldemort's agent. There is no consent and, in light of the surrounding circumstances (i.e., the possession), there is no conduct that could be reasonably seen as manifesting assent. The person possessed is more a zombie than an agent.[22]

Dementors raise a closer question. Certainly, for most of the Harry Potter saga they play a key role for the Ministry of Magic and arguably they act sub-

---

17. *See, e.g., Goblet of Fire* 154 (Hermione describing Mr. Crouch's house-elf as "[h]is *slave*") (emphasis in original).

18. *Chamber of Secrets* 14.

19. *Goblet of Fire* 380 (Dobby). Despite the strong case against considering house-elves to be agents, this essay will continue to do so. For one thing, without the house-elves, many of this essay's best examples will disappear. For another, any good lawyer must be able to "believe[] as many as six impossible things before breakfast." LEWIS CARROLL, THROUGH THE LOOKING GLASS at 89 (Plain Label Books 1956) (1871) (the Queen, speaking to Alice). And for a third, after liberation Dobby does choose to be employed by Hogwarts to perform work side-by-side with the Hogwarts house-elves.

20. RESTATEMENT (THIRD) OF AGENCY § 1.01, comment d (2006).

21. Latin: even more so.

22. *See, e.g., Order of the Phoenix* 500 (Ginny describing her experience being possessed by Voldemort: "When he did it to me, I couldn't remember what I'd been doing for hours at a time. I'd find myself somewhere and not know how I got there.").

ject to the Ministry's control.[23] However, it is not clear that the dementors have manifested assent to act "on behalf of" the Ministry. It is equally arguable that they are merely under contract: providing services to the Ministry in return for a macabre form of payment.[24]

Ending the Agency Relationship: Potteresque Variations on the Notion of Termination by Express Will

"An agency relationship may end in numerous ways,"[25] and the express will of either the principal or agent always suffices. The termination is effective when the manifestation of the express will reaches the other party. If the principal's "revocation" or the agent's "renunciation" breaches a contract between the parties, the termination will be wrongful and give rise to a claim for damages. Nonetheless, principal and agent each have the non-waivable power to terminate the agency.

Termination by express will has something important in common with the creation of an agency relationship. Both are assessed objectively; the relevant manifestation is interpreted from the perspective of a reasonable third person, and subjective intent is irrelevant. Thus, for example, Lucius Malfoy never intends to terminate Dobby's role as house-elf, but even the despicable Malfoy recognizes the objective significance of throwing a sock and having Dobby catch it.[26]

The distinction between an agent's right and power to renounce an agency is highly significant in the Muggleworld, but the distinction blurs substantially when Voldemort is involved. As explained previously, if an agent's renunciation is wrongful, then the principal's normal recourse is to seek damages. But when Voldemort is the principal, normalcy is not the norm, and the consequences of breach are far more serious (and final). As explained by Sirius Black, recounting the death of his brother: "[Regulus] was murdered by Voldemort. Or on his orders, more likely, ... [H]e got in so far then panicked about what he was being asked to do and tried to back out. Well, you don't just hand in your resignation to Voldemort. It's a lifetime of service or death."[27]

---

23. *See, e.g., Order of the Phoenix* 146–47 ("dementors are taking orders only from the Ministry of Magic").

24. Such a deal is plausible because the exchange provides dementors access to continuous pleasure without the risk of concerted opposition from magic folk.

25. Kleinberger, *supra* note 5, §5.1 at 153.

26. *Chamber of Secrets* 337–38 (attacking Potter and exclaiming, "You've lost me my servant, boy!").

27. *Order of the Phoenix* 112. In the Muggle world, there is one type of agent that lacks the power to immediately terminate the agency relationship. Business entity statutes typi-

The Agent's Duties to the Principal: Loyalty, Obedience, Good Conduct, House-Elves, and Snape

Agency is a "fiduciary relationship," and consequently the agent owes a duty of loyalty to the principal in all matters pertaining to the agency. "The agent's role is a selfless one, and the principal's objectives and wishes are dominant.... Except when the principal has knowingly agreed to the contrary or when extraordinary circumstances exist, the agent is obliged to prefer the principal's interests over its own and to act 'solely for the benefit of the principal in all matters connected with [the] agency.'"[28]

The agent's duty of loyalty includes a duty to: (i) not compete with or take opportunities from the principal; (ii) safeguard the principal's confidential information; and (iii) avoid conduct that would reflect poorly on the principal or otherwise injure the principal's reputation (the duty of good conduct). The agent is also obliged to obey the principal's instructions and avoid unauthorized acts. In addition, "[i]f an agent possesses information and has reason to know that the principal may need or desire the information, the agent has a duty to provide the information to the principal."[29]

The Half-Blood Prince contains a poignant acknowledgment of the agent's duty to provide information. In an attempt to extenuate Snape's betrayal of Harry's parents, Dumbledore says: "He was still in Lord Voldemort's employ on the night he heard the first half of Professor Trelawney's prophecy. Naturally, he hastened to tell his master what he had heard, for it concerned his master most deeply."[30]

Even a brief breach of the duty of loyalty can have egregious consequences, as illustrated by the opening chapter of *The Order of the Phoenix*. The wizard Mundungus is acting for the Order and keeping watch on Privet Drive. He deserts his post to pursue business of his own, and the dementors attack. Harry must defend himself (and his cousin) and, as a result, faces expulsion from

---

cally require an entity formed under the statute to have a "registered agent for service of process." These agents have the power to resign, but the resignation is not effective until either the entity designates a new agent or a statutory waiting period has passed. *See, e.g.,* Uniform Limited Partnership Act (2001), § 116(c) (agent's resignation takes effect 31 days after delivery to the appropriate government filing office, unless a new agent is designated sooner); Revised Uniform Limited Liability Company Act, § 115(c)(1) (same).

28. Kleinberger, *supra* note 5, § 4.1.1 at 117–118 (quoting Restatement (Second) of Agency § 387) (footnotes omitted).

29. Kleinberger, *supra* note 5, § 4.1.5 at 125.

30. *Half-Blood Prince* 549.

Hogwarts. Later in the book, with "a pleading note in his voice," Mundungus seeks to explain away his dereliction of duty: "See, I wouldn't 'ave left ... but I 'ad a business opportunity—'"[31] The excuse is lame as regards both common sense and the law of agency.

Not surprisingly, a glaring breach of duty can be found in Voldemort's brief experience as agent for Borgin and Burkes. Consider the incident of Hepzibah Smith, Helga Hufflepuff's cup, and Slytherin's locket. Despite Voldemort's protestation that "I am only a poor assistant, madam, who must do as he is told," Voldemort acquiesces when Hepzibah burbles, "I've something to show you that I've never shown Mr. Burke! Can you keep a secret, Tom? Will you promise you won't tell Mr. Burke I've got it?"[32]

When Voldemort reports neither this conversation nor Hepzibah's possession of the cup and locket, he breaches the agent's duty to provide information. His subsequent theft of the two items breaches both his duty not to usurp opportunities from his principal and his duty not to compete with his principal.[33]

As for the duties of good conduct and obedience, Hermione gives Ron a good reminder in the following colloquy on the role of prefects:

> Ron: We're supposed to patrol the corridors every so often and we can give out punishments if people are misbehaving. I can't wait to get Crabbe and Goyle for something ...
> Hermione [sharply]: You're not supposed to abuse your position, Ron!
> Ron [sarcastically]: Yeah, right, because Malfoy won't abuse it at all.
> Hermione: So you're going to descend to his level?
> Ron: No, I'm just going to make sure I get his mates before he gets mine.
> Hermione: For heaven's sake, Ron—[34]

---

31. *Order of the Phoenix* 82.
32. *Half-Blood Prince* 435.
33. Ms. Smith's heirs also have grounds to complain and, fearing to sue Voldemort, might argue that his employers (Borgin and Burkes) are responsible for his intentional tort [wrongful act]. Two agency law theories would be relevant: (i) that Borgin and Burkes were negligent (careless) in the hiring, training, supervising, or retention of Voldemort as an employee; and (ii) that Borgin and Burkes are vicariously liable because the tort occurred within the scope of Voldemort's employment. The negligence theory would turn on whether Borgin and Burkes had any reason to know of Voldemort's character (or lack thereof). The vicarious liability theory, which goes by the Latin name *respondeat superior*, is explained shortly; it would not win for the heirs in any Muggle jurisdiction other than perhaps Minnesota, where "Respondeat Superior [Has] Run Amok," 59 BENCH & B. MINN. 16 (Nov. 2002).
34. *Order of the Phoenix* 189.

Hermione is giving voice to a key principle of agency law. Although Ron's concern for his "mates" is commendable, he is obliged to obey the instructions of his principal and to avoid putting his principal "in a bad light." As a prefect, Ron acts on behalf of Hogwarts. His principal is the school, not any of his mates.

Perhaps ironically, it is Dobby (the house-elf) who seems to have best assimilated the agent's duty of loyalty. "We keeps their secrets and our silence, sir. We uphold the family's honor, and we never speaks ill of them."[35]

Dobby tries to maintain this attitude even after his agency ends (i.e., he ceases to be the Malfoy house-elf):

> Dobby could tell Harry Potter that his old masters were—were—*bad Dark wizards.*" Dobby stood for a moment, quivering all over, horror-struck by his own daring—then he rushed over to the nearest table and began banging his head on it very hard, squealing, "*Bad Dobby! Bad Dobby!*"[36]

On the other hand, the series' most striking example of grudging loyalty is Kreacher, another house-elf. Kreacher despises his duty to serve Sirius Black:

> "Kreacher lives to serve the noble house of Black ... [but] Master was a nasty ungrateful swine who broke his mother's heart.... Master is not fit to wipe slime from his mother's boots, oh my poor [deceased] Mistress, what would she say if she saw Kreacher serving him[?]"[37]

Kreacher is no happier when Harry inherits Sirius's house and with it Kreacher's obligation of service: " 'Kreacher will do whatever Master wants,' said Kreacher, sinking so low that his lips almost touched his gnarled toes, 'because Kreacher has no choice, but Kreacher is ashamed to have such a master, yes—' "[38]

Tragically, Kreacher's disdain for Sirius eventually becomes outright disloyalty. When Harry fears that Sirius is in danger at the Ministry of Magic,

---

35. *Goblet of Fire* 380.

36. *Goblet of Fire* 381 (emphasis in original). Arguably at least, Dobby's comments breach no duty because almost all aspects of the duty of loyalty end when the agency ends. However, the duty not to disclose confidential information obtained during the agency continues even after the agency. So, if Dobby obtained the secret "Dark wizard" information while serving as the Malfoy house-elf, Dobby is indeed "Bad Dobby" for disclosing that information to Harry. Otherwise, nothing in agency law restricts Dobby from bad-mouthing his former principal.

37. *Order of the Phoenix* 109.

38. *Half-Blood Prince* 189.

Kreacher breaches his duty to Sirius by making sure that Sirius is incommunicado and by concealing from Harry the fact that Sirius is still at home. As a result, Harry rushes off to the Ministry, fulfills Voldemort's plans, and finds himself confronting a detachment of Death Eaters.

Far worse — or so it seems — was Snape's treachery (a.k.a. breach of an agent's duty of loyalty) at the end of *The Half-Blood Prince*. However, the final novel reveals that Snape was, in fact, a *double* agent.[39]

Snape never intended actually to serve Voldemort, but agency law takes an objective approach to determining agency status. Each master wizard manifested to Snape a desire to have Snape "act on the principal's behalf and subject to the principal's control"[40] To each wizard, Snape "manifest[ed] assent or otherwise consent[ed] so to act."[41] Snape's heroic but secret intent to disserve Voldemort is immaterial.

As Harry eventually learns, Snape was fiercely (albeit secretly) loyal to Dumbledore and perfidiously disloyal to Voldemort. As a matter of agency law, Snape's duty to one principal (Dumbledore) does not excuse his breach of duty to his other principal (Voldemort). In this instance, however, technical disloyalty was heroic. Moreover, under relevant law, perhaps:

- Voldemort's claims for breach died with him, or
- Snape's liability does not survive Snape's death, or
- both.

If not, perhaps Snape's estate will benefit from "jury nullification."

An Agent's Good Faith Struggles with the Duty of Loyalty

Sometimes the duties of loyalty and obedience create a quandary for agents acting in good faith. Suppose compliance threatens the interests of others, or even the interests of the principal?

The Harry Potter novels contain examples of both types of dilemmas. As to the interests of others, several times the pre-liberation Dobby acts as if Harry's safety justifies disloyalty to the Malfoys. The Restatement (Second) of Agency recognizes that an agent may legitimately act against the principal's interest

---

39. *See Deathly Hallows.*
40. RESTATEMENT (THIRD) OF AGENCY § 1.01 (2006).
41. RESTATEMENT (THIRD) OF AGENCY § 1.01 (2006).

"in the protection of ... the interests of others,"[42] but Dobby is apparently unaware of this marvelously vague permission. He devises his own approach to acting adversely to his principal: transgressing in order to help Harry and then subjecting himself to appropriate discipline. In *The Chamber of Secrets*, for instance, Dobby explains: "Dobby will have to punish himself most grievously for coming to see you."[43]

Even without reference to the *Restatement (Second) of Agency*, Dobby's approach may be unnecessarily harsh. The Malfoys may have implicitly authorized Dobby to misbehave on condition that he then inflict commensurate punishment on himself. The evidence is in a brief conversation between Dobby and Harry Potter. Harry asks, "[W]on't they notice if you shut your ears in the oven door?" Dobby responds, "Dobby doubts it, sir. They lets Dobby get on with it, sir. Sometimes they reminds me to do extra punishments...."[44]

The Hogwarts Sorting Hat experiences the second kind of dilemma. The Hat acts as an agent for the school; it takes on the sorting function formerly performed by the school's four founders.[45] In the troubled times described in *The Order of the Phoenix*, the Hat fears that faithful performance of its duties may undercut the very purpose for which it was created:

> Though condemned I am to split you
> Still I worry that it's wrong,
> Though I must fulfill my duty
> And must quarter every year
> Still I wonder whether sorting
> May not bring the end I fear.
> ...
> For our Hogwarts is in danger
> From external, deadly foes
> And we must unite inside her
> Or we'll crumble from within
> I have told you, I have warned you ...
> Let the Sorting now begin.[46]

The Hat solves its problem by fulfilling another duty, that of providing to the principal information pertaining to the principal's interests and relevant to the

---

42. Restatement (Second) of Agency §387, comment d (1959).
43. *Chamber of Secrets* 14.
44. *Chamber of Secrets* 14.
45. *Goblet of Fire* 177.
46. *Order of the Phoenix* 206–07.

agency. As Nearly Headless Nick nearly succeeds in explaining: "The hat feels itself honor-bound to give the school due warning whenever it feels—[interrupted here by Professor McGonagall]."[47]

Dumbledore: Agent or Principal and, if Agent, Agent for Whom?

It is clear that the Death Eaters act on behalf of Voldemort, but what does agency law have to say about those "agents of the good" who rally around Dumbledore? No one in the Harry Potter novels engenders more loyalty (in the lay sense of the word) than Albus Dumbledore, Headmaster of Hogwarts, Order of Merlin First Class, Grand Sorcerer, Chief Warlock, Supreme Mugwump, International Confederation of Wizards. But loyalty in the lay sense does not necessarily signify an agent-principal relationship. For example, thousands of people in Chicago remain loyal to the Cubs, but those diehards are certainly not agents of the ball club.

To understand Dumbledore's role (or, as will be seen, roles) from an agency law perspective, it is necessary first to understand that, in the modern world (whether of wizards or Muggles), a principal need not be a human being. In fact, in the modern world many, perhaps most, principals are organizations—for example, corporations, partnerships, limited liability companies, and so forth. These organizations necessarily act through agents.

In the Harry Potter novels, Gringotts (the wizard's bank) is a good example of an organization that acts through its agents. According to Hagrid, the bank is "[r]un by goblins."[48] Presumably, some goblins function as the managing power that controls the organization, while others act as the bank's agents: doing "its" work, such as keeping accounts and providing security.

Hogwarts School of Witchcraft and Wizardry is another example. The professors and staff act on behalf of the School and are its agents. As Headmaster, Dumbledore has the authority to supervise and direct those agents, but he is not their principal. He is himself an agent of the School. In the nomenclature of the *Restatement (Third) of Agency*, §1.04(1) and (9), (i) he and the others are co-agents of Hogwarts; (ii) he is a superior agent; (iii) all the others are subordinate agents.

For example, it is Dumbledore who decides that Hogwarts will use Hagrid to notify Harry that Harry has been accepted as a Hogwarts student.[49] While

---

47. *Order of the Phoenix* 207.
48. *Sorcerer's Stone* 63.
49. *Sorcerer's Stone* 50–51.

Hagrid may experience himself as acting "for Dumbledore," viewed from an agency law perspective, Hagrid is "on Hogwarts business."

But if Dumbledore is "merely" an agent of Hogwarts and therefore subject to Hogwarts's control, who controls Hogwarts? The ultimate management power resides in the governors as a group (including, distressingly, Lucius Malfoy). As Malfoy explains to Minister Fudge, even "[t]he appointment—or suspension—of the headmaster is a matter for the governors."[50]

Accordingly, when Dumbledore dies, it is for the board of governors to determine whether to close the school and, if not, whom to choose as Dumbledore's successor. As Professor Flitwick says, "We must consult the governors.... We must follow the established procedures. A decision should not be made hastily."[51] Professor McGonagall, Deputy Headmistress of Hogwarts, agrees: "[T]he right thing to do is to consult the governors, who will make the final decision."[52]

Thus, when Dumbledore acts in his Hogwarts role, he acts as an agent and not as a principal. Whatever loyalty is extended to him in that role is either personal (i.e., loyalty in the lay sense of the word) or directed at him in his representative capacity (i.e., as the highest ranking agent of the school).[53]

And what of Dumbledore and the Order of the Phoenix? According to Hermione, the Order is "a secret society.... Dumbledore's in charge, he founded it. It's the people who fought against You-Know-Who last time."[54]

In legal terms, the Order is an organization, presumably a nonprofit association, and, again presumably, its members have ultimate control over its activities. Therefore: (i) Dumbledore is himself an agent of the Order; and (ii) the Order's adherents are not his agents, although they act under his direction. Thus, Dumbledore's role in the Order of the Phoenix parallels his role at Hogwarts. He is the highest ranking agent of the organization and thus superior to his co-agents, who are his subordinates.

Given the parallel between Dumbledore's roles and the overlap between the interests of Hogwarts and the concerns of the Order of the Phoenix, it is some-

---

50. *Chamber of Secrets* 263.

51. *Half-Blood Prince* 628.

52. *Half-Blood Prince* 629.

53. Those who ultimately control Hogwarts—i.e., the governors—are not themselves agents of the school because they are not subject to the organization's control. To the contrary, Hogwarts is controlled by its governors. (The governors temporarily cease to control Hogwarts during the period recounted in *The Order of The Phoenix*, when the Ministry of Magic enacts legislation allowing it to control the school; the Ministry exercises control through its agent, Dolores Umbridge, who is initially High Inquisitor, eventually Headmistress, and unfailingly a dangerous and nasty fool.)

54. *Order of the Phoenix* 67.

times difficult to determine for whom Dumbledore is acting. For example, when Dumbledore chooses Snape to teach Occlumency to Harry, is Dumbledore acting as the person who is "in charge" of the Order of the Phoenix, as Headmaster of Hogwarts, or as both?

Hagrid's sojourn with the giants provides another example of Dumbledorian complexity under the law of agency. Harry ascribes Hagrid's absence from Hogwarts to "his mission—the thing he was doing over the summer for Dumbledore."[55] The mission is certainly an agent's task (opening communication with the giants), but is Dumbledore personally the principal? It seems more likely that Dumbledore dispatches Hagrid on behalf of the Order of the Phoenix. It also seems likely that, acting as Headmaster of Hogwarts, Dumbledore gives Hagrid a leave of absence from his work as instructor in Magical Creatures. (Dumbledore's dual roles do not create a conflict of interest here, because in this situation the interests of both principals are in accord.)

Servants of Evil?

One of the most important subcategories of agent status is that of the "servant."[56] The importance comes from the consequences that attach to the label. When a "servant agent" harms a third party through a wrongful act within "the scope of employment," the principal (called the "master") is liable automatically for the harm. The liability is vicarious and applies without regard to the master's fault. *Respondeat superior*—literally: let the superior make answer. Or, to borrow Mr. Crouch's exclamation after the Dark Mark appears at the Quidditch World Cup, "If you accuse my elf, you accuse me...."[57]

The key factor for determining servant status is the extent to which the principal has the right to control the details of the agent's performance. The following colloquy among Dobby, Hermione, and Harry is illustrative, even though Harry had not exercised the detail of control that concerns Hermione. The discussion takes place in *The Half-Blood Prince*, following Dobby's and Kreacher's fruitless efforts to keep Draco Malfoy under surveillance:

---

55. *Order of the Phoenix* 202.

56. This usage of the term "servant" dates back centuries, and the Restatement (Third) of Agency uses the more modern label of "employee." However, most cases still use the older term. More importantly, "Agents of the Good, Employees of Evil" would make a far less catchy title for this chapter.

57. *Goblet of Fire* 137.

Hermione: What is this? ... What's going on, Harry?

Harry: Well ... they've been following Malfoy for me.

Kreacher: Night and day.

Dobby [proudly]: Dobby has not slept for a week, Harry Potter.

Hermione [indignant]: You haven't slept, Dobby? But surely, Harry, you didn't tell him not to—

Harry [quickly]: No, off course I didn't. Dobby, you can sleep, all right?[58]

Similarly illustrative is Hagrid's description of the tactics Dumbledore imposes for Hagrid's negotiations with the giants. Dumbledore scripts a multistage process of overtures, gifts, and promises: "Dumbledore wanted us ter take it very slow.... Let 'em see we kept our promises."[59]

The test for servant status is multifactored; not surprisingly, the close cases are matters of degree. For example, in *Sorcerer's Stone* Professor Quirrel may have begun as Voldemort's nonservant agent, but, as the Professor himself explains, "When I failed to steal the stone from Gringotts, he ... decided he would have to keep a closer watch on me."[60]

Although from an agency law perspective "the term *servant* has nothing to do with servile status or menial tasks,"[61] in the Potter novels many useful examples of servant status concern house-elves. As Winky explains in *The Goblet of Fire*, "House-elves does what they is told. I is not liking heights at all, Harry Potter ... but my master sends me to the Top Box and I comes, sir."[62]

In contrast, the Hogwarts Sorting Hat is likely a nonservant agent. The school has neither the right nor ability to control the manner in which the Hat makes its decisions. To the contrary, as the Hat itself proclaims, "The founders put some brains in me / So I could choose instead!"[63]

What about the Death Eaters? In *The Half-Blood Prince*, Dumbledore and Voldemort disagree as to the proper characterization. Voldemort calls them "my friends," and Dumbledore responds, "I am glad to hear that you consider them friends ... I was under the impression that they are in the order of servants." Voldemort rejoins, "You are mistaken."[64]

Dumbledore is most likely using the term "servant" in the colloquial sense; he is learned in many realms but likely not in the Muggle discipline of agency

---

58. *Half-Blood Prince* 451.

59. *Order of the Phoenix* 429.

60. *Sorcerer's Stone* 291.

61. Kleinberger, *supra* note 5, §3.2.2 at 81 (emphasis in original).

62. *Goblet of Fire* 99.

63. *Goblet of Fire* 177.

64. *Half-Blood Prince* 444.

law. Even so, in this—as in all his disagreements with the Dark Lord—Dumbledore is right. Control is the most important factor in the servant *vel non* analysis,[65] and "with respect to the physical conduct in the performance of the services [each Death Eater] is [undeniably] subject to [Voldemort's] control or right to control."[66]

The servant label also rests on two more specific factors. As to "the length of time for which the person is employed,"[67] as previously noted a Death Eater is "employed" by the Dark Lord forever—or until death, whichever comes first. As to "whether or not the parties believe they are creating the relation of master and servant,"[68] despite Voldemort's disingenuous reference to "friends," it is abundantly clear that those who join the Dark Lord do so as servants. The brand of the Dark Mark can mean nothing else.

A final example of Voldemort as master can be found in the Book One of the Harry Potter series. When Voldemort comes to share Professor Quirrel's body, the Dark Lord is on the spot to direct every aspect of the Professor's conduct. Quirrel is thus inescapably Voldemort's servant, and, when he addresses Voldemort as "Master," that label is apt. Fittingly, "The Man With Two Faces" personifies one of the most venerable maxims of agency law: *Qui facit per alium facit per se.*[69]

---

65. *Vel non* is Latin for "or not." Because so much of legal analysis involves "categories and consequences," lawyers often seek to understand whether or not a particular situation fits into a particular category.

66. RESTATEMENT (SECOND) OF AGENCY § 220(1) (1959).

67. RESTATEMENT (SECOND) OF AGENCY § 220(2)(f) (1959).

68. RESTATEMENT (SECOND) OF AGENCY § 220(2)(i) (1959).

69. Latin: Who acts through another, acts himself.

Professor Dumbledore's Wisdom and Advice

Darby Dickerson[1]

Introduction

Albus Percival Wulfric Brian Dumbledore.[2] Adorned with a long silver beard, midnight blue robes, and half-moon glasses, he was the greatest wizard of the modern age, if not all times. And he was Headmaster of Hogwarts Academy for Witchcraft and Wizardry. Although being a headmaster might not at first blush seem significant, his duties included interviewing and hiring faculty, entertaining foreign dignitaries, dealing with the press, and supervising a staff that included a werewolf, a half-Giant, a ghost, a possessed wizard, an ex-

---

1. Adapted from Darby Dickerson, *Professor Dumbledore's Advice for Law Deans*, 39 U. Tol. L. Rev. 269 (2008).

2. As one commentator has observed, "A look at Professor Dumbledore's name is very revealing." Specifically,

> **Albus:** *Albion* is an ancient literary name in Britain for "white," and *albescent* means "becoming white,".... Both words suggest that Dumbledore is a wizard who practices white (i.e., good) magic.
>
> **Percival:** Known for his virtue, he is, at least in the original telling, the only knight of King Arthur's Round Table who finds the Holy Grail; he's also the knight who, in pursuit of the Holy Grail, kills the Dark Knight (known as mortal sin) and the Red Knight (known as death).
>
> **Wulfric:** A Catholic saint born in 1154, Saint Wulfric was known for his miracles and prophecies....
>
> **Brian:** Of Celtic origin, this word means "strong"....
>
> **Dumbledore:** Rowling has gone on record saying that she liked this archaic name because it suggested the professor's easygoing, happy-go-lucky nature; she imagined him walking through Hogwarts' halls, humming to himself, like a bee. This obscure word, also spelled *dumbledor*, means "bumblebee."

George Beahm, Fact, Fiction, and Folklore in Harry Potter's World 91–92 (2005).

Auror with a magical eye, and a brilliant potions master who might be the Dark Lord's spy. He reported directly to a Board of Governors with many of the leading wizards of the day, and had to deal directly with the Minister of Magic at times. In performing his varied tasks as headmaster, Albus Dumbledore is an outstanding role model for those in positions of responsibility. We can learn a great deal from his life and career. Although Dumbledore's wisdom seems almost boundless, below are seven pearls extracted from the Halls of Hogwarts.

Dumbledore's CV

For those who might be wary of accepting advice from a slightly eccentric wizard, a review of his training and credentials should allay those doubts.

Albus Dumbledore was born in approximately 1845[3] to Percival and Kendra, both wizards. He had two younger siblings, Aberforth, the current bartender at the Hog's Head, and Ariana, who died as a child.

At age 11, Dumbledore matriculated at Hogwarts—the Oxford or Cambridge of the wizard world—and graduated seven years later. While a student, he was appointed Prefect in Gryffindor House and later Head Boy of the school; he also won the Barnabus Finkley Prize for Exceptional Spell-Casting, was selected as the British Youth Representative to the Wizengamot, and received the Gold Medal for Ground-Breaking Contribution to the International Alchemical Conference in Cairo. His classmate and long-time friend Elphias Doge wrote that by the end of Dumbledore's first year at Hogwarts, he was "nothing more or less than the most brilliant student ever seen at the school."[4] This observation was corroborated by Griselda Marchbanks, Head of the Wizarding Examinations Authority; she personally conducted Dumbledore's exams

---

3. Interview with J.K. Rowling (Oct. 16, 2000), http://www.accio-quote.org/articles/2000/1000-scholastic-chat.htm (Oct. 16, 2000) (indicating that, as of Book 4, Dumbledore was 150 years old); Wikipedia.com, *Chronology of the Harry Potter Stories*, http://en.wikipedia.org/wiki/Dates_in_Harry_Potter#1980 (last updated Aug. 15, 2007). Timelines in the Harry Potter series can be difficult to ascertain. For example, one source indicates that Dumbledore was actually born in 1881, Harry Potter Lexicon, *Albus Dumbledore*, http://www.hp-lexicon.org/wizards/dumbledore.html (last modified Sept. 1, 2007), while another sets his birth in 1851, Wikipedia.com, *Chronology of the Harry Potter Stories*, http://en.wikipedia.org/wiki/Chronology_of_the_Harry_Potter_stories (last modified Sept. 28, 2007).

4. *Deathly Hallows* 17.

in Charms and Transfiguration, and marveled that he had done "things with his wand I'd never seen before."[5]

After graduation, Dumbledore continued researching and writing, and his work was published in various academics journals, including *Transfiguration Today*, *Challenges in Charming*, and *The Practical Potioneer*. He was renowned for his discovery of the twelve uses of dragon blood, and for "his work on alchemy, with his partner Nicholas Flamel."[6] He also was an inventor, with the Deluminator being one of his creations.

In approximately 1891, Dumbledore became a Professor of Transfiguration and Head of Gryffindor House at Hogwarts. Many speculate that Dumbledore also served as Deputy Headmaster, because Hogwarts has traditionally had such a position and because he was involved in recruiting students, including Tom Riddle, aka Lord Voldemort.

By 1956, he had succeeded Armando Dippet as Hogwarts Headmaster. In Spring 1996, the Minister of Magic replaced Dumbledore with Dolores Umbridge as Hogwarts Headmaster because he refused to believe Dumbledore's warning that Lord Voldemort had returned. But Dumbledore was quickly vindicated and reinstated by the end of that same semester. In June 1997, Dumbledore was killed by Professor Severus Snape.

In addition to serving as Chief Warlock of the Wizengamot, Dumbledore also was selected as Supreme Mugwump of the International Confederation of Wizards. He founded and served as Secret-Keeper for the Order of the Phoenix, and held the Order of Merlin, First Class, for Grand Sorcery. According to his Famous Witches and Wizards trading card, found in packages of Chocolate Frogs, "Professor Dumbledore enjoys chamber music and ten-pin bowling."[7]

With his bona fides thus established, let's move to his advice.

One: Favor Charms, Not Curses

Albus Dumbledore realized that more can be accomplished through charms than curses. Although he battled the two most evil wizards to ever live, he abhorred Dark Magic, including the Unforgivable Curses. He even used jinxes, a lesser form of curse, with regret. Dumbledore's choice of magic reflects his

---

5. *Order of the Phoenix* 711.

6. *Sorcerer's Stone* 103.

7. *Sorcerer's Stone* 103. He also loves knitting patterns, *Half-Blood Prince* 73, and raspberry jam, *Half-Blood Prince* 62.

values and principles, which include respect, acceptance, cooperation, patience, trust, and love.

The wizard world has its own caste system.[8] Pure-blood wizards sit at the pinnacle, followed by half-blood wizards, Muggle-born wizards or mudbloods, and squibs, followed in no particular order by non-human beings of the magical world such as goblins, werewolves, house-elves, veelas, giants, merpeople, and centaurs. Although many wizards, including some in the valiant Order of the Phoenix, mistreat or disparage one or more of these "lesser" groups, Dumbledore treated them all with the utmost respect and kindness.

As his childhood friend Elphias Doge wrote in memoriam, Dumbledore "could find something to value in anyone, however apparently insignificant or wretched."[9] Illustrations of Dumbledore's kindness and respect are replete within the series. For example, he was unusual among wizards because he took the time and effort to master both Gobbledegook, the language of goblins, and Mermish, the language of merpeople. He sent Hagrid and Madame Maxime as emissaries to the giants, and instructed Hagrid to "show [them] some respect."[10] Earlier, Dumbledore had argued against killing the last giants in Britain. He showed compassion and helped house-elves Dobby and Winky. He did not hesitate before hiring Lupin the werewolf or Firenze the centaur.

---

8. Author J.K. Rowling has confirmed this caste system:

> Oppressed groups are not, generally speaking, people who stand firmly together— no, sadly, they kind of subdivide among themselves and fight like hell. That's human nature, so that's what you see here [in the books]. This world of wizards and witches, they're already ostracized, and then within themselves, they've formed a loathsome pecking order.

JOHN GRANGER, UNLOCKING HARRY POTTER 143 (Zossima Press 2007) (quoting J.K. Rowling). The caste system is also depicted in the "The Fountain of Magical Ministry" within the Ministry of Magic:

> Halfway down the hall was a fountain. A group of golden statues, larger than life-size, stood in the middle of a circular pool. Tallest of them was a noble-looking wizard with his wand pointing straight up in the air. Groups around him were a beautiful witch, a centaur, a goblin, and a house-elf. The last three were all looking adoringly up at the witch and wizard.

Order of the Phoenix 127.

9. *Deathly Hallows* 20. Doge met Dumbledore on their first day at Hogwarts. Doge "had contracted dragon pox shortly before arriving at school," and his "pock-marked visage and greenish hue did not encourage many [people] to approach [him]." But Dumbledore did. *Deathly Hallows* 16.

10. *Order of the Phoenix* 427. He urged the Ministry to "[e]xtend [the giants] the hand of friendship, now ... or Voldemort will persuade them, as he did before, that he alone among wizards will give them their rights and freedom." *Goblet of Fire* 708.

Dumbledore realized the true power of respect and acceptance. Not only did he understand that it was morally correct to treat all beings equally, but he knew that only through collaboration and true unity could the dark forces be defeated. And he understood it would take the cooperation of all magical beings and beasts to accomplish this important task. In a wizard world ripped apart by Voldemort's violence, he taught that "[u]nderstanding is the first step to acceptance, and only with acceptance can there be recovery."[11] In this endeavor, he knew it was critical to look past physical form, birth rights, language, and culture: "Differences of habit and language are nothing at all if our aims are identical and our hearts are open."[12] He also knew that those who are not respected will, in the end, rebel against their oppressors.

Dumbledore trusted his staff and treated them with the utmost respect. Indeed, he trusted some in the face of great skepticism by others. As just two examples, he trusted both Severus Snape, the former Death Eater, and the half-giant Hagrid with his life. Because of this trust, his staff reciprocated and were loyal to him even after his death.

In stark contrast to Dumbledore stands Lord Voldemort. Despite Voldemort's vast magical abilities, he ultimately failed because he did not love and respect others. And, as Dumbledore explained to Harry, "[t]hat which Voldemort does not value, he takes no trouble to comprehend."[13] In large measure, therefore, Voldemort's downfall was attributable to his own arrogance and prejudice. Because he disdained house-elves, he failed to recognize their significant magical powers, which ultimately saved Harry, Ron, and Hermione from certain death in the Malfoy Mansion. Because Voldemort did not love, he could not appreciate the power associated with a mother dying to protect her beloved son. Because the Death Eaters followed him out of fear, not respect, they were unable to overcome Dumbledore's Army and a unified Hogwarts.

Dumbledore was also patient. Unlike most readers and other Harry Potter characters, Dumbledore did not rush to judge others, which led him to appreciate the true characters of both Snape and Draco Malfoy. While his power of legilimency certainly helped in this regard, his patience was likely determinative.

Professor Dumbledore valued cooperation and collaboration. When they arrive at the castle, new Hogwarts students are sorted into one of four houses:

---

11. *Goblet of Fire* 680.

12. *Goblet of Fire* 723; *see also Goblet of Fire* at 708 (in which Dumbledore told Minister of Magic Cornelius Fudge, "You fail to recognize that it matters not what someone is born, but what they grow to be!").

13. *Deathly Hallows* 709.

Gryffindor, Hufflepuff, Ravenclaw, or Slytherin. Once sorted, students live, eat, attend class, and study primarily with those in their own house. Indeed, students from one house are restricted from the other houses, which are guarded by portraits that require passwords or, in the case of Ravenclaw, accurate answers to logic questions. The house system is competitive, with all vying for the House Cup and the Quidditch Cup.

Recognizing the dangers of division and competition, Dumbledore implored the students and faculty to work together: "[W]e are only as strong as we are united, as weak as we are divided."[14] It was not until the very end, however, when all houses united in the Battle of Hogwarts, that his dream for a united school became reality, albeit a bloody one. But when the houses did ultimately unite, together they were able to defeat Voldemort and bring peace to the wizard world.

We can draw many lessons from Dumbledore's choice of magic, and his core values. First, respect can be a key to our ultimate success. By celebrating differences and valuing each person based on talent, not titles, we can conjure our collective strengths to create a strong and vibrant educational environment.

As a step toward this goal, I suggest we emulate Professor Dumbledore and abolish the current caste system in legal education.[15] We have many gifted educators in our schools who teach the most critical lawyering and life skills. I use the term "educator" because many individuals on our campus teach our students important lessons. In addition to tenured and tenure-track faculty, clinicians, legal writing professors, librarians, student life professionals, career service professionals, admissions staff, and public safety officers, among many others, help transform our students into competent, caring legal professionals. But instead of championing these educators' abilities and dedication, we have too often ignored or downplayed their contributions—to the detriment of our students.[16] In many instances, we have branded them with lesser titles, banished

---

14. *Goblet of Fire* 723; *see also Deathly Hallows* 680 ("I sometimes think we Sort too soon....").

15. Kent D. Syverud, *The Caste System and Best Practices in Legal Education*, 1 J. ALWD 12, 13 (2001) (observing that "[t]here are seven castes in most American law schools, ranging from the elite Brahmins to the dalits, or untouchables," and that castes "include: tenured and tenure track faculty, deans, clinical faculty, law library directors, legal writing directors and faculty, and adjunct faculty. The untouchables, who are barely mentioned when we talk about what our institutions teach students, are, of course, the professional staff of law schools.").

16. Kent D. Syverud, *supra* n. 15, at 13.

them to segregated offices, and silenced them in our systems of shared governance.

As Dumbledore reminded us, "[d]ifferences ... are nothing at all if our aims are identical."[17] With this sage advice in heart and mind, we should not allow bias, budgets, or boggarts stand in the way of change, for improving the lot of some will not worsen the lot of others. Because we really can achieve more united than divided, schools that embrace respect as a core value will excel. They will excel because individuals who are respected will strive to give their best effort, day in, and day out. With a true team of educators giving the best of themselves to our students, excellence can be the only result.

While some may see creating a caste-free educational community as an overwhelming challenge in our Muggle world, we should remember that the most difficult problems in the wizard world are rarely solved by magic alone; instead, the wizards must also use "intelligence, reasoning, planning, courage, determination, persistence, resourcefulness, creativity, fidelity, friendship, and many other qualities traditionally known by the philosophers in our world as virtues."[18] So, even without wands and potions, we do have the power to create positive change.

Second, we should avoid the rush to judgment. In the bustle of daily activity, it is easy to jump to conclusions, to choose the path likely to bring short-term gain, and to shun that which we do not fully understand. It is only through patience like that exemplified by Dumbledore that we can carefully evaluate people, circumstances, and options in a way that best serves our institutional interests. So, as we rush through our days and semesters, we should try to remember that first impressions are often not the best, and that second chances can be better than the first.

Finally, and especially in light of tragedies in campuses across the country, we should strive to enhance collaboration. Stated differently, we must demolish "information silos" that impede communication and collaboration.[19] Information silos arise when individuals or departments, either intentionally or unintentionally, fail to share information, when communications falter, and when crucial constituencies are ignored. We should strive to build cultures in which we share critical information. Unfortunately, too many still view knowledge as

17. *Goblet of Fire* 723.

18. *See* TOM MORRIS, IF HARRY POTTER RAN GENERAL ELECTRIC xviii (2006) (urging corporate leaders to consider Professor Dumbledore as a role model).

19. Dept. of Educ., Dept. of Just. & Dept. Health & Human Servs., *Report to the President on Issues Raised by the Virginia Tech Tragedy* (June 13, 2007), available at http://www.hhs.gov/vtreport.pdf.

power and believe that, by being the sole source of information, they can elevate their position. Conversely, they worry that sharing information will weaken their own position.

Two: "Teach by Example and Lead by Encouragement"[20]

At Hogwarts, Harry and his classmates encountered teachers with a range of abilities, philosophies, and methods. The no-nonsense Professor Minerva McGonagall was stern and reserved, but fair; she focused on the fundamentals and emphasized the need to practice. With every gaze into her crystal ball, the spacey Professor Sybill Trelawney saw doom and disaster. Despite being the great-great-granddaughter of a celebrated seer, her inner eye, except on two occasions,[21] has proven rather blind. Lacking actual talent, she relied on techniques such as confusion and ambiguity. Severus Snape, a brilliant but brooding teacher who favored the Slytherins over all others, used insults, sarcasm, sneers, and withering glares. Bullied as a child, as a teacher he bullied his students. The rumpled Remus John Lupin genuinely loved children and teaching; he treated his students with respect, and patiently explained the reasoning behind magical spells. He dispensed praise regularly and balanced doctrine with skills. Dolores Umbridge was a rigid bureaucrat who attempted to disguise her black spirit with pink attire. She sought order, shunned creativity, and tried to control Hogwarts through punishment and rules.

Whatever their faults and differences, Harry learned important lessons from these teachers. But his primary mentor was Albus Dumbledore. Although Dumbledore had left the Transfiguration classroom decades earlier, he remained a master teacher. In this regard, Dumbledore's two primary qualities were teaching by example, and educating with encouragement. As one commentator noted,

> Dumbledore is Harry's most important teacher by the example he sets, as well as by the many interactions he has outside the classroom with this young wizard in training. Harry's other instructors provide him with many magical tools, but Dumbledore gives him the life instruction, guidance, and ongoing encouragement he needs for a proper use of those tools.[22]

---

20. Morris, *supra* n. 18, at 5.
21. *Prisoner of Azkaban* 324; *Order of the Phoenix* 840–44.
22. Morris, *supra* n. 18, at 4.

Dumbledore understood that the best teachers do not simply convey information. Instead, they teach by example and model the best qualities of their chosen profession. They value and do not punish curiosity.[23] They encourage students to explore, and provide them with maps, not directions, to find the answers. They do not force conclusions. They teach students how to teach themselves—how to become life-long learners; they afford students the latitude to experiment, but provide enough guidance to succeed.[24]

A classic example is how Dumbledore helped Harry to understand the intriguing Mirror of Erised, which shows people the "deepest, most desperate desire of [their] hearts."[25] In this situation, Dumbledore allowed Harry the opportunity to learn independently about the Mirror's effect. Later, he guided Harry in a discussion about how the Mirror worked. He ensured that Harry left with sufficient knowledge to face the Mirror successfully if he ever ran across it again (which Dumbledore suspected he would, and which Harry did). And, at the same time, he helped Harry to learn a larger life lesson: "It does not do to dwell on dreams and forget to live."[26]

Dumbledore took a similar tact regarding the Horcruxes. He provided Harry with some information about Horcruxes and took him on a journey to find one. But in the end, he provided Harry with the tools to continue the search, and a choice about whether to pursue the Horcruxes, or the Hallows.

While not all of us teach in the classroom, we can all teach by example. We can, with our words and actions, model those principles and values that are most important. Law school deans, for example, have the opportunity to mentor constituencies beyond their student body. As just a few examples, if a dean values scholarship, she can provide resources for faculty to produce high-quality scholarship, but she can also produce scholarship herself. If we value public service, the dean can ensure that faculty and staff have sufficient pro-bono opportunities, but the dean can also serve. If professionalism is valued, the dean can set a proper tone. If the dean wants the community to embrace the school, the dean and school can embrace the community.

The essence of teaching is not lecturing, or questioning, or grading assignments. The essence of teaching is helping others to reach their potential. And helping others to reach their potential is a job for everyone.

---

23. *Goblet of Fire* 597–98 ("Curiosity is not a sin....").

24. *Deathly Hallows* 684 ("It is essential that I give the boy enough information for him to do what he needs to do.").

25. *Sorcerer's Stone* 213–14.

26. *Sorcerer's Stone* 214 ("If you ever *do* run across it, you will now be prepared.") (emphasis in original).

Three: Stand up to Your Friends

Each of the four houses at Hogwarts is characterized by a particular virtue. Harry and most of his friends are in Gryffindor, whose emblem is the lion and whose virtue is courage. During Harry's first end-of-year feast, Professor Dumbledore expounds on the concept of courage. As he explains to the student body when describing the actions of Neville Longbottom, "There are all kinds of courage.... It takes a great deal of bravery to stand up to our enemies, but just as much to stand up to our friends."[27] Neville won Professor Dumbledore's praise because he attempted to stop Harry, Ron, and Hermione, his fellow Gryffindors, from wandering the castle halls at night. Even after Harry and Ron pleaded and cajoled, Neville stood his ground and was stopped only by Hermione's "Petrificus Totalus" spell.

It can be more difficult to say "no" to those who are our friends and allies than to those who are, well—shall we say—more problematic. But expediency is rarely the answer. As hard as it might be, we should not allow personal feelings to rule our decisions. Instead, we must always do what's best overall. By consistently using this touchstone, most will recognize the courage it takes to act for the greater good, and will respect, if not support, the decisions we must make.

Four: Even Wizards Are Human

Wizards bleed. They cry. And they die. They are, after all, human. Even Dumbledore, the greatest wizard of all times, had flaws and made mistakes. When Harry and Ron broke school rules after having been warned they would be expelled for additional violations, Dumbledore acknowledged the following: "I seem to remember telling you both that I would have to expel you if you broke any more school rules.... Which goes to show that the best of us must sometimes eat our words."[28]

Dumbledore also recognized that, because of his abilities and position, his mistakes could have tremendous consequences: "I make mistakes like the next man. In fact, being ... rather cleverer than most men, my mistakes tend to be correspondingly huger."[29] Indeed, at the end of *Order of the Phoenix*, Dumb-

---

27. *Sorcerer's Stone* 306.
28. *Chamber of Secrets* 330–31.
29. *Half-Blood Prince* 197.

ledore confides in Harry his greatest mistake: the failure to tell Harry about the Prophecy, which led to Sirius's death.[30]

Dumbledore also knew he lacked the power to "make other men see the truth,"[31] and that he could never please everyone. After the scheming journalist Rita Skeeter exposes Hagrid's half-giant heritage, Hagrid takes refuge in his cabin. In an effort to coax Hagrid out of hiding, Dumbledore shares,

> Really, Hagrid, if you are holding out for universal popularity, I'm afraid you will be in this cabin for a very long time.... Not a week has passed since I became headmaster of this school when I haven't had at least one owl complaining about the way I run it.[32]

Dumbledore often used cheer to cope with unfounded criticism. To Rita Skeeter, for example, he said with genuine delight, "I particularly enjoyed your description of me as an obsolete dingbat."[33] More importantly, Dumbledore recognized that perceived flaws might actually be strengths. When Dumbledore met with Harry following Sirius's death at the Ministry of Magic, he understood that Harry was angry, confused, mad, and sad. He realized that Harry was experiencing the pain of tremendous loss. And he said, "There is no shame in what you are feeling, Harry.... On the contrary ... the fact that you can feel pain like this is your greatest strength."[34]

Though imperfect and vulnerable, Dumbledore understood the antidote for imperfection: the willingness to ask for help. As he explained to Harry, "You will also find that help will always be given at Hogwarts to those who ask for it."[35]

Over and over again, this promise held true. When Harry asked for, and genuinely needed help, it arrived. In *The Chamber of Secrets*, having been bitten by the deadly Basilisk, and with Ginny on the verge of death, Harry asks for help, and Fawkes arrives to heal his wound and deliver the sword of Gryffindor. And in *The Deathly Hallows*, when Harry senses he is about to die, he asks for help and the bequeathed Snitch opens with the Resurrection Stone, which gives him the courage to face Voldemort once more.

Like wizards, all of us are only human. We have flaws and make mistakes. We cannot avoid all mistakes, and we cannot correct all flaws. Nor should we

---

30. *Order of the Phoenix* 826.
31. *Prisoner of Azkaban* 393.
32. *Goblet of Fire* 454.
33. *Goblet of Fire* 307.
34. *Order of the Phoenix* 823.
35. *Chamber of Secrets* 264.

try. But what we can do is to acknowledge those mistakes, take criticism constructively, understand that perceived flaws may actually be masking our strengths, and never be afraid to seek help when we need it.

Five: Humor and Reflection Place Most Events into Proper Perspective

Despite his many responsibilities and challenges, Albus Dumbledore almost always appeared calm, collected, and in control. He also had a whimsical air about him. And readers quickly learn that, in Dumbledore's case, appearance is reality. Wisdom, experience, and a level of confidence that comes only with mastery of a craft certainly contributed to his demeanor. But his keen sense of humor and knack for charming self-deprecation, coupled with his habit of taking time to reflect, helped him to place events and circumstances into their proper perspective.

Dumbledore's sense of humor is apparent from the first time we meet him. Arriving at Privet Drive soon after learning of the deaths of James and Lily Potter, Dumbledore immediately encounters a cat, the Animagus Professor Minerva McGonagall: "For some reason, the sight of the cat seemed to amuse him. He chuckled and muttered, 'I should have known.'"[36]

During this same exchange, he tries to convince Professor McGonagall to accept a lemon drop and also commented that "I haven't blushed so much since Madam Pomfrey told me she liked my new earmuffs."[37]

A connoisseur of both Muggle and magical sweets, Dumbledore shared this moment with Harry following Harry's confrontation with Voldemort over the Sorcerer's Stone:

> "Now, enough questions, I suggest you make a start on these sweets. Ah! Bertie Bott's Every Flavor Beans! I was unfortunate enough in my youth to come across a vomit-flavored one, and since then I'm afraid I've rather lost my liking for them—but I think I'll be safe with a nice toffee, don't you?"
> He smiled an popped the golden-brown bean into his mouth. Then he choked and said, "Alas! Ear wax!"[38]

Dumbledore was also a good sport. At Christmas lunch one year, he promptly donned a witch's hat, topped with a stuffed vulture, that popped out of a

---

36. *Sorcerer's Stone* 9.
37. *Sorcerer's Stone* 10–11.
38. *Sorcerer's Stone* 300–01.

cracker.[39] In addition, he could and did poke fun at himself. At the Yule Ball during the Triwizard Tournament, Dumbledore was speaking with Igor Karkaroff, a former Death Eater and headmaster of Durmstrang:

> "Well, Dumbledore," said Karkaroff, ..."Are we not right to be proud that we alone know our school's secrets, and the right to protect them?"
> "Oh I would never dream of assuming I know all Hogwarts' secrets, Igor," said Dumbledore amicably. "Only this morning, for instance, I took a wrong turning on the way to the bathroom and found myself in a beautifully proportioned room I have never seen before, containing a really rather magnificent collection of chamber pots. When I went back to investigate more closely, I discovered that the room had vanished. But I must keep an eye out for it. Perhaps it is only accessible at five-thirty in the morning. Or it may only appear at the quarter moon—or when the seeker has an exceptionally full bladder."[40]

Dumbledore also understood the importance and power of celebration. He hosted feasts at the beginning and end of the school year, on Halloween, and at Christmas. He also celebrated important events, such as the arrival of the foreign students for the Triwizard Tournament, and encouraged students to celebrate successes informally.

In addition to keeping matters in perspective through humor, Dumbledore took time to reflect on important events. Aided by the mysterious Pensieve, he could extract memories and review them later:

> I sometimes find ... that I simply have too many thoughts and memories crammed into my mind .... At these times ... I use Pensieve. One simply siphons the excess thoughts from one's mind, pours them into the basin, and examines them at one's leisure. It becomes easier to spot patterns and links, you understand, when they are in this form.[41]

With the Pensieve, he could gain valuable perspective about people and events. He could watch events with more care and objectivity. He could focus on important details that might be missed while in the moment "live," and could consider how these details fit onto the much larger canvas.

---

39. *Prisoner of Azkaban* 227–28 (in this context, a cracker is a noisemaker stuffed with a prize). The hat was identical to the one that appeared earlier in the book when Neville transformed the boggart into Professor Snape wearing the clothes of Neville's grandmother using the "Riddikulus" charm. *Prisoner of Azkaban* at 135.
40. *Goblet of Fire* 417–18.
41. *Goblet of Fire* 597.

In the press of life, we can be pulled in several different directions at once, confronted with unpleasant challenges, piled high with more work than hours in a day, and criticized for decisions we made in good faith. In the tough times, we need effective coping mechanisms. Taking our cue from Professor Dumbledore, humor, celebration, and reflection can help us gain perspective, rejuvenate, and focus on the positive.

Humor can help us keep our balance and grace as we wade through the daily muck of life. The importance of humor is almost axiomatic. Just type "importance of humor" into Google, and you'll be flooded with millions of results.

Thus, one power of humor is to remind us that the daily happenings in the dean's office,[42] and indeed at the law school, are rarely the most important matters of the day. In addition, humor can be used to calm tense situations, relieve stress, and celebrate success and joys. It is, in short, a versatile and potent remedy that we should never forget to utilize.

On a related point, celebrations can revitalize both individuals and organizations. One of the most successful U.S. companies is Southwest Airlines, which promotes a culture of celebration. In studying Southwest, two authors concluded that celebrations provide opportunities to build relationships, reduce stress, recognize milestones, and remove fear.[43] The Southwest and Hogwarts experiences suggest that we should stop every now and then and celebrate our accomplishments, both individually and collectively. Focusing on successes can reorient perspectives and allow us to achieve even more than we imagined.

Celebrations demonstrate that pausing, even briefly, can bring great perspective to any situation. The same is true for reflection. Finding time to reflect is essential for long-term personal and institutional well-being. Only with reflection can we understand the impact of our daily decisions and actions. Reflection helps us to separate the important from the trivial, to put events into context, to extract personal feelings from institutional decisions, and to plan more effectively for the future. Some build daily or weekly reflection time into their schedules. Others take breaks or vacations. Still others reflect with the help of colleagues or by keeping daily journals. Whatever the timing or method, reflection, like humor and celebration, can help us become and remain more effective.

---

42. *See* Allan W. Vestal, *"A River to My People ..." Notes from my Fifth Year as Dean*, 37. U. Tol. L. Rev. 179, 184 (2005) (identifying humor as one of the six lessons for being a successful law dean).

43. Kevin Feinberg & Jackie Feinberg, Nuts! Southwest Airlines' Crazy Recipe for Business and Personal Success chs. 13, 14 (1998).

Six: Banish Boggarts

A fascinating creature in the wizard world is the boggart. A boggart is a shape-shifter that assumes the form of its intended victim's worst fear. Boggarts hide in dark, enclosed places, and often settle in drawers and closets. Wizards are taught to approach a boggart in groups, so that it will have difficulty choosing which individual to target. But the best method to banish a boggart is with the "Riddikulus" charm, which will make it appear amusing.

Like boggarts, fears tend to reside in the dark crevices of our own minds. And, as Dumbledore explained to Harry, they often involve the unknown.[44] Fear, in turn can breed avoidance behaviors. As an example, most wizards and other magical creatures feared Lord Voldemort; and they feared him so much that they would not use his proper name. Instead, they referred to him as "He-Who-Must-Not-Be-Named" or "You-Know-Who." Even his followers referred to him as the "Dark Lord." But substituting these euphemisms for his name only increased the fear and panic.

Harry and Dumbledore were among the few to refer to Voldemort by that name or his given name, Tom Riddle. And Dumbledore was the only one to do so consistently. As Dumbledore instructed Harry, "Call him Voldemort.... Always use the proper name for things. Fear of a name increases fear of the thing itself."[45] Using Voldemort's actual name was a sign of courage that allowed these characters to reduce and even repel the fear.

We sometimes project our worst fears into situations before fully understanding them. In other words, we create our own boggarts. If we fail to acknowledge our fear, it inevitably will control us. On the other hand, if we openly name and confront our fear, we have taken the first step toward defeating it, because we have regained the power to act. Although it may seem easier to simply avoid our fears, avoidance only makes our fears more powerful.

Although the "Riddikulus" charm relies heavily on laughter, it also depends on faith: faith that we can face our fears, and faith that we have the ability to handle the situations presented. As Martin Luther King, Jr. related, "Fear knocked at the door. Faith answered. There was no one there."[46] Again, Dumbledore is our teacher. He had faith in Snape, and in Harry. And in the end,

---

44. *Half-Blood Prince* 566 ("It is the unknown we fear when we look upon death and darkness, nothing more.").

45. *Sorcerer's Stone* 298.

46. Martin Luther King, Jr., *The Strength to Love*, in THE ESSENTIAL WRITINGS AND SPEECHES OF MARTIN LUTHER KING., JR. 517 (James M. Washington ed., 1990).

that faith banished fear as symbolized by Voldemort. If we have faith in ourselves and in others, there will be no room for fear.

Seven: Our Choices Define Us

The last piece of advice relates to the first: In the end, it is not our ancestry, credentials, or aptitude that will define us. Instead, as Professor Dumbledore observed, "It is our choices … that show what we truly are, far more than our abilities."[47]

On several occasions, Dumbledore carefully highlights the importance of free will and choices. After Draco Malfoy disarmed him in the Astronomy Tower, he spent time speaking with Draco about his actions and asked Draco to "discuss your options."[48] With Draco feeling scared and trapped, Dumbledore attempted to explain that Draco did have a choice: he did not have to kill Dumbledore, as Dumbledore had already chosen how he would die—at the wand of Severus Snape.

The importance of choices was also central at the end-of-year feast following the Triwizard Tournament. In the last challenge of that Tournament, Voldemort kills Hogwarts competitor Cedric Diggory, a loyal and talented wizard, simply because he landed in the wrong place at the wrong time. Cedric did not even have time to defend himself. When eulogizing Cedric, Dumbledore encouraged the students to remember the power of choice:

> Remember, if the time should come when you have to make a choice between what is right and what is easy, remember what happened to a boy who was good, and kind, and brave, because he strayed across the path of Lord Voldemort. Remember Cedric Diggory.[49]

Dumbledore also discusses choices in the context of the Prophecy. The Prophecy did not name Harry as the person with the power to vanquish Voldemort. Instead, two boys fit the description: Harry and Neville. As the Prophecy foretold, Voldemort had a choice, and made his choice by marking Harry.

But the Prophecy also afforded Harry a choice. As Dumbledore explained to Harry, a Prophecy is not the truth; many prophecies are made, but not all are fulfilled. Harry's decision to face Voldemort was his own choice, made of free will; it was not a foreordained event outside of Harry's control.

---

47. *Chamber of Secrets* 331.
48. *Half-Blood Prince* 591.
49. *Goblet of Fire* 724.

"But, sir," said Harry, making valiant efforts not to sound argumentative, "it all comes down to the same thing, doesn't it? I've got to try and kill him, or—"

"Got to?" said Dumbledore. "Of course you've got to! But not because of the prophecy! Because you, yourself, will never rest until you've tried!"[50]

* * *

"[Y]ou are free to choose your way, quite free to turn your back on the prophecy!"[51]

And, in the end, Harry realizes other important choices as well. In their meeting in King's Cross, Dumbledore implies that Harry's choice to allow Voldemort to kill him actually allowed him to live. And Dumbledore explains to Harry that it's his choice whether to return to the living, or remain in the other world:

"I've got to go back, haven't I?"
"That is up to you."
"I've got a choice?"
"Oh yes." Dumbledore smiled at him.[52]

Harry is a brave and talented wizard, but, as Dumbledore predicted, in the end, Harry's greatness rested on the choices he made: he chose Gryffindor over Slytherin, he chose Ron and Hermione as friends, he chose to pursue Horcruxes over Hallows, and he chose to face Voldemort.

Similarly, we will be evaluated largely on our choices. As such, we must carefully evaluate how we make those choices, which ties back to the importance of values and principles. If we treat others with respect, teach by example, stand up to our friends, understand our limitations and ask for help when we need it, gain perspective from humor and reflection, and replace fear with faith, it is likely that, on the whole, our choices will be ones made in the institution's best interest and that support our critical missions.

Conclusion

Although we do not have the magical powers with which Professor Dumbledore was blessed, he still provides an ideal role. Indeed, as described above,

---

50. *Half-Blood Prince* 511.
51. *Half-Blood Prince* 512.
52. *Deathly Hallows* 722.

most of his virtues were non-magical. In the end, Dumbledore is memorable because he cared. Indeed, if all of his advice could be summarized, it would be to care for others. Dumbledore cared for his students, staff, and faculty. He cared for "undesirable" magical creatures and beasts. He cared enough to sacrifice time and physical well-being to stop the dark forces. His tremendous level of caring was evident in all that he did: his lessons with Harry, his decision to hide the contents of the Prophecy for so long, his refusal to allow Professor Trelawney to be banished from Hogwarts, and the list continues. Because he cared, he was able to have a positive and lasting impact on his school, and society. His legacy provides us with a clear roadmap of how to do the same.

Contributors

Benjamin H. Barton
Director of Clinical Programs and Associate Professor of Law, University of Tennessee, College of Law.

Mary Beth Beazley
Associate Professor of Law, The Ohio State University, Moritz College of Law. J.D., Notre Dame Law School; B.A., Bowling Green State University. Professor Beazley fell in love with the world of Harry Potter in 1998, when she read the first book aloud to her daughters.

Mark Edwin Burge
Legal Writing Professor, Texas Wesleyan University School of Law. J.D., University of Texas School of Law; B.A., University of Houston. Professor Burge teaches legal analysis and writing, commercial law, and contract drafting. His scholarship interests include methods of statutory interpretation, the changing role of stare decisis, and the implications of evolving interpretive methodologies and institutions for the practice of law and American legal education. Frankly, he views any opportunity to write about the relationship of such topics to *Harry Potter* as delicious and profoundly undeserved icing on his professional cake. Professor Burge would like to thank Frank Snyder for selecting his chapter over a competing essay by Horace Slughorn, and Rhonda West Burge for her delightful ability to give Hermione Granger a run for her money in Arithmancy.

Benjamin Davis
Associate Professor, University of Toledo College of Law. J.D.-M.B.A, Harvard; B.A., Harvard College.

Darby Dickerson
Vice President and Dean, Stetson University College of Law; Special Curator, Albus Percival Wulfric Brian Dumbledore Collection of Marvels and Mysteries, Hogwarts School of Witchcraft and Wizardry. Dean Dickerson would like to thank her research assistant, Casey Stoutamire, for her work on this chapter.

Joel Fishman

Asst. Director for Lawyer Services, Duquesne University Center for Legal Information/Allegheny County Law Library. Ph.D., University of Wisconsin-Madison. His chapter is a revised version of the paper published in 12 Tex. Wes. L. Rev. 452–456 (2005).

John Gava

Reader, Faculty of Law, University of Adelaide, Australia. Professor Gava can be reached at john.gava@adelaide.edu.au.

Eric Gouvin

Professor of Law, Western New England College School of Law. Among other things, Professor Gouvin teaches business organizations law and the regulation of financial services. His more traditional academic writings explore the intersection of corporate law and banking law in both domestic and international settings, so an chapter about the wizarding banking system was a natural area of academic inquiry. Prof. Gouvin has a special place in his heart for the Harry Potter series because over the course of several years he read them aloud with his son, Joe. He thanks his daughter Lucy for her research efforts in identifying reference to Gringotts throughout the books and to Patricia McCoy, Michael Malloy, and Heidi Mandanis Schooner for their comments on an earlier draft of this piece.

Daniel S. Kleinberger

Professor of Law; Director, Mitchell Fellows Program, William Mitchell College of Law. J.D., Yale; A.B. Harvard. His writing ranges from the theoretical (*Closely Held Businesses through the Entity-Aggregate Prism*) to the applied (*Guilty Knowledge; Respondeat Superior Run Amok*), and his writings have been cited by the 7th Circuit, the New York Court of Appeals, the Delaware Chancery Court, the California Court of Appeals, the federal bankruptcy court, and the American Law Institute. He delivered the keynote address at the 21st Century Commercial Law Forum in Beijing, China ("Two Decades of 'Alternative Entities'—from Tax Rationalization through Alphabet Soup to Contract as Deity.") His chapter was previously published in Daniel s. Kleinberger, Agency Partnerships and LLCs: Examples and Explanations (3rd ed., Aspen 2008). Reprinted with permission of the author and publisher. The author appreciates the advice of Potter enthusiasts Sonya Huesman, Lindsay Hutchins Matts, Kristina Shidlauski, and especially Sam, Rachael, and Carolyn Kleinberger.

Lenora Ledwon

Professor of Law, St. Thomas University School of Law. Ph.D., English Literature, Notre Dame; J.D., University of Michigan. Professor Ledwon has edited a textbook, LAW AND LITERATURE: TEXT AND THEORY and co-edited a casebook, LAW AND POPULAR CULTURE. Her articles have appeared in: HARVARD WOMEN'S LAW JOURNAL; YALE JOURNAL OF LAW AND FEMINISM; STUDIES IN LAW, POLITICS AND SOCIETY; and LITERATURE/FILM QUARTERLY, among others. She is currently working on articles dealing with internet fan fiction, and storytelling in graphic novels. She teaches Contracts, Evidence, Law & Literature, and Legal Storytelling. Professor Ledwon delivered an early version of her chapter, "Harry Potter Goes to Law School," at the 2000 Society of American Law Teachers Conference at NYU Law School.

Daniel Levy

Professor of Economics, Bar-Ilan University, Ramat-Gan, Israel; Emory University. Ph.D., University of California, Irvine. Professor Levy is the Director of the Aharon Meir Center for Banking Research at Bar-Ilan University, a Senior Fellow at the Rimini Center for Economic Analysis at the University of Bologna, and a member of the Academic Advisory Committee of the Israel's Central Bureau of Statistics. When not practicing his arithmancy and divination skills to better understand the Potterian Economy, he studies the behavior of prices, economic growth, and business cycles. Professor Levy expresses appreciation to the editors, Frank Snyder and Jeffrey Thomas, the student assistants who worked on the project, the two part time wizards (Avihai Levy and Eliav Levy) for help and comments, and Arye Hillman and Danielle Gurevitch for comments. He also gratefully acknowledges financial support from Adar Foundation of the Economics Department at Bar-Ilan University and support of the Economics Department at Emory University. All remaining errors are Neville Longbottom's.

Wendy Law

Assistant Professor and Law Library Faculty, Texas Wesleyan University School of Law; Adjunct Professor, Hogwarts School of Witchcraft and Wizardry, Ravenclaw House. J.D., Texas Wesleyan University, M.I.L.S., University of Michigan, B.A., University of Michigan. Professor Law would like to thank her co-author Anna Teller for all of her contributions and support, and she would like to thank Frank Snyder, Susan Ayres, Joan Stringfellow, and Cynthia Burress for their contributions in the development of her chapter. She dedicates her chapter to her Muggle family and friends, and thanks them for their support.

Sue Liemer

Associate Professor and the Director of Lawyering Skills, Southern Illinois University School of Law. Professor Liemer's sons grew up along with Harry Potter. For their willingness to e-chat about Harry Potter and related matters, she would like to thank Pablo Alvarez, Eli Bortman, Barbara Busharis, Hayley Gorenberg, Gabrielle Hoyt-Disick, Daniel Dye, Stephen Kastenberg, Neil Levine, Karin Mika, Donnica Moore, Michael Murray, Dan Real, Ruth Anne Robbins, Jennifer Scott, Wanda Temm, and Tom the Englishman.

Benjamin Loffredo

Yale College, class of 2012. Ben was one of two high school students who presented at the 2005 conference *The Power of Stories: Intersections of Law, Culture and Literature*, co-sponsored by Texas Wesleyan University School of Law, the University of Gloucestershire, and the City of Gloucester, England. Ben wrote his chapter when he was in high school. He thanks Frank Snyder and Jeffrey Thomas for organizing this project and for including his chapter in this book.

Andrew P. Morriss

H. Ross and Helen Workman Professor of Law and Business, University of Illinois, Champaign-Urbana; Professor, Institute for Government and Public Affairs. Ph.D., Economics, Massachusetts Institute of Technology; J.D. and M.Pub.Aff., University of Texas at Austin; A.B., Princeton.

Jeannie Marie Paterson

Senior Lecturer, Faculty of Law, Monash University, Australia. Ph.D., Monash University; BA/LLB with honors, Australian National University.

Geoffrey Christopher Rapp

Associate Professor, University of Toledo College of Law. J.D., Yale; B.A. Harvard College. Professor Rapp has also taught at the University of Utah, Michigan State University, and Wayne State University. He has taught Torts, Business Associations, Antitrust, Trusts & Estates and Sports Law. While in law school, Professor Rapp was a Notes Editor of the *Yale Law Journal* and a Head Teaching Fellow in the Department of Economics. He has written on the problem of wrongful conviction in *DNA's Dark Side*, published in the *Yale Law Journal* in 2001.

Ruth Anne Robbins

Clinical Professor of Law, Rutgers School of Law—Camden. This chapter appeared in slightly different and longer form as *Harry Potter, Ruby Slippers and Merlin: telling the client's story using the characters and paradigm of the archetypal hero's journey* 29 Seattle Univ. L. R. 767 (2006). Professor Robbins teaches lawyering courses at Rutgers School of Law in the shining metropolis of Camden, New Jersey. Those courses include advanced legal writing, first year legal writing and the law school's domestic violence clinic. She is proud to have been the president of the Legal Writing Institute (2008–2010 term). She also serves as a member of the editorial board of J. ALWD, and is a co-organizer of the applied legal storytelling conference series. Her legal scholarship relates to persuasion in two areas: story structure and visual impact.

Heidi Mandanis Schooner

Professor of Law, Columbus School of Law, The Catholic University of America. Professor Schooner thanks her research assistant Diana Norris (unrelated to the feline Mrs. Norris,) who reread the Harry Potter novels with great speed and seriousness. She also thanks her favorite wizards, Thor Mandanis Schooner and John Mandanis Schooner, who keep her focused on the importance of the fight between good and evil and who have given her the excuse to reread the Harry Potter novels many times. She also thanks some dear Muggles for their insights: Eric Gouvin, Alice Mandanis, Robert Rosenblum, and Steve Schooner and the participants at the Law and Harry Potter panel discussion at the Annual Meeting of the Association for the Study of Law, Culture and the Humanities at Syracuse University College of Law.

Aaron Schwabach

Professor of Law, Thomas Jefferson School of Law. Professor Schwabach would like to thank Jeffrey Thomas, Bridget Longridge, and everyone else involved in this project for the tireless dedication that made it possible, and Qienyuan Zhou and Veronica, Jessica, Daniel, Karen, Jennifer and Jon Schwabach—and the entire world of Harry Potter fandom—for their patience and endless willingness to talk about the wizarding world. His chapter was originally published in longer and somewhat different form as *Harry Potter and the Unforgivable Curses: Norm-formation, Inconsistency, and the Rule of Law in the Wizarding World,* 11 ROGER WILLIAMS U. L. REV. 309 (2006), and an excerpt appeared as "Unforgivable Curses and the Rule of Law" in Jeffrey E. Thomas et al., *Harry Potter and the Law,* 12 TEXAS WESLEYAN U. L. REV. 427, 443 (2006). Professor Schwabach can be reached at aarons@tjsl.edu.

Avichai Snir

Ph.D. candidate, Department of Economics, Bar-Ilan University, Ramat-Gan, Israel. Besides Potterian Economics, his research interests include price setting, income inequality, behavioral economics, English literature, and ski. Mr. Snir expresses appreciation to the editors, Frank Snyder and Jeffrey Thomas, the student assistants who worked on the project, the two part time wizards (Avihai Levy and Eliav Levy) for help and comments, and Arye Hillman and Danielle Gurevitch for comments. He also gratefully acknowledges financial support from Adar Foundation of the Economics Department at Bar-Ilan University. With his co-author, he attributes all remaining errors to Neville Longbottom.

Alison McMorran Sulentic

Associate, Baker Botts, L.L.P., Houston, Texas. J.D., Harvard; M.A., University of the Witwatersrand, South Africa; A.B. Harvard. Ms. Sulentic is an employee benefits lawyer whose practice includes advising clients on the design and regulatory compliance of qualified pension and profit-sharing plans, welfare benefit plans and executive compensation arrangements, and on privacy and security issues relating to employee benefit plans. Ms. Sulentic was a law professor at Duquesne University School of Law for twelve years, and has published numerous articles relating to legal and ethical issues in compensation planning. Needless to say, the views expressed in her chapter are those of the author and do not represent the positions adopted by Baker Botts, L.L.P. or its clients. To her knowledge, Ms. Sulentic has never met a wizard or a house-elf, but she would gladly support all efforts to bring justice for house elves and others to the wizarding world.

Anna K. Teller

Attorney, Law Office of Donald E. Teller, Jr., P.C. J.D., Southern Methodist University, M.L.I.S., University of North Texas, B.A., Spring Hill College. Ms. Teller would like to thank her co-author Wendy Law for inviting her to write with her, and Professor Susan Phillips for her support and encouragement.

Geoffrey R. Watson

Professor Law, Columbus School of Law, The Catholic University of America; aspirational Professor of Jurisprudence, Hogwarts School of Witchcraft and Wizardry, Slytherin House. J.D., Harvard; B.A. Yale, after achieving six OWLs and seven NEWTs at Hogwarts (Slytherin). Professor Watson was a law clerk to the Hon. Harrison L. Winter on the Fourth Circuit Court of Appeals, an Attorney-Advisor at the Department of State, and a faculty member at Seattle University before joining Columbus School of Law. He wishes, however, that he was on the faculty at Hogwarts, where he would teach (of course) Defense Against the Dark Arts, would develop close ties with colleagues at Durmstrang, and aspire to be Head of Slytherin House.

Danaya C. Wright

Clarence J. TeSelle Professor of Law at the University of Florida, Levin College of Law. Ph.D., Political Science, Johns Hopkins; J.D., Cornell; M.A, English Literature. St. John's College; M.A., University of Arizona; B.A., Cornell College. Professor Wright finds Harry Potter to be a delightful melding of her academic interests. Her scholarship focuses on the history of English family law from the late medieval period to the late nineteenth century. She also researches nineteenth-century American railroad law. She teaches property, wills and trusts, Constitutional law, and legal history and can hardly wait for her young toddlers to be old enough to enjoy Harry Potter.

Index

Note: *f* indicate footnotes